Science Smart

Science Smart

COOL PROJECTS FOR EXPLORING THE MARVELS OF THE PLANET EARTH

Discover the wonders of Earth science, geology and geography with these hands-on crafts

hot air balloons · camouflaged periscope · world drums · time zone maps · wave in a bottle · stepping stones · rock candy · spider webs and much more . . .

GWEN DIEHN, TERRY KRAUTWURST, ALAN ANDERSON, JOE RHATIGAN, & HEATHER SMITH

Main Street
New York

10 9 8 7 6 5 4 3 2 1

Published by Main Street, a division of Sterling Publishing Co., Inc.
387 Park Avenue South, New York, NY 10016
This book is comprised of the following titles published by Lark Books,
a division of Sterling Publishing Co., Inc.:
Science Crafts for Kids © 1994 by Gwen Diehn and Terry Krautwurst
Geography Crafts for Kids © 2002 by Lark Books
Geology Crafts for Kids © 1996 by Alan Anderson, Gwen Diehn and Terry Krautwurst
© 2003 by Sterling Publishing Co., Inc.
Distributed in Canada by Sterling Publishing
c/o Canadian Manda Group, One Atlantic Avenue, Suite 105
Toronto, Ontario, Canada M6K 3E7
Distributed in Great Britain and Europe by Chris Lloyd at Orca Book
Services, Stanley House, Fleets Lane, Poole BH15 3AJ, England
Distributed in Australia by Capricorn Link (Australia) Pty. Ltd.
P.O. Box 704, Windsor, NSW 2756, Australia

ISBN:1-4027-0514-X

Table of Contents

**Introduction to
Science Projects**   12

Science Log   14

Earth   16
Bird Hide   18
  Whatta-buncha-ologies   21
Camouflaged Periscope   22
  Cameo Creatures and
  How to Be One   23
Mold Garden   25
  The Fungus Among Us   27
  Fuzzy Wuzzy Was a Worm?   27
Wormery   28
Toad House   30
  Toad-ally Awesome   31
Root Viewer   32
Seed Cast Tiles   34
Buried Treasure
  In Search of the Lost Landfill;
  Adventures in Garbology   36
  Radioactive   37
  Dating; Fantastic Fossils 38
Spider Web   39
  Amazing Spiders and
  Incredible Webs   41
Hypsometer   42

Air   45
Clay Pot Wind Chimes   47
  What's That Sound?   48
Xylophone   49
  Totally Tubular   50
Sound Viewer   51
Nephoscope   53

Jiminey Cricket, It's Hot!   54
Hot Air Balloon   55
Rocket Jet Kite   58
  What Makes a Rocket Rocket? 60
Centipede Kite   61
  Hidden Air   63
Barometer   64
  Wind Facts That'll Blow You Away 65
Wind Sock   66
Hovercraft   68
Helicopter   70

Riding on Air 71

Wind Speed Meter 72

Admiral Beaufort's Wind

Force Scale 73

Thunder Stick 75

The Shocking Truth About;

Lightning and Thunder 77

Water 78

Wave in a Bottle 80

How Waves Work 81

Waterspout 82

Whirlpools and Rubber Duckies 84

Red Cabbage Indicator Paper 85

Acids and Bases and You 87

Marbled Paper 88

Backyard Mini-Pond 90

Underwater Viewer 92

Model Grist Mill 93

Gearing Up, Gearing Down 97

Skimmer Net 98

Water's Skin 99

Gluep and Oobleck 100

Water Lens 102

Powered Model Boats 104

Try This Puzzle 106

Clay Boats 107

What Makes a Boat Float? 109

Fire 110

Solar Clock 112

The Sun, Center of Life 114

Solar Oven 115

Polar Solar Collectors 119

Solar Food Dryer 120

Plant Tepee 122

Color Spinners 124

Mixed-Up Colors 125

Fire Clock 126

Dried Apple Garland 128

Light Catcher 129

Light and Color 131

Solar Stone 132

Geology Projects 134

All About the Earth 136

Geologist's Notebook 138

Planet Mobile 141

Molten to the Core 144

Why the Earth's Insides So Hot? 145

Earth Balls 146

Our Ever-Moving, Ever-

Changing World 148

Moving Liquid 150

Moving Liquid-Experiment #1 151

Experiment #2 152

Pangaea, Laurasia, and Gondwana   152
Jigsaw Puzzle   154
How Do You Spell Relief?
E-a-r-t-h-q-u-a-k-e!   156
Seismograph   158
Volcanoes!   160
Exploding Volcano   162
Nature's "Tea Kettles"   164
Pebble Mosaic Flower Pot   165
Mountains High, Valley's Low   166
Mountain Building   168
Landform Pop-Up Book   170

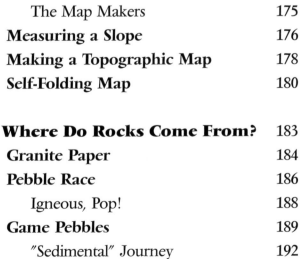

The Map Makers   175
Measuring a Slope   176
Making a Topographic Map   178
Self-Folding Map   180

Where Do Rocks Come From?   183
Granite Paper   184
Pebble Race   186
Igneous, Pop!   188
Game Pebbles   189
"Sedimental" Journey   192

Making Sandstone   193
Making a Conglomerate   194
Morphed   195
Faux Marble   197
Metamorphic Rocks   198
Weather Wear   200
Erosion Experiment   201
From Rock Into Soil; Don't
Forget Clay   203
Moss Rock Garden   204
Hunting for Clay   206
A Primitive Kiln   209
Clay Beads   212
Earth Crayons   214
Rocks That Grow   216
Limestone Cave   218
Garden Markers   220
Rock Jewelry   221
Fossils: Signs of Ancient Life   223
Fossil cast   225
Seed Cast Medallions   227
The Big Time Line   228
The Geologic Time Scale   230

Minerals, Minerals, Everywhere 232
   Building Blocks of Rocks 233
  Rock Candy 234
    Crystals and Their Shapes 235
    How Crystals Grow: The Birth and
    Growth of Quartz 236
  Crystal Theory Experiment 237
  Growing Crystals 238
  Paper Crystal Models 240
    A Mineralogist: The Sherlock
    Holmes of Geology; Moh's Scale 243
    What a Gem! 244
  Treasure Boxes 246
  Rock Mobile 247

**How We Use Rocks
and Minerals** 249
  Paperweight 250
  Sand Clock 251
  Trivet 253
    Rocks for Building 254
  Model Earth House 255
  Window Garden 258
  Tin Lantern 260

    Metals from Minerals 261
    Gold, Silver, and Platinum 263

Collecting Rocks and Minerals 264
  Sand Painting 265
    Gearing Up 268
    Finding Rocks and Minerals 269
  Backpack 270
    Safety tips to Remember 272
  Rock Collection Box 273

Geography Projects 274
Introduction: What is Geography
    for Anyway?
    Where in the World Are You? 281
Astrolobe 282
    Oh, Drat, the World Ain't Flat 285
Cross Staff 286
    Lost? Thank Your Lucky Stars 289
A Totally Useful Compass 290
    The Great Age of Discovery
    in Perspective 292
House Sundial Clock 294

Still, Still Lost? 296

Time-Zone Clock 297

Dream Travel Box 298

Before the World was a Spherical Planet
Orbiting the Sun . . . 299

Marco Polo Travel Journal 300

Worldly Place Mats 302

Maps, Maps, & Even More Maps 303

Become a Cartographer
in One Day 304

Antique Map & Case 307

Old Map Pillowcase or
    Adventure Backpack 309

Grid Art 311

Neighborhood Map 312

Family Maps 314

Globe Your Friends 315

Where the Rivers Flow 317

The Center of the World 318

The Flat Map Flap 319

Forget latitude and Longitude . . . 321

Topographic Map of a

Friend's Face 322

Strange Place Names in
the United States 324

Deep Map 324

Geographic Blunder: Naming Nome 325

Take a Deep Breath and Say . . . 327

Create a Favorite Novel Map 328

Mail Map 329

Recycled Map Shade 330

We Are Different; We Are the Same 332

The Tooth Rat? 333

"Made In . . ." Treasure Hunt 334

World Snacks 336

Stamp Box 338

Family Tree Batik Banner 340

Time Capsule 343

Clay Bowl 344

Baa, Moo, Kuk-kurri-kuu 346

World Drum 346

The Earth Shapes You   348

Where You Live Brochure   349

Hometown Detective   351

    Listen to Your Landscape   352

Salt Dough Landscape Model   353

    Predict the Future   355

Pangea Pudding Puzzle   356

    Serving Up Some plate Tectonics   358

Climate Study With Tree Rings   359

    Reading Tree Rings   360

Weather Station   361

    Making a Barometer   362;

    Making a Wind Vane   363;

    Building an Anemometer   364

    Cloud Chart   365;

    More Weather Forecasting Tips   366

Rain Map   367

You Shape the Earth   369

Solar Oven   370

Water Filter   372

CD Mobile   374

    Trash Trivia   376

Debate Book   377

    To Fish or Not to Fish: A Debate   380

    Food for Thought   381

World Hunger Banquet   382

    Population Numbers   384

Luminary of Earth at Night   385

    Earth from Space   386

    Top 25 Largest Cities on Earth   389

Native Habitat Garden   390

    Native Habitat Field Guide   392

    Toad House   393

    Twiggy Bird Feeder   393

    What's Up with All These Rabbits?   394

The Ultimate World Heritage Site   395

Templates   396

Index   398

METRIC CONVERSION CHART

Although the conversions aren't exact, there are about 2-1/2 centimeters in an inch.

So to convert inches to centimeters, just multiply the numberof inches by 2.5.

To convert feet to meters, divide the number of feet by 3.25.

CONVERSION CHART

INCHES	MILLIMETERS
1/8	3
1/4	6
1/2	13
3/4	19

INCHES	CENTIMETERS
1	2.5
1-1/4	3.2
1-1/2	3.8
1-3/4	4.4
2	5
3	7.5
4	10
5	12.5
6	15
7	17.5
8	20
9	22.5
10	25
11	27.5
12	30
13	32.5
14	35
15	37.5
16	40
17	42.5
18	45
19	47.5
20	**50**
21	**52.5**
22	**55**
23	**57.5**
24	**60**
25	**62.5**
26	**65**
27	**67.5**
28	**70**
29	**72.5**
30	**75**

INTRODUCTION TO SCIENCE PROJECTS

When you hear the word scientist, what sort of person does your mind's eye see? Is it someone in a lab looking at test tubes full of bubbling chemicals? Somebody studying complicated formulas? A person gazing into a microscope?

Some scientists do those things. Others search for lost cities, record the songs of whales and dolphins, study ancient medicines, look for undiscovered stars and planets, explore deep caverns, track the paths of caribou herds, walk in space, fit together dinosaur skeletons, find cures for diseases, and-well, you get the idea. There are lots of different kinds of scientists! All scientists, though, have one thing in common. They're absolutely, irresistibly, gotta-figure-it-out curious about how things work and why things happen.

Does that describe you, too? Do you wonder how the world works? Do you like to learn by doing as well as by reading and looking? Great. Then this book is for you.

All of the projects in *Science Smart* are fun and interesting and rewarding. Some are simple and will take just a few minutes to complete. Others are more complicated and challenging. But no matter which project you tackle, when you finish you'll have something you can be proud to call your own. And in the making, many of the projects will help you understand important scientific ideas. Others will help you create tools and instruments that you can use to conduct your own scientific studies.

So please: Don't just sit back and read this book. Use it. There are a lot of terrific crafts to make in these pages. And there are a lot of eye-opening discoveries to make about this amazing, wonderful world of ours. Let's get started!

A Few Tips About the Crafts Projects

* More than 2,000 years ago, Aristotle and other pioneers of science believed that everything in the universe was made up of just four kinds of elements: earth, air, water, and fire. These days, we know better. In honor of the beautiful simplicity of the idea, however, we've organized this first science section into earth, air, water, and fire sections. Feel free to skip around from section to section and project to project.

* Read the instructions all the way through at least once before you begin a project. As you read, imagine yourself actually doing each step.

If there's something you don't quite understand, go through a trial run using "pretend" materials. Substitute pieces of scrap paper for pieces of wood, for instance. Acting out the instructions usually makes things clear.

* Collect all the materials and tools listed under "What You'll Need" for your project, then start. If you don't have some of the items listed, try to think of things you do have that will serve just as well. Be creative! Use your ingenuity!

* Several projects involve the use of an electric appliance, such as a hair dryer or hot plate. Others require a sharp knife. In such cases, please use caution and your own good common sense. We haven't said "Be careful!" every time we ask you to pick up a pair of scissors. So when we do point out that you can get hurt unless you follow the instructions carefully, we're serious. Also, sometimes we suggest that you get an adult to help you with a certain step. We say that only when we think it's important.

* Some of the crafts may call for tools or materials that you've never used or even heardof before. Don't let that stop you! Tools aren't mysterious things used only by adults and unavailable to you. Stores carry them and sell them to people who aren't one bit smarter than you are. People who work there will know what an awl or hacksaw blade is, and will find it for you. After you go look at one, you'll know, too. With the right tool, a job that looks hard (maybe even impossible!) becomes easy.

* One notion we want you to get from this book is that science isn't just a subject you learn in a classroom. It's a way of looking at the world. Everything has its own interesting story to tell, of why it is the way it is. As you use this book, think of how the ideas you're reading about apply to the things around you. And never stop asking the most important question in science: "Why?"

Science Log

It's helpful to have a notebook to jot down plans, observations, lists of things you need for projects, and other information. This logbook is easy to make, and, because it has a ring binding, you can add pages when you need to. It also has a stiff cover, so you can use it as you would a clipboard when writing outdoors or away from a table.

What You'll Need

2 pieces of cardboard, each 6 by 9 inches

Pieces of leftover wallpaper or wallpaper samples*

White craft glue or rubber cement

A glue brush or an old paint brush

A razor knife

Scissors

About 10 sheets of white typing paper

About 5 sheets of grid paper (optional)

A hole puncher

An awl or a large nail

2 looseleaf rings, either 1- or 1-1/2-inch size

A piece of string about 2 feet long

A pen or pencil

14

*Paint stores that sell wallpaper will often give you their old sample books if you ask for them. If you can't find any wallpaper, you can use self-adhesive shelf paper instead.

What to Do

1. First make two book covers. To make a cover, lay one piece of 6- by 9-inch cardboard on the wrong side of a piece of wallpaper. Trim the wallpaper so that it is about 1-1/2 inches bigger than the cardboard on all sides.

2. Cover one side of the piece of cardboard with glue. Place the glue side down on the wrong side of the wallpaper, centered so that the 1-1/2-inch border is all around the cardboard. See Figure 1.

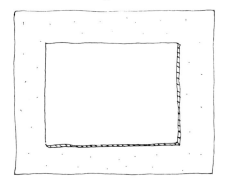

Figure 1

3. Trim each corner. See Figure 2.

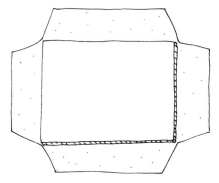

Figure 2

4. Place the cover on the table so that the wallpaper side is down and you can see the cardboard of the book cover. Put glue on each of the four corner flaps, and fold each one up to glue it to the cover. See Figure 3.

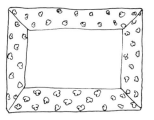

Figure 3

5. Cut a piece of wallpaper to fit 1/4 inch inside the edges of the cover. Glue this endpaper to the inside of the cover so that you can no longer see the cardboard. See Figure 4.

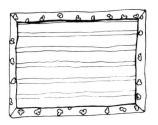

Figure 4

6. Repeat Steps 1 through 5 for the other cover.

7. Cut the pieces of typing paper and graph paper (if you are using it) crosswise in half so that each piece is 5-1/2 by 8-1/2 inches. Stack up the sheets.

8. Punch two holes in the front cover about 1 inch in from each side and about 1/2 inch down from the top edge. You may need to start the holes with the awl and use the tip of the razor knife to widen them if the cardboard and wallpaper are too tough for the hole puncher.

9. Pick up about five sheets of paper and carefully place them under the cover so that they are butted up against the top edge (the edge with the holes) and centered between the side edges. Use the awl or pencil to mark where the holes should be. See Figure 5. Carefully remove the cover, and use the hole puncher to punch two holes through all five sheets at one time. Repeat this step until all of the paper has been punched.

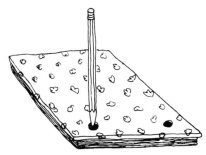

Figure 5

10. Stack up the cover and all of the paper. Arrange it so that the holes are all lined up. Place the stack on top of the other cover. Use the awl or pencil to mark the centers of the holes. Remove the top cover and stack of paper.

11. Use the hole puncher or the awl and razor knife to punch two holes in the bottom cover, where you've marked them.

12. Arrange the stack so that all holes line up. Slip a ring into each hole, and lock each ring closed.

13. Tie one end of the string to one of the rings. Tie the other end of the string around a pen or pencil so that it will be handy when you need to record something.

15

THE EARTH—

where would we be without it?
In this chapter, you can find out a
lot about Earth and its inhabitants.
Build a bird hide and a camou-
flaged periscope to watch the busy
comings and goings of colorful
birds….Grow a mold garden and
watch the "decomposers" at work—
without them, we'd be up to our
ears in all the garbage that ever
existed….Build a home for worms
and one for toads, and watch these
important garden helpers do their
work….Make a root viewer, so you
can see the beginnings of new
life….Craft a handy box for your
rock and mineral collection….Build
a hypsometer to measure the height
of your house and your favorite tree.
And feel closer to Mother Earth
than you ever have before.

EARTH

This little hut will let you get close to birds and small animals without scaring them away. It's easy to build and just as easy to take apart and move to a new location.

What You'll Need

4 strong, straight sticks about 4-1/2 feet long and 2 inches in diameter

6 lighter (but still strong) straight sticks about 2-1/2 feet long

2 forked sticks at least 2 feet long before the fork

100 feet of strong rope

Scissors

A small saw or strong branch cutters

An old sheet or bedspread from a double bed, preferably green or brown

Small leafy branches

What to Do

1. Lay two of the large sticks on the ground side by side and as far apart as the length of two of the smaller branches. Lash the smaller branches between the two large sticks, using about 6 feet of rope for each lashing. See Figure 1 and detail of Figure 1.

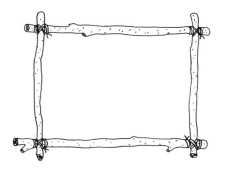

Figure 1

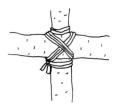

Detail of Figure 1

2. Do the same thing with the other two large sticks and two smaller sticks.

3. Ask a friend to help you hold the two stick frames up so that they're as far apart at the bottom as the length of the remaining smaller sticks. Tilt the two frames toward each other to form a tent shape.

4. Lash the two remaining straight sticks to the frames at the bottom. Lash the two frames together at the top.

5. Use the two forked sticks to make the structure sturdy. First saw or clip off the forks so that the forks are only 2 inches long. Leave the straight ends long. Lash one fork against one of the tilted strong sticks on each side of the frame. Be sure that the forked sticks are on opposite ends of the frame and opposite sides from each other. See Figure 2.

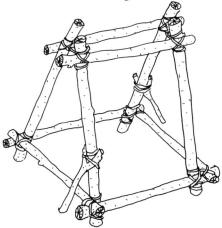

Figure 2

6. Drape the old sheet or bedspread over the frame. Feel

where the ends of the sticks are, and cut small slits in the cloth so that the stick ends poke out and anchor the cloth at the top as well as the bottom of the frame. See Figure 3.

7. Cut short slits to hold leafy branches in spots all over the cloth, and poke small branches through.

8. Cut viewing holes in the cloth at your eye level on the two large sides of the bird hide. Make the holes about 2 by 6 inches.

Figure 3

9. Bring a tree stump or a small stool to sit on, a bird or animal identification book, binoculars, and your notebook and pencil when you go bird or animal watching. It's also a good idea to pack some water and a snack!

Whatta-buncha-
ologies!

The word *science* comes from the Latin word for "knowledge." That makes sense, because scientists are always trying to learn more— to gain knowledge—about our world and universe.

But there are lots of different kinds, or branches, of science. (There's a lot to learn about our world and universe!) What to call them all?

In 1594, Otto Casmann, a European scholar, called the study of humans *anthropology*. The ending came from the Greek word for discussion: *logos.* It was the first time anyone had ever used "ology" (AHL-uh-gee) to refer to science. But it sure wasn't the last. People have been tacking "ology" onto the names of branches of science ever since.

Here's a list of just a few. How many of the sciences can you guess without looking at the right column?

Hint: As hard as some of these look to pronounce, you'll usually be right if you put the emphasis on the OL in "ology"—for example, for *pomology*, the study of fruit, say "po-MAHL-uh-gee."

Science	The Study of...
Anthropology	Humans
Apiology	Bees
Apology	(Sorry, just a joke. We apologize.)
Biology	Living Things
Cartology	Maps
Cetology	Whales
Conchology	Shells
Criminology	Crime and Criminals
Cryptology	Codes
Ecology	Environment
Entomology	Insects
Geology	Earth's Crust
Graphology	Handwriting
Herpetology	Reptiles
Hippology	Horses
Hydrology	Water
Ichthyology	Fish
Ideology	Ideas
Meteorology	Weather and Climate
Mycology	Fungi
Myrmecology	Ants
Nephology	Clouds
Ophiology	Snakes
Ophthalmology	Eyes
Ornithology	Birds
Otology	Ears
Paleontology	Fossilized Life Forms
Pedology	Children
Psychology	Mind and Behavior
Pyrology	Fire
Seismology	Earthquakes and Tremors
Sociology	Human Society
Speleology	Caves
Storiology	Legends and Folk Tales
Vulcanology	Volcanoes
Zoology	Animals

Camouflaged Periscope

With this device you can look around corners and spy on birds and small animals without scaring them away. Keep your periscope with you in your bird hide (see page 18) to extend the range of your eyes.

What You'll Need

A long, thin cardboard box, about 20 by 3 by 3 inches

Plastic package tape

A razor knife

2 pieces of cardboard as wide as the inside width of the box and 3 times as long

2 small mirrors, about 2 by 2 inches

Super glue

Acrylic paint

A paint brush

What to Do

1. Tape both ends of the box closed.

2. Lay the box on one of its long sides, and cut a square hole at one end. The hole should be as long as it is wide. See Figure 1.

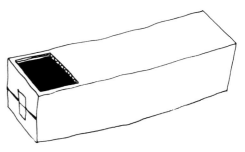

Figure 1

3. Turn the box over, and cut the same size hole at the opposite end of the box, on the opposite side.

4. Fold the two pieces of cardboard into right triangles. See Figure 2. Tape the triangles closed.

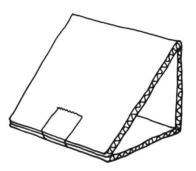

Figure 2

5. Glue a mirror to the slanted side of each cardboard triangle. See Figure 3.

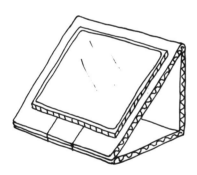

Figure 3

6. After the glued mirrors are completely dry, glue the triangular mirror bases inside the holes in the box. The mirrors must face outward. Wedge the

right-angled sides against the back and ends of the box. See Figure 4.

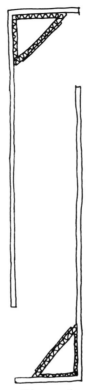

Figure 4

7. With acrylic paints, paint leaf shapes on all sides of the periscope. If the mirrors are in plastic frames, paint the frames, too.

8. To use the periscope, hide behind a tree, a bush, or a fence, and hold the periscope so that one of its openings sticks out so the creature you want to watch is in your line of vision. Look in the other opening. Move the periscope to bring various creatures into your line of vision. You can also stick the periscope out of the opening of your bird hide to extend the range of your eyes.

Camo Creatures
and How to Be One

Almost all birds and animals use camouflage—hide-and-seek tricks—to avoid danger or to help them sneak up on a meal without being seen. By understanding the ways nature's creatures hide, you can become a really good hider, too.

Have you ever seen a silhouette, or shadow picture, of a famous person or of someone you know? You can tell who it is just by the shape.

It's the same way in nature. Many birds and animals can't see colors at all—only shades of light and dark. But all wild creatures recognize shapes. If you're a bird, bug, or animal, it's your outline that makes you stand out.

That's why many living things have outline-hiding

"camo" clothes.) Also, remember that your eyes have a telltale round shape. Break up their outline by drawing a stripe or two next to each eye or from temple to temple—like a raccoon's striped "mask." Use a piece of charcoal to do the makeup. (Don't get the charcoal *in* your eyes, though!)

Another kind of natural camouflage is called *countershading*. Have you noticed that many birds and animals are dark-colored on top and light below? Squirrels, sparrows, lions, fish, whales, dogs, and cats (to name just a few) have lighter-colored stomachs than backs. That makes them much harder to see from a distance. Why? Because sunlight from above lightens the dark upper surface and shadows the under surface. So the two shades blend to make a single, less noticeable, neutral color.

Neutralizing your skin color will also help hide you (even if you have dark skin). Rub a light coating of dirt, clay, or dust on your hands, neck, and face to take the sun's "shine" off.

camouflage. They're covered with distracting patterns—spots, stripes, and other designs that "break up" their actual shape. Scientists call this trick *disruptive coloration*. The eye tends to see different patterns on an object as completely separate parts. When an animal is marked with lines and patterns that lead off into the lines and patterns of its surroundings, its outline "disappears." A spotted fawn

resting in leafy sunlight looks like a bunch of brownish plants. A zebra's stripes "scatter" the animal's outline into nearby trees and brush.

When observing nature, you can use disruptive coloration to hide *your* outline. Wear patterned clothing, such as plaid, in shades similar to the surroundings. (Outdoor and military stores also sell specially patterned

Also, remember that animals are aware of shadows and of any movement. When a squirrel hides on a tree limb or when a lion stalks prey, it hunkers down as low as possible to keep its shadow small, and stays absolutely still. Do the same when *you're* trying to be "invisible," and chances are you'll get a better, closer-than-ever look at the birds, animals, and other creatures sharing your world.

Mold Garden

The adults in your house are not going to like this project as much as you will. You may even have to guard it to make sure no one tries to throw it out with the garbage. If you explain that you are studying tiny organisms called molds, you might convince them to leave your project alone. But whatever you do, don't take the cover off of your mold garden when you're showing it to them!

What You'll Need

A plastic, aluminum, or ceramic container at least 2 inches deep and 6 inches square

A trowel or a large spoon

A few trowels of rich garden soil or compost

Orange peels, bread, cheese, and any other foods that you might have seen growing interesting-looking furry coats in the past (except meats)

A spray bottle full of water or a watering can

Plastic wrap to cover the container completely

A large rubber band or string to fit around the container

A magnifying glass

Tweezers

A piece of white paper

A piece of black paper

What to Do

1. Fill the pan about 1 inch deep with soil or compost.

2. Lay the orange peels, bread, cheese, and other foods on top of the soil. You might consider placing them in some kind of design if you want a really handsome garden.

3. Lightly water the garden.

4. Cover the garden with plastic wrap. Hold the wrap firmly in place with the rubber band or string.

5. Put the garden in a warm, dark place. After a day or two, check on it. Continue to watch the garden for changes. If nothing happens after a few days, give it some more water. Make sure the plastic wrap is completely sealed. Put the garden back in the warm dark.

6. When the garden blooms, carefully remove the cover. Be prepared for a smell! Use tweezers to pick up small bits of the mold. Put light mold down on the black paper and dark mold on the white paper. Use the magnifying glass to get a better look at your mold.

7. When you're finished with the mold garden, throw it into a compost heap or bury it in the garden. Throw away the plastic wrap and rubber band. You can wash and reuse the container.

The Fungus *Among Us*

What's black and yellow and orange and brown and red and white and green and blue…gobbles up anything in its path except metal…and lives everywhere—in the air, inside animals, on plants, underneath the ground, in your shoes, and even (eck!) in your ears and mouth? You guessed it: the fungus among us.

There are more fungi (pronounced FUNJ-eye) in our world than any other kind of plant. The mold that grows on food, the yeast that's used to make bread, and the mushrooms that pop up on your lawn are only a few of more than 100,000 different types of fungi. The soil in a small garden contains at least 10 times as many fungi as there are people on Earth!

Most plants make their own food, but fungi can't. So instead they eat other plants and animals—just like people do. The difference is, we eat our food first and then digest it. Fungi do the opposite. They give off chemicals that turn their meal-to-be (a nice fresh banana, for instance) into yucky mush. Then they suck up the liquid.

Their odd eating habits make fungi both friends and foes to us human types. For one thing, we have to go to a lot of trouble to keep fungi from eating our food before we do. Refrigerators help, because most kinds of fungi prefer warm surroundings. But even in cold temperatures hungry fungi will eventually turn the good, solid food *we* like into the nasty, oozy stuff *they* like.

Fungi also make it tough for people to grow food. Most of the plant diseases that give farmers and gardeners trouble are actually hungry fungi digesting roots, leaves, and stems. Even your feet are a treat to certain kinds of fungi that cause the itchy-skin disease known as athlete's foot.

On the other hand, if it weren't for fungi, we'd all be up to our necks in dead plants and animals. Fungi break down, or decompose, plant and animal remains and turn them into plant food and soil. Molds also help us make such foods as cheese and vinegar. And the green mold that you've probably seen growing on oranges or other fruit? That's the famous fungus *Penicillium*. Revolting as it may look, that mold provides us with penicillin, which has probably saved more human (and animal) lives than any other medicine in history.

Plus, we humans turn the tables on at least some of the fungus among us and eat them. Every year we gobble up millions of pounds of mushrooms grown on underground "farms" in caves and old mines.

Some ants are fungus farmers, too. Workers carry bits of leaves into the nest, where smaller ants chew them up and add them to the fungus garden. The insects tend their crop constantly, weeding out any foreign fungi and harvesting the kind they like to eat.

Fuzzy Wuzzy Was a… *Worm?*

You don't usually think of an earthworm as fuzzy, but if you rub your fingers very lightly from back to front along a night crawler's sides, you can just barely feel tiny hairs (called *setae*). There are eight hairs on each ring, or segment, of the worm's body. Earthworms have muscles that can tilt the bristles forward or back, like the oars on a rowboat. They use the hairs to help them move ahead or backward. They also use the hairs to grab onto the soil. That's why it's so hard to pull an earthworm out of its burrow!

27

A Wormery

The design of this wormery makes it easy for you to trace the tunnels of the residents and observe each day's new diggings.

What You'll Need

A piece of 1 by 2 lumber 22 inches long

A saw

A ruler

A pencil

Sandpaper

Acrylic paints

A brush

Wood glue

2 pieces of plexiglass each 5 by 7 inches

Super glue

A brace and bit, or a hand drill and a small drill bit

4 narrow screws between 3/8 and 1/2 inch long and slightly wider than the drill bit

A screwdriver to fit the screws

Silver or colored duct tape

Black puffy paint (optional)

A trowel or a large spoon

Sand

Dark garden soil or compost

Leaf mold

Cellophane tape

Sheets of tracing paper

A soft, dark cloth about 2 by 2 feet

What to Do

1. Saw the lumber into three pieces. Two of them should be 7 inches long, and the third should be 5-7/8 inches long.

2. Sand the three pieces of lumber.

3. Use wood glue to glue the two 7-inch pieces of wood to the ends of the shorter pieces of wood.

4. When the glue is dry, paint all surfaces of the wood with acrylic paints.

5. When the paint is dry, lay the U-shaped form down flat, and super glue one of the pieces of plexiglass to the top surface. The plexiglass edges should overlap the wood on three sides by about 1/2 inch.

6. When the glue is dry, turn the wormery over and glue the other piece of plexiglass to the other side in the same manner.

7. To reinforce the glue, drill a starter hole halfway down each side about 1/4 inch in from the edge of the plexiglass.

8. Put a screw in each hole. Tighten it down with the screwdriver. Turn the wormery over and repeat Steps 7 and 8 on the other side.

9. Put duct tape along all the edges where plexiglass and wood come together. Use scissors or a razor knife to help with this job. If you want to decorate the wormery, now's the time to draw puffy paint worms crawling along the edges.

10. Fill the wormery with layers of sand and soil. Make each layer about an inch deep. Place a few earthworms below the final layer. Top off the layers with a layer of leaf mold. Lightly sprinkle the layers with water.

11. Cover the wormery with the dark cloth when you aren't observing it.

12. To check and record the progress of the worms, tape a piece of tracing paper to one side of the wormery each day, and trace the layers and tunnels. Put a date on each piece of paper so that you can keep track of the papers and compare the changes that take place from day to day.

13. After a week or so, dump the entire contents of the wormery out into the garden or compost heap and start over. Worms are happier in the earth than in a wormery!

Toad House

A toad is a gardener's friend because it eats a *lot* of insects. Toads like to live in dark, cool holes or hollows in rocks or under debris. You can invite a toad to live in your garden by making a toad house.

What You'll Need

A medium-sized clay flower pot

Acrylic paints

A paint brush

A trowel

What to Do

1. Wash and dry the pot if it has been used.

2. Paint leaf and flower shapes in greens, browns, and other earth colors all over the outside of the pot, including the bottom.

3. When the paint is completely dry, go outside to the garden and find a sheltered spot among your plants. Lay the pot on its side. Use the trowel to bury it halfway beneath the soil. Put some dead leaves and other garden debris in the bottom of the toad house. Check back after a few days to see if any of the debris has been moved. If you're patient, you may catch a glimpse of your toad sometime. If no toad seems to come to your toad house, try moving it to another location.

Toad-ally Awesome

Next time you see a toad, pick it up and get better acquainted. No, you *won't* catch warts. You'd better be gentle, though, or your hand will get slimed.

See those ugly oval lumps behind the toad's eyes? Those are called *parotoid glands.* When a toad is roughly handled, those glands (and others on its skin, including those warty bumps) give off a gooey liquid. The stuff won't hurt your skin. But it does burn and irritate sensitive membranes—like the ones inside an animal's mouth. That's why dogs, cats, and most other creatures that try snacking on a toad spit it out fast. Pretty good self-defense, for a little guy with pop eyes and webbed feet!

Some people confuse frogs and toads, but they're really quite different. Frogs have long legs and smooth, shiny bodies. Toads have short back legs and wide, bumpy, dull bodies.

Frogs are nervous and—well, jumpy. To get somewhere, they leap. Toads are more relaxed and slow-moving. They'll hop if they have to, but they'd rather walk.

Frogs live in and around water. Toads spend most of their time on land.

Also, toads are smarter than frogs. In laboratory experiments, scientists have found that toads can figure out mazes much more quickly than their frog relatives.

Most people think toads are homely but still lovable. To an insect, though, a toad is Godzilla. Do you know how many beetles, grubs, and other bugs an average toad snaps up during the summer? About 110 a day, or roughly 3,300 a month!

To invite a toad into your garden, give it a cool, shady place to live (like the flowerpot toad house on the opposite page). Toads drink by sitting in water and soaking the liquid through their skin. So put a shallow pan of "drinking" water nearby, somewhere private and out of view. And to *really* pamper your pet, put a battery-operated night light near its home, to attract moths and other tasty toad snacks.

Root Viewer

What goes on in the dark under the soil, when the first roots of a baby plant are bursting out of the seed and uncoiling, reaching and stretching and searching for food? This special planter will give you a front-row seat for one of nature's great performances.

Figure 1

What You'll Need

A 1-quart, square-bottomed, plastic freezer container

A sharp knife or razor knife

A piece of plexiglass
5 by 7 inches

Plastic tape 1 inch wide

A piece of black paper the same size as the plexiglass

Cellophane tape

A handful of small stones or broken clay flowerpot pieces

Potting soil

A few beans or other seeds

What to Do

1. Carefully cut from a top corner of the plastic container straight down to the middle of the bottom of the same side. See Figure 1.

2. Make the same kind of cut on the opposite side of the container. Now make a straight cut across the bottom. Remove the cutout piece of plastic.

3. Using the plastic tape, tape the piece of plexiglass to the open side of the container. Be sure that all edges are completely covered with tape and that there are no holes or gaps between the container and the plexiglass.

4. With cellophane tape, tape the piece of black paper to the top edge of the plexiglass so that it can be lifted and lowered.

5. Place the stones in the bottom of the container to improve drainage. Add potting soil to fill the rest of the container. Push a few seeds into the soil about 1/2 inch back from the plexiglass edge.

6. Flip the black paper down. If necessary, tape the bottom edge so that it stays down. Water the seeds, and place the container in a dark spot until the seeds sprout. After they have begun to grow, place the container in the light, and lift up the black paper every day or so to check on the roots. In a few days you should be able to see them and watch their progress. Since roots tend to grow straight down, the slanted, clear side of this container should make the roots clearly visible.

Seed Cast Tiles

When you walk through the woods or across a field in autumn, you'll find pods and other seed heads with interesting shapes. Clay casts are a nice way of collecting these intricate and beautiful objects. See page 227 for Seed Cast Medallions.

What You'll Need

Low-fire potter's clay*

A rolling pin

Dried seed heads from plants

A table knife

A paper clip for each tile

A board about 1 by 3 feet

White conte crayon** or white chalk

Acrylic matte medium**

A soft paint brush

*Clay can be bought in a craft supply store.

**Both conte crayons and acrylic medium are available from an art or craft supply store.

What to Do

1. Before making the tiles, you need to wedge the clay—that is, get rid of air bubbles that could cause the tiles to break in the kiln. To wedge the clay, pound and knead it for about 10 minutes.

2. Roll the clay out to a 1/4-inch thickness.

3. Cut the slab into rectangles or squares the size that you want the finished tiles to be.

4. With your fingers, press a seed head into each tile. If the seed head is prickly, wear garden gloves to do this part of the job. Lift the head off. It's okay if pieces of it stick to the clay. They'll burn away during firing, leaving their impression.

34

5. Unbend the paper clips into S shapes. Bend each S into a slight angle, and slip it into the center of the back of each tile, about 1 inch below the top edge. This will be the hook from which you'll be able to hang the tiles. If you don't want to hang the tiles, skip this step.

6. Place the tiles on the board in a cool, dry place for about a week. When the tiles are dry and no longer feel cold when held up to your cheek, carefully place them in a pit kiln (see page 209) to fire them.

7. After the tiles are fired, rinse them off to remove any remaining ash. Color across the surface of each tile with chalk or white conte crayon. Be careful to keep the chalk out of the seed head impression. If crumbs of chalk fall into the impression, blow them out.

8. When you have enough white on the surface of the tile that the black or gray impression shows clearly, gently brush the entire surface with acrylic matte medium to keep the chalk from smearing.

In Search of the Lost...
Landfill?

When you think of an archaeologist, you might think of a person who searches ancient pyramids for mummies of the long-ago rich and famous, or who discovers lost gold in deep-in-the-jungle Incan tombs.

Well, many archaeologists *do* lead exciting lives. But often the "treasure" they find isn't exactly in a spectacular place.

An archaeologist's job is to study the way people lived in the past by examining the objects they left behind. Works of art from a great king's burial site may tell part of the story—but they don't always say much about the day-to-day lives of ordinary citizens.

So to an archaeologist, everyday things—a broken cookpot, a bit of burned food, a worn tool—are really important finds. Each is a piece in the who-were-these-people-and-how-did-they-live puzzle.

Now, think about it: Where would an archaeologist exploring your town 500 years from now find the greatest number of everyday objects from the greatest number of people, all in one place? That's right: the local landfill, or dump. To a scientist studying the past, there's no richer "treasure trove" than the place where the people threw away their trash.

In many early societies, that place was the community or family fire pit, where meals were cooked and the leftovers tossed in to burn. Bits of charred bone and food such as grains and nuts tell an archaeologist what kind

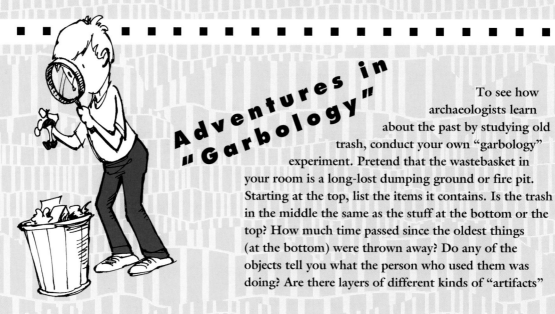

Adventures in "Garbology"

To see how archaeologists learn about the past by studying old trash, conduct your own "garbology" experiment. Pretend that the wastebasket in your room is a long-lost dumping ground or fire pit. Starting at the top, list the items it contains. Is the trash in the middle the same as the stuff at the bottom or the top? How much time passed since the oldest things (at the bottom) were thrown away? Do any of the objects tell you what the person who used them was doing? Are there layers of different kinds of "artifacts"

of diet the people ate, what sorts of animals and plants lived in the area, and much more.

Finding the site of the village pit kiln reveals another kind of "trash pile," where potters tossed pottery that came out of the kiln broken or imperfect. Sometimes a pit kiln site is littered with hundreds of clay-vessel pieces. Each is a valuable clue about the humans who lived there.

Some archaeologists study more recent times. In many cities today, urban archaeologists dig through turn-of-the-century garbage dumps, unearthing such things as old toys, tools, newspapers, medicine bottles, and even clothing. Their discoveries help explain city life 100 years ago.

And where do you suppose archaeologists studying early farm life dig for trash treasure? Country families didn't have landfills. They threw things away in a completely different sort of place: the outhouse!

■ ■ ■ ■ ■ ■ ■ ■ ■

for different parts of the week or times of day? If you compared the trash in your room with the trash in your best friend's room, what would be different? What would be the same?

An archaeologist learns to "read" objects almost as though they were words in a book. The more you read, the better you understand the whole story.

Radioactive Dating

"Radioactive dating" sounds like something teenage space aliens do. But actually, it's how curious earth creatures called scientists figure out the ages of fossils, rocks, and artifacts.

All living things have radioactive atoms inside them called *carbon 14*. The atoms aren't dangerous. They come from the carbon dioxide in air. Plants "breathe" it in, animals eat plants, and people eat plants and animals. So we're all a little bit radioactive.

When something dies, it stops taking in carbon 14. And the radioactivity already in the plant or animal starts to gradually decay, or fade away.

Scientists know exactly how fast (well, actually, how slow) carbon 14 loses its "buzz." After 5,730 years, half the radioactivity is gone. And after about 50,000 years, there's none left at all.

By measuring how much radioactive carbon 14 is still in a piece of wood, shell, bone, or fossil, scientists can tell how long ago it was a part of something alive. And if it has no radioactivity, they know that it's more than 50,000 years old.

Of course, rocks don't eat or breathe so they don't contain carbon 14. But when most rocks are formed they do pick up other kinds of radioactive atoms, which also decay at a certain speed.

When lava from a volcano hardens, for instance, it almost always contains brand-new radioactive potassium 40. It takes 1.3 billion (1,300,000,000) years for a rock to lose half its radioactive potassium 40 atoms. Those atoms don't really go anywhere, though. As they decay, they turn into a kind of un-radioactive atoms called argon 40.

So, to figure the age of volcanic rock, scientists compare the number of potassium 40 atoms with the number of argon 40 atoms. A rock that's half and half is 1.3 billion years old. (Can you guess how old a rock is if it has twice as many potassium 40 atoms as argon 40 atoms?)

Fantastic *Fossils*

Fossils are the remains of animals and plants that lived long ago—*really* long ago. Dinosaur fossils are at least 65 million years old. The earliest fossils known, tiny bacteria from ancient sea deposits in southern Africa, are 3-1/2 *billion* years old.

Most things that die are eaten up by animals or bacteria before they get a chance to *be* fossils. But sometimes mud or sand quickly covers the dead animal or plant. The soft parts decay, but hard parts, such as bones, teeth, shell, or wood, last longer. Over the ages, minerals from soil or water seep into the buried parts, making them tougher. Eventually they're hard as rock. They become *petrified*, like the stone logs in Arizona's Petrified Forest National Park, or the dinosaur bones and eggs at Utah's Dinosaur National Monument.

Other times, even the hard parts dissolve. The entire plant or animal disappears, but it leaves an impression of itself in the rock—a *mold*, much like the seed tiles you can make on page 34. Fossilized footprints are another type of mold. Sometimes minerals fill in the mold and make a *cast* fossil. (If you poured plaster of Paris into a footprint in your backyard, you would be making a cast.)

By comparing fossils from different places around the world and from different layers of rock, scientists can "read" about Earth's development.

Often, the stories fossils tell are surprising. Fossilized sea life, for instance, has been found in rock at the top of Mt. Everest. So we know that what is now the world's highest mountain was once the bottom of an ocean. And where do you suppose scientists have found the remains of a lush tropical forest? Buried under miles of ice and snow—at the South Pole!

Actually, if it weren't for fossils, you'd have a hard time believing most of the crazy stories you hear about life on Earth millions of years ago.

A reptile four stories high and as heavy as 15 elephants? A fish as long as an 18-wheeler, with the head of a huge snapping turtle?

Yeah, right!

Ferns as tall as oak trees? Twenty-foot-long centipedes? Dragonflies with 2-1/2-foot wingspans?

Get outta here!

But scientists know that all these things—and a whole lot more about Earth's incredible history—are absolutely, undeniably true. They're facts written in stone: fossils. For more fossils see page 223.

Spider Web

The orb-web spider makes a sturdy web that covers a large area yet uses little material and energy. The spider makes a spiral path beginning at the center. After you make this model web, you'll never look at a spider web in the same way again!

What You'll Need

A piece of cloth 12 by 12 inches*

An iron and ironing board

A 10-inch wooden embroidery hoop**

A needle

Silver or white embroidery thread

Scissors

*Look for cloth that's made for counted cross-stitch or embroidery, in a color that you like. Or you can use any medium-weight to heavy-weight cloth that's not textured and not silky.

**Get this at a craft or sewing store.

What to Do

1. Iron the cloth if it is creased or wrinkled.

2. Loosen the adjusting screw on the embroidery hoop, and separate the two parts of the hoop. Lay the cloth, centered, over the inner (smaller) hoop; then place the outer hoop over the cloth and the inner hoop,

and push down equally all around. The cloth will be stretched tightly by the hoops. Tighten the screw when the outer hoop is in place to lock the whole arrangement. You can then gently pull out any wrinkles or loose spots in the cloth.

3. Thread the needle with several feet of thread. Pull the two ends of thread together and knot them. You will be using a double strand of thread. When you run out of thread, just tie a knot on the back of the cloth, and start a new piece of thread just as you did this first piece.

4. An orb-web spider begins its web by laying down a bridge line between two upright supports, such as branches or fence posts.

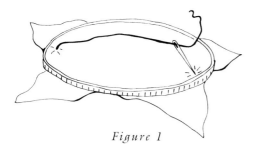

Figure 1

You'll do this by poking your needle from the back to the front of the cloth at any spot as close to the edge as you can. Bring the needle and thread across the circle of cloth, and put the needle in as close to the hoop as you can on the opposite side of the circle. See Figure 1. Now stick the needle back out toward the front, very close to the spot where you just came from. Swing all the way across the circle, and put the needle back in very close to where the bridge line began. You should now have a double thickness of bridge line, and the needle should be on the back side of the cloth.

5. The orb-web spider next attaches a strand near the middle of the bridge line and reels out silk to drop to another anchoring point, pulling on the bridge line so that a Y shape is formed.

You'll do this by bringing the needle and thread (on the back side of the cloth) to a spot on the edge midway between the two anchoring points, poking the needle through, and looping it up and around the bridge line. Just poke the tip of the needle through, so that if it isn't in the right spot, you can easily pull it out and try again until it comes out exactly where you want it. Now bring the needle across the front side of the cloth, and stick it back in at a spot on the edge

midway between the other two anchoring points. Pull a little on the thread (and be sure that it loops around the bridge line) so that it pulls the bridge line into a slight Y shape. On the back of the cloth, travel up to the center again, poke the needle through, and retrace the bottom leg of the Y so that it has double thickness like the other bridge lines. See Figure 2.

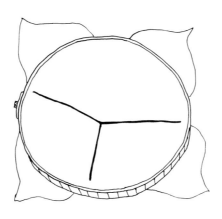

Figure 2

6. The next thing the orb-web spider does is to lay out a framework of spokes that move outward from the center of the web.

To copy her, move the needle over about 1 inch from the bridge line, staying at the outside edge of the circle, and poke the needle through to the front side. Then bring the needle across the front of the cloth to the center, and poke it through to the back. Take the needle to the edge of the cloth, about 1 inch from the spoke you just made, and poke it through to the back. Repeat these huge stitches until you've made spokes all the way around the web. Each time you come back to the center, bring the needle out as close to the same place as you can. See Figure 3.

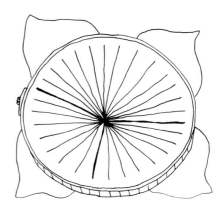

Figure 3

7. After all the spokes are in place, the orb-web spider builds a spiral outward from the center. As the spiral turns, the distance that the web moves out along the spokes remains the same with each turn.

In your case, make a spiral by poking the needle through so that it comes out the center on the front of the cloth. Move out about 1/4 inch and poke the needle through *right next to* any spoke. On the back side, feel around with the needle until you find the spot just on the *other* side of the spoke from where you went in, and poke the needle back to the front. See Figure 4.

Figure 4

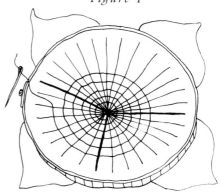

Figure 5

8. Continue moving in a spiral. Study Figure 5 carefully. As you move, try to keep the spaces that you move along the spokes the same. The spaces between the spokes will, of course, grow larger as you move out from the center.

9. When your web is the size you want it to be, add a few more anchoring threads. The outer edges of spider webs are never perfectly smooth.

10. If you've enjoyed making an orb-web spider web, study some other spiders as they build webs. Draw their webs, and make some notes about what they do first and how they proceed to build their webs. Then embroider their webs the same way you did the orb-web. You can make a collection of spider web models.

Amazing Spiders and Incredible
(Edible?) Webs

Did you know that some spiders live *underwater*, in little air-filled spider-web balloons? Or that some capture their meals by hurling gluey spitballs at passing bugs? Others lasso their prey with spider-silk rope!

Spiders are among the most amazing creatures on earth. Scientists think there are somewhere between 30,000 and 50,000 different kinds in the world. Even the most common types, such as garden spiders and other members of the family known as orb weavers, are anything but ordinary.

Orb weavers spin the kind of web you think of when you picture a spider web: a round or triangular net of silky threads. Next time you see one, take a closer look.

See those wispy, almost invisible silk strands spiraling round and round the web? Each is less than 1/100 of an inch thick, yet stronger, by weight, than steel. If you look at one of the strands under a microscope, you'll see little drops of sticky liquid strung along it, like beads. That's what bugs get stuck in. Inside each tiny bead is more spider silk, coiled up like a spring. When a trapped insect struggles, the coils unwind and the strand stretches, so the bug can't break free. Sticky spider silk can stretch more than four times its length without breaking!

Have you ever wondered why spiders don't get caught in their own webs? It's because not all the threads are sticky. In an orb web, the strands that extend outward from the center like spokes on a wheel are dry. When a spider runs to a trapped insect, it steps only on the dry strands and not the gluey ones.

Most orb webs contain about 60 feet of silk and take a spider about half an hour to build. If a part of the web gets damaged, the spider eats up all the wrecked pieces and patches the holes with new silk. Some orb weavers gobble up their old webs and build new ones every day!

Hypsometer

How in the world can you measure something as tall as a large tree or a skyscraper? A hypsometer (hip-SOM-uh-ter) is the answer. This clever instrument uses triangles to measure the height of very tall things.

What You'll Need

A cardboard tube about 2 feet long

Acrylic paints

A paint brush

A piece of corrugated card-board about 6 by 6 inches

A pencil

A razor knife

An awl or a large nail

Colored plastic tape

Scissors

A needle

2 feet of black or other dark-colored thread

A yardstick

A piece of heavy poster board

or cardboard 18 inches long by 1-1/2 inches wide

2 heavy rubber bands

A piece of wood, such as molding, about 2 feet long by 1/4 inch thick by 3/4 inch wide

A fine-tipped black permanent marker

3 feet of heavy thread or kite string

A fishing weight or a washer or other small weight that can be tied to the thread

A stapler

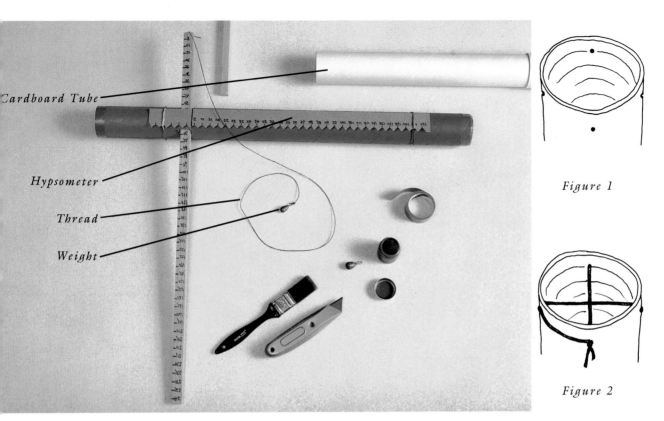

Cardboard Tube

Hypsometer

Thread

Weight

Figure 1

Figure 2

What to Do

1. First paint the tube if you want your hypsometer to be fancy and decorated. If you don't want to decorate it, skip this step.

2. After the paint is completely dry, stand the end of the tube on the piece of cardboard and trace around the circular end with a pencil. Use the razor knife to cut out this circle.

3. Punch a small hole in the exact center of this circle with the awl or large nail. Then tape the circle to one end of the tube with plastic tape.

4. Use the awl or nail to poke four small holes in the other end of the tube. The holes should be about 1/4 inch down from the opening and spaced equally around the opening. See Figure 1.

5. Thread the needle with dark-colored thread. Poke it through one of the holes and pull the thread from the outside, through the hole, across the opening of the tube, and into the hole on the opposite side. (Hold the tail of the thread with your finger to keep it from sliding through the holes.) Now, without cutting the thread, bring the needle to one of the other two holes. Poke the needle in and pull the thread from the outside, through the hole, across the opening of the tube, and through the hole on the opposite side of the opening. You should now have a cross made of thread in the opening. Tie the ends of the thread together and trim the remaining thread. See Figure 2.

6. Wrap plastic tape around the outside of the opening in this end of the tube to hide the holes and thread ends.

7. Now make the height measure. Lay the piece of poster-board alongside the yardstick and mark off every 1/2 inch, using the permanent marker. Make each mark 1/2 inch long. Do NOT number the marks yet. See Figure 3.

8. Use scissors or the razor knife to cut a sawtooth edge. Begin each cut between two marks, cut at a slant to the bottom of one mark, then cut at a slant up to the spot halfway between the next mark and the mark you are on. See Figure 4.

9. Use the rubber bands to fasten the height measure to the tube. See Figure 5.

10. Now make the distance measure. Lay the piece of wood next to the yardstick, and make the same marks as you did on the poster board height measure. Number these marks, beginning with 0 and going by 5s until you run out of marks.

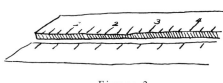

Figure 3

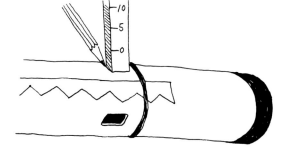

Figure 6

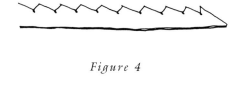

Figure 4

Figure 5

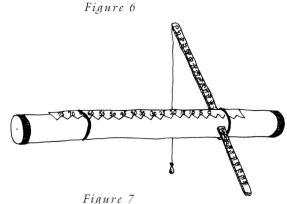

Figure 7

11. Hold the wooden distance measure with one of its ends against the tube, about 6 inches down from the end with the crossed threads and right beside the height measure. See Figure 6. Trace around the end of the wooden piece. Use the razor knife to cut this shape out of the side of the tube. Now trace the end of the wooden piece on the cardboard tube on the other side of the sawtooth measure. Figure 6 also shows you where this place is. Use the razor knife to cut out this shape, too.

12. Slide the wooden distance measure through the two shapes you have just cut out of the tube. The wooden measure should be firmly held in place, yet it should easily slide up and down through the cutout shapes.

13. Tie one end of the heavy thread or kite string to the fishing weight (or whatever you are using as a weight). Staple the other end of the string to the 0 end of the wooden distance measure.

14. Now you are ready to number the height measure. Start numbering at the first mark after the place where the distance measure is inserted into the tube. Going from right to left, begin with 0 and number by 5s until you run out of marks. There will be a few notches and marks on the other side of the wooden measure. Just leave those without numbers. See Figure 7.

15. To use the hypsometer, measure the distance from where you are standing to whatever it is you want to measure. You could use a long tape measure or a yardstick. (Note: You must be on level ground or at least on the same level as the object you are measuring.) Slide the wooden distance measure so that the number of feet you are from the object is at the opening where the wooden measure goes into the tube (away from the sawtooth edge). Hold the hypsometer so that you can look through the pinhole while the weighted string swings freely on the same side of the hypsometer as the sawtooth edge. Turn the hypsometer until the string hangs free.

Look through the pinhole so that the top of the object to be measured is at the cross point of the crossed threads. Now gently turn the tube so that the freely hanging weighted string catches on the sawtooth edge. Carefully lower the hypsometer, making sure that the string does not move from the tooth in which it is caught. Add your height to the number on the height measure where the string was caught. The sum is the height of the object. Note: If you are measuring the object in feet, be sure to add your height in feet.

44

THE AIR

around us—we breathe it every minute of every day. Yet air is important to us in other ways, too. If you build some wind chimes from clay pots, you can discover how sound travels through the air....Make a xylophone, and listen to the different notes that come from tubes that hold different amounts of air....Build a nephoscope to help you track the clouds as they move across the sky....Make a hot air balloon and a rocket jet kite—why should rocket scientists have all the fun?...Build a barometer, and tell your friends what the weather will be like tomorrow....Or make a new-tech hovercraft, a helicopter, and a wind speed meter—and learn even more about the air around us.

AIR

Clay Pot Wind Chimes

These chimes have a nice, musical sound on a breezy spring or summer day. Play around with different sizes of pots to get different tones.

What You'll Need

Several clay flowerpots of different sizes

Scissors

Rope

Monofilament fishing line

Broken pieces of pottery or seashells

A paint brush

Acrylic paints

What to Do

1. Wash and dry the pots, if they have been used.

2. Cut a piece of rope about 3 feet long, and tie two or three knots right on top of one another at one end. The knots should make a big lump.

3. Thread the unknotted end of the rope through the hole in the bottom of the pot, from the inside out. See Figure 1. The knot should stop the rope from coming out of the pot.

4. Cut a piece of monofilament

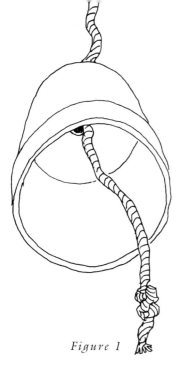

Figure 1

about 8 inches long. Tie one end of it to a piece of broken pottery or a shell.

5. Reach into the pot and pull the knotted rope out so that you can tie the other end of the monofilament to it. See Figure 2. Adjust the length so that the bottom edge of the clapper hangs out of the pot by about 1 inch.

6. Make as many bells as you want, perhaps using different sizes of pots and different materials for the clappers.

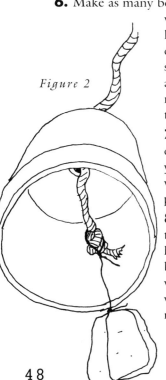

Figure 2

7. Paint designs on your bells with acrylic paint.

8. When they are dry, hang the bells outside where the wind can move them.

What's That Sound?

Throw a rock into the middle of a pond, and circles of waves ripple outward. Blow your nose in the middle of a room, and circles of a different sort of waves ripple outward. You can't see them, but you hear them: H-O-N-K.

When you blow your nose you make it vibrate, and when it vibrates, your schnozzola makes the surrounding air vibrate, too. Waves of air molecules, some thick and some thin, go rushing outward in a special you-blowing-your-nose pattern. When the waves reach your ear, they make your eardrum vibrate in exactly the same pattern. Your inner ear changes those vibrations to electrical messages and passes them along to your brain. H-O-N-K.

All sounds happen like that. When something vibrates, it wiggles back and forth in its own special way. As the vibrating thing pushes forward into the air, the air molecules in front are squashed together and the molecules behind are thinned out. When it pushes back again, it squishes together the molecules behind it and thins out the ones in front. Every time the object vibrates, it pushes out more thick and thin

groups of air molecules: sound waves. Different patterns of sound waves produce different sounds.

An object that vibrates slowly (your nose, for instance) makes a low sound. Things that vibrate fast have a high

sound. We call how high or low a sound is its *pitch*, and the number of times something vibrates per second its *frequency*. Which would have a higher pitch: something that vibrates 100 times a second, or something that vibrates 300 times a second?

You can change an object's pitch by changing its thickness. Have you ever noticed that some of the strings on a guitar are thicker than others? The thickest string vibrates the slowest and has the lowest pitch. The thinnest string vibrates faster, and makes a high note.

You can also change an object's pitch by changing its length. Shorter things vibrate faster and produce a higher sound. If you're playing a guitar, you can make a string sound a higher note by pressing down on the string and shortening its length. (Check out the two photos above.) Look at the xylophone on page 49. When you bonk one of the tubes, the metal and the air inside the tube vibrate and send out sound waves. Which tubes make the highest notes: the long ones or the short ones?

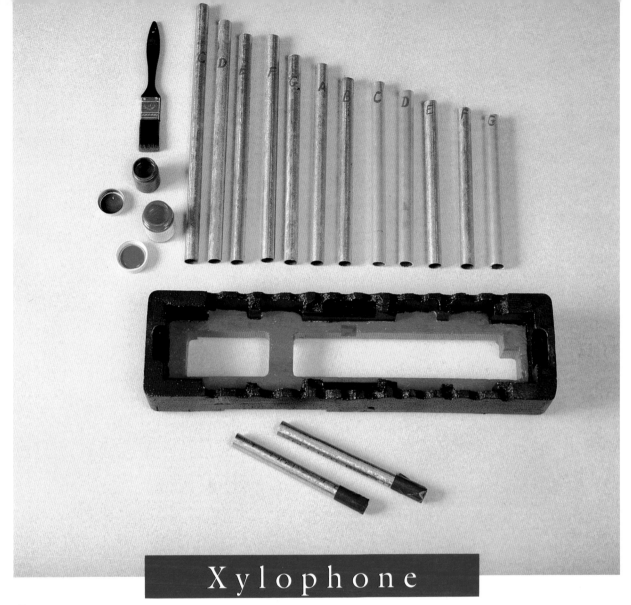

Xylophone

A xylophone with clear, ringing tones can cost a lot of money. You can make this one for very little cost, and you'll enjoy playing your favorite songs, as well as inventing new tunes.

What You'll Need

12 feet of 5/8-inch aluminum or steel pipe*

A ruler

A hacksaw

A metal file

A plastic foam packing form at least 16 inches long by 5 inches wide with an open center, or 2 pieces of foam packing form 16 inches long by 1 inch wide. Whichever of these that you use should be between 1 and 2 inches high.

A razor knife

Acrylic paint

A thin paint brush

A wide paint brush

12 inches of colored plastic tape

Scissors

*Metal pipe is available from a hardware store.

What to Do

1. Saw the pipe into the following lengths: 14-1/4 inches, 13-1/4 inches, 12-1/2 inches, 12-1/4 inches, 11-1/4 inches, 10-3/4 inches, 10 inches, 9-3/4 inches, 9-1/4 inches, 8-3/4 inches, 8-1/2 inches, 8 inches, 7-1/2 inches, and 7-1/2 inches.

2. Use the file to smooth the sawn ends.

3. Arrange the pipes in order from long to short. Keep the two 7-1/2- inch pieces out of this arrangement. Using the thin paint brush, paint each of these letters on the end of a pipe, starting with the longest pipe: C, D, E, F, G, A, B, C, D, E, F, and G.

4. Use the knife to cut two shallow resting places for each pipe on the foam forms. See Figure 1.

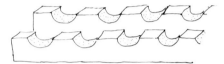

Figure 1

5. Paint the foam base your favorite colors, using acrylic paints and a paint brush.

6. Arrange the pipes in their resting places, beginning on the left with the longest pipe, C.

7. Wrap 6 inches of tape around one end of each 7-1/2-inch pipe. Hold the short pipes by the taped ends when you play the xylophone.

Totally
Tubular

Every minute of every day, you're surrounded by background noise: a hodgepodge of sound waves, with all sorts of frequencies and pitches. Usually, you hear all the sounds at once, jumbled together. But here's a way to partially sort them out.

Save the cardboard tubes from a roll of wrapping paper, a roll of paper towels, and a roll of toilet tissue. Or better yet, cut several long tubes into a variety of lengths—say, 6, 12, 18, 24, 30, and 36 inches. Now put an end of each tube to your ear, one at a time, listen into the end of it, and compare the sounds.

Why do you hear only low, soft sounds in the long tubes, and only higher, louder sounds in the shorter tubes?

All things have their own *natural frequency*, or range of frequencies, at which they vibrate. One way to make that happen is to hit or (in the case of a rubber band or guitar string) pluck the object. But that's not the only way. If sound waves come along that have the same frequency as an object's natural frequency, the waves will make the object vibrate, too. Scientists call this *resonance*. Maybe you've noticed it when you've been listening to a stereo and a certain note made something in the room vibrate and buzz.

That's what's happening in the tubes. The "object" that's vibrating is the column of air inside each tube. Because each tube is a different length, the air column inside "hears," or resonates with, only the sounds that match its frequency range. So it picks up the background sounds that it "likes," and ignores the rest.

Sound Viewer

With this easy-to-make device, you can create a light show that will let you *see* sound.

What You'll Need

A small, empty can, such as a tomato paste can or a baking powder can

A can opener

Acrylic paint

A paint brush

A large balloon

A heavy rubber band

Scissors

Tiny pieces of broken mirror, or small pieces of very shiny silver foil paper

Super glue

What to Do

1. Remove both ends of the can and wash it out.

2. Paint the outside of the can with acrylic paint to decorate it.

3. After the paint is dry, make a rubber membrane by cutting a section out of the balloon and stretching it across one of the open ends of the can. Hold the rubber membrane in place with the rubber band. Adjust the rubber band so that it is tight, and pull out any wrinkles from the membrane so that it is smooth and tight across the opening.

4. Use a tiny bit of glue to glue a small piece of mirror or shiny silver foil to a spot near an edge

of the membrane. The mirror or foil should not touch the edge of the can.

5. When the glue is dry, go to a sunny window, and hold the sound viewer so that it reflects a spot of light onto a wall while you hold the open end of the can up to your mouth. You may have to move around some to find the right position.

6. Now talk and hum into the can while pressing it up against your face around your mouth. Notice what happens to the light when you sing very high notes, when you talk in a deep voice, when you sing a musical scale.

7. Try making a second sound viewer. This time glue several pieces of mirror or foil to the rubber membrane in a design. Watch what happens when you sing or talk into this viewer.

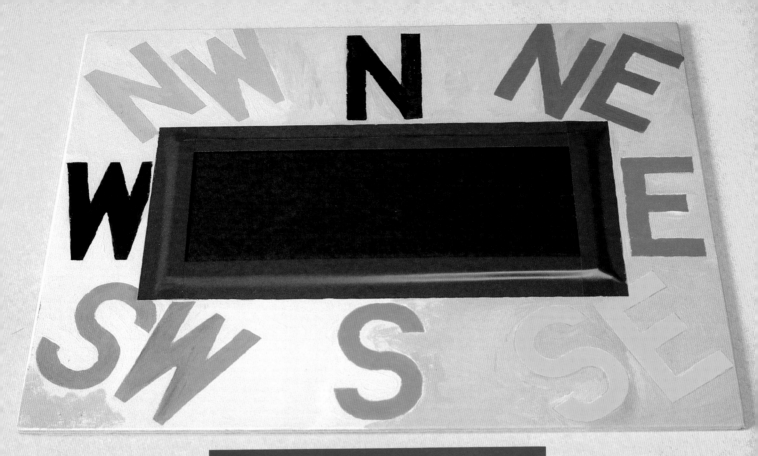

Nephoscope

A nephoscope is an instrument that makes it easy to see which direction clouds are traveling in—which can be hard to do with the naked eye. You can make this nephoscope in just a few minutes.

What You'll Need

A piece of glass or plexiglass about 5 by 10 inches

A piece of black paper the same size as the glass or plexiglass

A piece of plywood, Masonite, or heavy cardboard about 12 by 18 inches

Plastic tape, 1 inch wide

Sandpaper

A magnetic compass

Acrylic paints

A paint brush

Stencils for letters (optional)

What to Do

1. Lay the piece of black paper in the center of the board, and place the glass or plexiglass on top of it, so that the paper is completely covered by the glass.

2. Carefully tape the glass and the paper to the board. Cover all of the edges of the glass with tape.

3. Smooth the edges of the board with sandpaper. Brush

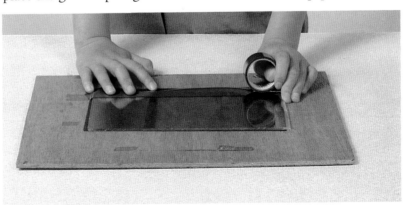

off all the dust from sanding. (If you are using cardboard, you can skip this step.)

4. Use acrylic paints to paint the letters N, S, E, W, NW, NE, SW, and SE on the board in the same positions in which they appear on a compass. Stencils will make it easier to paint the letters, but you can also do them freehand. If you want

to, paint a background around the letters.

5. To use the nephoscope, go outside and hold the board so that N points to north when the board is held flat. Look in the glass, and you will see a reflection of the sky. Watch the clouds float across the mirror surface; you will be able to see the direction from which the clouds come.

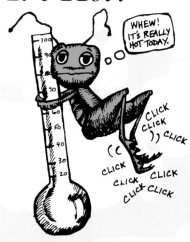

Jiminey Cricket, *It's Hot!*

Have you ever listened to the pleasant chirping of crickets on a summer's night? If you're wearing a watch, the crickets will not only sing to you but also tell you the temperature!

How? Just count the number of chirps a cricket makes in one minute. Then divide that number by four, and add 40. More often than not, the figure you get will be within two or three degrees of a thermometer's air-temperature reading.

Like other insects, crickets are cold-blooded creatures. In other words, their body temperature is always at the same temperature as their surroundings. Crickets are more active in warm weather. They chirp by rubbing the bases of their back legs together. And the warmer the temperature, the faster they rub!

Hot Air Balloon

This is a tricky project but well worth the fine-tuning it takes to get your balloon aloft. The trick is to be sure the air outside the balloon is much cooler than the air you put into the balloon.

What You'll Need

12 pieces of colored tissue paper, each 20 by 30 inches

White craft glue

A stapler

A marker

A ruler or yardstick

Sharp scissors

Old newspapers

A hair dryer

What to Do

1. Run a thin bead of glue along the short edge of a piece of tissue paper, 1/4 inch from the edge. Overlap a second piece of paper over the glue so that the two pieces are joined and make one long piece of tissue paper 20 inches wide and about 5 feet long. See Figure 1.

Figure 1

2. Repeat Step 1 five more times until you have six long sheets of paper.

3. Fold each long sheet of paper in half lengthwise, and stack the six sheets exactly on top of one another. Keep all folded edges on the same side.

4. Be sure all edges are even; then staple the stack together along the unfolded edges and at the top and bottom. See Figure 2. Put the staples about 10 inches apart, and be sure not to put any staples on the folded edge. The staples will make it easier to cut the pieces of

55

paper all at one time.

5. Use the marker and ruler to mark the top sheet of tissue paper like Figure 3. (Just put the dots. No need to write the measurements. The measurements just tell you how far to put the dots from the folded edge and from each other.)

6. Join the dots with a curving line. See Figure 4. You should have a gentle curve. Carefully cut through the whole stapled stack of paper at once along the curved line. You will have cut off the stapled pieces and will be left with a stack of folded papers.

7. Put the first folded piece of paper on top of some sheets of old newspaper. Put a piece of newspaper between the two layers of tissue, to keep the glue from seeping through. Run a thin bead of glue along the curved edge of the top sheet.

8. Place the second piece of folded tissue paper on top of the first, gluing the curved edges together. See Figure 5.

9. Slip newspaper between the two layers of tissue paper on piece number two.

10. Repeat Steps 7, 8, and 9 for the rest of the six sheets of

tissue paper. You should end up with a stack of tissue paper sheets folded on one edge and glued together like an accordion on the other, curved edge. Let the glue dry completely before going on. See Figure 6.

11. When the glue is dry, carefully take out all of the newspaper. Some of it will be stuck to the tissue paper, and you will have to peel it away in the stuck spots.

12. Open out the bottom piece of tissue.

13. Put a thin bead of glue all along the curvy edge, just as you did in Step 7.

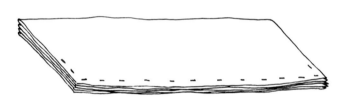

Figure 2

Figure 5

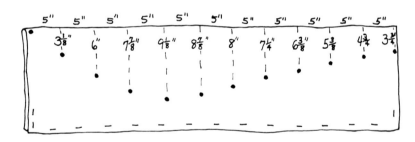

Figure 3

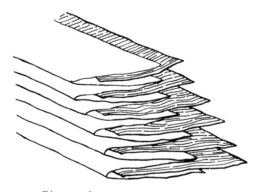

Figure 6

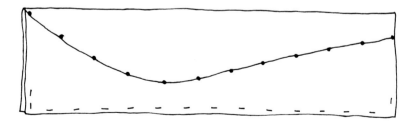

Figure 4

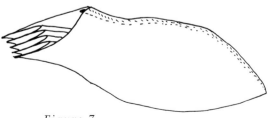

Figure 7

14. Unfold the top piece of tissue paper and press its curvy edge all along the bead of glue. See Figure 7. The balloon pieces are now all joined.

15. Wait for the glue to dry completely before inflating the balloon. While you are waiting for the glue to dry, you can glue tissue paper streamers to the bottom edge for decoration if you like. Cut thin strips about 24 inches long, and glue one to each of the six sections of the balloon.

16. Ask a friend to help you hold the balloon upright while you carefully place a hair dryer just inside the open bottom of the balloon. (If you put the dryer too far into the balloon, the dryer will overheat and turn itself off.) When the balloon is inflated and all puffed out, it should rise to the ceiling.

17. Fly your balloon outside only on cool or cold days when there is no breeze. Use an extension cord to plug in the hair dryer. If you are flying your balloon outside, you might tie a kite string to it as a tether to keep it from getting away from you. Be sure to fly it in an area without trees.

When you fly your balloon inside, try to find a cool room with a high ceiling so you can watch the balloon lift as if by magic. When the air inside it cools and the balloon comes down, simply inflate it again with the hair dryer. *Happy flying!*

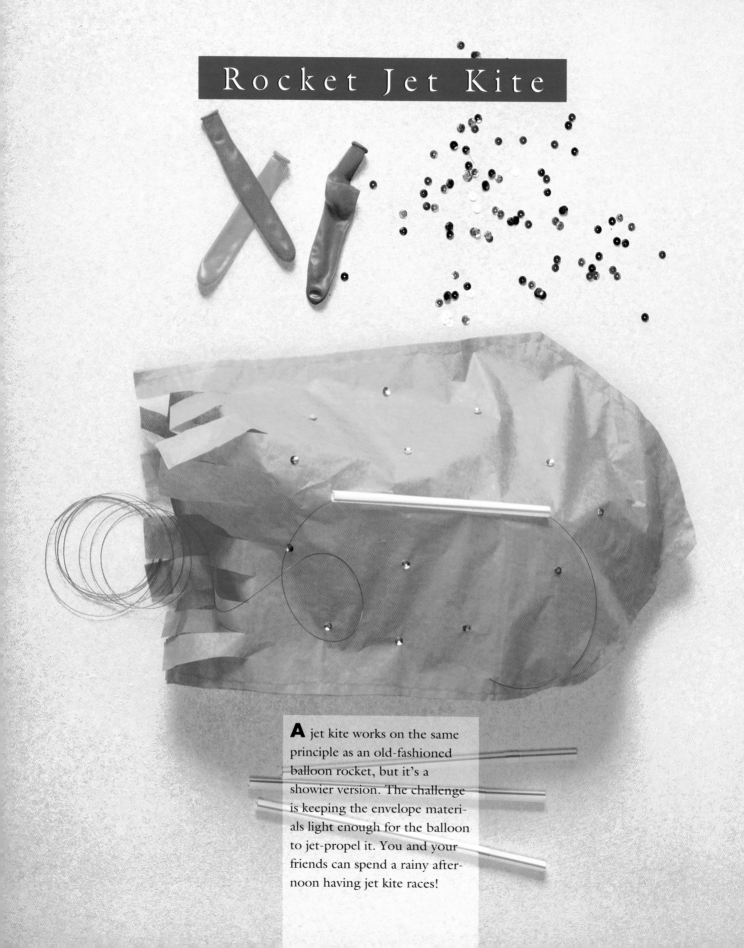

Rocket Jet Kite

A jet kite works on the same principle as an old-fashioned balloon rocket, but it's a showier version. The challenge is keeping the envelope materials light enough for the balloon to jet-propel it. You and your friends can spend a rainy afternoon having jet kite races!

What You'll Need

A supply of long, skinny balloons

A cloth tape measure

Sheets of colored tissue paper

Scissors

White craft glue or a glue stick

A plastic drinking straw for each kite

Cellophane tape

A reel of monofilament fishing line or kite string

What to Do

1. Blow up a balloon. Ask someone to hold it closed while you measure it around its fattest width. Write down the measurement. Now measure its length, and write down that measurement, too. Let the air out of the balloon for now.

2. Put two sheets of tissue paper on top of each other. On the top piece, draw a rectangle that is as long as your blown-up balloon and 2 inches wider than *half* of your balloon's width. Find the mid-point of one of the short sides of the rectangle, and draw lines from that point to points 1/3 of the way down each of the long sides. See Figure 1.

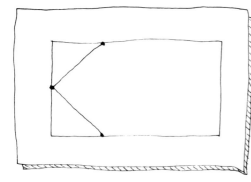

Figure 1

3. Cut out the two pieces of tissue paper at the same time.

4. Run a thin bead of glue along both long sides and the pointy end of one of the tissue paper shapes. Lay the other shape on top of the first shape, and press the gluey edges together. If you want to decorate the kite, use a small dot of glue to glue on sequins or pieces of other colors of tissue paper. Be careful not to let the kite get too heavy.

5. After the glue has dried, cut fringe along the unglued edge of the tissue paper envelope.

6. Cut the plastic drinking straw to a 6-inch length. Tape it to one side of the tissue paper envelope with 2 small pieces of cellophane tape. See Figure 2.

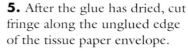
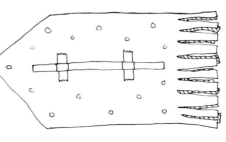

Figure 2

7. Thread one end of the monofilament through the straw. Tie that end to the back of a chair. Pull the monofilament tight and out about 20 feet. Cut it, and tie this end to the back of another chair.

8. Blow up the balloon. While holding the neck tight, slip the balloon inside the tissue paper envelope. Move the jet kite down to one end of the monofilament line. Be sure the kite's pointy end is facing the long part of the string.

9. Count "One! Two! Three! Go!" and let your jet kite fly. If you want to have races, each kite will need its own line.

What Makes a Rocket *Rocket?*

"...three...two...one... ignition...liftoff!" With a roar of fiery engines and a huge cloud of smoke and vapor, the space shuttle rises from Earth's grasp and heads for outer space.

"...three...two...one...*brrrazzel errrt*...plop!" With a burst of whoopee-cushion noise, a toy balloon careens crazily through the air and lands with a thump on the sofa.

Believe it or not, both "rockets" use the same sort of "engine" to make them fly. Scientists call it the action-and-reaction principle. It says that for every action, there is always an equal but opposite reaction.

When you blow up a balloon and hold the end shut, all the air inside pushes outward evenly against the balloon's walls. The balloon doesn't go anywhere because the push on each side of the balloon is equal to the push on the opposite side. All the forces are equal. Nothing is moving.

When you let go of the end, though, everything changes. The push on the front of the balloon isn't balanced by air pushing at the back. Instead, there's no push at the back. So the balloon leaps forward. The action of the air rushing out in one direction causes an equal reaction in the other direction.

The same thing happens inside a rocket. Rocket engines produce hot gases inside a cham- ber that has an open end. The hot gases push against the chamber's walls and rush out the open end with tremendous force. That action causes the spectacular reaction we've all witnessed: *whoosh!* Another rocket soars into space at thousands of miles per hour!

Centipede Kite

A centipede kite is a wondrous thing to see. Follow carefully the directions for building the kite, but let your imagination run wild when you decorate its face and arms.

What You'll Need

A piece of poster board cut into 11 strips 28 inches long and 1 inch wide

Scissors

A stapler

A pack of colored tissue paper

A light-colored pencil or a piece of chalk

Glue (rubber cement, glue stick, or other glue that won't wrinkle paper)

A black marker

Scraps of white typing paper

11 very thin bamboo garden stakes about 26 inches long

A hole puncher or an awl

Kite string

What to Do

1. Staple each strip of poster board into a ring.

2. Lay one ring down on a piece of tissue paper, and carefully trace around the circle with chalk or a light-colored pencil.

3. Draw another circle 1 inch outside of the first circle you

drew. Cut out the second (larger) circle.

4. Make cuts from the edge of the cutout circle to the inner circle about 1-1/2 inches apart. These will be glue tabs.

5. Put a bead of glue all around the outside of the poster board ring.

6. While the glue is still wet, set the ring on the inner circle of the tissue paper circle. Press the glue tabs up all around the ring so that the tissue paper is stretched smoothly all around the ring.

7. Repeat Steps 2 through 6 for each of the 11 rings.

8. Make one of the rings into a face, using markers, white paper scraps, and tissue paper scraps. Add ruffles around the edge, streamers, or whatever looks good to you.

9. With the hole puncher or awl, punch three holes in each ring—one at the top and one at

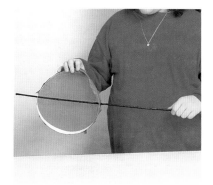

each side. Be sure the side holes are exactly across from each other at the center of the ring.

10. Carefully push a bamboo stake through the side holes of each ring. Center each stake, so that its side arms are of equal length.

11. Glue tissue paper scraps to the ends of the bamboo arms for more decoration.

12. Cut 30 pieces of kite string, each about 8 inches long.

13. To assemble the centipede,

use the arms of a chair or the sides of a big cardboard box to balance all the armed rings. Put the rings in the order you want them to be in the finished kite. Tie three strings between every two rings. See Figure 1.

14. Make a bridle on the face ring. Cut three strings, each a foot long. Tie one to each arm where the arm meets the ring, and tie the third string to the hole in the top of the face ring. Bring the ends of the three strings together in front of the face. Tie the strings together. See Figure 2.

15. You can hang the kite from the bridle and one or two other rings. Or you can tie the bridle strings and one or two other rings to the tops of poles for a parade. Your centipede will move like a wave in the breeze if you hang it near a window. It will make a fine, fierce mascot at the front of a parade.

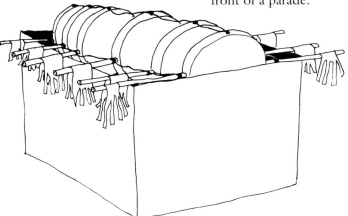

Figure 1

Figure 2

Hidden
Air

Riddle: You can't see me, but you can see the space that I fill. What am I?

Answer: air that hides in liquid.

You probably know several liquids that have air hiding out in them. How about cola drinks? Hard cider? Root beer? Ginger ale? Ginger beer? Fizzy liquids have carbon dioxide in them. (Carbon dioxide is one of the gases that make up our air.)

How does the air get in there? One way is through a process called *fermentation.* Some drinks, such as ginger beer, are made by mixing tiny, one-celled plants called yeasts with fruit juice or sugary water.

Yeasts are plants with no chlorophyll, so they can't make their own food the way green plants can. Instead, they must get their food from their surroundings. In the case of ginger beer, the yeasts eat sugary lemon juice and water. While eating, the yeasts breathe out carbon dioxide, the same gas that humans breathe out. And since the yeasts are living in a liquid, the carbon dioxide makes a space for itself in the liquid—tiny air bubbles.

As the yeasts eat and breathe, they also multiply, and soon they release many bubbles of carbon dioxide into the liquid. As long as the bottle is kept tightly capped, the air stays in the liquid. But as soon as the bottle is opened, the carbon dioxide begins to escape, causing the tingly feeling that fermented drinks give your tongue.

Barometer

A barometer is a basic weather-forecasting tool. Once you've begun to take note of changes in air pressure, you'll have a good idea of what to expect of the weather over the next day or so.

What You'll Need

A large balloon, 11-inch size or larger

Scissors

A quart-sized (or larger) glass jar with a wide mouth

About 12 inches of strong string or yarn

2 plastic drinking straws

Super glue

Two straight pins, extra long if possible

A shallow cardboard box, about 15 by 10 by 2 inches

Acrylic paints

A paint brush

A permanent black marker

What to Do

1. Cut off the neck of the balloon and stretch the balloon over the neck of the jar. Pull the balloon tight so that there are no bubbles or dimples in the surface. Tie the balloon to the neck of the jar with string. Wrap the string several times around so that it holds the balloon tightly. See Figure 1.

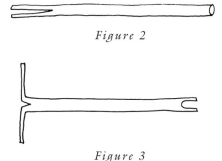

Figure 1

2. Cut a 4-inch length of one of the straws. Slit up one end about 1-1/2 inches. See Figure 2. Bend the slit ends to form a base for the straw. Notch the uncut end of the straw to form a resting place for the other straw. See Figure 3.

Figure 2

Figure 3

3. Glue the bent base of the straw to the center of the balloon with Super glue. While the glue is drying, trim one end of the other straw to a point. This will be the pointer of the barometer.

4. After the glue is completely dry, place the second straw sideways through the notched end of the upright straw. The pointer end should be on the right. Hold this straw in place with a pin. See Figure 4.

Figure 4

5. Remove any flaps from the box, and decorate it with acrylic paint. When the paint is dry, stand the jar apparatus in front of the box. With the top straw in a level position, stick the second pin through the straw about 1 inch to the right of the first pin. Stick this second pin all the way through the straw so that it sticks out the other side and into the box, loosely holding the straw to the box. You will have to push the jar as close as possible to the box. Even so, the upright straw may slant slightly inward. There should still be about 1 inch of pin between the straw and the box.

6. Place the barometer in or near an open window. Watch what happens to the pointer end of the top straw as the weather changes. Use the marker to record the position of the pointer and the weather at the time the straw was in that position. After a few days you should be able to see some relationship between the position of the straw and the weather. The pressure of the air in the room on the balloon causes the straw to move up and down. What happens when there is high pressure? What happens when the pressure is low?

Wind Facts That'll *Blow You Away*

The highest wind speeds on earth are produced by tornados. Meteorologists believe that some tornados produce winds as high as 400 miles an hour. The scientists don't know for sure, though, because the twisters always wreck their wind-speed instruments.

The strongest side-to-side wind ever recorded blew on April 12, 1934, at a weather station on Mount Washington, New Hampshire, USA. Observers measured a gust blowing 231 miles an hour!

The windiest place in the world is Commonwealth Bay, King George V Coast, in Antarctica. Winds average more than 70 miles an hour most of the year. You definitely wouldn't want to be there during a storm. Winds come howling in at 200 miles an hour!

The human body produces some impressive wind speeds, too. When you breathe normally, air moves in and out at a respectable five miles an hour. When you sniff, air comes gusting in at 20 miles an hour. That's a Force 5 on the Beaufort Scale; enough, according to the Scale's description, to make "small trees sway and small waves develop on lakes and rivers."

And when you sneeze hard: Stand back! That blast of air is moving 100 miles an hour—faster than many hurricanes!

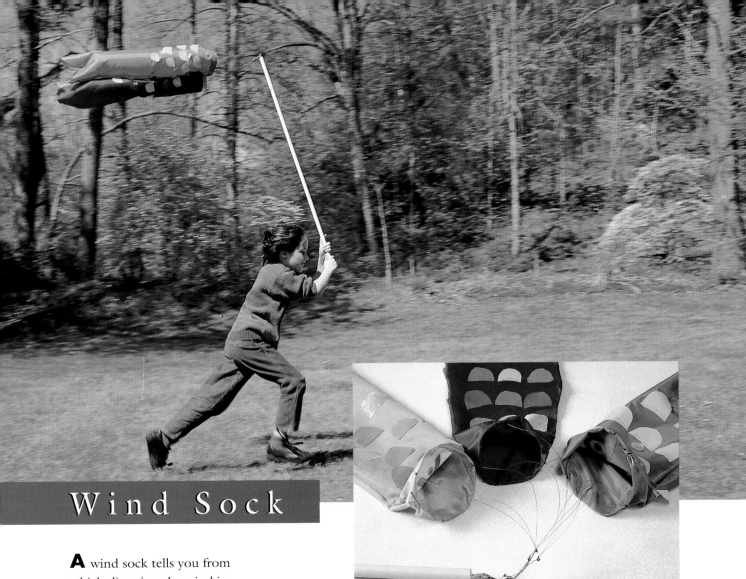

Wind Sock

A wind sock tells you from which direction the wind is coming. This one looks like a school of fish darting and swimming together.

What You'll Need

1/2 yard each of 3 different colors of taffeta or ripstop nylon

Scissors

Old newspapers

Fabric glue*

Scraps of other colors of light-weight material for decoration

6 plastic glue-on eyes**

About 36 inches of 14-gauge galvanized steel wire or other easy-to-bend wire

Wire cutters

Monofilament fishing line or kite string

An awl or a big nail

A cup hook

Pliers

A swivel hook

An old broom handle or a piece of 3/4-inch dowel, about 48 inches long

*Fabric glue is available in fabric stores.

**Eyes can be bought in craft stores.

What to Do

1. First make the fish. Begin by folding one of the pieces of taffeta or ripstop in half length-

Fold Line

Figure 1

wise. Cut a fish shape, as shown in Figure 1, being careful not to cut into the fold of the cloth. Your fish's body should be about 30 inches long. Save any scraps of material to use as decoration on other fish. Unfold the fish. Put a layer of newspaper under the entire piece of cloth.

2. Cut scales and other shapes out of other colors of cloth. Glue these in place with fabric glue. Also glue on two eyes. See Figure 2.

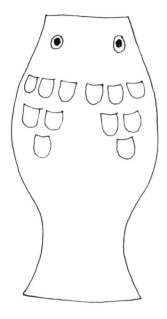

Figure 2

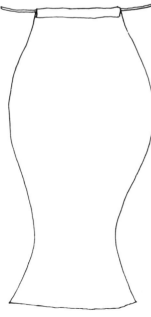

Figure 3

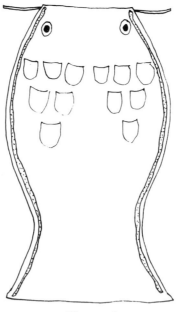

Figure 4

3. When the glue has dried (about 20 minutes), turn the fish over so the decorated side is against the table. Cut a piece of wire 4 inches longer than the width of the mouth end of the fish. Run a bead of glue all along the edge of the mouth end. Lay the wire just inside the line of glue. Fold the fabric over to cover the wire. See Figure 3.

4. When this glue has dried completely, turn the fish back over so the decorated side is up. Run a bead of glue all along the outside edges. See Figure 4.

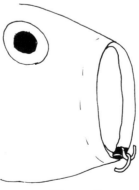

Figure 5

5. Fold the fish over so that the other outside edge is pressed against the bead of glue and the fish has been glued into a sort of fish-shaped tube. Do not glue

the mouth or tail end closed. As you get close to the mouth end, you will have to bend the mouth wire into a hoop. Bend the wires that are sticking out of the mouth end so that they lock together and hold the mouth into a round hoop. See Figure 5.

6. Use the awl or nail to start three holes around the hoop, just inside the wire. Into each hole thread an 18-inch-long piece of monofilament or kite string. Tie these strings to the hoop; then gather the free ends of the strings and tie them together to form a bridle. Make a second knot about an inch down from the first gathering knot. See Figure 6.

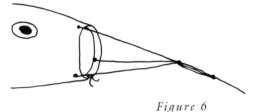

Figure 6

7. Repeat Steps 1 through 6 for the other two fish.

8. Next you'll make the pole. Hook the cup hook through the plain loop end of the swivel hook (the end that doesn't open). Use pliers to squeeze the cup hook closed.

9. Use the awl or nail to start a hole in the flat end of the dowel. Then screw the cup hook (with swivel hook attached) into the end of the dowel. Clip the three fish to the clasping end of the swivel hook. See Figure 7.

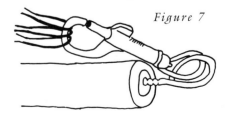

Figure 7

10. Hang the school of fish out of an upstairs window or from a flagpole.

Hovercraft

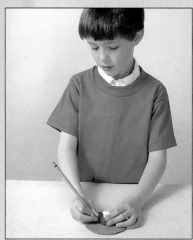

Every day, people travel from the eastern shore of Great Britain across the English Channel to Europe in a strange boat-plane called a hovercraft. The hovercrafts that cross the English Channel have many air jets under them. The pilot fires up an engine that sends so much air out of the jets that the hovercraft actually rests on a thin cushion of air. This air reduces friction and lets the hovercraft scoot freely over the water.

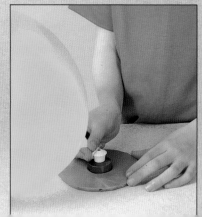

What You'll Need

A piece of corrugated cardboard about 6 by 6 inches

A pencil

Something to use as a pattern for drawing a circle 4 or 5 inches in diameter, such as a large mug or an upside down cereal bowl

A razor knife

Self-adhesive shelf paper

Scissors

A cap from a squirt bottle of liquid detergent—the kind of cap that can be pressed down to close and pulled up to open

White glue (optional)

A 10- or 11-inch round balloon

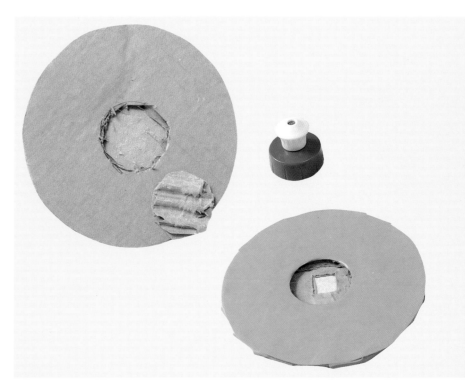

What to Do

1. Tracing around the pattern, draw a circle about 4 inches in diameter on the cardboard. Cut out this circle with the razor knife.

2. Place the bottle cap in the exact center of the cardboard circle, and trace around it with the pencil.

3. Corrugated cardboard has three layers: a top paper layer, a middle layer of ribbed paper, and a bottom paper layer. In this step you will be cutting through ONLY the top and middle layers of the corrugated cardboard. Use the razor knife to gently slice through the top paper layer just inside the small circle you have traced around the bottle cap. Remove that paper. Now carefully slice through the middle layer of ribbed paper. Be very careful not to cut through the bottom layer of paper. Remove the scraps of the inner layer. You should now be able to see the bottom layer.

4. Use the tip of the razor knife to cut a small square (with 1/4 inch sides) out of the remaining layer of corrugated cardboard inside the small circle.

5. Cover both sides and edges of the cardboard circle with self-adhesive shelf paper. Leave the small cutout circle and the cutout square on the other side uncovered.

6. Wedge the bottle cap down inside the cutout circle. It should fit snugly. If it is loose, put a thin bead of glue around the edges of the small circle, and then wedge the cap in the circle.

7. Press down on the cap to close it. Blow up the balloon. Twist its neck to hold the air in while you fit the opening of the balloon over the valve (top part) of the bottle cap. Be sure that the balloon stands straight up from the cap. Pull on the neck of the balloon to adjust

it. If the balloon leans over, the hovercraft won't work. Release the neck of the balloon. It will release a little air into its neck and then should stand straight up.

8. Grasp the neck of the balloon and the valve and pull up on the valve to open it. Place the hovercraft down on a smooth surface, such as a kitchen counter top or a smooth tile floor, and watch the hovercraft scoot.

9. Try sending the hovercraft down a sliding board on a playground. Compare its speed and performance without the balloon and with the balloon. Try making different sizes of hovercrafts. Try skimming the hovercraft over water. Fill a tub or sink. Let the surface of the water settle until there are no waves or ripples. Place the hovercraft gently on the surface of the water at the same time that you pull up on the valve of the cap. Experiment until your hovercraft stays afloat.

Helicopter

Everyone knows that when you run with a pinwheel the wheel will spin. What happens if you turn a pinwheel on its side and put it on top of a helicopter body? Try dropping this model off an upstairs porch or down a tall stairwell.

What You'll Need

A 6- by 6-inch square of paper

Scissors

Colored markers

A long, straight pin with a round head

A 1/2-inch-long piece of plastic drinking straw

A cork

What to Do

1. Fold the paper once into a triangle. Unfold it, and then fold it into the opposite triangle.

2. Unfold the paper. It should have creases going from corner to corner, forming an X. The center of the X is the center of the square. Make a cut from each corner halfway to the center along each crease. See Figure 1.

Figure 1

3. Use markers to color both sides of the paper and the entire cork.

4. When the paper has dried completely, make the wheel. Pick up any point; stick the pin through the point about 1/4 inch in from the point; skip the next point, but pick up the next and thread it onto the pin just as you did the first point. Continue around the square, threading every other point onto the pin until you have four points threaded onto the pin and four points lying flat. Now stick the point of the pin through the center point of the square. See Figure 2.

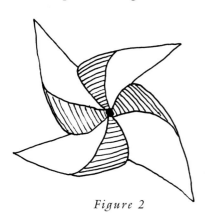

Figure 2

5. Slip the piece of drinking straw onto the sharp end of the pin while holding all the points on the pin; then push the end of the pin into the side of the cork about 1/4 inch from one end. Push the pin in firmly, but not all the way in. The straw should be able to move up and down slightly, and the wheel should feel springy.

6. Throw the helicopter up and watch what happens as it drops. The longer the drop, the better, so look around for good launching places such as stairwells, upstairs porches, and balconies.

Riding on *Air*

Have you ever been flying comfortably along in an airplane, enjoying the view above the clouds, when suddenly a small, sensible-sounding voice inside you pipes up: "Hey, how can this heavy thing be up here in the air? How come we don't just drop to the ground like a rock?" So much for a carefree trip!

Next time that happens, close your eyes, take a deep breath, and repeat the magic word: Bernoulli. Bernoulli. Bernoulli. (Pronounced Bur-NOO-lee.)

No, Bernoulli isn't an Italian magician. Actually, he was a Swiss scientist (his first name was Daniel) more than 250 years ago. And he figured out something important: Liquids and gases (air, for instance) have less pressure when they're moving. The faster they move, the less pressure they exert.

So what? Take a look. Cut two strips of paper 8 or so inches long and about 1-1/2 inches wide. Hold a strip by one end in each hand, so they hang down side by side in front of you, about 2 to 3 inches apart, with their edges facing you. Now blow hard between the strips, about 2 inches up from the free ends. The strips move *toward each other*—because the moving air between them has less pressure than the still air on either side. The side air pushes harder and shoves the strips inward.

OK, now on to airplanes. Take one of the paper strips and fold it in half. Now scoot the top end back about 1/2 inch and tape or glue it to the bottom. The resulting curved-on-top, flat-on-the-bottom shape is called an airfoil. Look familiar? It's the shape of an airplane's wing.

Slip the folded end of your paper wing over a pencil, and blow hard at the fold. The wing rises and stays there until you stop blowing. What's happening?

When you blow at the wing, your breath divides to pass over and under it, just like air passes over and under the wing of a moving plane. And because the wing's upper surface is curved, the air that goes over the top has to travel farther and faster than the air underneath to get to the other edge. Faster air on top means less pressure on top—and better yet, *more* pressure on the bottom. The bottom air pushes harder and forces the wing upward. The force is called *lift*—but if you're on an airplane, you can just call it reassuring.

Helicopter blades also have an airfoil shape. A plane has to rush forward through air in order for its wings to create lift. But a helicopter has to move only its blades. When they move around fast enough to create a pressure difference, up the 'copter goes.

Wind Speed Meter

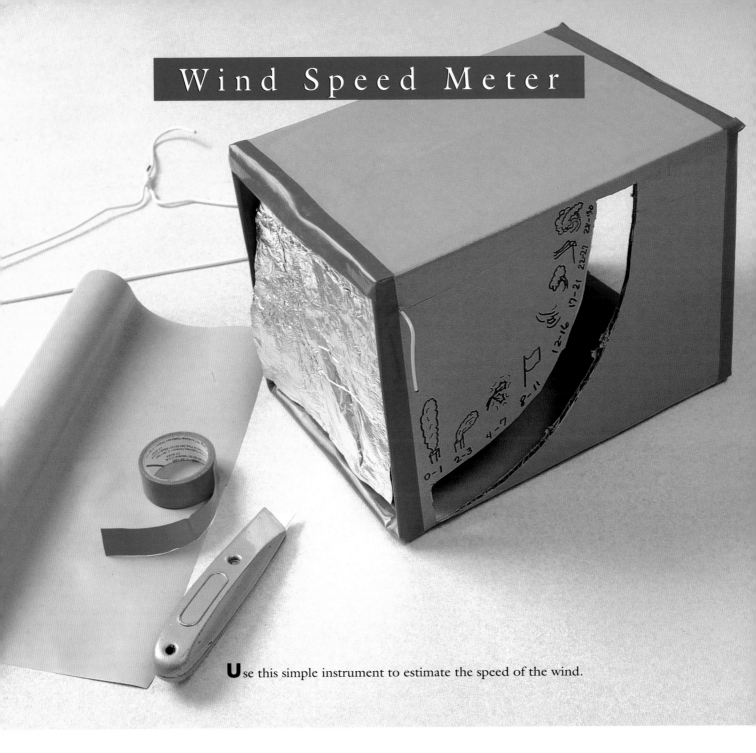

Use this simple instrument to estimate the speed of the wind.

What You'll Need

A cardboard box about
7 by 7 by 10 inches

A razor knife

Plastic tape about 1 inch wide

Self-adhesive shelf paper

A coat hanger

Wire cutters

A piece of aluminum foil
about 6 by 8 inches

Scissors

Cellophane tape

A fine-point permanent marker

A Beaufort Wind Force Scale
(see page 74)

What to Do

1. Cut off both ends of
the box. Use tape to reinforce
any pieces that get loose when
the box is cut.

2. Cover the inside and outside
of the box with self-adhesive
shelf paper.

3. Cut a straight piece of wire about 8 inches long from the coat hanger.

4. Poke the piece of wire into the side of the box 1/2 inch in from the open end and 1/2 inch below the top. Push the wire straight across the opening

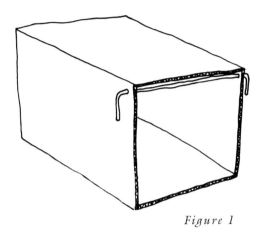

Figure 1

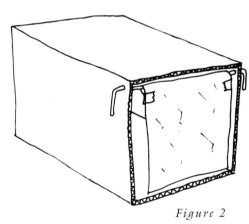

Figure 2

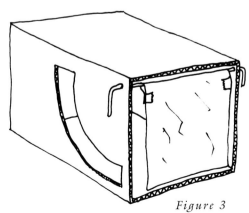

Figure 3

and out the other side. Make sure the second hole is directly opposite the first. Bend the ends of the wire down. See Figure 1.

5. Slide one of the 6-inch edges of the aluminum foil over the wire and make a fold about 1 inch deep all along the folded edge. Tape the fold with cellophane tape so that the foil hangs down like a curtain. Be sure that the curtain can move freely on its rod. See Figure 2.

6. Push on the bottom of the curtain with one finger so that you can see the curved path that the bottom of the curtain follows as it swings inward. Cut a curving slot about 1 inch wide that goes from the bottom of the side of the box to the top, following the path of the bottom of the curtain. See Figure 3.

7. Finish off the edges of the box with plastic tape.

8. To calibrate the meter, place it outside so that the curtain faces the wind. Make a mark where the bottom of the curtain appears. Using the Beaufort Wind Force Scale (see the sidebar on page 74), estimate the wind speed and draw a symbol and/or mark showing the number of estimated miles per hour that the wind is blowing when the curtain is in that position.

It will take several days to completely calibrate the meter; you will have to observe it in many different kinds of wind conditions to fill in the chart. When it is calibrated, you will be able to place it in the wind and estimate the wind speed by reading the position of the bottom of the aluminum foil curtain.

Amazing Easy-To-Use
Wind Force Scale

To measure wind speeds exactly, weather scientists use an instrument called an anemometer (an-uh-MOM-ih-ter). But you can get a pretty good idea of how fast the wind is blowing just by looking around you.

In 1805, Rear Admiral Sir Francis Beaufort (pronounced BO-fert) came up with a numbering system to describe how hard a wind was blowing by its effect on a Royal Navy ship. For instance, he classified a Force 2 wind as "that in which a well-conditioned man-of-war, with all sail set, and clean full, would go in smooth water from one to two knots." A Force 12 wind was "that which no canvas could withstand."

Today, the Beaufort Wind Force Scale—shown on page 74—also includes descriptions of how wind moves things on land. People all over the world use it to estimate wind speeds.

Force Number	Wind Description	Wind Effects On Land	Miles Per Hour	Kilometers Per Hour
0	Calm	Smoke rises vertically.	Less than 1	Less than 1
1	Light Air	Wind direction is shown by drift of smoke.	1-3	1-5
2	Slight Breeze	The wind is felt on face. Leaves and twigs rustle. Wind vanes move.	4-7	6-11
3	Gentle Breeze	Leaves and twigs are in constant motion. Light flags extend.	8-12	12-19
4	Moderate Breeze	Dust and loose paper blow about. Small branches sway.	13-18	20-28
5	Fresh Breeze	Small trees sway. Small waves develop on lakes and rivers.	19-24	29-38
6	Strong Breeze	Large branches sway. Umbrellas are hard to use.	25-31	39-49
7	Moderate Gale	Whole trees sway. It's difficult to walk against the wind.	32-38	50-61
8	Fresh Gale	Twigs break off trees. Walking becomes very difficult.	39-46	62-74
9	Strong Gale	Slight damage to buildings. Shingles may fly off roofs.	47-54	75-88
10	Whole Gale	Considerable damage to houses and other buildings. Whole trees are uprooted.	55-63	89-102
11	Storm	Widespread damage. (Winds this strong are very rare.)	64-73	103-117
12	Hurricane	Violent destruction.	More than 74	More than 117

Thunder Stick

Also called "rain sticks," thunder sticks are musical instruments that were first made in Africa. They were originally made of bamboo. This version is made out of different materials but has a sound very similar to that of the original instruments.

What You'll Need

5 feet of PVC (plastic) pipe with a 2-inch inside diameter (2" schedule 40)*

36 inches of 1/4-inch dowel

A saw

A brace and bit or a hand drill with a 1/4-inch bit

Sandpaper

6 or 8 pieces of corrugated cardboard, each about 2 by 6 inches

2 large corks, 2 inches in diameter at their smaller ends

Colored plastic tape

1/2 cup uncooked rice

Acrylic paints

Erasers designed to be put over the ends of pencils (optional)

Fat pencils with erasers (optional)

*You can get PVC pipe at a hardware store.

What to Do

1. PVC pipe is usually sold in 10-foot lengths. Ask the sales person to cut the pipe into two 5-foot lengths.

2. Drill a 1/4-inch hole through both sides of the pipe about 8 inches down from one end. Drill another pair of holes 2 inches and a quarter turn farther down the pipe. Drill two more pairs of holes the same distances apart. See Figure 1.

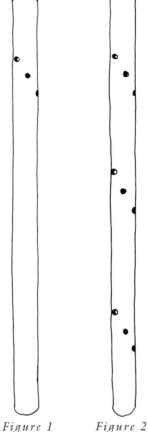

Figure 1   *Figure 2*

3. At the other end of the pipe, drill the same pairs of holes, the same distances apart, as you did in the first end.

4. Drill a third series of pairs of holes in the middle section of the pipe. See Figure 2.

5. Put a dowel through the first pair of holes that you drilled. See Figure 3. It should fit snugly. Saw it off where it comes out of the sides of the pipe. See Figure 4. Sand the pipe and the ends of the dowel smooth. Fill

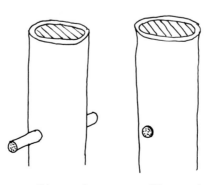

Figure 3   *Figure 4*

all the pairs of holes with dowels in the same way.

6. Fold one of the pieces of cardboard into an accordion fold. See Figure 5. Stuff it

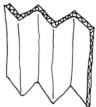

Figure 5

down one end of the pipe until it stops at the first dowel. Fold another piece of cardboard the same way, and stuff it on top of the first piece of cardboard. Put in as many pieces of cardboard as will fit.

7. Plug a cork into the end of the pipe, and tape the cork securely to the end so that it can't come out.

8. Pour the rice into the open end of the pipe. Fold cardboard and stuff it into this end of the pipe just as you did on the other end. Put in all the cardboard that will fit snugly. Cork and tape this end.

9. Decorate the thunder stick with colored plastic tape and acrylic paints. The design on the thunder stick shown here was made by spreading paint in the bottom of an old pie tin and then pressing the flat end of a pencil eraser into it to print the solid circles. The open circles were printed with the open end of an eraser designed to be put over the end of a pencil.

10. To use the thunder stick, practice tilting it slowly back and forth until you can keep a steady pattering sound going. Close your eyes, and listen to the gentle rain.

The Shocking Truth...
About Lightning and Thunder

Lightning is a giant spark in the sky, created by static electricity—the same kind of electricity that makes your hair crackle when you brush it, or that gives you a small shock when you walk across a carpet and then touch a metal object (ouch!). If the room was dark, you might've even seen a spark. How'd that happen?

When your feet rubbed on the carpet, you picked up some extra *electrons*—negatively charged pieces of atoms—from the rug. You charged yourself. Then, when your finger came close to metal, you discharged yourself—the wayward electrons flowed through your body and leaped across the air between you and the object with enough force to blow the air atoms apart and give off light and sound.

The same kind of thing happens, only on a *much* more powerful scale, when water droplets and ice particles move and swirl around inside a thundercloud. Scientists don't all agree on exactly how those bumping, blowing, freezing, and thawing particles supercharge a cloud with static electricity. But there's no arguing about the result: Sooner or later, there's a lot more electricity in the cloud than it can hold, and—c-r-r-a-a-a-c-k—like the spark that jumped from your hand, lightning streaks from the cloud to another cloud, or to the ground, a building, a tree, or (gulp) sometimes even a person. (The best place to be in a thunderstorm is *out* of the storm, indoors and away from windows.)

Lightning releases a huge amount of energy. A big flash can cause the temperature of the air around it to rise as high as 54,000° F (30,000° C). That's more than five times hotter than the surface of the sun! The extreme heat makes the air expand suddenly and spread out in powerful waves, like the air around an exploding bomb. Ka-boom! Thunder.

You usually see lightning before you hear its thunder, but actually they happen together. It's just that light travels much faster than sound. To tell how close a thunderstorm is, count the seconds between the lightning and the thunder. It takes sound five seconds to travel a mile. So if you count 10 seconds between the flash and the boom, the storm is two miles away.

Our planet's atmosphere is a shockingly electric place. Scientists say there are about 45,000 thunderstorms in the world every day, or about 16 million a year. In fact, at any given moment there are 1,800 thunderstorms flashing and crashing in our sky. Lightning strikes the Earth 100 times a second!

WATER—

the stuff of oceans and lakes, rain and snow, cold drinks and hot baths. Make a wave in a bottle, and hold the ocean in your hands....Create a waterspout, and some litmus paper to help you tell acids from bases....Decorate some colorful marbled paper, and build your own backyard mini-pond....Make an underwater viewer, so you can watch underwater life in streams and ponds, and a skimmer net to help you catch it....Build a model grist mill, and you'll discover how we humans have turned grain into flour for centuries....Mix up some gluep and oobleck—wonderful water-based materials that are fun to touch and even more fun to play with....Then make boats from clay or from wood—and watch them skim over the surface of the water.

WATER

Wave in a Bottle

Peek into this model while you tip it back and forth to see firsthand how waves are formed and break up. You control this tiny ocean. You can create a calm, sunny day, or whip up a storm at sea!

What You'll Need

A glass bottle*

Vegetable oil

Water

Food coloring

A cork to fit the bottle (or the bottle's own cap)

*A flat bottle, such as an old whiskey bottle, works best, but any clear bottle will do.

What to Do

1. Wash out the bottle, and remove the label by soaking the bottle in warm water.

2. Fill 1/2 of the bottle with water. Add a few drops of food coloring (stop when you like the color). No need to stir it.

3. Fill the remaining space in the bottle with vegetable oil.

4. Cork the bottle. If you have a screw-on cap for the bottle, put the cap on the bottle tightly.

5. Turn the bottle on its side, and let it settle for a few minutes. The water should sink to the bottom, and you should be able to see clearly the line between the colored water and the oil. Now begin to tip the bottle back and forth. Experiment to see what kind of waves you can make. If the oil starts to get bubbly, let the bottle rest for a few minutes.

How Waves Work

Ah, the beach. Soaring seagulls. Sun and sand. Waves rolling to the shore and crashing, one after another after another after another, in endless watery rhythm.

As you watch, you might think that the water in the waves is rushing toward you. But it's not. When a wave passes through the water, the water simply rises up, and then comes down again in pretty much the same place. Only the wave itself travels forward. You can see the same effect at home. Ask a friend to hold one end of a rope while you hold the other. Now, shake the rope up and down. Waves travel through the rope. But the rope stays put in your hands.

In open water, waves can travel for thousands of miles. But when a wave approaches shore and passes through shallower water, it slows down. The lower part of the wave starts to drag along the bottom. Meanwhile, the top part keeps going. So the wave curls over itself—and "breaks."

Most waves are formed by the wind blowing across the water's surface. The harder and longer the wind blows, the higher the wave. Earthquakes and other violent underwater movements of the Earth sometimes cause huge waves called tsunamis (soo-NAH-meez). A tsunami can speed through the ocean at nearly 500 miles an hour. Just before it strikes land, a tsunami sucks water up into itself and away from the coast, sometimes for several miles. The wave can rise as high as a 20-story building. Then the wall of water slams into the shore, causing great destruction.

Scientists have set up an early warning system in parts of the world, such as the Pacific, where tsunamis are most likely to happen. If they think a giant wave is coming, the scientists broadcast an alert so people can go to a safer place.

Waterspout

You can buy a special gadget to connect two plastic bottles, but for just a few pennies you can make this waterspout-maker. Warning: Once you make one waterspout, you'll probably have to make another one for your friends, or you'll never get a chance to play with yours!

What You'll Need

Two 2-liter plastic drink bottles

A flat washer with a 3/8-inch hole

Pipe thread seal tape*

Soft, flexible, plastic tape or electrician's tape

Scissors

*You can buy this at a hardware store or discount mart.

What to Do

1. Fill one of the bottles about 2/3 full of water.

2. Place the washer on the opening of this bottle. Wrap pipe thread tape around the edge of the washer and the edge of the opening of the bottle until the washer is completely sealed to the bottle opening. See Figure 1. Do not cover the opening in the washer. A good seal should take four or five turns of the tape. (The tape isn't sticky like most tapes; you must press it against the surface you want it to hold onto.)

3. Balance the empty bottle on top of the sealed washer and bottle. Hold the bottle in position, and put pipe thread tape around the place where the two bottle openings come together. See Figure 2. Wrap the tape several times so that there is no crack left.

4. Wrap plastic tape or black electrician's tape around the two bottle necks, making a strong joint. You'll need to wrap it several times. Completely cover the pipe thread tape and all the neck space of the two bottles. See Figure 3.

5. Turn the bottles over so that the filled bottle is on top. Check the joining for leaks. The water should just barely drip from bottle to bottle.

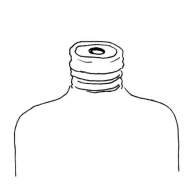

Figure 1

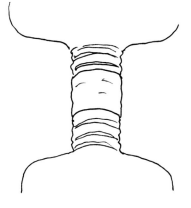

Figure 2

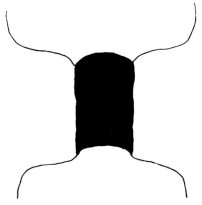

Figure 3

6. When you are sure the bottles do not leak, hold the filled bottle in one of your hands, and hold the joined bottle necks in your other hand. Holding the bottles horizontally, roll them in a circu-lar motion a few turns; then quickly hold the bottles upright, with the filled bottle on top. If the waterspout does not appear, give the bottles a few more turns. Try turning them in the opposite direction. Within a few tries, you should see a waterspout, a tiny tornado in the water, form. Watch how it draws the water down into itself as the water rushes from one bottle to the other.

Whirlpools and *Rubber Duckies*

You're enjoying a nice, relaxing bath in the world's biggest tub. You lean back and close your eyes. Aahhhh, this is livin'.

Yikes! All of a sudden somebody pulls the plug! Instantly you're swept toward the drain into a swirling cur-rent. As you spin crazily round and round, you lean over and look down into the whirlpool's middle. Haalllp! There's nothing but a hole! You're being sucked into empty space! You can't get away! You...

Whoa. Enough of this nightmare. Things like that just don't happen—unless you're a rubber duckie or some other bath toy. Right?

Well, not exactly. There actually *are* places in oceans, lakes, and rivers where rotating currents called *whirlpools* give boats and people trouble. Usually, the currents are formed when fast-moving water runs into a curved bank, or when incoming and outgoing tides move through a narrow passage at the same time. Small ships can get stuck and damaged in a whirlpool, but the water doesn't actually suck them into a hole.

In a bathtub, the spiral of water running down the drain is called a *vortex*. A tornado is a kind of vortex, too. If you make the waterspout project on page 82, you can watch a vortex in action and figure out what's happening. Here's how.

Without rotating or spinning the bottles, turn them over quickly so that the filled one is on top. Glug. Glug. Water drips slowly into the empty bottle, one glug at a time, and then stops completely. Why doesn't the water all run out at once? Because its "skin," or surface tension, holds the liquid back at the small hole where the two bottles meet. Besides, the empty bottle isn't really empty.

It's full of air. The water has to push some of that air out of the way in order to get in.

So every time water glugs into the bottom bottle, it shoves a bubble of air up into the top bottle. And the water level in the upper bottle goes down. Eventually there's not enough water to push down hard enough to shove air aside. Everything stops. (In fact, if the top bottle isn't almost full to begin with, it may not drip water at all.)

Rolling the bottles before you turn them upright, though, puts a new spin on the situation. The water in the top bottle starts rotating. At the same time, gravity pulls the water down toward the narrow drain hole. What happens? The same thing that happens when rotating ice skaters suddenly pull their arms in—they start spinning very fast. The closer to the neck the water gets, the faster it spins. A funnel-shaped vortex forms, with a hole in the middle. Presto: The hole lets air in from the lower bottle and water out from the upper bottle, all at once. Whoosh.

The same kind of thing can turn a bad thunderstorm into a tornado. All strong storms create powerful updrafts of moist air. When conditions are right, crosswinds put spin on the updrafts—just like when you rolled the bottles to make the water rotate. The result is a whirling column of upward-moving air called a "mesocyclone" (MEZ-o-SIGH-klone). Not all mesocyclones turn into tornados. But sometimes, as a mesocyclone spins upward, it becomes much narrower at the bottom than at the top. *That* speeds up the spin. (Remember the ice skater?) The result is a vortex of winds that can whirl faster than 200 miles an hour. If the vortex touches ground, it's a tornado. If it comes down over water, it's a waterspout.

Now, back to your bathtub. When you first pull the plug, water glugs out and then stops, just like the water in the bottles before you rotate them. But then a whirlpool starts, and the water drains freely.

So what makes the vortex? What puts the spin on the water going down the drain? Why, the planet Earth, of course! We're spinning all the time—at over 600 miles an hour!

Red Cabbage Indicator Paper

This kit will let you test liquids to see if they are acids or bases (see the sidebar on page 87). You'll also be able to compare liquids to known acids or bases to see which ones the liquids are most like.

What You'll Need

A red cabbage

A grater

2 bowls

Water

Scissors

Blotter paper (or any heavy, white, non-shiny paper)

An empty potato chip can with its lid

Colored self-adhesive paper

White typing or drawing paper

Markers or colored pencils

Various liquids to test, including lemon juice, vinegar, baking soda, water, milk, orange juice, tap water

Clear self-adhesive paper

What to Do

1. Grate up the cabbage, and let the gratings sit in a bowl of water for several hours.

2. Meanwhile, cut the blotter paper into strips around 6 inches long by 1/2 inch wide.

3. Cover the potato chip can with colored self-adhesive paper.

4. After several hours, drain the red cabbage water into another bowl. (You can use the grated cabbage to make coleslaw.)

5. Soak the strips of blotter paper in the red cabbage water for a few minutes until they turn bluish purple. Lay the wet strips flat on a counter top or other smooth surface.

6. Test some liquids with the indicator strips. (You can do this while they are either dry or wet.) Using markers or colored pencils and the white typing paper, copy the color that the paper strip turns. Draw a picture or write the name

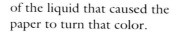

of the liquid that caused the paper to turn that color.

7. Use your notes to make a chart that shows the different colors that different liquids turn the indicator strips. When you test a liquid of unknown acidity, compare the color of its indicator strip with a known liquid's

strip color. Try testing rain, melted snow, stream water, and soil mixed with water.

8. You can attach the chart to the can using clear self-adhesive paper.

9. Keep the indicator strips in the can, where it is dry and dark.

Acids and Bases
and You

Acids and bases play important roles in our lives. They are in the foods we eat and the medicines we take. They are used to make virtually every product people use, from soap to glass to dyes for our clothes (as shown in the photo at right). Of all the different chemicals in the world, most are either an acid, a base, or a combination of the two.

Acids are sour-tasting chemicals. Lemon juice and vinegar contain acid. So do green apples, grapefruit, tea, and yogurt.

Not all acids are safe to eat, or even touch. Some of the most important acids are so powerful they can burn holes in skin and clothing. Nitric acid and sulfuric acid are two examples. They're used to produce such things as plastics, dyes, fertilizers, and explosives. When mixed with enough water, however, even "industrial" acids can be harmless. Hydrochloric acid is so powerful it will dissolve metal. But watered-down hydrochloric acid is in your stomach right now. Your body makes it to help digest food.

Bases are bitter-tasting chemicals that often have a slippery feel. Soap is made from a base. Egg whites and ammonia are bases. So is your blood. Oven cleaners and drain uncloggers contain the powerful base known as lye, or sodium hydroxide. It, too, can burn skin.

An important idea to remember is that acids and bases are chemical opposites. When you mix them together in the right amounts, they *neutralize* each other. For instance, if you put a drop of lemon juice (an acid) on your tongue, it will taste sour. But if you add a pinch of baking soda, which is a base, the sour taste will disappear.

Many kinds of vegetables and flowers won't grow well in soil that is too acid. So gardeners neutralize acid soil by mixing in calcium hydroxide, a base commonly known as *lime*.

You can tell if a substance is an acid or a base by testing it with an indicator such as the red cabbage paper described on page 85. An acid, such as lemon juice or vinegar, will turn the paper red. A base (try a tablespoon of baking soda dissolved in a small glass of water) turns it purplish green. Different liquids produce different shades, depending on how concentrated the acid or base is. For starters, try aspirin, flour, and toothpaste (mix each with a little water first).

Here's another experiment: Find an anthill and, using a stick, stir up a small section to alarm the ants (be careful not to get bitten). Now put a piece of indicator paper over the ants and wait a few minutes. Pretty soon tiny pink spots will appear on the paper—from the formic acid that ants spray into the air when they feel threatened!

Marbled Paper

There are many ways to marble paper. This is one of the simplest and requires only a few easy-to-find supplies.

What You'll Need

A disposable aluminum cake or lasagna pan

Water

Oil-based enamel paints*

Toothpicks

Several sheets of white and/or colored paper, small enough to lie flat in the aluminum pan

Old newspapers or waxed paper

*You can get small amounts of different colors if you buy paints for model cars and airplanes at craft stores or discount marts.

What to Do

1. Fill the aluminum pan with water.

2. Use a toothpick to stir the oil-based paint; then drip small amounts of paint onto the surface of the water. Use toothpicks to move the paint around; you can swirl it, mix several colors, add drops. Use your imagination, but work rather quickly because the paint will soon form a film on the top of the water. When that happens it will be hard to move the paint around without its clumping and breaking apart.

3. When the design on the surface of the water looks good to you, lay a sheet of paper flat on top of the water. Gently press it to make sure there are no air bubbles. Then slowly lift the paper, starting at one end and rolling it off of the surface of the water. Lay the paper face up to dry on a piece of newspaper or waxed paper.

4. When the paper and paint are completely dry, you can use a warm iron to flatten any pages that are curled or wrinkled. Use your paper for covering small books, making collages, making note cards, or covering small boxes. With experience, you will be able to marble larger and larger sheets. Experiment with different kinds of paper and also with small plastic containers, pencils, and other small objects that you would like to marble.

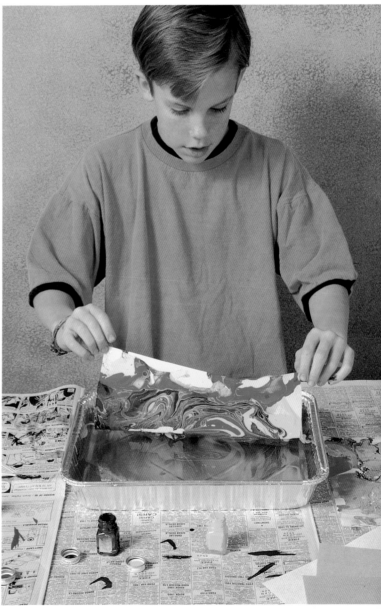

This tiny pond doesn't take up much room, but it makes a nice home for some pond plants—even for a frog and a fish or two.

What You'll Need

A plastic, 30-gallon garbage can (preferably green, brown, or black)

A yardstick or tape measure

Strong scissors

A shovel

Water

Large stones

Goldfish

Floating pond plants

What to Do

1. Select a flat spot for the pond. Either a sunny or shady place will do.

2. Trim off the top few inches of the can, leaving 20 inches of garbage can.

3. Dig a hole as wide and almost as deep as the can. Plan on having 2 inches of the can sticking out of the ground.

4. Place the can down in the hole, and fill in any gaps around it with some of the soil you dug out. Pack it firmly.

5. Fill the pond with water.

6. Place stones around the edge of the pond to hide the rim of the garbage can. Pack soil under and between the stones so that they are firmly held in place.

7. After 24 hours you can add floating pond plants and a goldfish or two. Ask the pet store for the kind of goldfish that can live in an outdoor pond. Follow directions from the pet store about introducing the fish to the pond. You'll need to feed the fish a few grains of fish food once a day at first, but before long the pond will become home to many small creatures, and the fish will find plenty to eat on their own. If you put in a few elodeia plants (ask at the pet shop), they will add oxygen to the water and make it healthier for your fish.

8. From time to time, scoop out fallen leaves and debris. During dry weather you may need to add water; otherwise the pond will take care of itself. In the winter the top of the pond may freeze, but the fish will swim down to the bottom and partially hibernate. They will stop eating and swim very slowly. When the weather warms up, the pond will thaw and the fish will return to active living. Be sure to keep your pond filled, because if the water is shallower than 18 inches it will freeze completely, and your fish will not be able to live.

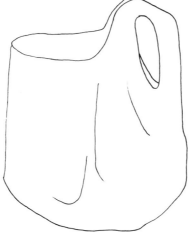

What's happening underwater? This viewer lets you put your eyes closer to the action without getting your face wet.

What You'll Need

A plastic 1/2-gallon milk jug

A razor knife or other sharp knife

Clear plastic wrap

A heavy rubber band

Acrylic paints

A brush

What to Do

1. Carefully cut away the top of the jug, leaving the handle. See Figure 1.

Figure 1

2. Cut away the bottom of the jug.

3. Decorate the outside of the jug with acrylic paints.

4. Cut a piece of plastic wrap 12 x 12 inches. Stretch the plastic wrap over the bottom hole of the jug, and hold it in place with the rubber band. Adjust the plastic so that there are no wrinkles and it is held tightly in place.

5. To use your underwater viewer, hold it by the handle, then press it underwater so that the water comes up the side of the jug but not into it. Peer down through the cut-away top at the stream bottom creatures and plants. The water slightly magnifies things, so everything you spy through your viewer will look slightly larger than life.

For centuries water has been used to do work. One of the main uses of water power years ago was to turn wheels in order to grind grain into flour. There aren't very many water-powered grist mills left today, but you can make a working model of one yourself. This model takes time and patience, but when you're finished, you'll be able to see clearly one way that water power can be harnessed to do work.

What You'll Need

Tools

A jigsaw*

Medium-grit sandpaper and a sanding block

2 C-clamps

A pencil

A drill or a brace and bit

A 1/4-inch drill bit

A 1/2-inch drill bit

A 1-inch expansion bit

Wood glue

A ruler

A hammer

A flathead screwdriver

A can opener

A crosscut saw

Materials

2 by 2 feet of 1/4-inch plywood

36 inches of 1/4-inch dowel

11 inches of 1-inch dowel

10 inches of 2- by 4-inch lumber

10 by 6 inches of 1/8-inch plywood

4-1/2 feet of 1- by 4-inch lumber

Balsa Wood Grinding Wheels

Frame

Pin Gear

Water Wheel

Lantern Gear

Plastic Washer

13 inches of 3/4-inch doweling

6 inches of 3- by 1-inch balsa wood

A 1-inch or 1-1/2-inch long wood screw with a flat head

A washer to fit the screw

1 plastic washer

A large, empty tuna can, with both ends removed

1 inch of 1-1/2-inch plastic pipe or hose

Several scraps of 1/8-inch plywood

*A power jigsaw is optional but very helpful.

What to Do

1. First make the *lantern gear.* Using the jigsaw, cut out two circles with 3-inch diameters from the 1/4-inch plywood. Sand their edges smooth.

2. Clamp the two circles together onto a workbench. Before you tighten the C-clamp, put a piece of scrap wood that is larger than the circles between the workbench and them. Mark the exact center of the top circle. Then put 11 marks 1 inch apart around the circumference of the circle, 1/4 inch in from the edge. See Figure 1.

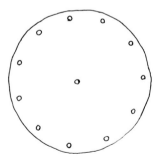

Figure 1

3. With the 1/4-inch bit in the drill or brace, drill the 11 edge holes through both circles at the same time. Then put the 1/2-inch bit in the drill, and drill the center hole through both circles at the same time.

4. Saw the 1/4-inch dowel into 11 1-1/2-inch lengths. Sand the edges.

5. Unclamp the circles. Glue the short dowels into the holes of the bottom circle. Be sure they are standing straight up. Put a dot of glue on the end of each dowel, and carefully fit each hole of the second circle onto the end of each dowel. See Figure 2.

6. Poke the 1/2-inch dowel into the center holes of the two circles so that the dowel sticks 1 inch out of the bottom of the bottom circle. Put aside the lantern gear for now.

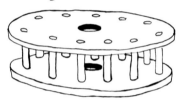

Figure 2

7. Next assemble the *pin gear.* Cut a circle with a 6-inch diameter from the 1/4-inch plywood. Sand it smooth.

8. Mark the exact center of this circle, and also make 19 marks 1 inch apart all around the circumference, 1/4 inch in from the edge.

9. Saw the 1/4-inch dowel into 19 1-1/2-inch pieces. Sand the cut edges.

10. Clamp the circle to the scrap wood and the workbench. With the 1/4-inch drill bit, drill the 19 holes around the edge.

11. Glue the 19 short lengths of dowel into the holes. Be sure the dowels stand straight up. Put aside the pin gear for now.

12. Assemble the *water wheel.* Cut two pieces of 1/8-inch plywood 10 by 3 inches each. Sand them smooth.

13. Mark the center of each of these pieces with a line. Cut halfway along the line. See Figure 3.

Figure 3

14. Fit the two pieces of wood together in an X. If the cut is too narrow for the pieces to fit, make another cut the same length on either side of the first cut to widen it. See Figure 4.

Figure 4

15. Clamp the 1-inch dowel to the workbench with 2 inches of it sticking over the edge. Make two 1-inch-deep cuts at right angles to each other. See Figure 5.

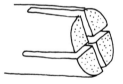

Figure 5

16. Slip the crossed wooden paddles into the crossed cuts on the dowel end. Enlarge the cuts on the dowel if necessary. See Figure 6.

17. Place the crossed paddles on a table with the dowel standing up. Place the tuna can over the dowel, and then center it on the paddles so that the dowel is in the center of the can. Mark the paddles where the tuna can crosses them.

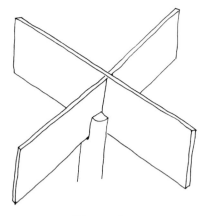

Figure 6

18. Draw a 2-inch line inward on each paddle beginning at the spot where the tuna can mark is.

19. Take the dowel off the paddles and uncross them. Saw each paddle along the 2-inch lines. See Figure 7.

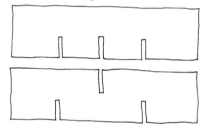

Figure 7

20. Reassemble the paddle wheel. Cross and lock the paddles; slip on the dowel end. Then slide the tuna can into the new cuts. The wheel should be sturdy now. See Figure 8.

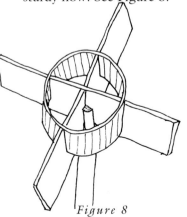

Figure 8

21. Now make the two *grinding wheels*. Draw two circles with 3-inch diameters on the wide surface of the balsa wood. Use the jigsaw to cut out the two circles. Since the balsa wood is thick, be careful to saw straight up and down. (It's okay if the circles aren't cut perfectly round.) Sand the circles to smooth them. Then drill a 1-inch hole in the center of one of the circles. Drill a 1/2-inch hole in the center of the other circle. Put these aside for now.

22. Next build the *frame*. Cut the following pieces of lumber:

From 2 x 4 lumber: Cut 2 pieces, each 5 inches long.

From 1 x 4 lumber: Cut one piece 8-3/4 inches long, one piece 8 inches long, one piece 10-3/4 inches long, one piece 12-1/2 inches long, and one piece 13-3/4 inches long.

From now on, we'll refer to all these pieces by the letter names on Figure 9.

23. Using a 1-inch expansion bit, drill a 1-inch hole in A and B, 1 inch down from the top, in the center of each piece. Drill a 1-inch hole in the exact center of E and F.

24. Nail the frame together as shown in Figure 9.

25. Assemble the mill. First, slide the plastic washer onto the dowel of the paddle wheel; then slide the dowel through the holes in A and B so that the washer and wheel rest against the outside of the mill frame.

Slip the 1-inch piece of plastic hose over the 1-inch dowel where it sticks out of the piece A. Now screw the pin gear onto the end of this dowel. Slip the washer onto the screw before putting it into the center of the

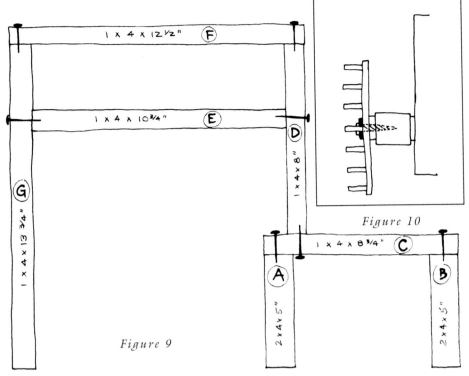

Figure 9

Figure 10

pin gear. See Figure 10.

Glue the balsa wood circle with the 1-inch hole in it onto F, on the top of the frame.

Slide the lantern gear dowel up through the holes in E and F and through the balsa wood circle, as shown in the photo. Adjust the gears so that the short dowels, or gear teeth, of the pin gear connect with the teeth of the lantern gear.

Force the other balsa wood circle over the end of the 1/2-inch dowel. It should fit snugly and hold the lantern gear in place.

If the lantern gear wobbles too much, glue scraps of plywood to hold it in position, as shown in Figure 11.

26. Use acrylic paints to paint the mill.

27. To use the mill, place it on a table with the paddle wheel hanging over the edge. Turn the paddle wheel with your hand. Watch how the gears work together to change the direction of motion. Imagine that the two

balsa wood circles are heavy mill stones. Corn and other grains could be ground between the bottom stone and the turning upper stone.

Try the mill in a stream. You'll need to build a dam to force the water into a narrow, fast-moving channel, or mill race. Experiment with the position of the mill and with different ways to speed up and slow down the water in the mill race. Listen to the rhythm of the grinding mill wheels as the water races around the paddle wheel!

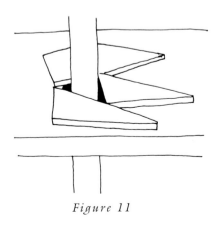

Figure 11

Gearing Up, *Gearing Down*

Gears are wheels with extra bite: teeth that help transfer movement from one part of a machine to another part, so the machine can do its job.

Sometimes gears change the *direction* of movement. Look at an eggbeater. When you turn the crank, your hand moves around in an up-and-down circle. So does the big gear wheel. But the smaller gears on either side change the direction of the movement. The beater blades rotate horizontally, from side to side.

Water wheels use gears to do the same thing. The gears change the wheel's up-and-down motion into the sideways, round-and-round motion needed to turn millstones and grind grain into flour.

Gears also change the *speed* at which machines run, and the amount of *force*, or push, they produce. If two gears fitted together end-to-end are the same size around and have the same number of teeth, they rotate at exactly the same speed and with the same amount of force. But suppose one gear has 40 teeth, and the other is only half as big and has 20 teeth.

One turn of the large wheel will make the small one go around two times, or twice as fast. But each turn

will have only half as much force. On the other hand, if you turn the small gear first, the bigger gear will go around only half as fast, but with twice the force.

By arranging gears of different sizes in different combinations, engineers and inventors can make the moving parts in machines speed up, slow down, or work harder.

Skimmer Net

This net is stronger and more flexible than most nets, because the handle and hoop are all made of one piece of wire. Use it for scooping up water creatures from your pond or from a creek.

What You'll Need

A piece of 14-gauge galvanized steel wire about 3-1/2 feet long

A ruler or tape measure

Wire cutters

Plastic-coated tape

Scissors

A pair of tights or pantyhose (lighter colors are best)

Straight pins

A needle

Heavy cotton thread

What to Do

1. Bend the middle of the wire into a circle about 5 inches across. Twist the wire at the base of the circle to hold the shape.

2. Twist the two long ends of wire together to make a single twisted length of wire. See Figure 1.

3. Bend the long twisted wire in half to form a handle. Then twist the single ends of wire around the section of wire just below the circle. See Figure 2.

4. Tightly wrap tape around the length of wire between the circle and the handle. See Figure 3.

5. Cut a piece of pantyhose as long as the circumference of the circle and about 6 inches wide.

6. Pin the piece of pantyhose net to the circle, turning under about 1/4 inch of cloth as you go. See Figure 4.

7. Pin the side and bottom seams of the net. See Figure 5.

8. Sew the net to the circle where it is pinned. Take out the pins as you sew.

9. Sew the side and bottom seams.

10. When you aren't using your net, hang it up by the loop in its handle. Happy scooping!

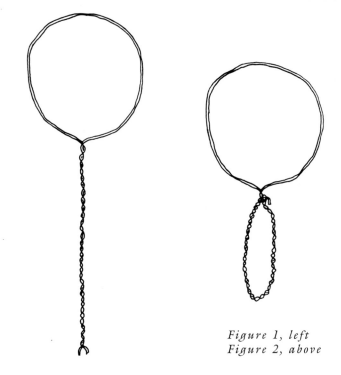

Figure 1, left
Figure 2, above

Figure 3

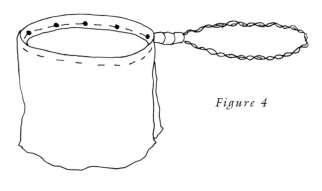

Figure 4

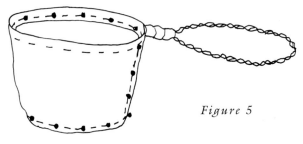

Figure 5

Water's *Skin*

Most people think that water is pretty ordinary stuff, but scientists know better. Plain old water isn't plain at all. One of water's unusual properties is its strong "skin," or what scientists call *surface tension*.

You've probably noticed it when you've put too much water in a glass. Just before the water overflows, it bulges above the rim of the glass, almost as though the liquid at the top is trying to hang on for dear life.

Why? Because water molecules—the tiny particles that make up water—have an especially strong attraction for one another. They're constantly pulling inward on each other from all directions, in order to stay together. But the poor molecules at the surface don't have anything above them to hang onto except air. So they pull together more strongly on each side. And the water molecules below pull them down especially hard. The result is a kind of elastic skin of you're-not-going-anywhere water particles. Actually, all liquids have surface tension, but water's skin is tougher than most. You can even float steel on it. Fill a bowl with water, and lay a small piece of paper towel on the surface. Now, put a pin or paper clip on the towel. Then use another pin or clip to *carefully* poke the wet paper away. Presto! You've made steel float!

In nature, water's surface tension is a regular stomping ground for pond insects. Water striders and beetles skate across the surface looking for prey. And underwater, mosquito larvae hang upside down from the film, like tiny, buggy bats in a liquid cave!

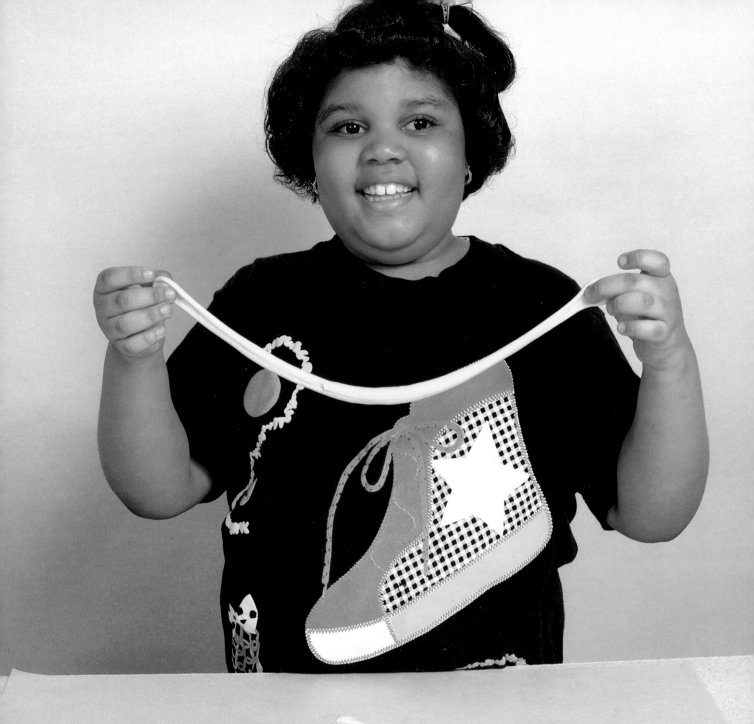

Gluep and Oobleck

"**G**luep" and "oobleck" are two wonderful substances that you can make when you add water to some common household chemicals. You'll want to play with oobleck for hours! You can make up a batch of gluep to keep and play with for several days.

What You'll Need

For gluep:

Borax*

Water

Measuring spoons

2 bowls

Tacky glue or Elmer's white craft glue**

Food coloring (optional)

For oobleck:

A large bowl half filled with cornstarch

Water

*You can get borax where laundry detergents are sold.

**Don't use Sobo white glue for this project. While it's a very good craft glue, for some reason it doesn't work well in gluep.

What to Do

To make gluep:

1. Make a solution of 6 tablespoons of water and 1 teaspoon of borax. Mix the solution well.

2. In a separate bowl, mix 1 tablespoon of glue and 1 tablespoon of water. If you want colored gluep, add 1 or 2 drops of food coloring.

3. Stir a scant 2 teaspoons of the borax solution into the glue-water. Continue stirring until the mixture gets thick.

4. Knead the gluep until it's pliable. Then the fun begins! Bounce it. Stretch it. Roll it.

Pull it into a thin sheet. Pop it. Snap it. Figure out as many things to do with it as you possibly can! To save it, put it in a plastic bag in the refrigerator, so it won't dry out.

To make oobleck:

1. Simply pour water into the bowl of cornstarch. Stir the resulting mixture with your hands or a spoon.

2. Pick up a fistful of oobleck. Squeeze it. Open your hand and hold the oobleck on your palm. Roll a ball of it between your two hands to make a snake. Hold the snake by its tail and watch what happens. Try punching the oobleck in the bowl. Pick up some and rub it together until it crumbles. Pick up the crumbs and let them sit on your palm for a few seconds. See what else you can do with oobleck! You won't want to stop playing with it!

Water Lens

This simple instrument shapes clear water into a lens and lets you get a good look at small creatures and objects.

What You'll Need

An oatmeal box or other wide cylindrical cardboard container

A razor knife or other sharp knife

Plastic wrap

A heavy rubber band

Acrylic paint

A paint brush

Water

What to Do

1. Remove the lid and turn the box over. Use the knife to cut away the bottom of the box.

2. Carefully cut out three rounded shapes from the wall of the box, leaving an uncut ring at the bottom.

3. Decorate the outside of the box with acrylic paints.

4. Cut a piece of plastic wrap about 12 x 12 inches. Use the rubber band to hold the plastic wrap to the top of the box, leaving the plastic wrap loose and somewhat droopy. (This is where the water will go.)

5. Pour water in the droopy part of the plastic wrap. To use the lens, place it in a lighted area; then put the object you want to look at inside the bottom ring of the box. Peer down through the water.

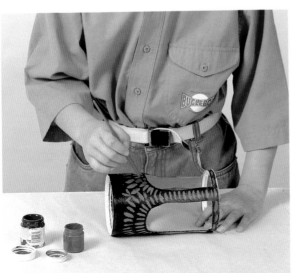

Powered Model Boats

Make a flotilla of boats to help you investigate how boats move through the water. Some of these boats are powered by propellers; others move by means of paddle wheels. Once you understand the basic principles, you can invent some designs of your own.

What You'll Need

A ruler

A pencil

Pieces of lumber of assorted sizes *

A couple of wood clamps

A saw

Sandpaper

A hammer

A 1/2-inch to 1-inch wood chisel

A very narrow wood chisel

A razor knife

Carpenter's glue or balsa wood cement

Rubber bands of various sizes

Tiny screw hooks

Plastic propellers**

Acrylic paints and a brush

*Pine and balsa both float well and are easy to work with. Balsa wood is available at craft stores.

**You can get propellers at a hobby shop that sells model airplane supplies. There are many kinds; look for the smallest and lightest ones that have plastic clips.

What to Do

1. Using the pencil and ruler, mark the lines where you want to cut the pieces of wood for hulls. Look at Figure 1 for ideas for hull shapes.

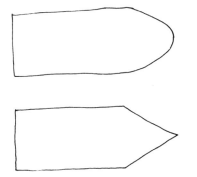

Figure 1

2. Clamp the boards to a work bench or other work surface, and saw along the lines you've drawn. Sand all cuts.

3. Cut out the places where paddles will be attached if you want to build paddle wheel boats. Cut out the propeller mount spaces if you are making propeller boats. See Figure 2.

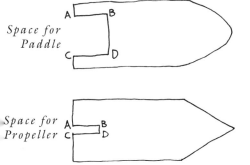

Space for Paddle

Space for Propeller

Figure 2

To cut out these shapes, first mark them with ruler and pencil. Then make the saw cuts from point A to point B and from point C to point D. To cut line B-D, hammer the chisel along the line you've drawn. This will give you a shallow cut.

Deepen the cut by hammering over the line some more. When the line is about 1/8 inch deep, hammer inward from the end of the hull toward line B-D. See Figure 3. Pieces of wood should lift up. Remove these pieces of wood, and then hammer another, deeper line from point B to

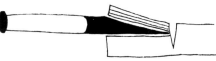

Figure 3

point D. Continue to hammer line B-D and then chisel up from the end of the hull to the line until the entire space is cleared out. See Figure 4.

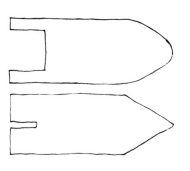

Figure 4

4. Cut out paddle wheels and paddles with a razor knife or saw, depending on the kind of wood you are using. Balsa wood cuts easily with a knife if it is thin enough. See Figure 5 for shapes.

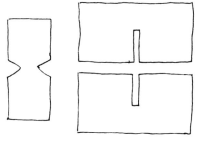

Figure 5

5. If you are using some paddle wheels, assemble them as in Figure 6.

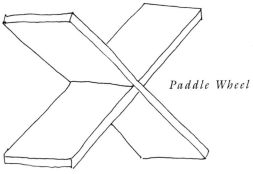

Paddle Wheel

Figure 6

6. Cut out propeller mounts if you are using propellers. See Figure 7.

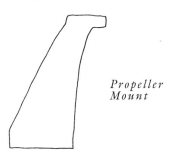

Propeller Mount

Figure 7

7. Assemble the boats. Tie rubber bands into thirds. Slip the two end loops over hull points, and slip the paddle or paddle wheel into the middle loop. See Figure 8. Mount propellers as in Figure 9.

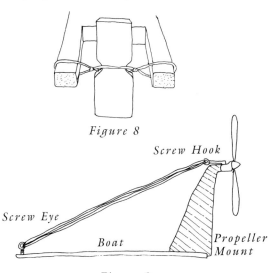

Figure 8

Screw Hook

Screw Eye

Boat

Propeller Mount

Figure 9

105

8. Paint the boats with acrylic paint. When the paint has dried completely, test out your fleet. You'll notice some interesting things about what happens when you spin a propeller in different directions. What other discoveries can you make? What other designs can you dream up?

Try This Puzzle!
(*Water You Weighting For?*)

The two glasses you see here are identical. They're both full right up to the rim with water. But one has a block of wood floating in it. If you weighed each of the glasses, which would be heaviest?

Answer: First read "What Makes a Boat Float" on page 109 and see if you can guess.

(Okay...the answer is at the bottom of page 109.)

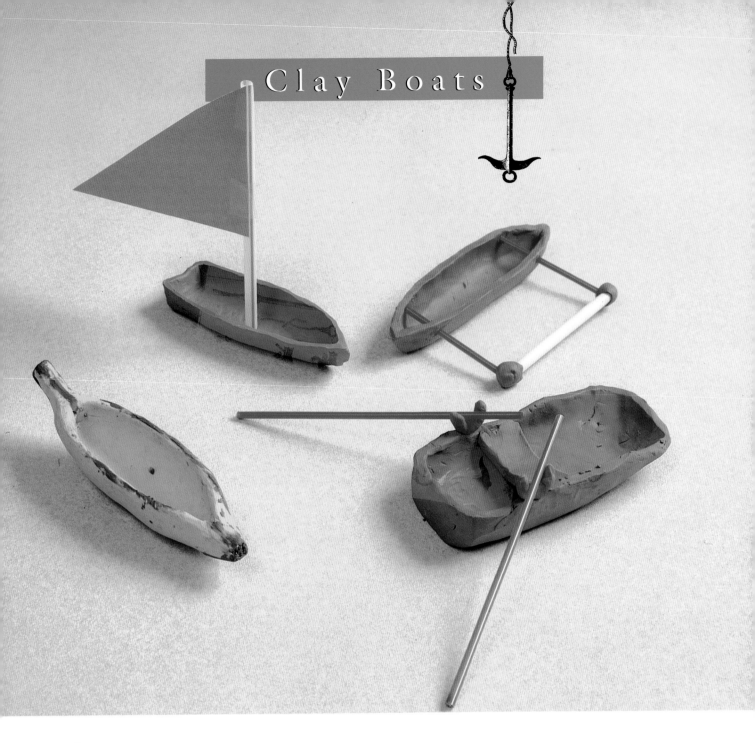

Clay Boats

Drop a ball of clay into a tub of water, and watch it sink like a stone. Now shape the ball of clay into a boat, and watch it float! What's going on here? In this project, you'll make some discoveries about when and why clay can float.

What You'll Need

A tub of water

Modeling clay (also called plasticine clay—NOT pottery clay)

Small sticks (toothpicks or matchsticks)

Small pieces of paper

Scissors

An awl or large nail

Tools to help form clay, such as plastic knives and spoons

What to Do

1. Fill the tub with water. Spend some time playing with different clay shapes to learn which shapes float best.

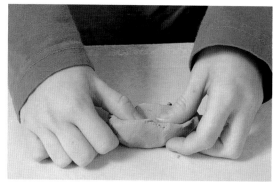

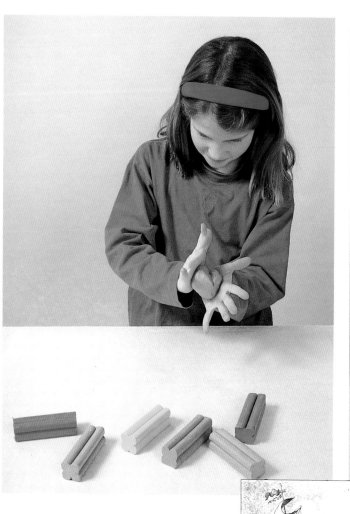

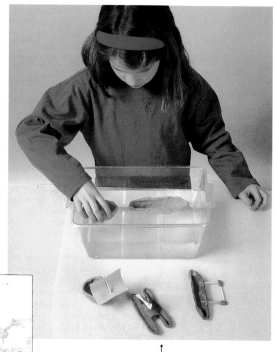

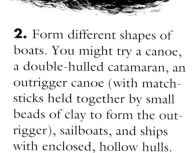

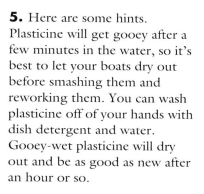

2. Form different shapes of boats. You might try a canoe, a double-hulled catamaran, an outrigger canoe (with matchsticks held together by small beads of clay to form the outrigger), sailboats, and ships with enclosed, hollow hulls. Test all of your boats.

3. As you begin to discover

which shapes float best, refine your designs. Build the biggest boat you can that will float; build the smallest. Make sails out of paper with matchstick masts.

4. Look at the boats in the photograph. Which designs do you think will float? Which are probably sinkers?

5. Here are some hints. Plasticine will get gooey after a few minutes in the water, so it's best to let your boats dry out before smashing them and reworking them. You can wash plasticine off of your hands with dish detergent and water. Gooey-wet plasticine will dry out and be as good as new after an hour or so.

What Makes a *Boat Float?*

If you throw a chunk of steel into water, it sinks like a rock. But if you weld 600,000 tons of steel into the shape of a supertanker, it floats. How can that be?

Whether a boat, a cork, a rock, your Uncle Bill, or anything else floats depends on two things: how much it weighs, and how big it is. Scientists call those two things—the heaviness of an object for its size—*density.*

When you put something in water, it pushes down on the water with as much force as its own weight. And it shoves aside—or *displaces*—enough water to make room for itself.

If the object isn't any heavier than the amount of water it shoves aside, no problem. It floats. The liquid that was holding up the water supports the object instead. But if the whatever-it-is weighs more than the water it displaces, it sinks.

A chunk of metal sinks because it's a lot heavier than the little bit of water it pushes aside. The liquid that was holding up that little bit of water can't possibly hold up the metal.

A 1,000-foot-long, 200-foot-wide, 600,000-ton steel supertanker is a different story. It floats because it's not only heavy, it's *big.* And it isn't solid. There are lots of rooms full of air, which weighs almost nothing.

When a supertanker is launched, it sinks down until the amount of water it pushes aside (and it pushes a *lot* of water) equals the weight of the ship. The rest of the ship floats above the surface. When cargo is loaded, weight is added and the ship sinks a little lower. But as long as the boat and cargo weigh less than the water the ship is pushing aside, it will float.

As for your Uncle Bill: He can float in a lake or pool—but not in a bathtub. Why? Because in a pool, there's enough room for Uncle Bill to push his own weight in water out of the way and still have plenty of water left beneath to support him. But in a tub, there's probably not enough water for Uncle Bill to push aside his weight, and certainly not enough left underneath to hold him up. So he sinks.

Answer to puzzle on page 106: In order to float, the block of wood had to push aside its own weight in water. That water spilled over the edge of the glass. So the weight of the two glasses is the same.

FIRE—

*the heart and soul of our sun.
That blazing ball of fire is the center
of all life on Earth, the source of heat
and light. Use the sun as we humans
have always done. Arrange some stones
into a solar clock to help you track
the seasons, as ancient people did at
Stonehenge....Cook your food in a solar
oven, and preserve it in a solar dryer....
Grow some plants in a tiny greenhouse....Then play with the sun's light—
make color spinners and light catchers....
Find your way by the sun's light, just as
your ancestors did—make a solar stone,
an astrolabe, a cross staff....Finally,
look at other, more distant suns with
your star magnitude gauge.*

FIRE

Solar Clock

Early people watched the sky more than most of us do today. They watched movements of the sun, moon, and stars that many of us never notice. Some people even developed gigantic sky clocks that helped them keep track of changing seasons. Stonehenge in southern England is thought to be one of these.

For ancient people in the northern hemisphere, the summer solstice was a very important time of the year. It was the time when the sun was most directly overhead and the days were longest. Plants grew strongest at this time of year. It was a time of great feasting and ceremony. It was important to know when the solstice was coming.

In this project, you will make a small solar clock that will help you learn to notice some important movements of the sun.

What You'll Need

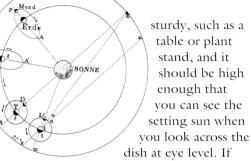

A large, shallow dish, such as a dish that goes under a very large clay or plastic flowerpot

Soil to fill the dish

A trowel

7 pointy-topped rocks, each one about 2 to 3 inches tall

A calendar

Mosses (optional)

What to Do

1. You'll have to begin this project at a certain time of year. The equinoxes—the days when night and day are of equal length—are around March 21 and September 21. The summer solstice—the day when the sun is in the sky for the longest period all year (if you live in the northern hemisphere)—is around June 21. The winter solstice—the shortest day of the year in the northern hemisphere—is around December 21. You should begin this project at one of these times: March 18 or 19, June 18 or 19, September 18 or 19, December 18 or 19.

2. The most important step in this project is finding the right location for your clock. You need a place from which you can see both sunrise and sunset all year round. It's best if you can see the distant horizon, the place where the sky and land seem to touch each other. If the sun sets behind trees or mountains where you live, you can still make a solar clock, but it will work best if you can see a distant horizon.

3. Once you've settled on a place, set up a stand for the dish. This should be something sturdy, such as a table or plant stand, and it should be high enough that you can see the setting sun when you look across the dish at eye level. If you think the stand and dish might be disturbed from time to time during the year, make a mark on the side of the dish and on the table so that you can reposition the dish if someone should move it.

4. Place the dish on the table or stand, and fill it with soil. Place a rock on top of the soil in the exact center of the dish. We'll call this your *center stone.*

5. On one of the four dates, go outside in the evening at sunset. Find the place on the near edge of the dish from which you can look directly at the sun across the center rock. Place a rock just inside the rim to mark this spot. We will call this your *spotting stone.*

6. Place a second rock inside the rim nearest the setting sun as you look from your spotting stone across the center rock. This is your *rim stone.* See Figure 1.

7. On the next evening, go outside and again look at the setting sun from your spotting stone across the center stone. Move the rim stone if you need to so that it lines up with the setting sun. You probably won't notice much change, if any, but it's a good idea to check your placement.

8. Continue checking the placement of the rim stone until the solstice or equinox has passed. Another reason to start checking a few days before the actual date is to increase your chances of catching at least one sunset in case there are some cloudy days around the event. The actual date of the event should be on a calendar.

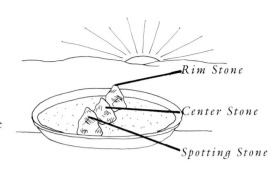

Figure 1

9. Watch your calendar until a few days before the next big solar event—equinox or solstice—and repeat Steps 5, 6, 7, and 8. Be sure to place the dish in the same position each time. You'll notice that you will need to place a new spotting stone as well as a new rim stone.

10. Repeat the process for the next two solar events.

11. Here are a couple of interesting facts that you may want to check by getting up early enough to view a sunrise.

The spotting stone for the winter solstice sunset will be the rim stone for the summer solstice sunrise; the rim stone for the winter solstice sunset will be the spotting stone for the summer solstice sunrise.

The spotting stone for the summer solstice sunset will be the rim stone for the winter solstice sunrise; the rim stone for the summer solstice sunset will be the spotting stone for the winter solstice sunrise! What can you discover about the equinox stones?

12. If you want to, decorate your clock by planting mosses around the stones.

The Sun,
Center of Life

Most of us don't give the sun much thought. It rises in the morning, sets in the evening, and makes summer days hot, right?

Right. But it also keeps us alive. All life on Earth depends entirely on the sun. In fact, without the sun life never would have existed here.

The sun's gravity holds Earth and all the other planets in our solar system in orbit. Its light gives green plants the energy to grow and produce oxygen for us to breathe. Its heat drives the winds, rains, and ocean currents. The sun provides food for us to eat and gives us the materials we use to build our homes and clothe ourselves. The fuel we use to drive our cars and heat our houses contains the sun's energy. Wood blazing in a fireplace gives off the power of sunlight stored by a growing tree. The energy in oil, gas, and coal is the sun's, captured millions of years ago by plants and animals.

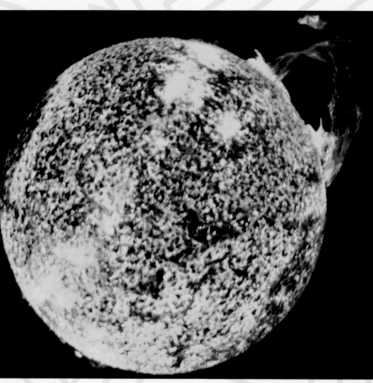

Everything about the sun is as dazzling as the star itself.

☛ The sun weighs as much as 332,946 planets the size of Earth.

☛ More than one million Earths could fit inside the sun!

☛ The sun is about 4-1/2 billion years old. Scientists say it will last at least another five billion years.

☛ Gravity is much more powerful on the sun than on Earth. If you weighed 100 pounds on Earth, you'd weigh 2,800 pounds on the sun!

☛ The sun is about 93 million miles from Earth. If you decided to travel to the sun, you'd be in for a long trip. It would take about 193 years to get there in a car going 55 mph. You'd get there a little sooner if you took a 100-mile-an-hour express train, though: just 106 years. A Boeing 737 going 450 miles an hour would make the trip in 24 years. Even a spaceship traveling at 25,000 miles an hour would have to fly more than five months to get to the sun!

☛ The sun is our nearest star. If the thickness of this page stood for the distance between Earth and the sun, the distance between Earth and the next nearest star would be a stack of paper 71 feet tall!

☛ It takes only about eight minutes for light and heat from the sun to reach Earth.

☛ The temperature of the sun's core is 27 million degrees Fahrenheit (15 million degrees Centigrade). In just one second the sun gives off more energy than people have used since the beginning of mankind.

Solar Oven

This is the simplest design for a solar oven that you are likely to find anywhere. All of the materials are things you can easily find. On a bright, sunny day, you can bake a batch of cookies in your oven while your family and friends watch in amazement! See page 370 for a pizza box solar oven!

What You'll Need

2 cardboard grocery boxes*

A razor knife

White craft glue

A bowl to mix glue and water

A 1- or 2-inch-wide soft paint brush

About 2 rolls of large-size aluminum foil

Scissors

A flat piece of cardboard 7 inches longer and 7 inches wider than the length and width of the outer box

Several other flat pieces of cardboard the same size as, or larger

than, the walls of the inner box

2 large, clear plastic, turkey-roasting bags

Paper tape (the kind that you have to wet in order to make it stick)

Self-adhesive shelf paper

A stick about the same length as the width of the outer box

An aluminum cookie sheet or oven bottom liner

A can of flat black latex spray paint

115

*The ideal inner box is 19 by 23 by 8 inches. The ideal outer box is a little wider, longer, and taller: 23 by 27 by 9 inches. If you can't find these exact sizes, look for an inner box that fits inside the outer box with about an inch of space on all sides and the bottom. Boxes that are bigger than the ideal are better than boxes that are smaller; rectangular boxes are better than square ones. The inner box should be as shallow as possible, but taller than the pots you will use. The pots can't touch the window.

What to Do

1. Cut the flaps off the inner box. Leave the flaps on the outer box.

2. Pour about a cup of glue into the bowl, and add about the same amount of water. Stir well. Using the paint brush to apply the glue, glue aluminum foil to the entire inside and outside surfaces of the inner box and to the entire inside surface of the outer box. Also cover both sides of the flaps on the outer box. Do your best to keep the aluminum foil smooth.

3. Cut little pieces of cardboard 1 inch by 1 inch. You will need enough to make six stacks, each of them 1 inch tall. Glue the pieces together to make the six stacks. Glue the stacks to the inside bottom of the outer box. See Figure 1.

4. Put a bit of glue on the top of each stack, and carefully place the inner box on the stacks. Arrange it so that there is about 1 inch of space between the four walls of the inner box and the four walls of the outer box. See Figure 2.

5. Cut flat pieces of cardboard to fit in the spaces between the walls of the two boxes. These

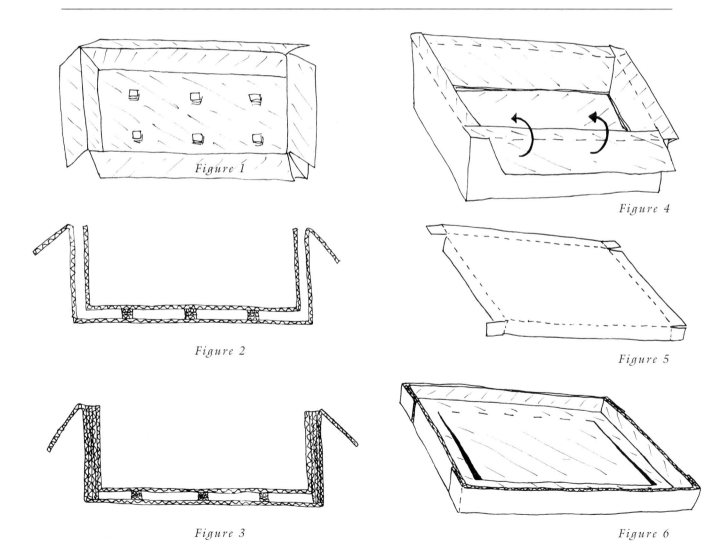

Figure 1

Figure 4

Figure 2

Figure 5

Figure 3

Figure 6

pieces will be the insulation. Glue aluminum foil to one side of each flat piece. When the glue has dried, slip the flat pieces into the spaces between the box walls. Face the shiny side toward the outside. When all the pieces of insulation are in place, the inner box should fit snugly inside the outer box. See Figure 3.

6. Fold the flaps of the outer box up and around the inner box walls. Trim the flaps to fit. These flaps should be covered with aluminum foil on both sides. See Figure 4.

7. Glue the flaps in place.

8. Glue foil to one side of the large flat piece of cardboard that you will use for the lid. Center this piece of cardboard over the boxes, foil side down. Fold the edges over the finished box for a good fit. Cut and fold corner flaps and glue them. See Figure 5.

9. Remove the lid, and place it inside up on a table or the floor. Draw a window opening in the center of the lid the size of the opening of the inner box. Be sure this opening is a little smaller than the turkey roasting bag.

10. Cut three sides of the window, leaving one long side to fold up for a reflector. See Figure 6.

11. Spread glue along the edge of the window frame and stretch the turkey roasting bags in the opening. (You will be using four layers of plastic.) Pull the bags tight so that the plastic stretches smoothly across the window opening.

12. Replace the lid on the oven. Open the reflector lid. Trim the stick so that it is the

right length to prop open the lid at different angles.

13. Completely cover the outside of the box and lid with self-adhesive paper.

14. Spray-paint the aluminum cookie sheet black, and allow it to dry.

15. To use the oven, place it outdoors in a sunny spot. Place

the black sheet in the bottom of the oven. Mix cookies according to your favorite recipe, and place them on a dark aluminum or nonstick baking sheet. Put the baking sheet on the black cookie sheet on the floor of the oven.

If your oven seems too deep for the cookies, place a couple of aluminum pie pans upside

down on the black cookie sheet, and place the baking sheet of cookies on them. That way, the cookies will be closer to the window. Place the lid on the oven. Angle the oven so that the sun shines directly into the center of the box. Adjust the reflector angle to focus sunlight in the oven. It will take several hours to bake the cookies, depending on how warm the day is and how bright the sun is. Check on the oven from time to time, and adjust the angle of the oven and of the reflector to keep the sun shining inside the oven. Don't open the lid until you think the cookies are done, as heat will quickly escape once you open it. Use a hot pad to handle the cookie pan. It will get very hot! Your solar oven will heat up to about 275 degrees F on a hot, sunny day when there are many hours of sunlight.

16. Experiment with cooking other things in your oven. Here are some hints: Put food into dark-colored, covered pots (although cookies don't need to be covered). If you are cooking fresh vegetables, don't add water. For other foods, start with the recipe you usually use, and adjust it if it isn't cooking right. Smaller pots of food will cook faster. The thinner the sides of the pot, the faster the food will cook. Small pieces of food will cook faster than large ones.

Polar
Solar Collectors

You've probably heard of solar collectors—devices that "catch" the sun's warmth and use it to heat water or even an entire house. If you live in a sunny part of the planet, your home may have a solar collector. It's probably up on the roof, where it can be aimed at the sun to capture the most heat.

But did you know that one of the world's best "solar collectors" isn't manmade at all, and works even in the coldest places on Earth? This solar collector has fur, four legs, and weighs over 1,000 pounds. It's a polar bear!

Polar bear hairs are like tiny, see-through pipes. They're hollow and completely transparent. The fur only looks white to us because the inside wall of each hollow hair reflects visible light—the part of sunlight we can see. But the hairs also do something else. They trap ultraviolet light—one of the parts of sunshine that we *can't* see. Ultraviolet light is the invisible energy that gives people suntans.

The bear's hollow hairs grab the ultraviolet radiation and lead it, like hot water in a pipe, to the animal's skin—which, under all that fur, is black. Black absorbs solar energy. So the bear soaks up the sun's energy like a sponge and stays warm in weather that would give almost any other creature the cold shivers. Manmade solar collectors have to be pointed at the sun to make them grab as much heat as possible. But polar bear fur traps light coming from any direction. And the animals lose very little heat, because the hairs are strictly one-way: Ultraviolet energy can flow toward the animal's skin, but never away from it.

No wonder solar engineers are studying polar bears! They're trying to figure out how to use the bear-hair's heat-catching tricks in manmade designs. Who knows? Maybe someday all solar collectors will be white and fuzzy!

Solar Food Dryer

This food dryer will let you preserve food for later...or turn your favorite fruits into handy snacks.

What You'll Need

A cardboard box about 12 by 16 by 24 inches, open at one end

A razor knife

Aluminum foil

Cellophane tape

Black plastic tape about an inch wide

Clear plastic wrap or a clear plastic paint drop cloth

About a yard of vinyl window screen cloth or cheesecloth

1 or 2 cake cooling racks

Acrylic paints

A paint brush

What to Do

1. Lay the box down on one of its large sides.

2. Make a cut from the top corner of the open end of the box straight along the edge until the cut is about 2 inches from the closed end of the box. Make an identical cut along the other top edge. See Figure 1.

3. "Score" a line between points A and B on Figure 2. (Score means to cut just deeply enough to leave a groove. DON'T cut all the way through the cardboard.) The top of the box should now bend easily to a slant, touching the bottom of the box. See Figure 2.

4. Trim the sides of the box so that they follow the slant of the top. See Figure 3. Trim off any flaps that stick out on the bottom past the place where the slanting top touches the bottom.

5. Carefully cut three windows, one in each side and one on the slanting top of the box. Leave a frame about 1-1/2 inches wide around each window. See Figure 4.

6. Cut pieces of aluminum foil big enough to line the inside bottom, back, and sides of the box. Tape the foil in place with loops or strips of cellophane tape.

7. Cut out two triangles of screen or cheesecloth slightly larger than the two side windows.

8. Tape the screen or cheese-cloth to the outside of the windows with black plastic tape.

9. Cut a piece of plastic slightly larger than the slanted top opening. If you need to, use cellophane tape to tape two smaller pieces together to get a big enough piece.

10. Stretch and tape the plastic to the outside of the top window, using black plastic tape. See Figure 5. The entire frame—top and sides—should now be covered with black tape.

11. Paint the top and back of the box with black acrylic paint. If you want to add some designs to the box, do that now, but be sure to leave most of the box black so that it will absorb heat more readily.

12. Place the oven racks inside the food dryer. To use the dryer, lay thinly sliced fruit or vegetables (apples, sweet potatoes, pears, apricots) on the racks. Close the dryer and place it in a sunny spot indoors or outdoors. The fruit will dry in 10 days to two weeks, depending on how dry the weather is. If you place the dryer outside, be sure to bring it in at night or in rainy weather.

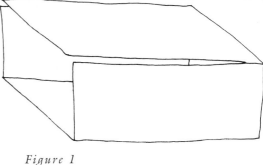

Figure 1

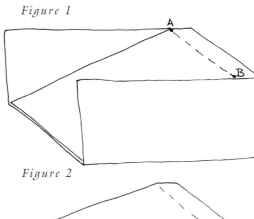

Figure 2

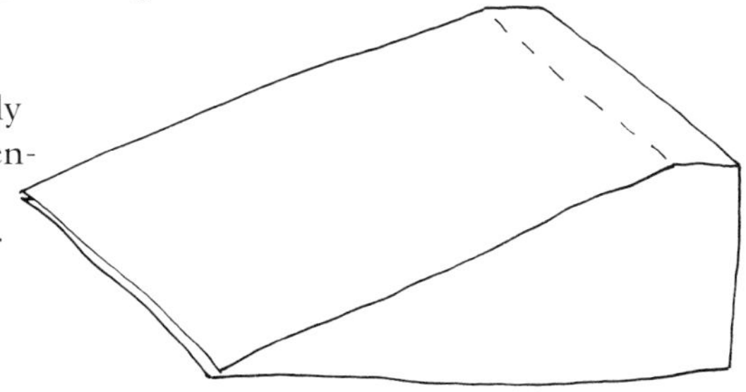

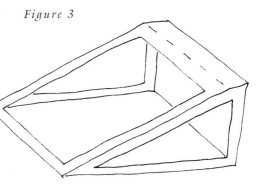

Figure 3

Figure 4

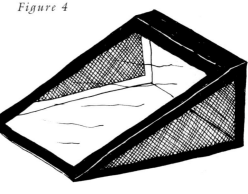

Figure 5

This mini-greenhouse will keep plants warm and cozy all winter long. If you put it in a sunny spot, you'll be able to pick lettuce for a salad in January! In spring, you can simply lift up the tepee and fold its legs together for easy storage.

What You'll Need

3 pieces of edge molding, each 36 inches long*

Enamel spray paint

A hammer

A nail

3 screw eyes**

4 inches of soft wire

A permanent marker

Scissors

Clear plastic (either an old shower curtain or a heavy plastic paint drop cloth)

A staple gun

3 clothespins

*Edge molding is a kind of lumber that is cut to wrap around edges of walls. If you look at the end of a piece, it will be curved (see Figure 1). You can buy edge molding at a large hardware store or a lumberyard.

Figure 1   *Figure 2*

**A screw eye is a small ring attached to a screw (see Figure 2), available at hardware stores and discount marts.

What to Do

1. Spray-paint the three pieces of edge molding completely.

2. After they're dry, use the hammer and nail to make a starter hole in one end of each of the sticks.

3. Place a screw eye in each starter hole, and screw it in with your fingers. (Or thread the nail through the screw hole, and turn it like a faucet to tighten it.)

4. Tie the three screw eyes loosely together with the wire. See Figure 3.

5. Spread the three pieces of wood to form a triangular framework around your plants. Push the ends of the sticks into the ground, about an inch deep, to anchor them. Make sure that the 1/4-inch edge of the molding is facing outward

on the piece that will be the door. The clothespins will then be able to grip that edge.

6. Use markers and scissors to cut three triangular pieces of plastic to fit over the three sides. Leave about an inch of extra plastic on each edge for stapling to the framework.

7. Ask a grown-up to help you staple two of the triangular pieces of plastic to the frame. Then staple ONE SIDE only of the third piece, leaving one side open for a door.

8. Use clothespins to fasten the loose side when you want the door closed. Open the door and clothespin it back on warm days.

9. If you live in a place where the winters are very cold, use two layers of plastic for all of the walls of the tepee.

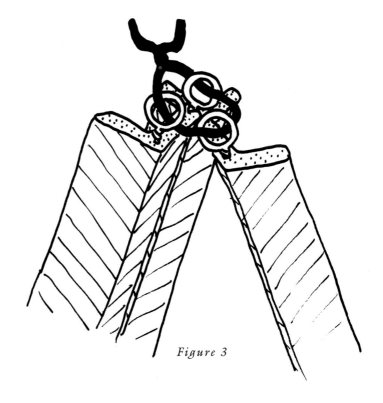

Figure 3

Color Spinners

When you spin these, you'll see colors change in front of your eyes as if by magic!

What You'll Need

Corrugated cardboard (such as the flaps from an old box)

Something round to use as a pattern to draw a circle (such as a quart-sized paint can or an upside down bowl)

A pencil

A razor knife

A piece of 1/4-inch dowel, about 7 inches long for each spinner

Red, blue, and yellow acrylic paints

A brush

A saw

A pencil sharpener (optional)

An awl or a large nail

What to Do

1. Tracing around your pattern, draw a circle about 4 inches in diameter on the cardboard.

2 Cut the circle out, using the razor knife.

3. Paint the circle, using two of the colors. Paint pie-shaped wedges in alternating colors, until you completely fill in the circle. (The easiest way to make wedges is to draw straight lines across the circle so that they all cross exactly in the center.)

4. Use the awl or nail to poke a starter hole in the exact center of the cardboard circle.

5. Saw off a 7-inch-long piece of dowel, and sharpen one end either with the razor knife or in a pencil sharpener.

6. Poke the sharpened end of the dowel through the hole in the center of the circle. Push about 3 inches of the dowel through the hole.

7. To spin the spinner, make a loose circle with the fingers of one hand, and slip the pointy (bottom) end of the spinner dowel through the hole in your hands. Rest the pointy end on a table top or the floor. Use your other hand to spin the top of the dowel. Loosely support the bottom of the spinner with your bottom hand while you continue to spin the spinner with your other hand. Watch what happens to the colors.

8. Make other spinners using other combinations of colors. Try making one with all three colors. Try using white and a color or black and a color. Experiment!

Mixed-Up *Colors*

Magenta *Yellow* *Cyan*

Have you ever painted with watercolors? Then you probably know that if you mix blue paint and yellow paint, you get green paint. But wait a minute. If you shine a blue light and a yellow light together, you get *white*. Why?

Colored lights and colored paints mix completely differently. Paints, inks, and dyes contain *pig-*

ments that soak up all the colors of the rainbow except the ones they reflect. For example, blue paint absorbs all of the spectrum except blue.

Every time you mix two colored paints together, you make a paint that absorbs more of the spectrum than before. The new color is always a little closer to black, which of course doesn't reflect any color at all.

The primary colors for pigments are yellow, cyan (pronounced SY-ann—a greenish blue), and magenta (purple-red). Printers and painters mix yellow, cyan, and magenta inks or paints to make all of their colors.

Mixing colored light is the opposite of mixing paints. White light contains all the colors of the spectrum. So every time you combine one colored light with another, you make a color that's a little closer to white.

The primary colors for light are red, green, and blue. By mixing just those three colors of light in different amounts, you can make any color in the world. Scientists say it's possible to create more than a million distinct colors of light!

For one example of how people use light's primary colors, check out a color TV screen. Look very closely, or through a magnifying glass. (Don't hurt your eyes. Look for just a few seconds.) Surprise! All of the colors on the screen are actually made up of thousands of tiny red, blue, and green stripes or dots.

The color spinners on page 124 can help you understand the ways colors mix. Try making a blue and yellow color spinner. If the two paints happen to overlap a bit where the wedges meet, they'll combine to make a greenish color. That's because you mixed their pigments and created a paint that absorbs more of the spectrum. But when you spin the spinner, you combine the blue and yellow *light* reflecting off the card. The moving spinner looks white. Likewise, if you make a red and green spinner, any mixed-up paint will be blackish. But when you spin the card, the red and blue reflected light combine to make yellow!

Fire Clock

The ancient Chinese made clocks that worked by burning a candle. This fire clock uses an incense stick instead of a candle, so it will smell sweet as it helps you tell time.

What You'll Need

A ball of plasticine clay (modeling clay) the size of your fist

Several sticks of incense

A flat, heat-proof dish or tray (such as an aluminum baking pan)

Thread

Scissors

About 10 small jingle bells

A clock or watch

A match

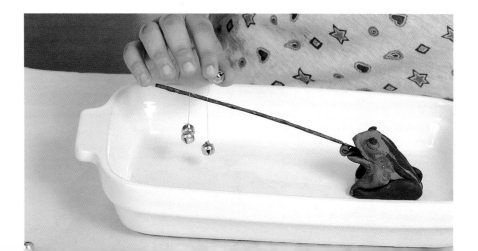

What to Do

1. Make a simple figure out of the clay, such as a bird, a person, or an animal standing on its hind legs. Or simply shape the clay into a cylinder or wedge. The figure or shape should be about 3 inches tall.

2. Push the handle of a stick of incense into the figure's mouth or somewhere else near the top. Be sure the stick is held firm, with about 1 inch of it sticking into the clay. The stick should slant slightly upward.

3. Stand the figure with the incense stick at one end of the heat-proof dish. The stick should reach across to the other side of the dish but not stick over the edge.

4. Cut pieces of thread about 4 inches long. Tie a jingle bell to each end so that you have five or six pairs of bells on strings.

5. Ask an adult to help you light the stick of incense. Drape a pair of bells over the incense stick about 1 inch down from the lighted tip. Use a watch or clock to see how long it takes for the stick to burn to the thread. When the burning tip reaches the thread, it will burn through it, and the bells will drop to the dish, making a tinkling sound. After you've seen how long it takes the incense to burn a certain distance—for example, 1 inch—you can place the other pairs of bells along the stick at the spaces you want. You might want a pair of bells to drop every 15 minutes. Or you might want to use the clock to time something that needs to go on for an hour. Experiment with extra sticks of incense. You'll soon figure out how to set your clock to go off when you want it to.

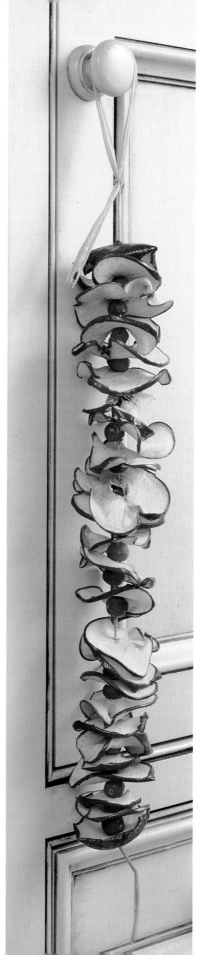

Dried Apple Garland

After you've built a solar food dryer (see page 120), you can make a dried apple garland with some of the slices your dryer turns out. Experiment with making other kinds of garlands, too. You might try dried sweet potato slices with raisins (dried grapes), or pears and pineapple spears.

What You'll Need

Raffia*

A big-eyed needle

Dried apple slices

Whole cranberries or other firm, edible berries

*Raffia is sold in craft stores.

What to Do

1. Thread the needle with a thick strand of raffia. Tie a big knot about 2 inches from the end of the strand.

2. Poke the needle through either a cranberry or an apple end slice (if you have one).

3. Thread apple slices and cranberries until you run out of apple slices. Finish off with either a cranberry or another apple end slice.

4. Tie a loop in the end of the raffia and cut off the rest of it.

5. Hang the garland in a dry, shady place, and snack off it until all that's left is the raffia.

Light Catcher

When you join 12 five-sided figures, called pentagons, to form a three-dimensional solid, the solid is called a dodecahedron (doh-dek-uh-HEE-dron). If you cover the 12 surfaces of a dodecahedron with shiny paper, it will gather and reflect light and fill your room with pieces of the rainbow.

What You'll Need

A piece of heavy paper, such as lightweight poster board or bristol board

Tracing paper

Carbon paper

A sharp pencil

Sharp scissors or a razor knife

A ruler or straightedge

A table knife

Rubber cement

Pieces of shiny paper, such as wrapping paper or foil

Dental floss or monofilament fishing line

A needle

What to Do

1. Make a template from one of the shapes given in Figure 1. Choose either the large or the

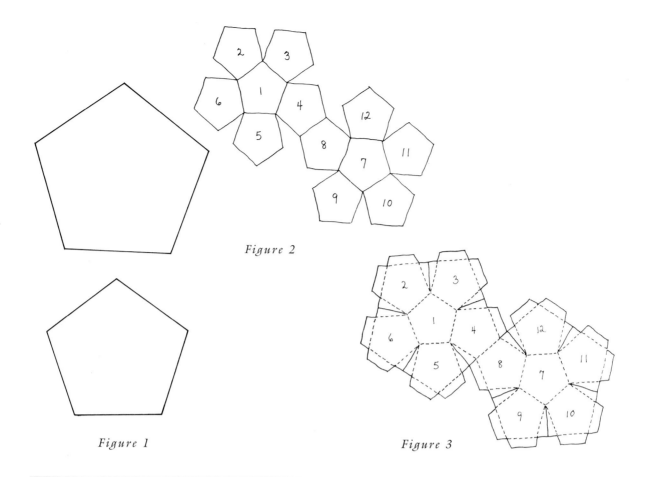

Figure 1

Figure 2

Figure 3

small shape, but use the same shape for all of the pentagons of each dodecahedron.

To make a template, trace the shape onto tracing paper. Use a ruler to make sure the lines are perfectly straight. Then put a piece of carbon paper between the tracing paper and a piece of heavy paper, with the carbon side facing the heavy paper. Draw over the figure you have traced. You should now have a copy of the shape on heavy paper. Carefully cut out this shape, making sure all lines are perfectly straight.

2. Use the template to draw the pentagons as shown in Figure 2. Notice that each pentagon shares at least one edge with another pentagon. The numbers in Figure 2 are to help

you keep track. You do not need to write the numbers on your drawing.

3. Draw the tabs as shown by the solid lines in Figure 3.

4. With sharp scissors or a razor knife, carefully cut out the figure. Be sure to cut ONLY along the outside of the tabs. Do NOT cut the tabs off the figure.

5. Using the table knife, score all of the lines between pentagons and between pentagons and tabs. (These are the dotted lines in Figure 3.) To score lines, place a ruler along the line and draw a table knife along the line so that the line is pressed down but not cut. Scoring a line makes it easier to fold.

6. Carefully fold all the tabs down in the same direction.

Then fold all the outer pentagons down. Fold the line between the two units of pentagons so that the two units face each other.

7. Put rubber cement on the top surface of each tab. Let it dry. (It will look dull when it is dry.) When the cement is dry, press the tabs that are next to each other together, causing the two groups of pentagons to come together and form angular bowls, as in Figure 4. Be careful as you press the tabs together, because once dry rubber-cemented surfaces are joined, they can't be pulled apart.

8. Now join the two bowls by pressing together the tabs that face each other on the two units. Again, be careful, because dry rubber cement can't be moved.

130

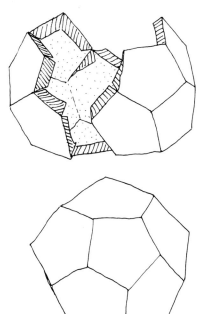

Figure 4

9. You now have a dodeca-hedron, but not a light catch-er. To make a light catcher, use the template that you made to draw pentagons on shiny paper or foil. Cut out each shiny pentagon. Coat each pentagon on the dodec-ahedron with rubber cement, and coat the back of each shiny paper pentagon with rubber cement. When the cement has dried, press the shiny pentagons onto the dodecahedron.

10. Thread a needle with dental floss or monofilament. Pierce a small hole in the cor-ner of one shiny pentagon, and pull the floss through. Tie a knot to hold the floss in place. Hang the dodeca-hedron in a sunny window.

Light
and Color

When you hear the word *reflection,* you probably think of what you see when you look in a mirror. But actually, almost *everything* you see is a reflection of light bouncing off an object and into your eyes. Have you ever been in a super-dark place? A place so dark you couldn't see your own hand when you held it in front of your face? Your hand was there, of course. But you couldn't see it because there was no light reflecting from it.

Light from the sun or some other source is called *white* light, but it is really a mixture of seven colors: red, orange, yellow, green, blue, indigo, and violet. These make up the spectrum—the colors you see in a rainbow. The seven colors usually travel together, combined as white light, until they are reflected by something. Then the light rays bounce back into our eyes.

But not all objects reflect all the colors back in equal amounts. Some things absorb part of the spectrum and reflect only what's left. That's why our world is such a colorful and interesting place. When you look at a green leaf, you're seeing the green part of white light reflected by the leaf. The other colors have been absorbed by the leaf. When sunlight strikes a red rose, the flower "soaks up" all the colors in the spectrum except red, which it bounces back into your eyes. The polka dots on Uncle Fred's tie are white because they reflect all the colors in light. The black background of the tie is black because it soaks up all the colors. And that little yellow spot of spilled mustard is there because it reflects the yellow part of the spectrum—and because Uncle Fred is a sloppy eater!

Solar Stone

The Vikings had a simple stone or wooden instrument called a solar stone, or bearing dial, that helped them find north, which was home for the Vikings. You can use your solar stone to navigate around your neighborhood or when you're exploring new territory. It can also help you find your way around the sky at night.

What You'll Need

A piece of corrugated cardboard about 5 by 5 inches

Something to use as a pattern to draw a circle with a 4-inch diameter

A pencil

A razor knife

A straight-sided cork

A 5-inch length of 1-inch-diameter dowel

A hacksaw

Super glue

An awl or a large nail

Two 1-1/2-inch-long finishing nails (They have very small heads.)

Acrylic paints and a brush

A permanent black marker or puffy plastic paint in a squeeze bottle

What to Do

1. Make the dial by tracing a 4-inch circle onto the cardboard and then cutting it out with the razor knife.

2. Find the exact center of the circle, and center one end of the cork over that spot. Now trace around the cork. Carefully cut out this small circle. Test the size of the small circle by sliding the cork into it. If the

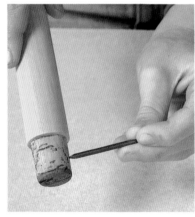

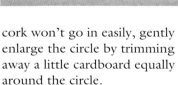

design, make four points for the four directions—north, south, east, and west. Use black marker or puffy paint to label the four directions.

8. Paint the handle, including the cork.

9. Assemble the solar stone by sliding the dial over the cork. Then push a finishing nail into the top hole and one into the side hole.

10. You can use the solar stone both during the day and at night to find north. Here's what you do. Go outside at noon and point the side nail, or pointer stick, in the direction in which you are walking. Now hold the stone so that the top nail, or shadow stick, casts a shadow on the dial. Turn the dial so that "north" lines up with the shadow. Since the sun's shadow points north at noon in the northern hemisphere (line the shadow up with "south" if you live in the southern hemisphere), you can tell the direction in which you are heading, as well as other directions.

At night, set the pointer stick so that it points in the direction in which you are heading, then hold the dial at eye level so that you can sight the North, or polar, Star with the shadow stick. You may have to turn around until you find the star. When you find the star and are able to sight it, turn the dial so that north points in the direction of the star. You can now read the direction that the pointer stick is pointing. That is the direction in which you are heading. You can also read where north, south, east, and west are.

This instrument works best in the far north. Why might that be?

cork won't go in easily, gently enlarge the circle by trimming away a little cardboard equally around the circle.

3. Saw off a 5-inch length of dowel.

4. Saw the cork in half. Be very careful to make a straight cut so that the cork will stand flat on its cut end.

5. Glue the sawn end of the cork to one end of the dowel.

6. After the glue is dry, use the awl to make a starter hole in the very center of the top of the cork and another on the side of the cork, about halfway between the top of the cork and the place where the cork and dowel meet.

7. Paint the dial in a fancy design. Somewhere in the

Geology Projects

All About the Earth

This planet of ours called Earth is a really amazing place. Here we are on a rocky, spinning ball that's whizzing through space at almost 45,000 miles (72,000 km) an hour. (Whoa! Hold on to your hat!) The eight other planets in our solar system are traveling that fast, too. But as far as anybody knows only Planet Earth is carrying the likes of cheeseburgers, skateboards, Godzilla movies, and about six billion two-legged creatures who like to call themselves "intelligent life."

Over the years, some of the most inquisitive creatures, known as scientists, have learned a lot about Earth and its place in the universe. For instance, we know that our solar system is just one of more than 100,000 million other solar systems in our galaxy. And there are at least 10,000 million other galaxies in the universe!

When you look at it that way, Earth seems awfully tiny. Even compared to the four largest planets in our own solar system, Earth is small. But here at ground level, Earth is more than big enough to give scientists and other curious people (like you) a lot to learn and discover.

After all, our planet's surface—its continents and oceans and mountains and valleys and deserts and all the rest—covers nearly 197 million square miles (512 million sq km). The Earth is 24,902 miles (39,843 km) around at the equator, and 24,859 miles (39,774 km) around at the poles. If you walked every day and every night without stopping to rest, it would take you more than a year to walk all the way around the globe!

Earth is so big that it fools our eyes. To a five-foot human, a mile-high mountain is huge. And look at the Grand Canyon! Now that's a big hole! So most people think that our planet is rough and bumpy. But for its size, Earth is actually surprisingly smooth. If you were to shrink it down to the size of a bowling ball, it would be even smoother than the real thing.

Here's another way Earth tricked our ancestors' eyes. For hundreds of years people thought that the Earth was flat because the world looks flat when you gaze at the horizon. Of course, these days we know better. The world is round, right? Umm, well, not exactly. Actually, because it's slightly bigger at the equator than at the poles, Earth isn't truly round. It bulges in the middle and flattens just a bit at the top and bottom. Scientists call anything with this particular shape a *geoid* ("earth-shaped").

A fantastic view of the sphere of the Earth as photographed from the Apollo 17 spacecraft during the final lunar landing mission in NASA's Apollo program

In this chapter, we're going to learn how old the Earth is, what it's made of, why its insides are so hot, how and why earthquakes happen, what causes mountains to rise, and much more. So fasten your seat belt and get ready to ride…to the tops of mountains…to the bottoms of oceans…and down deep inside the fiery core of Planet Earth!

How Old Is Earth? How Old Is That?

Scientists think that our planet is about 4.6 billion years old. Obviously, that's really, really old—but just how old?

To help you get a better idea of how long ago 4.6 billion years is, imagine that Earth is ten years old instead of 4.6 billion.

Ten years ago our newborn planet was just beginning to form an outer crust. It was mostly a big, molten ball of dust and gas left over when a much, much larger ball of dust and gas collapsed on itself and formed the hot, shining star we call the Sun. Back in those days there were a few other leftover balls circling the Sun, too. Some were smaller than Baby Earth, some larger. Some were closer to the Sun, some farther away. Today we call them the planets. Together they make up our Solar System.

You wouldn't have wanted to be anywhere near Earth during those first couple of toddler years. Talk about the Terrible Twos! There were no seas or land. You couldn't breathe the air. Virtually everything was hot and molten. Meteorites and asteroids and comets kept crashing into the red-hot planet.

Eventually, about **eight years ago**, things cooled down. Rocks began to form, creating a thicker crust. Water from steam collected on the surface, forming shallow seas. And the first signs of life—bacteria—appeared.

A little more than a billion years later—about **five of our imaginary years ago**—you were really hot stuff if you were pond scum. You and other members of the blue-green algae family were the most advanced forms of life on earth.

It wasn't until **last year** that the first plants on land showed up. Meanwhile, giant sea scorpions as much as nine feet long roamed the oceans.

About **eight months ago**, lush swamps of mosses and tall-as-trees ferns covered the land. Today, their fossils make up most of the world's coal beds.

Six months ago, the first dinosaurs appeared. **A month and a half ago**, they became extinct.

Our earliest ancestors, big-brained hairy creatures who could actually walk on two legs instead of four, showed up about a **day and a half ago.**

The first true humans, or animals who looked more or less like your Uncle Bill when he gets up in the morning, started tromping around in East Africa and Asia about **two hours ago.**

Eleven minutes ago the last Ice Age, when glaciers covered most of the Northern Hemisphere, finally ended.

Late afternoon over the Andes Mountains with sun glare, heavy cloud illumination, and sunlight against the Pacific Ocean

Thomas Jefferson signed the Declaration of Independence **15 seconds ago.**

Neil Armstrong, the first human on the moon, took a small step for man and a giant leap for mankind a little less than **two seconds ago.**

And you? How long have you been around?

Wink your eye once, fast. If you actually are ten years old, that's how long you've lived compared to the long, long, long life of Planet Earth.

GEOLOGIST'S Notebook

THIS BOOK IS MODELED AFTER AN OLD JAPANESE STYLE OF BOOK. IT MAKES AN EASY-TO-CARRY FIELD NOTEBOOK. DECORATE THE COVER WITH GRANITE PAPER (SEE PAGE 184) OR ANY OTHER FANCY PAPER.

WHAT YOU NEED

- *Ruler*
- *Pencil*
- *Scissors*
- *12 to 15 sheets of white paper, 8½ by 11 inches (22 by 28 cm)*
- *Light, bendable cardboard such as poster paper or railroad board or tagboard for the cover, cut the same size as the page papers PLUS an extra ½ inch (1.5 cm) in width. The cover for the book shown here is 4½ by 11½ inches (11.5 by 29.5 cm).*
- *Paper clip*
- *Fancy paper to wrap the cover, sized slightly smaller than the cover itself. The granite paper on the cover of the book measures 4 by 9½ inches (10 by 24.5 cm).*
- *Large metal paper clamp*
- *Several pieces of scrap cardboard to use as a surface for hole poking*
- *Awl (sold at hardware stores)*
- *4 feet (1.2 m) of string or heavy thread*
- *Sewing needle with a large eye*
- *1 bead (optional; learn how to make one on page 212)*

WHAT YOU DO

1. Stack four or five sheets of paper neatly and fold them in half with a strong crease. Tear or cut the paper at the fold line. Repeat this with more paper until you have 21 pieces. Use the ruler and pencil to measure one piece of paper so that it is 4½ by 11 inches (11.5 by 28 cm). You can make the book any size, but keep in mind that the paper will be folded in half, so it must start out measuring twice as wide as the book pages will be.

2. Pick up six pieces of page paper at a time, stack them evenly, and fold them in half all at once. You will do this three times. You should now have three folded stacks of paper (called signatures) and three leftover sheets.

3. Place one of the signatures against one end of the outside of the cover cardboard with the folded end toward the middle of the cover. **1**

4. Use the rounded edge of the paper clip to press or score a line on the cover cardboard along the folded edge of the signature. Move the signature out of the way. Hold the ruler along the scored line and score this line hard several more times to make sure the line is straight. Scoring a line makes it fold more easily.

5. Place the signature against the other end of the cover **2**, and score a second line along the folded edge, just as you did before. Now your cover looks like figure **3**.

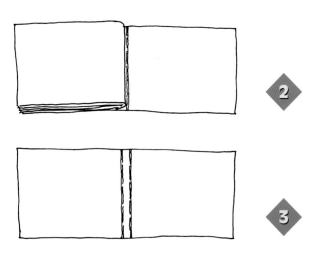

6. Lay the fancy paper, outside facing up, over the cover cardboard so that it is centered evenly. You should be able to see the ends of the scored lines above and below the fancy paper. **4** Lay the ruler

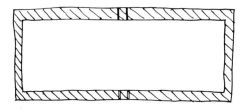

along the scored lines, over the fancy paper, and score the fancy paper along the scored lines in the cover. **5**

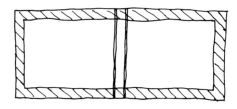

7. Carefully fold both the cover cardboard and the fancy paper together along the scored lines. Slip the three signatures inside the cover, pushing them firmly against the folded spine of the notebook. **6**

8. Trim 1 inch (2.5 cm) off the end of each of the three leftover pieces of paper, and slip these into the notebook at the back. They will stick out beyond the end of the book for now.

9. Clamp the entire book together with the large paper clamp so that nothing can move during the next part of the process.

10. **Ask an adult to help you with this step.** Use the awl to poke two holes about 1 inch (2.5 cm) down from the top and bottom edges, and ½ inch (1.5 cm) in from the spine of the notebook. You or an adult will have to screw the awl back and forth to make it go through all the thicknesses of paper. **7**

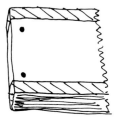

11. Turn the book over while it is still clamped and widen out the holes from the back.

12. Thread the needle. Stick the needle into either hole. Pull the thread until a tail 12 inches (30 cm) long is left. Hold that tail in place while you wrap the thread around the outside of the book and go back into the same hole. Pull tight.

13. Tie the two ends of thread together tightly on the spine of the notebook. **8**

14. Repeat steps 12 and 13 for the other hole.

15. Cut the tails off evenly and either thread a bead through one thread (such as in the book shown here) or braid the tails, or fray them, or tie them together, or make bows, or cut them off short. Fold the three pages that are sticking out of the book in half so that their folded edges line up with the rest of the pages in the book. Use these extra long pages when you need a bigger sheet of paper.

PLANET
Mobile

THIS PAPIER-MÂCHÉ MOBILE SHOWS
YOU EARTH'S SIZE COMPARED TO
THE OTHER PLANETS IN OUR SOLAR
SYSTEM, AS WELL AS THE RELATIVE
DISTANCE OF ALL THE PLANETS FROM
THE SUN. IF YOU HANG THE MOBILE
IN A SUNNY WINDOW, YOU CAN WATCH
THE REAL SUN LIGHT UP ONE SIDE OF
EACH PLANET, LEAVING THE OTHER
SIDE IN DARKNESS, JUST LIKE DAY
AND NIGHT ON EARTH.

WHAT YOU NEED

- *Old broomstick, mop handle, or 1-inch-wide (2.54 cm) dowel, at least 42 inches (107 cm) long*
- *Old newspapers*
- *Spool of heavy thread or container of waxed dental floss*
- *Scissors*
- *Package of aluminum foil*
- *1 green pea*
- *8 paper clips*
- *1 small lime*
- *1 marble*
- *1 large cabbage*
- *1 orange*
- *1 grapefruit*
- *Water*
- *Mixing bowl or plastic dishpan*
- *2 cups (250 g) of all-purpose white flour*
- *Measuring cup*
- *Large cooking pot*
- *Spoon*
- *Acrylic paints*
- *Paintbrushes*
- *Old aluminum pie pan*
- *2 nails, ½-inch (1.3 cm) long*
- *Hammer*
- *Piece of colorful, sturdy yarn, 5 feet (1.5 m) long*

WHAT YOU DO

1. It helps to do this project if you first set up a convenient work space. Find two chairs that are the same height and move them about 3 feet (91 cm) apart, so that you can rest the broomstick, mop handle, or dowel across the backs of the chairs. Spread old newspapers on the floor under the broomstick.

2. First you must make an *armature* for each planet. An armature is an inside framework that keeps you from needing too much heavy, wet papier-mâché. You will make your armatures out of aluminum foil. Begin by cutting nine pieces of thread or dental floss, each at least 3 feet (91 cm) long. Tie a very fat knot (or several knots, one on top of the other) at the end of the first string. Now make a ball of aluminum foil around this knot. The ball should be the size of the green pea. You now have an armature for the planet Mercury hanging from the end of a thread. Eat the green pea and move onto the next planet.

3. For all the rest of the planets you will begin by tying a paper clip to the end of a piece of thread. You will then make a ball of aluminum foil around the paper clip. The size of the balls are as follows:

> **Venus**—a small lime
>
> **Earth**—a slightly bigger lime
>
> **Mars**—a marble
>
> **Jupiter**—a large, 9-inch (23 cm) cabbage
>
> **Saturn**—an 8-inch (20 cm) cabbage
>
> **Uranus**—an orange
>
> **Neptune**—a grapefruit
>
> **Pluto**—a marble

4. Tie the planets onto the broomstick like this: First make a mark 2 inches (5 cm) from the left end of the broomstick. Call this mark the sun. (Later you can paint that end of the broomstick yellow or orange.) Tie Mercury ½ inch (1.2 cm) away from the sun; Venus 1 inch (2.5 cm) from the sun; Earth 1½ inches (4 cm) from the sun; Mars 2 inches (5 cm) from the sun; Jupiter 5 inches 12 cm) from the sun; Saturn 9½ inches (24 cm) from the sun; Uranus 19½ inches (50 cm) from the sun; Neptune 30 inches (75 cm) from the sun; and Pluto 39¾ inches (102 cm) from the sun.

5. Now it's time to make the papier-mâché. First you must tear three or four sections of old newspaper into strips about 1 inch (2.5 cm) wide and 3 inches (8 cm) long. Put these strips in warm water in the mixing bowl to soak for two hours while you take a break.

aluminum foil and to round and smooth out the surfaces of the planets. You should put the papier-mâché on in layers, and let it dry completely every time you have built up a layer of ⅛ inch (.5 cm) or so. You don't want it to get too thick or heavy or it will take too long to dry. It shouldn't take more than two layers to finish your planets. Many of the planets themselves have craters and mountains, so it's fine if your model planets do, too.

9. After the planets have dried completely, paint them. You can also paint the broomstick. Be sure to paint the left end of the broomstick up to the "sun" mark a bright yellow or orange to show where the sun is in relation to the planets. The colors of the planets that we can see with our bare eyes are as follows:

Mercury—lead gray

Venus—silver

Earth—blue and green

Mars—red

Jupiter—whitish yellow

Saturn—yellow

Uranus, **Neptune**, and **Pluto**—Because these planets can't be seen by earthlings using just our eyes, paint them gray or dull silver.

6. After your break, drain the water from the bowl of newspaper strips. Then mix 1 cup of flour (125 g) with 6 cups (1.5 l) of water in the cooking pot. **Ask an adult to help you put the pot onto the stove over moderate heat.** Stir the paste until it gets as thick as melted ice cream, then remove the pot from the heat and let it cool slightly.

7. Pour the lukewarm paste into the wet newspaper strips and mix thoroughly. You can mix with your hands or the spoon. It feels good to work with the warm paste, so don't cool the paste completely.

8. Now you will put strips and globs of papier-mâché all over your planets to completely cover the

10. Hammer a nail into each end of the broomstick or dowel. Tie the yarn to these two nails so that you can hang the mobile.

Molten to the Core

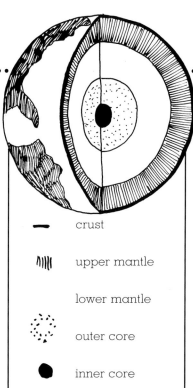

—	crust
٨١١١(	upper mantle
	lower mantle
⁖⁖	outer core
●	inner core

No matter where you are right now, there are about 8,000 miles (12,800 km) of Planet Earth beneath your feet, and almost all of it is rock. True, water covers more than two-thirds of the globe's surface. But even the deepest parts of the oceans reach less than seven miles (11 km) to the sea floor. Compared to the thousands of miles of rock beneath them, our oceans don't amount to much more than a thin film of moisture—about as much as the morning dew on an apple! (That's why it's so important to take good care of the water we have.)

Scientists call the planet's water layer—our oceans, rivers, lakes, and streams—the *hydrosphere*. The air above, of course, is called the *atmosphere*.

The solid parts of our planet are made up of layers, too. When Earth was formed, gravity sorted out all the ingredients. The heaviest materials, such as iron, were pulled toward the center. Lighter elements stayed closer to the surface.

That's why Earth's *crust*—the planet's outer layer—is made up of fairly "light" rocks. The upper or *continental crust* forms the continents and is made of granite and other ancient rock that has been pushed and

Pot holes eroded in columnar basalt

shoved and jumbled around a lot over the years. This part of the crust is as much as 60 miles (96 km) thick. The lower or *oceanic crust*, the part beneath the oceans, is much thinner, only about three miles (4.8 km), and is made of younger rock called *basalt*.

Earth's crust is the part we know the most about, because, after all, we live on it. Compared to the rest of the planet the crust is as thin as the skin on that apple we mentioned. And it's comfortably cool, too—unlike Earth's sizzling inside layers.

Below the crust is a layer of hot, heavy rock about 1,800 miles (2,880 km) thick. Scientists call this layer the *mantle*. Together, the crust and the upper part of the mantle are called the *lithosphere*. It's really toasty down there—between 1,600 and 5,500°F (870 to 3,035°C)! It's so hot, in fact, that in places the mantle rock isn't quite solid. It's thick and flexible—like Silly Putty™. Scientists think that some of these parts ooze in currents, like gummy rivers.

Beneath the mantle is an even heavier, hotter layer called the *outer core*. It's made mostly of the metals iron and nickel—liquid iron and nickel, that is. The entire outer core is melted through and through, and no wonder. The temperature is a scorching 5,500 to 7,200°F (3,035 to 3,978°C)!

Finally, at the very center of Earth is the *inner core*, a ball of solid iron nearly 800 miles (1,280 km) thick from its outside to its middle. Whew! Somebody open a window! The coolest part of the core is about 6,000°F (3,312°C), and the hottest part is nearly 12,000°F (6,642°C)—that's hotter than the surface of the sun!

But wait a minute. If Earth's inner core is so hot, how come it's solid instead of molten, like the outer core? Because so much weight is pushing in on the core from all directions, its molecules don't have any room to move apart. They stay packed together—solid as a rock.

Why Are Earth's Insides So Hot?

Eruption of Mount Kilauea. Hawaii National Park, 1969

You don't have to look much further than the steaming lava erupting from a volcano to know that Earth's insides are hot—super hot. But why? What makes all that heat? Is there a fire down there somewhere?

Scientists think most of inner Earth's heat was trapped billions of years ago, when the planet was being formed from chunks of space matter. Because of gravity, materials piling up on the outside squeezed materials inside. The squeezing generated heat. Plus, the searing-hot meteors and asteroids that were crashing into earth stayed hot as their pieces were pushed deeper into the planet.

The pressure from Earth's outer layers pushing inward still produces a lot of heat. And as radioactive materials inside the Earth decay, they give off even more heat.

In a way, then, there is a fire down there—a fire that's been burning for more than three billion years!

EARTH
Balls

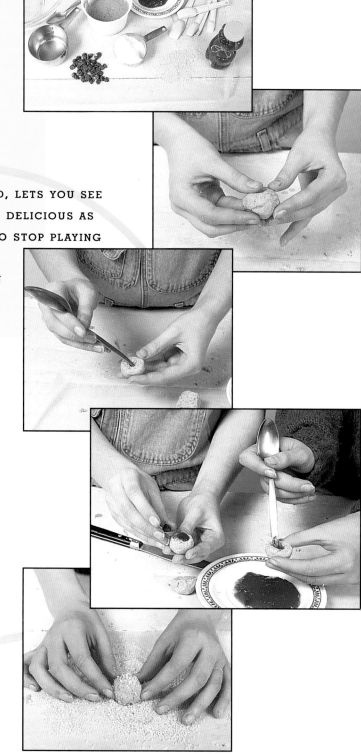

Here's a geological model that's fun to build, lets you see what the inside of the earth looks like, and is delicious as well as nutritious to eat! If people tell you to stop playing with your food, explain that you're actually learning geology, and then invite them to join you for a snack of yummy earth balls.

WHAT YOU NEED

For 6 to 8 earth balls:

- *Large bowl*
- *Spoon*
- *Measuring cups*
- *¼ cup (31 g) of powdered milk (noninstant is best, but instant will do)*
- *½ cup (170 g) of creamy peanut butter*
- *¼ cup (100 g) of honey*
- *Waxed paper*
- *Dull dinner knife*
- *½ cup (170 g) of strawberry, cherry, or raspberry jam*
- *½ cup (110 g) of chocolate chips*
- *½ cup (70 g) of sesame seeds or graham cracker crumbs*

146

W HAT YOU DO

1. Wash your hands.

2. Put ½ cup (170 g) of peanut butter and ¼ cup (31 g) of powdered milk into the bowl. Mix it with the spoon or with your hands. Add 1 teaspoon of honey in order to make a stiff dough. You may need more (or less) honey depending on how stiff or runny the peanut butter is. Keep adding honey a little at a time until the dough feels like clay dough.

3. Scoop up a small, round spoonful of dough and roll it into a ball.

4. Put the ball down on a piece of waxed paper and carefully cut the ball in half. Be careful not to squash the ball when you cut it.

5. Use the tip of the spoon handle to scoop out a small hole in the center of each half of the ball. The hole should be about the size of the tip of your little finger.

6. Use the spoon handle tip to put a small amount of jam into the holes you have scooped out. Now place a single chocolate chip in the middle of the jam in one of the halves of the ball. Don't put a chocolate chip in the other half. You now have created the core of the earth (the chocolate chip), surrounded by the hot, molten outer core (the jam)—all surrounded by the semiliquid magma (peanut butter mixture)!

7. Place the two halves of the ball back together and roll it a little in your hands to seal the seam.

8. Pour out about ½ cup (70 g) of sesame seeds or graham cracker crumbs onto another piece of waxed paper. Roll the ball around in the seeds or crumbs to thoroughly coat it. This coating is the rocky crust of the earth.

9. To complete the experiment, carefully cut the ball in half again so that you can see the layers: core, outer core, magma, and crust. Think about the real earth and its layers as you slowly chew your earth ball. Earth balls are so delicious that you'll want to make more to snack on and give to friends. Stored in the refrigerator in a closed container, they will keep for a long time.

Our Ever-Moving, Ever-Changing World

$\mathbf{T}$ry this: Go outside and jump up and down a couple of times. Did you feel the Earth shake? Now try this: Stand very, very still. Did you feel the ground moving? Of course not. We humans aren't sensitive enough to notice. But the ground beneath your feet actually is (s-l-o-w-l-y) moving all the time. Every once in a while it moves too noticeably—in an earthquake, for instance.

Solid as it seems, Earth's crust is a not-quite-connected crazy quilt of huge pieces, or *plates*, dozens of miles thick, restlessly pushing and shoving and bumping and scraping and pulling apart and jamming together. Each plate is attached to a piece of Earth's upper mantle, and together they ride on top of the partly molten, putty-like layer in the mantle called the *asthenosphere* (az-THEN-uh-sfeer).

Heat from Earth's core and lower mantle causes currents of oozing rock in the asthenosphere. These currents, called *convection cells*, slowly rise and fall, moving the plates above. (Check out the experiments on pages 20 to 22 for a firsthand look at the ups and downs of convection cells.) The study of how the pieces of Earth's crust move is called *plate tectonics* (tek-TAHN-iks).

Most of the action in Earth's crust happens at the seams, or cracks, where plates meet. In the Pacific Ocean, at least five large plates come together. That's why there are so many volcanoes and earthquakes in China, Japan, Hawaii, and California. There are a lot of places where chunks of the Earth are grinding together or moving apart.

Geologists think that different types of plate seams cause different kinds of Earth-changing actions. One happens in the oceans, along underwater ridges that stretch for thousands of miles. In these places, the Earth constantly grows new crust. Molten rock from the mantle oozes up through the crack between plates and into the sea water, where it cools and hardens and becomes part of the plates on either side. Convection currents in the mantle drive the plates apart. Then, new, hot material rises into the widening crack. **1**

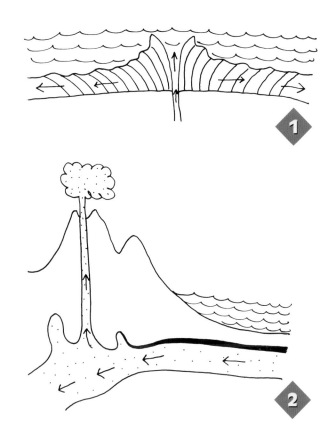

Meanwhile, in other places, the edges of ocean plates (which are made of heavy rock) are pushed under continental plates (which are lighter). The old ocean crust is shoved back down into Earth's mantle, where it melts as it sinks deeper into the planet's insides. Eventually, the hot, gooey rock will rise back up in a convection cell at an oceanic ridge and become part of Earth's crust again. Or it might find its way to a "hot spot," where it can gush upward through a long, deep opening and erupt on the surface. We call those places volcanoes. **2**

When plates push against one another, something's got to give. If they collide head-on, the edges of both plates slowly buckle upward, forming mountains. That's how the Alps and the Himalayas came to be. Not all plates push straight into each other, though. The plates along California's famous San Andreas Fault grind against each other sideways. Most of the time, neither side moves

Rockslide avalanche on Sherman Glacier, caused by Alaska earthquake, 1964

much. The plates stay pressed together. Every once in a while, though, the plates slip apart—and then lock together again. Usually the plates slip just a little, not even enough for a person to notice. But sometimes the plates jerk apart with a lurch, making the ground shake or, when the plates slip a lot, causing earthquakes and landslides.

This sort of push and pull is happening all the time, in places all over the world where plates of Earth's crust meet. Our planet is constantly recycling its rock and reshaping its surface.

MOVING *Liquid*

A MODEL CONVECTION CELL

To try to understand pressure changes and movement in the earth's crust, geologists study what is called the *convection current theory*. The difference in temperature between the extremely hot center or core of the earth and the cooler mantle (molten rock) causes slow movement of the rocks that form the earth's crust.

Here's how geologists think that works: Hot molecules dance around faster than cool ones do. This fast movement causes the molecules to spread farther apart and to be less densely packed than cooler molecules. When a liquid is heated, it is, therefore, lighter and less dense than when it is cool. We know that lighter, less dense objects tend to float on top of denser, heavier substances. The hot core of the earth is constantly heating up the mantle that is closest to it. This hot liquid rock, being less dense and therefore lighter, rises very slowly toward the crust, or surface, of the earth. As it rises it cools and becomes heavier, and therefore sinks back down. This rising and sinking forms what scientists call giant convection cells in the earth's mantle. The plates of the earth's crust, riding on the mantle, move along very slowly on the convection cells— a few inches a year at most—like giant rafts floating on very slowly moving water.

The following two experiments will let you see how heat can move a liquid. Keep in mind that liquid rock moves much more slowly than water does, but the process is the same.

Experiment #1

W HAT YOU NEED

- *Large clear glass container, such as a glass mixing bowl, at least 7 inches (18 cm) tall*
- *Container of cold water*
- *Small glass jar, no more than 2 or 3 inches (5 or 8 cm) tall*
- *Handful of marbles or clean pebbles*
- *Container of very hot water*
- *Food coloring*
- *Piece of aluminum foil 4 by 4 inches (10 by 10 cm)*
- *Rubber band*
- *Towel*
- *Notebook*
- *Pencil*

W HAT YOU DO

1. Fill the large bowl with cold water, at least 6 inches (15 cm) deep. A good plan is to fill it and then put it in a refrigerator or freezer for a few minutes while you're getting the jar ready.

2. Put a layer of marbles or pebbles in the bottom of the jar to weight it. Fill the jar with very hot water. Try filling it with hot tap water and then sitting it in a pan of even hotter water for a few minutes. Ask an adult to help you prepare and pour the very hot water.

3. Add several drops of food coloring to the water in the jar. Tear a small hole, about the size of your thumbnail, in the center of the piece of aluminum foil. Cover the jar with the aluminum foil, centering the hole. Press the foil to fit the jar opening, and then hold it in place with the rubber band. What you are doing is making a smaller opening for the hot water to come out of.

4. Remove the bowl of cold water from the refrigerator. Holding the jar right side up and with your thumb over the hole, quickly place the jar on the bottom of the bowl, under the level of the cold water. You'll probably see and hear a few bubbles as air rushes out of the jar.

5. Now watch what happens. You can tell where the hot water is because it is colored. Use the towel to wipe the beads of moisture from the outside of the bowl in order to have a clear view of what's happening.

6. If the jar represents the hot core of the earth, what happens to the liquid rock that has been heated up by it? Where does this "hot rock" go? What happens after that "hot rock" cools down? Watch the surface of the water for currents. Is the water in motion? What's causing the motion in your model convection cell? Make notes in your notebook about this experiment.

Experiment #2

THIS EXPERIMENT SHOWS HOW HEAT MOVES WATER AND ALSO HOW A MATERIAL FLOATING ON A MOVING LIQUID MOVES WITH IT. IMAGINE THAT THE WATER IS THE SLOWLY MOVING BOTTOM LAYER OF THE EARTH'S CRUST.

WHAT YOU NEED

- *2-quart (1.9 l) cooking pot, full of water*
- *Stove*
- *Some dried herbs, such as rosemary, basil, or oregano—or some dry sawdust*
- *Notebook*
- *Pencil*

WHAT YOU DO

1. **Ask an adult to help you with this experiment** because you will need to use a hot stove and boiling water. Place the pot half on and half off one of the burners. (You are trying to make one part of the pot hotter than the other.)

2. Turn on the stove burner to high. As the water begins to boil (you'll see tiny bubbles forming on the bottom of the pot), sprinkle a thin layer of dried herbs or sawdust on top of the water. Watch what happens. Think of the dry particles as the earth's crust plates riding on the liquid mantle of the earth.

3. Notice where the herbs or sawdust go. Where do the particles gather? Do they gather over the hotter or the cooler part of the pot? Why? What does the movement of the herbs or sawdust tell you about the movement of the water? How is this a model of a convection cell? The dry particles gather where the cooler current sinks and move away from the spot where the hotter water rises. Why does this happen? Make notes in your notebook about this experiment.

Pangaea, Laurasia, and Gondwana

Earth's plates have been moving around and pulling apart and bumping into each other for a long time. It's no wonder the world has gone through a lot of changes.

Take our continents, for instance. You may have looked at a globe or map of the world and thought, gosh, those continents look like puzzle pieces. If you moved them around, some of them would fit together. Look at South America and Africa—if you pushed them towards each other, they'd match up perfectly side by side! Maybe they were connected once, and then just sort of, er, you know, floated apart.

Floated apart? The continents? Millions of tons of rock? Get outta here! Until recently, that was pretty much how most scientists reacted when anyone suggested that maybe the continents had been connected long ago and then somehow moved apart. A German scientist, Alfred Wegener, was the first to study the idea and say that it might be true. He came up with some pretty convincing evidence, too. He discovered that the same types of rock, and fossils of the same kinds of creatures, could be found in places where the continental "puzzle pieces" fit, even though those places were separated by hundreds of miles of oceans.

But it wasn't until 20 years after Alfred Wegener's death that geologists realized he was right. The continents

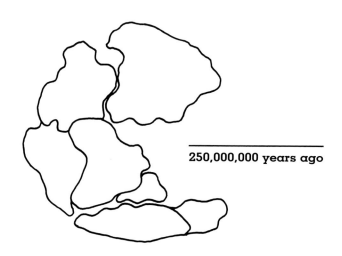

250,000,000 years ago

and ocean floors really do "float" on moving rock plates, and have been for millions of years.

They're floating right now. If you're ten years old, North America and Europe are about one foot farther apart today than they were on the day you were born. In some places the continents are moving about an inch (2.54 cm) a year. In other places, they're drifting as much as four inches (10 cm) a year.

Over time, continents drifting a few inches a year can make a b-i-g difference.

About 250 million years ago, all the continents on Earth were connected in a single land mass near the equator. Alfred Wegener called it *Pangaea* (Pan-GEE-uh), which means "all earth."

Around 200 million years ago, Pangaea split into two super-continents that gradually drifted apart. *Laurasia*, in the north, included the land that would become North America, Europe, and Asia. *Gondwana*, in the south, included South America, Africa, India, Antarctica, and Australia.

Over the next 100 million years, the land that was to become India drifted northward and eventually crashed into Asia, creating a huge pileup of rock we call the Himalayas. Australia broke away from what would be Antarctica. A split opened between South

Snow-dusted ranges on the Tibetan Plateau, showing the Vale of Kashmir in northern India, the major valley within the Himalaya Mountains

America and Africa, and also between North America and what would be Europe and Asia. The narrow strip of seawater in the middle was a baby ocean. It's a lot wider now. We call it the Atlantic.

With the help of computers, geologists are using their knowledge of how and where plates move to figure out what our world might look like in the future. Some predict that the Mediterranean Sea will disappear, that the Red Sea will become a new ocean, and that Australia will float to the equator. Don't hold your breath, though. These changes will take about 75 million years to happen!

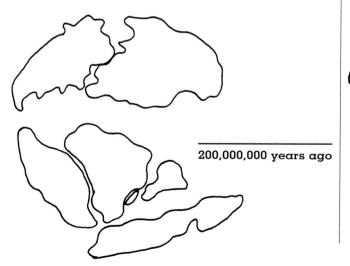

200,000,000 years ago

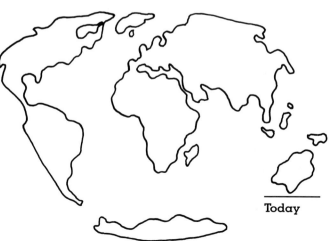

Today

153

JIGSAW Puzzle

IT'S FUN TO THINK OF THE ANCIENT CONTINENTS FITTING BACK TOGETHER LIKE GIANT JIGSAW PUZZLE PIECES. IT'S EVEN MORE FUN TO MAKE A MODEL OUT OF SALT DOUGH AND SEE FOR YOURSELF HOW THEY USED TO BE CONNECTED.

WHAT YOU NEED

- *Several sheets of tracing paper*
- *Pencil*
- *Scissors*
- *2 cups (250 g) of flour (plain white, unbleached, or bread flour work best)*
- *2 cups (192 g) of table salt*
- *2 tablespoons of dry wallpaper paste*
- *Spoon*
- *Large bowl*

- *2 cups (473.2 ml) of water*
- *Rolling pin*
- *Dull table knife*
- *Cookie sheet or pizza pan*
- *Oven*
- *Hot pad*
- *Acrylic paints*
- *Paintbrush*

154

WHAT YOU DO

1. Enlarge the pattern on a copier as indicated. Carefully trace it and cut out the pieces. Set them aside.

2. Mix the flour, salt, and wallpaper paste in the large bowl. Add 1 cup (236.6 ml) of water and mix, then slowly add as much of the rest of the water as you need to make a firm dough. The dough should not be runny, but should feel like stiff clay.

3. When the dough is sticking together but is still pretty crumbly, dump it out onto a floured countertop or table and knead it for about five minutes. Here is how to knead dough: Starting with a mound of dough, squeeze it and push it away from you at the same time, then pull it toward you, folding the top toward you as you pull. Next, turn the dough mound partway around and repeat what you did before. Continue to push, pull, and turn. It takes a little practice to get into the rhythm of kneading. Sprinkle the dough with a tiny bit of water if the dough seems too dry, or a tiny bit of flour if it gets too sticky.

4. Roll the kneaded dough out onto a lightly floured countertop or table until it's ¼ inch (1 cm) thick all over.

5. Place one of the paper pattern pieces on the dough slab and carefully cut the dough with the dull knife, following the edges of the pattern piece. Peel off the tracing paper pattern. Gently lift up the cutout dough and place it on the cookie sheet or pizza pan. Cut out all the other pieces the same way. Peel off the tracing paper pattern after you cut out each piece.

6. Salt dough must be dried very slowly or it will crack. It must also dry completely or it will get mushy and start to rot. **Ask an adult to help you put the pan in a 170°F (76.6°C) oven for one hour.** (If you are using a gas oven, leave the oven door halfway open during the entire hour. Do not use a microwave to dry salt dough.) After an hour, turn the oven up to 200°F (93°C) and dry the dough for 30 minutes more. (If you are using a gas oven, leave the door a quarter of the way open during this baking time.) After 30 minutes, turn the oven up to 250°F (121°C) and dry the dough for another 30 minutes. (If you are using a gas oven, keep the door closed during this baking time.) **Ask an adult to help you take the pan out of the oven.**

7. Let the puzzle pieces cool for 30 minutes, then tap one piece to see if it sounds hollow. If it does, it's completely dry.

8. Paint the pieces with the acrylic paints and let the paint dry. Be sure to wash out your paintbrush when you are done.

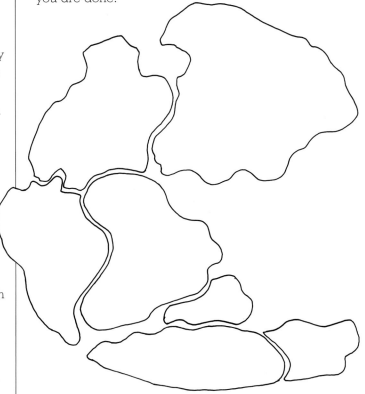

Enlarge pattern by 200%

How Do You Spell Relief? E-a-r-t-h-q-u-a-k-e!

There's a lot of tension in this world, what with the Earth's plates constantly pushing and shoving and grinding into each other, all fighting for position. Usually it's more or less a standoff, with no plate gaining or losing much ground. But sometimes the strain gets to be too much. Rocks in the Earth's crust just can't take it any more. They slip or break apart for a moment (aah, relief!)—and then lock together again in a new position.

That moment of relief for the Earth's crust isn't always relaxing for us, though. When the rocks shift, they release all their built-up energy in the form of shock waves. Those shock waves ripple through the ground and deep into the earth, causing the shake, rattle, and roll we know as an earthquake.

Not all earthquakes cause damage. Hundreds of rock-relieving jerks happen every day along *fault lines*, which are breaks or weak spots in the Earth's crust. In most cases we can barely feel these "miniquakes." But every once in a while a whole lot of tension builds up at a fault line, and when the rocks finally give, they give big. The shock waves are so powerful they make the ground roll and sway and vibrate violently in all directions for dozens or even hundreds of miles. Streets crack. Bridges buckle. Buildings shake themselves to pieces. If a strong earthquake happens near or in an ocean, it might cause a *tsunami* (soo-NAH-mee), or tidal wave. A tidal wave can travel through the sea at almost 500 miles (800 km) per hour. By the time it reaches land, it can be as tall as a 20-story building!

Places near the edges of Earth's crustal plates, such as California, Japan, China, Italy, Greece, and Mexico, get the most earthquakes. But a quake can happen almost anywhere. Some of the strongest earthquakes in North America's history happened in Missouri, right in the middle of the United States, in 1811 and 1812.

By the way, Earth isn't the only shaky place in our solar system. Scientists have recorded thousands of "moonquakes," and several "Marsquakes," too!

Left: Montana earthquake area, 19-foot (6 m) displacement, 1959

Right: This landslide in Anchorage, Alaska, was caused by an earthquake, and destroyed many homes in the city.

RECORD-SETTING EARTHQUAKES

This whole-lot-of-shakin'-goin'-on planet of ours produces between 500,000 and one million earthquakes a year! Most are mild and do little or no harm. From time to time, though, an especially strong earthquake causes a lot of damage.

Here are facts about six Big Ones:

■ **1556, Shaanxi Province, China:** One of the worst disasters ever, this earthquake killed more than 800,000 people.

■ **1755, Lisbon, Portugal:** Scientists think this was one of the strongest earthquakes in history. More than half the city was destroyed and the shocks were felt as far away as Norway. The quake created a giant tidal wave that swept half a mile in from shore and washed away everything in its path.

■ **1906, San Francisco, California:** This famous earthquake created enormous landslides, opened up huge cracks in the ground, and caused many fires. Most of the city's buildings either collapsed or burned to the ground.

■ **1923, Sagami Bay, Japan:** Even though it started underwater, this powerful quake destroyed almost three-quarters of the buildings in Tokyo, 70 miles (112 km) away, and completely demolished Yokohama, 50 miles (80 km) away.

■ **1960, Chile:** Starting in May, this series of enormous earthquakes rocked Chile's coast and flattened most of the buildings in the region. Mud slides and tidal waves caused even more damage. Geologists rank the strongest quake at 9.0 on the Richter scale. That's equal to the explosive power of almost 200 million tons of TNT!

■ **1964, Alaska:** This was the strongest quake in North American history. In some places the ground was lifted 30 feet (9.2 m) higher. Many buildings in Anchorage and surrounding towns were destroyed by the shocks and by the tidal waves it caused.

Seismograph

A SEISMOGRAPH IS A DEVICE THAT RECORDS VIBRATIONS OF THE EARTH. IT IS USED TO MEASURE THE INTENSITY OF EARTH-QUAKES. WHEN YOU DO THE EXPERIMENT DESCRIBED HERE, YOU WILL GET AN IDEA OF HOW A SEISMOGRAPH GIVES SCIENTISTS A PICTURE OF THE TREMORS OF THE EARTH DURING AN EARTHQUAKE.

WHAT YOU NEED

- *Sturdy cardboard box, about 8 by 8 by 11 inches (20 by 20 by 28 cm) or slightly larger*
- *2 pieces of heavy string, each 2 feet (61 cm) long*
- *Scissors*
- *Brick*
- *Awl or large nail*
- *Small block of wood, about 1 by 2 by 3 inches (2.54 by 5 by 8 cm)*

- *Several sheets of typewriter or copier paper*
- *Glue stick*
- *Heavy-duty tape, such as duct tape*
- *3 rubber bands*
- *Pencil with soft lead (number 2) or a stick of vine charcoal (sold at art-supply stores)*

1. Place the box on its side on a table. Tuck in the side and top flaps to strengthen the box. Fold out the bottom flap to form a tray to catch the paper.

2. Tie one string to each side of the brick. If the brick has holes in it, you can tie the strings through the holes in the brick. Tie double knots.

3. Punch two holes, about 4 inches (10 cm) apart, in the center of the top of the box. **1**

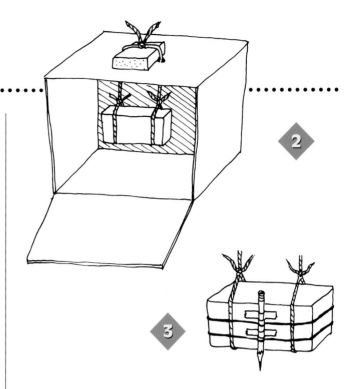

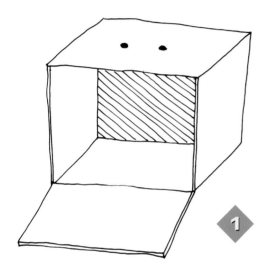

4. Push the ends of the strings through the holes you have poked. You may need to push them first through the holes in the flaps, then through the holes in the actual box. Then, with the brick resting on the bottom of the box, tie the strings together on the top of the box. Pull the strings tight enough so that there is no slack, and tie a double knot.

5. Slide the block of wood under the knot of the string to lift the brick off the bottom of the box. Adjust the string so that the brick hangs evenly. **2**

6. Cut sheets of paper in half and glue them together end to end so that you have a long sheet of paper. You can make this sheet as long as you want, but be sure to make it at least 3 feet (91 cm) long. Roll up the paper when the glue is dry.

7. Slip the roll of paper behind the brick so that the leading edge of paper is on the bottom of the box. Pull out the edge of the paper until it reaches the end of the front flap of cardboard.

8. Use tape and rubber bands to attach the pencil or charcoal to the front flat side of the brick. Make sure that the point comes in contact with the paper so that it can make a mark when the paper is pulled under the brick. Test it out before taping the pencil in position. This is the trickiest part of this project. The pencil must strike the paper hard enough to make a mark, but not so hard as to catch the paper and keep it from being pulled through. You may need to try several different kinds of pencils or charcoal and adjust each several times before you find one that works. Use the rubber bands to hold the pencil or charcoal while you are adjusting it. Once you have found the right position, tape it in place. **3**

9. Place the seismograph on a small table, such as a kitchen table or a coffee table. Ask a friend to cause a table-quake by shaking one of the legs of the table while you slowly pull the paper under the pencil. Pull evenly, and watch your seismograph record the quake. Try different kinds and speeds of shaking and see what results you get.

Volcanoes!

Have you ever given a bottle of soda a really hard shake and then popped the cap? WHOOSH! All those bubbles of gas in the soda push themselves and most of the liquid right out the top.

That's how a volcano erupts, too. *Magma*, which is a mixture of gases and hot molten rock, collects in a chamber deep inside the earth. As more and more magma enters the chamber, more and more pressure builds. The magma pushes hard against the surrounding rock, opening up cracks wherever there are weak spots. Eventually one of the cracks opens almost all the way to the surface. This becomes the volcano's *main tube*, or *pipe*. As the magma rises through the tube and gets closer to the surface, the gases in the molten rock form bubbles, like the bubbles you made when you shook the soda bottle. The bubbles push even harder against the "cap" (the Earth's crust) until—KABOOM! WHOOSH!—they blast through,

blowing a hole right through the surface. Hot steam, ash, and gases come bursting out, pushing huge chunks of rock and big globs of *lava* into the air. Then even more lava spills over the top.

A volcano can erupt many times over the centuries. After each eruption, the lava and ash around the opening, or *crater*, cool and harden. Layer after layer, eruption after eruption, the volcano grows. This is how most of the world's tall, cone-shaped volcanoes, such as Mount Vesuvius in Italy and Mount Fuji in Japan, came to be.

Some volcanoes don't erupt with a huge explosion of dust and gas. Instead, the lava bubbles and boils and spurts to the surface and then flows down the sides, like a huge pot of thick soup that's been left on the stove too long. These are known as "quiet" volcanoes (even though their eruptions can be anything but)! Their lava flows build gently sloping, dome-shaped mounds. Most of Hawaii's great volcanoes, such as Mauna Loa and Kilauea, are dome-shaped volcanoes.

There are nearly 850 active volcanoes in the world. At least 80 are beneath the oceans. When the edge of one ocean plate is pushed beneath another, the rock that has sunk into the mantle melts and rises, bubbling upward into the sea through weak spots in the other plate. When the lava touches water it cools and hardens. In some places so much lava has built up that it sticks far above the water. That's how volcanic islands in the Pacific Ocean, such as the islands of Japan, were formed.

Most volcanoes, like most earthquakes, happen near the edges of Earth's crustal plates. If you mark all the volcanoes in the world on a map and draw lines between them like a connect-the-dots puzzle, you'll have a pretty good sketch of Earth's pushiest plates. There are so many active volcanoes around the edges of the five big plates in the Pacific, that geologists call the area "The Ring of Fire"!

Opposite top: Mount St. Helens eruption with rising ash clouds, Washington, 1980

Opposite bottom: Arching lava fountains. Mount Kilauea, Hawaii, 1970

AMAZING VOLCANO FACTS

■ Erupting volcanoes cause lightning! Ash clouds pick up electrical charges even better than water clouds do. So eruptions often trigger big thunder and lightning storms.

■ In 1883 the volcano Krakatoa, in Indonesia, exploded with one of the most powerful eruptions of all time. Rock pieces were thrown 34 miles (54 km) high. People on the island of Rodrigues, nearly 3,000 miles (4,800 km) away, heard the volcano and described the sound as "the roar of heavy guns." Within two weeks, ash from the volcano had completely encircled the Earth!

■ The largest active volcano on earth is Hawaii's Mauna Loa, a dome volcano only 13,680 feet (4,209 m) high but more than 75 miles (120 km) long and 30 miles (29 km) wide.

■ The largest known volcano isn't on Earth at all. It's on Mars! The volcano Olympus Mons is 17 miles (27 km) high—that's three times taller than Mount Everest, the tallest mountain on Earth!

Lava drapery hardened over a sea cliff, formed during an eruption of Kilauea Volcano in Hawaii

EXPLODING Volcano

THIS IS THE POPULAR SODA AND VINEGAR EXPLODING VOLCANO EXPERIMENT, WITH A COUPLE OF NEW TWISTS. GATHER A FEW FRIENDS TO WATCH WHEN YOU FIRE OFF YOUR VOLCANO!

WHAT YOU NEED

- *Small glass or plastic bottle with a narrow neck*
- *Piece of cardboard, about 12 by 15 inches (30 by 38 cm)*
- *Modeling clay*
- *Funnel or piece of heavy paper to roll into a funnel*
- *Measuring cup*
- *1 pound (454 g) box of bicarbonate of soda (baking soda)*
- *Red food coloring*
- *1 quart (946 ml) bottle of vinegar (any kind will do)*
- *Spoon*

162

WHAT YOU DO

1. Remove the lid from the bottle if it has one and stand the bottle in the middle of the piece of cardboard.

2. Use flat slabs of clay to model a volcano around the bottle. Leave the mouth of the bottle open.

3. Use the funnel (or the piece of paper rolled into a cone) to pour about ¼ cup (50 g) of baking soda into the mouth of the bottle. The amount you pour in will depend on how big the bottle is. You want to fill the bottle about halfway.

4. Pour a few drops of red food coloring into ½ cup (118.3 ml) of vinegar and stir or swirl it to mix it.

5. Now the excitement begins! Place the volcano on a countertop or table that is okay to get wet. You could also try putting the volcano in the bottom of an empty bathtub or someplace flat outdoors. Carefully pour some vinegar into the mouth of the volcano—and stand back!

6. You can make several explosions without adding more soda simply by pouring in more vinegar each time the "lava" stops flowing. Notice where the lava flows. Does it flow in the same place each time? Does it flow in different places? Why might that be? What effect would this volcano have on the land, plants, buildings, and people nearby? In which ways is this model like a real volcano? In which ways is it different?

7. When you are finished using the model, lift the clay from the cardboard, and gently pull on the bottle until it comes out. Then rinse out the bottle and dry it. Pat the clay mountain shape dry, and replace the bottle. You can use this volcano many times.

Nature's "Tea Kettles"

Our planet's insides are so fiery that in some places the heat just naturally boils out. Water from rain or underground streams flows through a spot where Earth's mantle is especially close to the surface. The rocks there are hot enough to make the water hot, too. These places are called *hot springs*. The steaming water that bubbles to the surface is great for bathing. People come from all over the world to special resorts, such as the one in Hot Springs, Arkansas.

A *geyser* is a different sort of hot spring. You wouldn't want to take a bath in one! Instead of bubbling to the surface, the water in a geyser comes out in a rush of scalding steam. Then the geyser quiets down again. More water collects in an underground chamber to replace the water that steamed out. The rocks around the chamber heat the new water until, eventually, it becomes super hot and erupts too. Some geysers, such as Old Faithful in Yellowstone

Above: Minerva Hot Springs. Yellowstone National Park, Wyoming

Left: Riverside Geyser in eruption. Yellowstone National Park, Wyoming

National Park, erupt "faithfully" over and over again, spitting out between 10,000 to 12,000 gallons (37,850 to 45,420 l) of hot vaporized water every 30 to 90 minutes! Most geysers, though, aren't as predictable. Some take days, weeks, or even years to erupt again.

Most of the world's hot springs and geysers are in only three countries: New Zealand, Iceland, and the United States. People in Iceland are especially good at using the naturally hot water to make their lives easier. Water heated by the Earth is piped directly to radiators and hot water tanks in homes and office buildings. Almost 100 percent of the city of Reykjavik, the capital of Iceland, is heated with hot springs.

PEBBLE MOSAIC
Flowerpot

PEBBLES AND PLANTS ARE MADE FOR EACH OTHER. THEIR COLORS LOOK GOOD TOGETHER, AND THEIR BEAUTIFUL ORGANIC SHAPES REMIND US OF THE NATURAL WORLD. TRY COVERING A SMALL FLOWERPOT WITH SOME OF YOUR FAVORITE PEBBLES.

WHAT YOU DO

1. Cover your work surface with two sheets of newspaper. Make a small puddle of glue on one piece of newspaper. Lay out a few pebbles. Use your finger to place a blob of glue on the flat side of each pebble. Let the glue dry and thicken for a few minutes.

2. Turn the flower pot upside down on the other piece of newspaper. Place gluey pebbles next to each other all over the pot. Begin by placing the rim pebbles. If you build up from the rim, the pebbles will rest on the ones beneath them and will not slide. If they begin to slide, let the glue dry a little longer. Sometimes it will be necessary to hold a pebble in place for a few minutes until the glue sets. It helps to lightly tap each pebble with the tip of your fingernail, much like a brick mason taps each brick, to help it sit more firmly in the mortar.

3. Let the pot dry for several hours. The glue should dry clear: it won't be necessary to clean up any extra blobs or drips.

4. Pot your favorite plant in its nice new home.

WHAT YOU NEED

- *Old newspapers*
- *White waterproof craft glue*
- *Collection of pebbles, preferably ones that have at least one flat side*
- *Small clay flower pot*

Left: Bridal Veil Falls, an outstanding example of a waterfall flowing from a hanging valley. Yosemite National Park, California

Opposite: Grand Canyon in the morning light. Grand Canyon National Park, Arizona

Mountains High, Valleys Low

You might say that Mother Nature just can't make up her mind: First she builds mountains, then tears them down and scatters the remains.

On page 18 we saw how the tectonic plates of the crust move and collide with each other and give birth to mountains. When one plate dives deep, the rock gets hot in the mantle and then sizzles up to make volcanic mountains, like the Andes in South America. Plates also make mountains when they collide and buckle their edges, like a rumpled rug. This is what raised the Alps in Europe and the Himalayas in Asia.

Mountains are also born in the ocean. The Hawaiian Islands, such as Mount Kilauea, are the tops of submarine volcanoes that have risen several miles out of the sea floor.

Almost as fast as mountains rise up, *erosion*, the world's demolition expert, wears them back down.

The most important tool of erosion is water. Rainfall seeps into rocks and helps them break apart and dissolve; ice expands when it freezes and forces rock apart. Streams and rivers carry rock particles downstream and dump them in lakes or oceans, sometimes hundreds of miles away.

The higher the mountains, the faster the demolition. The Himalayas, including Mount Everest, are very steep and young mountains (about 45 million years old). They are still rising today and eroding very fast. The Appalachian mountains, which run from Alabama to Newfoundland, are old mountains (nearly 400 million years old) which have been lowered and smoothed by erosion.

If you've ever seen the Grand Canyon, you've witnessed what erosion can do in 15 or 20 million years! The Colorado River has cut through rock more than a mile deep, breaking many millions of tons into sand

and carrying it downstream into Lake Mead, which was built in 1936 to create Hoover Dam.

Most erosion happens during big floods, when a mass of mud may suddenly slide down a bank; or a landslide may bring down part of a mountain; or a river may gouge into its banks. A fast stream can cut into solid rock like a sandblaster, scouring the bedrock with its load of sand, gravel, and rock.

The land is also reshaped by *glaciers*, mountain-sized masses of ice that flow downhill a few inches or feet every day. Glaciers act like huge, slow-motion snowplows, pushing sand and gravel and rocks before them, smoothing off hills, polishing solid rock, and carving U-shaped valleys through mountains! When they stop and melt, they leave piles of sediment called *moraines*. Cape Cod, Massachusetts, and Long Island, New York, are moraines bulldozed hundreds of miles southward by glaciers.

Glaciers can also make the kind of landscape we see on picture postcards. The last Ice Age in Europe and North America, which ended about 10,000 years ago, left behind rolling hills, small lakes, and fertile fields. They also brought several feet of rich topsoil to the American Midwest—which makes midwestern farmers happy, but doesn't thrill Canadian farmers!

A third powerful tool of erosion is wind, which can quickly reshape the face of the Earth. A powerful windstorm can move enough sand to bury a house; windblown sand can chip away at solid rock. In large dust storms, a cubic mile (4 cubic km) of air may carry 4,000 tons (4,408 metric tons) of dust! Parts of the central United States are covered by more than 25 feet (7.7 m) of wind-carried soil called *loess*.

MOUNTAIN Building

Here are three experiments that demonstrate the process by which many mountain ranges were created. Of course, it takes hundreds and hundreds of years for a mountain range to develop, but these simple experiments will let you imagine how great slabs of the earth's crust moving toward each other could push up mountains.

What You Need

- *2 large chunks of clay (either ceramic clay or plasticine), each twice as big as your fist*
- *Rolling pin*
- *Dull table knife*
- *2 pieces of aluminum foil, each about 5 inches (13 cm) long*
- *Fat dowel or a piece of an old broomstick*

168

$\mathbb{W}$HAT YOU DO

1. Work the lumps of clay with your hands until they are soft and easy to bend and shape.

2. Roll each chunk out until it is about 8 inches (20 cm) long, 4 inches (10 cm) wide, and 2 inches (5 cm) high. Trim the chunks with the knife so that they look like bricks.

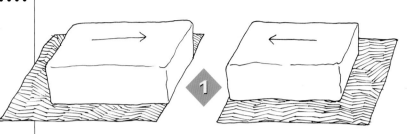

3. Place each clay brick onto the edge of a piece of aluminum foil. Each brick will represent a land mass.

4. Place the two land masses—each riding on its aluminum foil plate—about 12 inches (30 cm) apart on a smooth table or countertop.

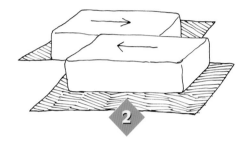

5. For the first experiment, hold each land mass at its far end and slam them together as hard as you can. **1** Try this several times. Describe what happens. Describe how the clay after the collision is like the edge of a continent that has had a collision with another continent. In what ways was your experiment like real life? In what ways was it different?

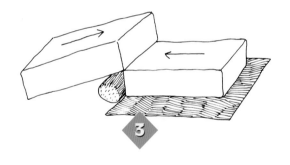

6. Separate the clay and form it into bricks again. For the second experiment, place the long side of each brick along an edge of its aluminum foil. **2** Push the two bricks so that they brush against each other as they travel past each other. Describe what happens. How is the edge of the clay like an edge of a continent that has had another land mass slide alongside it?

7. Often, one land mass is heavier than the other, and it sinks under the lighter land mass as the two collide. In the third experiment, you will use a dowel to lift one clay brick over the other. First, make the clay into two bricks again. Sit one of them on a piece of aluminum foil. Place the other brick facing the first brick, but with one of its short end tilted up so that it rests on the dowel. **3** Slide the two bricks toward each other and jam them together. What happens as they hit each other? How is this collision different from the first or second one that you tried? What kind of land forms would be the result of a collision like this?

LANDFORM Pop-Up BOOK

It's fun to discover ways to use pop-ups to show different landforms. Here are directions for four different kinds of pop-ups. Try combining them or changing them to create your own book of landforms.

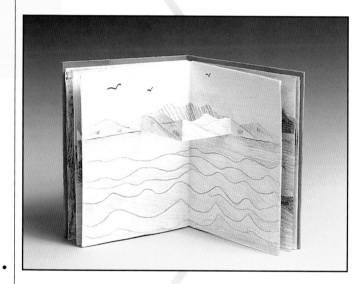

WHAT YOU NEED

- *Unlined white paper, such as typing or copier paper, 8½ by 11 inches (22 by 28 cm)*
- *Pencil*
- *Scissors*
- *Ruler*
- *Glue stick*
- *Colored pencils or crayons*
- *1 sheet of colored construction paper, 9 by 12 inches (23 by 30.5 cm)*
- *Paper clip*

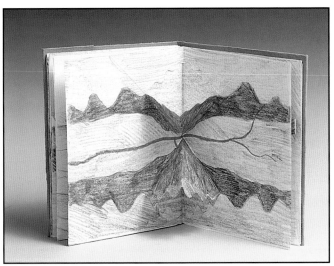

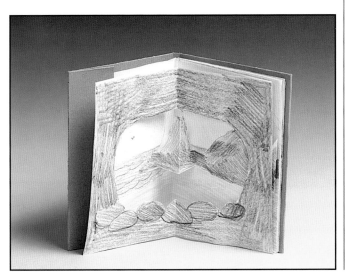

W HAT YOU DO

1. Decide which landforms you want to include in your book. Some ideas to start with are a mountain, hills, a butte, a river valley, a sea cave, stalactites and stalagmites, cliffs, a volcano, or sand dunes. Make a simple drawing of the landform on white paper and decide which kind of pop-up would best show it.

2. Fold a sheet of white paper in half from top to bottom and cut it along the fold line. You will now have two pieces of paper, each measuring 5½ by 8½ inches (14 by 22 cm). Fold each of these in half, as in figure **1**. This is the first step in making any of the four pop-ups that follow.

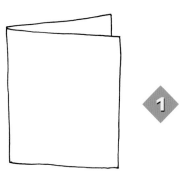

To make a pop-up from the center of the page:

a. Draw a straight line from the folded edge halfway across the page. Make this line where you want the bottom of your pop-up to be. **2**

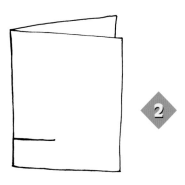

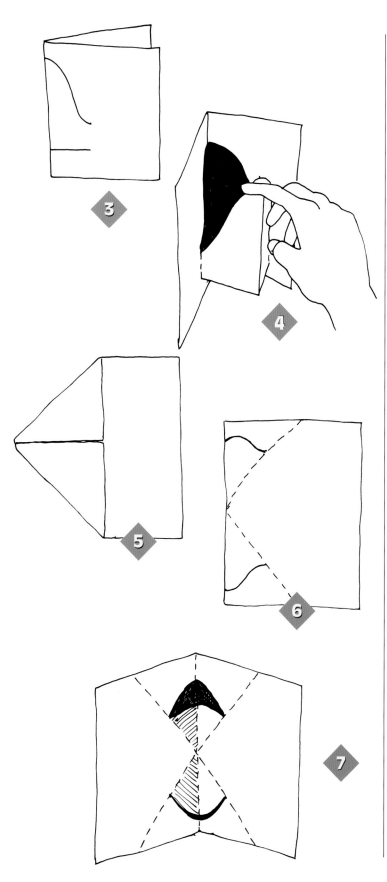

b. Draw the top edge of the pop-up in whatever shape it needs to be to show the landform you are making. Don't go past the middle of the page. Remember that you are drawing half of the landform. So, for example, you would draw a mountain like this: **3**

c. Cut along both lines.

d. Open the page and gently pull the pop-up toward you. **4**

e. Close the page with the pop-up folded on the inside and press to crease all the folds.

To make two pop-ups from the center of the page:

a. Fold the top and bottom corners of the folded side of the paper down so that they meet, forming two triangles. **5**

b. Unfold the triangles and draw the top edge of the pop-ups from the folded edges of the paper to the fold lines you have just made. **6**

c. Cut along the lines you have drawn.

d. Open the page and gently pull the pop-ups toward you along the fold lines you made in step a. **7**. You will have to reverse the direction of the folds.

e. Close the page with the pop-ups folded to the inside. Press hard to make sharp creases.

To make a pop-up that sticks out past the edge of the paper:

a. Fold a triangle down from the top corner of the folded edge, like this: **8**

b. Open the page and gently pull the triangle to the inside. Close the page again, with the triangle inside. Press to crease the folds.

c. From a scrap of paper, cut out a triangle with a 2- to 2½-inch (5 to 6.5 cm) base and fold it in half.

d. Glue the cutout triangle to the triangle that is folded inside the page. Match the fold lines. **9**

e. Close the page. If the new triangle sticks out, trim the tip so that it fits completely inside the folded page.

f. Draw the landform on the two triangles. You may want to trim the tip to make it some other shape to suit your landform.

To make an opening that comes forward:

a. Trim 1 inch (2.5 cm) off one short edge of the sheet of paper. Fold the paper in half.

b. Draw the opening that you want (a cave? a rock arch?). Cut out the opening, being sure to leave the edges around the opening uncut. **10**

c. Put a ½-inch (1.5 cm) strip of glue along each of the two side edges of the pop-up on the back side of the paper. Glue these edges to the edges of another sheet of 5½-by-8½-inch (14 by 22 cm) folded paper. Since the cutout page is shorter than the underneath page, you won't be able to open this pop-up completely, but as you open it, the top page will come forward. **11**

d. Try making another pop-up in the inside of this pop-up. You will make the inside pop-up just like any other pop-up. It's a good idea to make the inside pop-up before gluing the front pop-up to the inside page. Glue the inside pop-up to its back page first, then glue the front pop-up to the inside page.

3. **For all pop-ups, this is the next step:** Glue the pop-up page inside another folded page of 5½-by-8½-inch (14 by 22 cm) white paper. When you are gluing, be sure to put glue everywhere except on the back of the pop-up part.

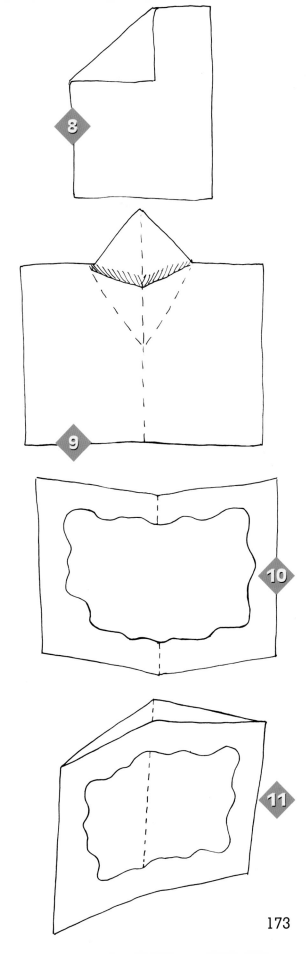

4. Open the pop-up page and finish drawing and coloring the landform as well as the page around it to make an environment for the landform. Color the paper that shows behind the pop-up so that it blends in with the scene you have drawn.

5. To make a book out of all the pop-up pages, begin by stacking all the folded pop-ups in the order you want them to be in the book. Put glue all over the outside back page of the first pop-up, and then lay it on top of the outside front page of the next pop-up. Repeat this step until all the pages are glued together. **12**

6. Fold two blank 5½-by-8½-inch (14 by 22 cm) sheets of paper. Glue one to the top and one to the bottom of the stack of pages.

7. To make a cover for your book, lay a sheet of colored construction paper on the table. Use a ruler to find the center, and draw a line to mark the center of the paper. **13**

8. Use the paper clip and ruler to score two lines, each ¼ inch (1 cm) away from the center line on either side. To score, simply press hard with the rounded end of the paper clip. Scoring makes it easier to fold stiff paper. Fold the paper along the scored lines to make a spine for the book. **14**

9. Slip the stack of pages inside the cover, pushing it all the way in against the spine. Open the cover, keeping the pages in place. Use the ruler and paper clip to score lines across the top and bottom of the stack of pages. Fold the cover along these scored lines. **15**

10. Again slip the stack of pages inside the cover against the spine. Score a line along the outer edge of the pages, then move the page stack over to the other side of the spine, and score another line along the outer edge of the stack. Fold the cover along each of these two newly scored lines. **16**

11. Slip the first and last pages of the page stack into the space inside each cover fold over. **17** Decorate the cover to finish the book.

The Map Makers

Look at a regular highway map: You can see where roads, towns, and cities are, along with a few really big natural features, like lakes and rivers. But a highway map doesn't give a clue about hills or valleys, let alone the rocks below the surface.

So geologists make their own maps. It's sort of like making a map of your backyard. You'd show the lawn, bushes, driveway, tree house, and fence. A geologist's backyard is much bigger, and a geological map shows whole rock formations—the kind of rock, how thick it is, how it rises or falls, and what kind of rock lives next door.

The map may have different colors for different kinds of rocks. Granite might be red; shale, green; sandstone, sandy; limestone, light blue; marble, dark blue, and so on.

And it will have curvy lines all over it. These are *contour lines*, which show whether the land is steep or level. Every point on a contour line is at the same altitude above sea level. The line next to it is either higher or lower by a number that's written on the map—usually an amount between 20 and 200 feet (6 and 61 m). When the land is steep, like on a mountainside, the lines are very close together. When the land is level, the lines are far apart.

Geologists draw little symbols to show whether rocks are tilted up or down (this is called *dip*) and the direction of dip (*strike*). Dip and strike are important because they show how the crustal plates have shifted and heaved whole rock formations and mountains around. Rocks that used to lie level may be tilted steeply and even turned on end. That's like turning your floor into a wall!

There are other symbols geologists use to mark things: mines, folded rocks, mineral veins, loose rocks or pebbles, landslides, gemstones, fossils, grooves cut in rocks by glaciers, and other interesting features.

What a geological detective really wants to look at is an *outcrop* of *bedrock*, the thick, unbroken rock of the crust that lies under everything else. But how can you

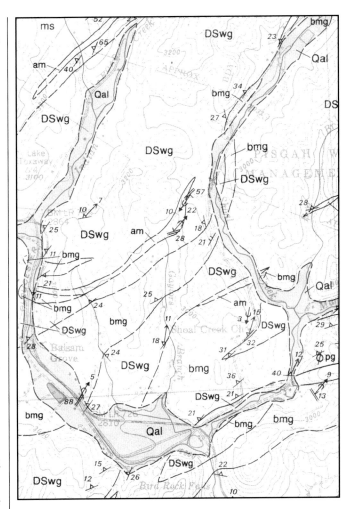

see bedrock when it's hidden under plants, soil, sand, water, and buildings? Unless you want to do a lot of digging, you have to search for an outcrop where bedrock pokes through the surface. You can also use places where someone else has done the digging for you— highway and railroad cuts, quarries, and abandoned mines. Other good places to see bedrock are cliffs and some river banks. Once you find bedrock in one place, you can compare it to other places you find bedrock and begin filling the blanks on your map.

Why go to all the trouble to make a geological map? This is how a geologist tries to understand how the surface of the Earth got to be the way it is.

You can get an idea of what a geological map looks like in most libraries, or you can order them from the U.S. Geological Survey or other public agency.

175

MEASURING a Slope

Have you ever wondered how high a hill is? One way to find out is to use a process called leveling. This is a very old way of measuring the height of a slope. In earlier days, people actually used this method to measure the height of some of the highest mountains. Here's how you and a friend can use a homemade instrument to measure a slope.

What You Need

- *Quart-size (946 ml) glass jar with a lid, half filled with water*
- *Wide rubber band*
- *Pointed stick about 2 feet (61 cm) long*
- *Notebook*
- *Pencil*
- *Tape measure*

WHAT **Y**OU **D**O

1. Place the jar of water on a level table or level ground. When the water stops sloshing around, carefully place the rubber band around the jar at exactly the level of the water.

2. You'll need a friend to help with the next steps. Stand at the bottom of the slope you want to measure. Give your friend the stick. Hold the jar in front of your face so that you look straight across the water. Use the rubber band to see when the water has stopped sloshing and is level. (Make sure the water level and the rubber band are in

the same place. If the top of the water is in a different place from the rubber band, tip the jar until they are in the same place. Now look across the leveled water.)

3. While you are looking across the water, spot a place on the slope, and ask your friend to put the tip of the stick there as a marker.

4. Record "1" in your notebook.

5. Now climb up the slope and stand where the point of the stick is touching the ground. Place your feet on either side of that spot, and look through the leveled water for the next place on the slope to mark. Ask your friend to move the stick to the new mark. Record another mark in your notebook.

6. Repeat step 5 until you reach the top of the hill or as far up the slope as you want to measure.

7. Add up all your marks and write the sum in your notebook.

8. Ask your friend to help you use the tape measure to measure the distance from your eyes to the ground beneath your feet. Multiply the number of marks you recorded by the distance between your eyes and the ground. The answer is the height of the slope you just measured.

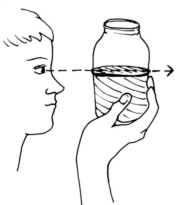

Making a Topographic Map

A TOPOGRAPHIC MAP SHOWS MOUNTAINS AND VALLEYS, HIGH PLACES AND LOW PLACES. PEOPLE WHO KNOW HOW TO READ THESE MAPS CAN TELL BY LOOKING AT ONE JUST HOW STEEP A CERTAIN HILL IS. THEY CAN PLAN THE EASIEST PLACE TO BUILD A ROAD THAT MUST CROSS A MOUNTAIN RANGE OR THEY CAN USE THE MAP TO HELP FIND THE BEST PLACE TO BUILD A LOOKOUT TOWER. THIS PROJECT WILL HELP YOU UNDERSTAND HOW TO READ A TOPOGRAPHIC MAP.

What You Need

- *Lump of clay twice as big as your fist*
- *Piece of cardboard or large tile, 12 by 12 inches (31 by 31 cm)*
- *Wire coat hanger*
- *2-foot (61 cm) long piece of dental floss*
- *2 sticks, each about 3 inches (7.6 cm) long*
- *Ruler*
- *Piece of white paper*
- *Pencil*

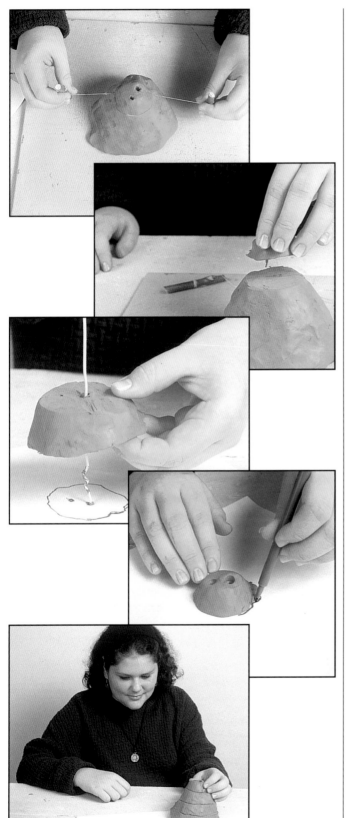

WHAT YOU DO

1. Make a mountain out of the clay and place it on the cardboard.

2. Straighten out the coat hanger. Use one end to poke two holes straight down through the center of the mountain. Make sure your two holes go all the way through the mountain.

3. Tie each end of the dental floss to one of the short sticks and stretch the dental floss until it is taut. Hold onto the handles and use the dental floss to cut through the mountain around 1 inch down from the peak.

4. Remove this clay slice and place it on the paper. Use the pencil to carefully trace around it. Push the pencil through one of the holes in the clay and make a dot on the paper; do the same with the other hole. Put the slice aside, but don't squash it. You'll need it again later.

5. Cut a second slice, 1 inch (2.5 cm) down from the first. Lay the second slice over the tracing of the first one, being careful to place the holes in the second slice over the dots on the paper. To line up the holes precisely, poke the coat hanger through one of the holes in the slice until it touches one of the dots on the paper; do the same with the other hole. Carefully trace around the second slice. Your tracing will form a circle outside the tracing of the first slice.

6. Cut as many more slices as you can, each 1 inch (2.5 cm) down from the one before it. Line up the holes with the dots and trace each as you cut it.

7. When you have traced all the slices, stack them back up in order on the cardboard. Be sure the holes line up.

8. Compare the topographic map you have made to the model mountain. Why are some of the traced lines closer together than others? What kind of slope gives you lines that are close together? What kind gives lines that are far apart? On your topographic map, where are the steepest slopes? Where would be the best place to build a trail to climb to the top of the mountain?

$\mathscr{S}$elf-$\mathscr{F}$olding Map

$\mathbf{T}$HIS IS A POCKET-SIZE MAP THAT NOT ONLY UNFOLDS EASILY BUT ALSO FOLDS ITSELF BACK UP. YOU CAN DRAW YOUR OWN MAP ON IT OR GLUE ON A MAP THAT YOU WANT TO USE ON A ROCK COLLECTING TRIP.

$\mathbf{W}$HAT YOU NEED

- *A sheet of heavy-weight paper for the map cover*
- *Pencil*
- *Ruler*
- *Scissors*
- *Sheet of plain white paper, 8½ by 11 inches (22 by 28 cm) to use for the map (If you want to use a map that is already drawn, cut it to 8½ by 11 inches (22 by 28 cm) and use it in place of the plain white paper.)*
- *Glue stick*

1. Use the pencil and ruler to mark the cover sheet so that it is 5 by 11 inches (13 by 28 cm), and then cut it out. Put this sheet aside for now.

2. Fold the plain white paper in half so that it measures 5½ by 8½ inches (14 by 28 cm). If you are using a map that is already drawn, fold it so that the map is on the inside.

3. Turn the paper so that the fold runs across the top. Fold the two top corners down as though you were making a hat. Be sure to leave a ¼-inch (1 cm) space between the two flaps. **1**

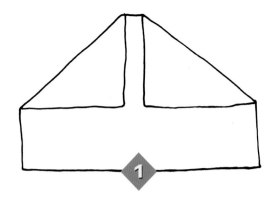

4. Press all the creases, then unfold the paper completely, with an 11-inch (28 cm) edge at the top. Keep the map side facing up if you are using a map that is already drawn. About 3½ inches (9 cm) in from the left side, make a fold that goes from top to bottom. Press the crease.

5. Repeat step 4 on the right side. Unfold the paper again. You should have creases that look like **2**.

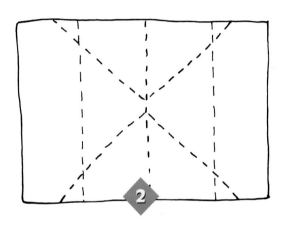

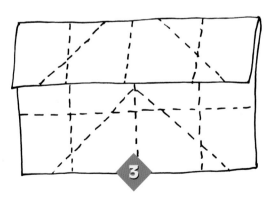

6. Two inches (5 cm) down from the top, make a fold that goes evenly across the paper. The middle of the top should come to the point of the bottom V. **3**

181

7. Repeat step 6 two inches (5 cm) up from the bottom.

8. Unfold the paper, keeping the map side up if you are using a map that is already drawn. It should have creases that look like figure **4**.

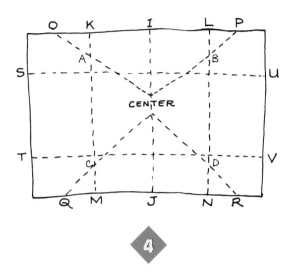

9. Now that you have made all the creases you will need, it's time to refold the paper. You will have to fold a few of the creases back in the opposite direction, but you will be using the same fold lines. Here's how to do it: Pull points I and J so that they come up off of the table while points A, B, C, and D stay on the table. Crease again the folds that go from the center to I and from the center to J, so that points I and J lift up and bring with them creases I-center and J-center.

10. Now lift points O, P, Q, and R up toward you one at a time, reversing the creases that go from O to A and from Q to C.

11. At this stage of folding, points I, J, O, P, Q, and R should all be lifting off the table. Hold the paper with your left hand at point I and your right hand at point J. Push these two points towards each other and down toward one side. The rest of the points should also come towards each other, and one whole side of the paper should be trying to fold over on top of the other side. You should help the paper do just that. Let go of points I and J and press the side that wants to be on top onto the rest of the paper. **5**

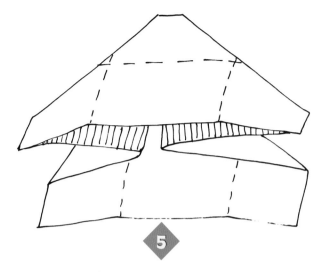

12. Fold and unfold the map a few times to be sure it works, fixing creases as necessary. To glue the map into the cover, first fold it up. Then put glue all over the outside of the top side of the folded map. Open up the cover paper. Press the flattened point of the sticky side of the folded map into the fold of the cover. **6** Press the map to help it stick to the cover.

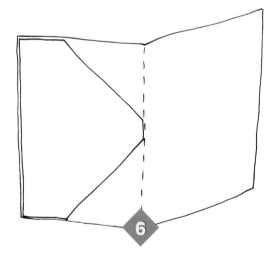

13. Now put glue all over the other surface of the folded map.

14. Bring the unglued cover of the map folder over on top of the glued surface and press down hard to help stick the glue. Press the map under a heavy book while the glue is drying. If you haven't yet drawn a map on the paper, do so now, or wait until you are out walking in the area you want to map.

Where Do Rocks Come From?

By now you know that Earth is a very active place. The crustal plates scrape and collide and dive beneath each other, causing earthquakes and volcanoes, and building mountains. As they do this, the plates play a nonstop game with the Earth's rocks that is as dynamic as a great video game, but much s-l-o-w-e-r! Part of the game is to change all three kinds of rocks—igneous, sedimentary, and metamorphic—into other kinds of rocks.

In this chapter we'll see how rocks can be created deep in Earth's mantle, raised slowly to the surface, destroyed by water and wind, and created again, and again, and again. These changes are part of what is called the *rock cycle*.

The rock cycle moves in such slow motion that geologists measure those movements in *geologic time*. To a geologist, a million years is just a blink of an eye. In fact, there have been about 4,500 million-year blinks since the Earth was formed! With that kind of time to play with, it's not hard to imagine how a rock formed at the bottom of the ocean can end up on a mountaintop—many millions of years later.

The flat, neat layers on top were formed when molten rock erupted through volcanoes and then cooled and hardened. Below these layers are much thicker deposits of eroded shale, formed when silt and mud sank to the bottom of a lake or ocean and became rock. Colorado's Mount Garfield

Granite PAPER

When you stop to look carefully at rocks, you'll begin to notice and appreciate their many beautiful colors and interesting shapes and textures. This paper is designed to look like granite, with its multicolored surface. The top photograph shows a good example of granite.

What You Need

- Rough cement sidewalk or a concrete block or any flat concrete surface
- Colored pencils or crayons
- Piece of granite or a photograph of a piece of granite
- Plain white paper

Sweetwater Granite, showing structures stripped of outer layers. Granite Mountains, Wyoming

HAT YOU DO

1. Brush off any loose pieces of concrete or other debris from the concrete surface you plan to use.

2. Choose three or four colors of crayon or colored pencil that you can see in the piece of granite or the photograph of granite. Lay a sheet of white paper on the concrete.

3. Use one hand to hold the paper firmly in place while you gently and evenly color over the entire area that you want to look like granite. Use a medium or light color for this first layer.

4. Move the paper slightly so the little concrete bumps will be in different places and then color with a different color. Be sure to hold the paper in place and to color evenly.

5. Continue moving the paper and then holding and coloring it with the different colors that you see in the rock you are using as a model. Stop when the paper looks like granite.

6. Use your granite paper to cover books (see page 138), to wrap gifts, or as note cards.

PEBBLE Race

Small flat pebbles make nice markers for games. They can be used to play tic-tac-toe as well as race games, such as the one described here.

1

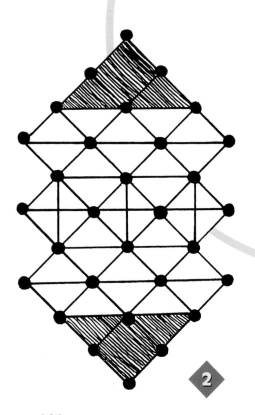

2

Enlarge game board pattern on a copier by 200%

WHAT YOU NEED

- Old sock without a hole in the toe
- Scissors
- Shoelace or leather thong, about 12 inches (31 cm) long
- Piece of paper, 10 by 10 inches (25 by 25 cm)
- Pencil
- Colored markers
- Piece of lightweight cardboard, 10 by 10 inches (25 by 25 cm)
- Glue stick
- 6 flat, round dark-colored pebbles
- 6 flat, round light-colored pebbles

WHAT YOU DO

1. First make a bag in which to keep your markers. Cut off the toe end of the sock, leaving the sock as long as possible without including the heel. Make a straight cut across the sock so that the heel is cut off.

2. Cut eight small holes around the cut edge. These are for the lacing. **1**

3. Thread the shoelace or leather thong through the holes, and your bag is ready to use.

4. Enlarge the game board pattern **2** as indicated. Color over the game board dots and lines with a black marker, and color the two triangular "home bases" with a colored marker.

5. Glue the paper to the piece of cardboard.

To play Pebble Race:

〜 Two people at a time can play Pebble Race. One player places the dark-colored pebbles on the dots of his or her home base, and the other player places the light-colored pebbles on the dots of his or her home base.

〜 The winner is the first player to get at least three pebbles across the board and safely into the other player's home base. The pebbles may be placed on any of the six dots that are in the home base.

〜 Players take turns making their moves. Pebbles can be moved only along the lines that connect the dots, and they can be moved only in a forward or sideways direction. They may not be moved backwards.

〜 A pebble can jump a pebble that is next to it as long as it follows the lines that connect the dots and moves in a

straight line during the jump. If a player jumps his or her own pebble, the jumped pebble stays where it is. But if a player jumps the other person's pebble, the jumper captures the jumped pebble and removes it from the board. It is okay to jump more than one pebble at a time, and the pebbles jumped can be from both players. In other words, I can jump (and capture) your pebble, and if that move puts me next to my own pebble, I can jump it, too, in order to move my pebble farther along the board.

〜 A player can lose three pebbles and still win the game, but once someone captures more than three of the other player's pebbles, the other player can't win. Play should continue, however, because it is still possible for the second player to capture the other player's pebbles so that he or she can't win, either, causing the game to end in a draw.

Igneous, Pop!

Did you ever put a stone into a campfire? It doesn't melt, does it? But inside the Earth's mantle it's hot enough to melt rock! Only when this hot liquid rock gets near the cool surface does it harden (or *crystallize*) to form *igneous rock*. Igneous (IG-nee-us) comes from the Latin word for fire.

In Sechon one we learned that plates of the Earth's crust can dive down into the red-hot mantle. If they dive deep enough, they melt into magma. After a long time, this liquid magma may rise through older, harder rocks toward the surface—as fast as a mile a day.

Some of the magma pops right through the surface as a volcano. But most of it stops underground to form huge masses called *plutons* (named for Pluto, the Roman god of the underworld). Plutons take thousands or even millions of years to cool. While they're cooling, they heat everything around them, including the groundwater. This water may turn to steam and shoot up as geysers, like Old Faithful in Yellowstone National Park.

Magma is a very hot, thick soup of water, carbon dioxide, silicon, aluminum, iron and many other dissolved chemicals. When it cools, it can form many kinds of igneous rock. The magma under oceans usually produces *basalt*, whose dark colors can be seen in pictures of Hawaiian volcanoes. Magma rising under continents

Devils Tower, an igneous intrusive body exposed by erosion. Devils Tower National Monument, Wyoming

usually produces *granite*, which is lighter-colored and grainier than basalt. The volcanoes around the Pacific "rim of fire" come from *andesite magma*, which is partway between basalt and granite; andesite was named after the Andes mountains.

As a rock cools, it grows crystals; the slower a rock cools, the larger its crystals. Plutons cool slowly, because they are deep in the Earth, and plutonic crystals may be large enough to see by eye; some are several inches or feet long. Volcanic rock cools quickly in the ocean or atmosphere, and its crystals may be too small to see. Some lava cools very fast when it is thrown into the air, making a dark glass called *obsidian* which has no grains at all.

Here's a puzzle: If most granite is formed underground in plutons, why do we see so many granite rocks lying around on the ground? The answer is that igneous rocks like granite are very hard, but the sedimentary rock above is softer. Eventually this softer rock breaks down in the rain and wind, exposing the granite below.

Igneous rocks that have been smoothed by water

SMALL ROUND PEBBLES HAVE
BEEN USED FOR GAMES FOR
HUNDREDS OF YEARS. A
PAINTING ON THE WALL OF
AN ANCIENT ROMAN HOUSE
SHOWS PEOPLE PLAYING A
GAME WITH SMALL STONES.
THE GAMES DESCRIBED IN
THIS PROJECT ARE SIMILAR
TO THOSE PLAYED LONG AGO.

GAME Pebbles

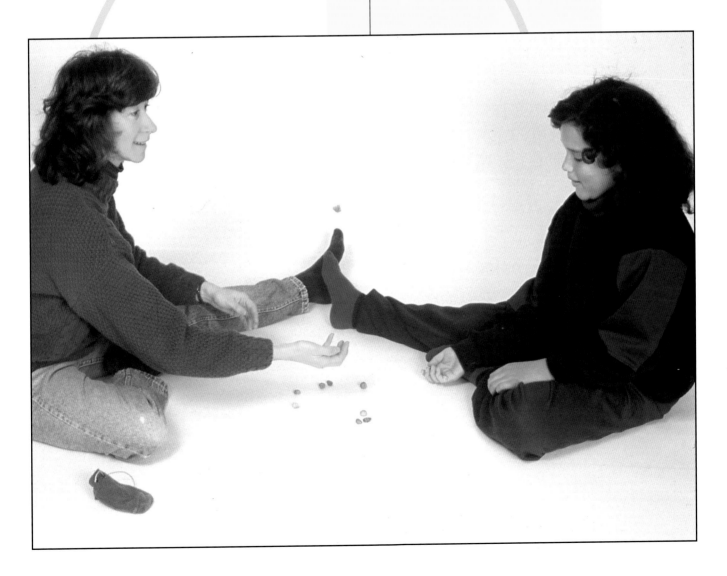

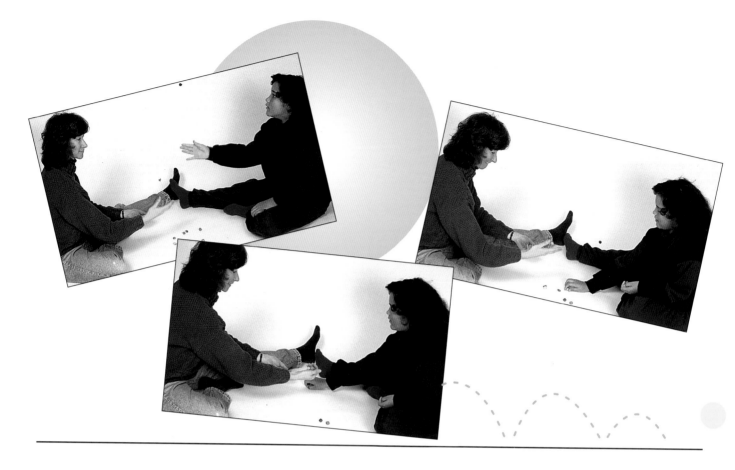

What You Need

- *Old sock without a hole in the toe*
- *Scissors*
- *Shoelace or leather thong, about 12 inches (31 cm) long*
- *11 small, round stones; choose ones that are easy to pick up*

What You Do

1. To make a bag in which to keep your pebbles, see the directions on page 187.

2. The following games include some that are easy and others that are more challenging. Experts at these games usually trade their beginner stones in for smaller and more round stones to make the games even more challenging.

Practice Moves:

a. First practice throwing a stone up and catching it with the same hand. Sit on the floor to do this, and concentrate on throwing the stone about 12 inches (31 cm) into the air. When you are very good at catching the stone, try practice move b.

b. Practice throwing a stone up and catching it on the back of your hand without letting it roll off. When you can do that, you're ready for move c.

c. Practice holding five stones in your two hands, throwing them all up at one time, and catching them all on the backs of your two hands held together. Practice until you can catch all five stones without any rolling off.

d. Practice throwing up one stone and picking up another stone while the first stone is in the air, and then catching the first stone without dropping the second one. When you can do that, you're ready to play some games.

Scratches

THIS GAME COMES FROM THE CZECH REPUBLIC, AND IT IS ONE OF THE EARLY GAMES ON WHICH OUR MODERN GAME OF JACKS IS BASED. THE GAME IS STILL PLAYED IN THE CZECH AND SLOVAK REPUBLICS.

1. Play this game with a friend or by yourself for practice. You will need five stones. The first move is called Slugsnail. To play Slugsnail, place four of the stones at the corners of an imaginary square on the floor in front of you, and put the fifth stone on the back of your hand. Keeping the fifth stone on the back of your hand, gather up the four other stones, holding them in the palm of your hand until all four have been picked up. If the stone rolls off the back of your hand, you lose your turn, or, if you are playing by yourself, you must start over.

2. The next part of the game is called Ones. To play Ones, throw down all five stones. Pick up any one and toss it into the air. While it is in the air, you must pick up one other stone and hold it in the palm of your hand while you catch the tossed stone. Put one of these stones into your other hand, and toss the remaining stone while you pick up another stone. Repeat until you have picked up all the stones, one at a time. If you miss or drop a stone, you lose your turn. If you are playing alone, start over if you miss. A variation is for two people to play at the same time with their own stones. They should both start at the same time, and the one who finishes first without a miss wins the round.

3. The rest of the rounds are called Twos, Threes, and Fours. They are played the same as Ones, except that you must toss a stone and then pick up two, three, or four stones at one time.

4. Another move is called Horse. To play Horse, throw all five stones in the air at once and try to catch them on the back of your tossing hand. Then toss into the air any stones that have stayed on your hand, and catch them in the palm of your hand. The winner is the player who catches the most in his or her palm.

5. An advanced move is called Thumber. To play this you'll need an extra stone called the "thumber." Place it in the crotch of your thumb—where your thumb and index finger come together. Hold the thumber in place while you do all the other moves in the game. It must not fall out or be put down with the other stones during the entire time of the game.

Leopard jasper

Knucklebones

THIS GAME COMES FROM THE ISLAND OF MAURITIUS IN THE INDIAN OCEAN.

1. Each player needs ten stones plus a master stone. Each of the ten stones should be about the size of the end of your thumb and easy to pick up. It helps if they are somewhat flat on some surfaces.

2. Hold all ten stones in one hand, toss them, and catch as many as possible on the back of your tossing hand. The ones that you don't catch should be left on the ground. The next play is made with the stones you were able to catch.

3. Toss the stones from the back of your hand into the air, and try to catch them all in the palm of your hand. If you drop any, you lose your turn. If you catch them all, lay those aside in a pile of your winnings.

4. Now repeat steps 2 and 3 using the stones that were dropped in the first step. The winner is the person who picks up all his or her stones in the fewest tosses.

"Sedimental" Journey

*L*ike a restless housekeeper, nature is constantly sweeping up loose bits of dirt and rock, carrying them away, and dropping them as *sediment*. Sediment may be as large as a rock rolling down a mountainside or as small as the dust you find on your windowsill. Nature is a remarkable magician, and can turn all kinds of sediment—pebbles, sand, clay, even the bodies of tiny, dead animals and plants—into rock.

Most sedimentary rock forms under water. In a flooding river, a large rock will get carried just a few feet, while a smaller pebble may bump along for half a mile

ment begins with a thick bed of sand that is changed into *sandstone*. Next, a thin bed of clay is added and hardens into *shale*. This is followed by another bed of sandstone. If you cut through this sedimentary layer cake years later, as rivers or highway builders often do, you can see the beds clearly. You may also see beds that have been tilted by rising magma or folded like an accordion by Earth's moving plates.

Other sedimentary rock is laid down at the bottom of the ocean by the skeletons of tiny floating plants and animals called *plankton*. These creatures may be too small to see, but there are so many of them that when they die their skeletons make thick layers of rock called *limestone*.

A third kind of sedimentary rock is made when the water of a lake or ocean evaporates, leaving behind its minerals. This is how we get table salt for our food: salt water evaporates and leaves the salt called *sodium chloride*.

Intricate crossbeds in Navajo Sandstone. Arches National Park, Utah

before settling and waiting for the next flood. Sand may be swept along for miles, and the mud that turns the river brown may travel all the way to the ocean before it gradually settles to the bottom.

How can all these particles turn into rock? The process may take millions of years as sediment is slowly buried by more sediment piling on top. As the pile gets heavier, the particles near the bottom are squeezed closer and closer together and warmed by the heat of the earth. Groundwater brings new minerals that act like cement to bond the particles together into *sedimentary rock*.

How can you tell if a rock is sedimentary? Often, it is laid down in layers or beds. Imagine that our pile of sedi-

Sometimes a sedimentary rock has no obvious bedding. How can a geologist tell it from an igneous rock? One way is to look at the rock through a microscope. Sedimentary rock grains are smoothed by their travels and surrounded by mineral "cement." Igneous rock grains are jagged and locked together without cement.

You may also wonder: If sedimentary rock usually forms under water, how does it turn into dry land? Remember how active the Earth's crust is? Over million of years, sedimentary rock is pushed upward by rising magma, or the oceans dry up, leaving it behind. In whatever way it becomes dry land, this thin blanket of sedimentary rocks covers most of the Earth's continents.

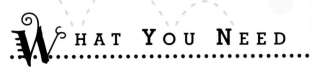 WHAT YOU NEED

- ½ cup (118 ml) of water
- 2 paper cups
- 2½ tablespoons of Epsom salts
  (sold at drug stores)
- Spoon
- ½ cup (100 g) of dry sand

WHAT YOU DO

1. Put 1½ inches (4 cm) of water in the bottom of one of the paper cups.

2. Dissolve the Epsom salts in the water. Keep stirring until almost all the salt has disappeared. The salt will cement the particles of sand together, just as certain minerals cement sand particles together in real sandstone.

3. Put 1½ inches (4 cm) of sand in the bottom of the other paper cup.

4. Pour the salt mixture into the sand and stir until the sand is completely wet.

5. Let the wet mixture sit undisturbed for about one hour. Then carefully pour off all the water that has risen to the top. You will have to pour off water several times during the first day of the experiment. Keep the paper cup in a place where no one will disturb it for at least one week. Do not cover the cup.

6. When the sandstone has dried completely, tear the paper cup away from it. If you discover that the sides and bottom are still damp, let the sandstone sit undisturbed until it is completely dry. Then, it will feel like real sandstone.

MAKING Sandstone

READ HOW SANDSTONE IS FORMED (PAGE **192**) AND THEN MAKE SOME OF YOUR OWN. IT WILL TAKE A WEEK OR MORE FOR YOUR SANDSTONE TO HARDEN, BUT THAT'S EONS SHORTER THAN THE TIME IT TAKES REAL SANDSTONE TO FORM!

MAKING A
Conglomerate

*L*IKE SANDSTONE,
A CONGLOMERATE
CONSISTS OF PARTI-
CLES OF MINERALS
CEMENTED TOGETHER
BY ANOTHER MINERAL.
YOU CAN MAKE YOUR
CONGLOMERATE OUT
OF PEBBLES AND SAND.
DECORATE THE SUR-
FACE WITH PRETTY
SEASHELLS YOU FIND
ON THE BEACH OR
SMALL ROCKS AND
YOU'LL HAVE MADE
AN ATTRACTIVE
PAPERWEIGHT.

Conglomerate in
ancient creek bed.
Sevier County, Utah.

194

WHAT YOU NEED

- *Water*
- *Paper cup*
- *2½ tablespoons of Epsom salts (sold at drugstores)*
- *Spoon*
- *2 tablespoons of sand*
- *2 tablespoons of gravel*
- *Several seashells or small rocks*

WHAT YOU DO

1. Pour 2 inches (5 cm) of water into the paper cup. Add the Epsom salts and stir until dissolved.

2. Add the sand and gravel to the watery mixture, and stir until the sand and gravel are completely wet and mixed. Let the cup sit undisturbed for one hour.

3. After an hour, water will have risen to the top; carefully pour it off. You will have to repeat this step several times during the first day of the experiment as more and more water rises to the top of the sand and gravel.

4. When no more water rises to the top, but the conglomerate is still very wet, push a few seashells or pretty stones into the top of the conglomerate. Half bury them so they'll become part of the conglomerate, but leave part of each sticking out so you can see them.

5. Leave the conglomerate in a place where no one will disturb it for at least one week. It will take a week or longer for the conglomerate to dry and harden.

6. After it is dry, tear the paper cup away from the conglomerate.

Morphed

*W*e've learned that rocks can be molten liquid (page 188) and can be formed from sand, clay, and the skeletons of tiny, dead animals (page 192). But there are even more amazing facts in Rocky's Believe-It-or-Not.

Very, very old and cold igneous or sedimentary rocks can be changed by tremendous heat and pressure into different kinds of rocks altogether! Known as *metamorphic rocks* (from the Greek for "change of shape"), these new or "recycled" rocks change into different minerals, shapes, and colors.

How is it possible for solid rocks to be reheated and metamorphosed? This mystery was solved only a few decades ago when geologists found that Earth's crustal plates are always sliding and crunching into each other. All this bashing around can create metamorphic rocks in different ways. When two crustal plates collide, the rocks at the edges of the plates are squeezed and metamorphosed. When one plate is forced under

Specimen of wavy folds in schist. Riverside Mountain, California

Hard metamorphic slate that started out as shale, a soft sedimentary rock

another, its rock is plunged into the hot mantle and metamorphosed. When magma rises, it heats and metamorphoses the older rock around it.

Metamorphic rock does not melt, like igneous rock. Instead, it is "baked" under high pressure into a new kind of "bread." Imagine a rock that spends millions of years ten miles (16 km) below the surface! Talk about your hot rocks! There the temperature might be 700°F (370°C) and the pressure 5,000 times as high it is on the surface. It's not surprising that minerals can be "cooked" into new ones, squashed into "layers," and later bent into wavy shapes!

You can get an idea of how this works the next time it snows. Scoop up a handful and make a snowball; press it as tight and hard as you can. The crystals of snow start out light and fluffy, but they get harder and denser because of the heat and pressure of your hands.

Rocks may begin to change even at shallow depths. When sedimentary shale, or mudstone, is baked gently, it becomes smooth, fine-grained *slate*. (Flat beds of slate can be split into shingles for roofs or flagstones for paths. Slate often has fossils in it.)

Deeper down, the shale forms *schist*, which has larger grains and wavy patterns instead of flat ones. These wavy patterns are caused when flat layers are crumpled by pressure, the way you might bend a thin piece of licorice by pushing on both ends.

Rocks called *gneiss* (nice) form under conditions so powerful that the rock becomes almost like plastic and its layers can be bent into S-curves. The dark layers of gneiss are usually *mica*, which form bands between thicker layers of pale or shiny minerals like *quartz* and *feldspar*. Gneiss comes from a German word meaning "sparkle."

Limestone may be metamorphosed into *marble*, which we cut and polish into statues, gravestones, and building blocks. Marble may be almost pure white, or it may have beautiful patterns of green or black minerals such as *olivine* and *serpentine*.

You can see some of the world's most ancient metamorphic rock in the northern United States and Canada—formed more than a billion years ago. Why was so much metamorphic rock made then? Because the Earth was much hotter than it is now, and there was more tectonic activity.

Faux Marble

POLISHED MARBLE HAS BEEN VALUED FOR ITS BEAUTY FOR MANY YEARS. PEOPLE USE MARBLE FOR TABLE-TOPS, FLOORS, MANTLEPIECES, WINDOWSILLS, AND MANY OTHER THINGS. MARBLE IS VERY EXPENSIVE, BUT YOU CAN MAKE FAUX (MEANING "FALSE") MARBLE THAT LOOKS AS INTRICATELY DESIGNED AS THE REAL THING, WHICH IS PICTURED BELOW.

What You Need

- *Something to put a marble finish on, such as a light switch plate, wooden box, wooden or plastic picture frame, small bookshelf, or chest of drawers*
- *Fine grit sandpaper*
- *Flat black, gray, or white latex paint*
- *1-inch (2.5 cm) flat paintbrush*
- *3 old pie tins*
- *Flat or semigloss white latex paint (base coat)*
- *2 other colors of flat or semigloss latex paint, one light and one dark: Choose colors that you like and that look good with your project. Pinks, greens, and browns will look the most like real marble.*
- *3 feathers*

1. If the object you plan to marble is wood or metal, sand it all over to make it smooth. If it's plastic, wash it to remove any grease or dirt.

2. Paint the object with the base coat—black or gray or white. Let it dry overnight. Meanwhile, study the picture of marble on page 197 to get an idea of how marble looks.

3. Pour the two colors and the white paint into the three tin pans. Start with the lighter of the two colors. Dip the tip of a feather into the paint, and then tap and drag it across the surface of the object you want to marble. As the feather gets wet it will stick together. When that happens, keep tapping. The tip will swirl around some and make nice patterns. Keep tapping until there is no more paint coming off the feather, and then dip it in the paint again.

4. Next dip the second feather into the darker color, tap and drag it across the surface. It's okay to cross some of the lighter marks. Keep working until you can see nearly equal amounts of the base color and the other two colors.

5. Dip the third feather into the white paint. Make a few long, jagged veins across the piece. These marks will cross over the other colors. They are the characteristic vein marks that make marble look like marble.

6. Let the piece dry overnight before using it.

METAMORPHIC Rocks

LIKE METAMORPHIC ROCKS, THESE BAR-SHAPED COOKIES ARE FORMED PARTLY BY PRESSURE AND HEAT. YOU'LL BE ABLE TO SEE THE LAYERS OR STRATA IF YOU LOOK AT THE CUT EDGES AFTER YOU SLICE THEM INTO SMALL SQUARES. TRY CHANGING THE INGREDIENTS OR REPEATING THE LAYERS TO MAKE YOUR OWN SPECIAL METAMORPHIC ROCKS. THIS IS ONE KIND OF ROCK YOU CAN SAFELY CHEW ON WITHOUT BREAKING YOUR TEETH!

WHAT YOU NEED

- *Oven*
- *Glass or aluminum baking dish, about 9 by 6 by 2 inches (23 by 15 by 5 cm)*
- *Measuring cup*
- *¼ cup (60 g) of butter or margarine*
- *Hot pad*
- *1½ cups (200 g) of cookie and/or graham cracker crumbs: To make your own, put cookie or graham cracker pieces between two large sheets of waxed paper and crush them with a rolling pin.*
- *6 ounces (250 g) of sweetened condensed milk*
- *3½ ounces (100 g) of flaked coconut—or crushed wheat cereal or chopped raisins*
- *4 ounces (110 g) of shelled and chopped nuts— or unsalted sunflower seed kernels*
- *4 ounces (110 g) of semisweet chocolate chips—or try butterscotch, mint chocolate, or milk chocolate*
- *3½ ounces (100 g) of granola*
- *Waxed paper*
- *Dull knife, such as a butter knife*
- *Spatula*

WHAT YOU DO

1. Preheat the oven to 325°F (163°C) for a glass pan or 350°F (176°C) for an aluminum pan.

2. Place the butter or margarine in the pan. **Ask an adult to help you put the pan in the oven** for a few minutes to melt the butter.

3. Use the hot pad to remove the pan from the oven. Sprinkle the cookie or graham cracker crumbs on top of the melted butter. Here we used half of each type of crumbs.

4. Pour the condensed milk evenly over the crumbs, trying not to disturb them.

5. Sprinkle on a layer of each of the following ingredients in this order:

   -shredded coconut, crushed wheat cereal, or raisins

   -chopped nuts

   -chocolate chips

   -granola

6. Place a piece of waxed paper on top of the mixture and press down all over. Either use the palm of your hand or the bottom of the measuring cup.

7. Peel off the waxed paper. Use the hot pad when you put the pan back in the oven. Bake the cookies for 25 to 30 minutes until the top layer is lightly browned.

8. Let the pan of cookies sit out for 15 minutes and then refrigerate for one hour.

9. When the cookies are cool, slice them into bars with the knife. Use the spatula to lift the bars out of the pan. Yum! If you have any left to store, keep them loosely covered in the refrigerator.

Weather Wear

Left: Good example of the effect of weather on rock. Rainbow Bridge National Monument, Utah

Below: Dramatic example of erosion. Polk County, Tennessee

Have you ever studied an old tombstone in a cemetery? Often the rock has worn down so much you can hardly read the names and dates.

This is a good example of *weathering*—the wearing down of rock by the weather and other natural forces. If you see how much a tombstone changes outdoors after only 100 years, you may understand how whole mountains can disappear over millions of years.

Nature uses many tricks to break down rock. The first is to create small and large cracks in rock. Cracks may form as rock cools or as heavy rock on top of it erodes away. These cracks are enlarged when water gets inside them, then freezes and expands. Salt crystals may also expand in the cracks.

Plants are powerful weathering agents. You've probably seen how tree roots can break up sidewalks. Roots can do the same thing to layers of rock, wedging apart even large boulders and opening them to more weathering. If a tree blows over in a storm, it exposes more rock and pries others loose.

Another powerful weathering agent is fire, which can cause rocks to shatter. You may think that natural fires are rare, but remember that geologic change takes a long time. In almost every area with grasses or trees, lightning causes many wildfires over the course of millions of years.

There are also many kinds of *chemical weathering*. Rainwater carries many kinds of chemicals that can dissolve minerals from rock. As these minerals are removed, the rock weakens and weathers more rapidly.

Weathering is a very important part of the rock cycle. It helps to break old rocks and even mountains into the sediment that forms new sedimentary rock. Even more important for us, some of this sediment produces the soil that allows us to grow crops, grasses, and trees.

Erosion Experiment

Spend a few minutes poking around in the garage or basement and you're sure to find all you need to set up an erosion table. Then get your scientific mind in gear as you devise experiments to show the effects of rocks, plants, and contouring on the way water erodes land.

What You Need

- *Something to use as a container: A paint roller pan is perfect, or try a dishpan, long wallpaper pan, baby bathtub, long plastic windowsill planter or planter trays, or old lasagna pan.*
- *Piece of wood, 2 by 4 inches (5 by 10 cm) or a brick (if you are NOT using a paint roller pan)*
- *Bucket of soil or sand; sandy soil works best*
- *Trowel*
- *Plastic knife, putty knife, or a flat stick for shaping the soil*
- *Large nail*
- *2 paper cups*
- *Water*
- *Rocks, small blocks of wood, small clumps of moss, twigs from short-needled evergreen trees, lichens, pebbles, model railroad trees—or any other objects that you can use to imitate plant growth*

WHAT YOU DO

1. If you are not using a paint roller pan, place the brick or piece of wood under one end of your container so that it will have a slope and water can drain away from the landform you will build.

2. Build a hillside at the high end of the container. Fill the entire end of the container, and build the hill at least 5 inches (13 cm) high.

3. Use the nail to poke four or five holes in the bottom of one of the paper cups. Space the holes evenly so that the bottom of the cup looks like a watering can spout. Fill the other paper cup with water.

4. For your first experiment, hold the holey paper cup about 12 inches (30 cm) over the hill, and pour water into it from the other cup. Move your hand around so that rain falls evenly on the hilltop. Watch to see what happens to the hill as rain falls on it. Make some notes in your notebook or draw a picture of the before and after.

5. Let the water drain to the low end of the container, then carefully pour only the water out. The soil should stay at the other end of the container. Now put the container back on its brick or piece of wood, and rebuild the hill. This time, add some rocks to the hill. Create another rain shower, and watch what happens to the hill. Make notes or drawings.

6. Keep emptying water and rebuilding the hill each time you change the experiment. Try planting trees made of moss or evergreen twigs; try contouring the hillside in different ways, much as farmers do when they plant crops on hillsides. Each time, build the hill as much as possible as it was built at first, and note what happens when it rains. Try placing some small blocks of wood (houses) on the hillside in different places, and watch what happens to them when it rains. What does this experiment show about the effect of plants, rocks, and different kinds of contouring on erosion?

From Rock Into Soil

$\mathcal{A}$ soft coating of soil covers most of Earth's continents like a blanket. But even on the best farmlands, this blanket is only a few feet thick. Without it, Earth would look like a hard ball of rock—no trees or bushes, and—most likely—no people.

The process of making soil begins with weathering, which breaks rock into small particles. Rocks weather fastest where it's rainy and warm. That's why a desert has only a few inches of soil or none at all. Antarctica is a dry, frozen land with practically no soil.

But soil is more than just little pieces of rock. It's softened by a mixture of decayed plants and animals known as organic matter, or *humus*. This humus is needed to hold water and nourish the roots of trees, crops, and other plants.

Soil also has living ingredients—countless numbers of ants and worms, gophers and moles, and billions of tiny organisms too small to see. The activities of these creatures help to break down leaves and branches into more soil.

One way to understand soil better is to cut a deep trench in the ground. First you'll see the darkest soil with most of the humus, which geologists call the *A-horizon*. This zone is full of life, and the soil looks and smells alive. Next you'll find the *B-horizon*, where the soil is rougher and there is little life or organic matter. Below that is the C-horizon, which is mostly broken and decayed bedrock mixed with some clay. Under the *C-horizon* is rock—all the way to the center of the Earth.

The recipe for making good soil is complex. First you take plenty of rainwater and chemicals to soften up the rock. Then you add the decaying bodies of dead plants and animals to make humus. Finally, you let the earthworms, gophers, and beetles dig around and mix the soil so the bits of rock break down faster.

Even for the best "cook," working in the best "kitchen" with plenty of rain and mild temperature, it may take more than 200 years to make enough soil to grow a forest. In dry climates, even thousands of years aren't enough to form fertile soil.

That's why it's so important to protect our topsoil from washing away or eroding. We need good soil to grow our food, and it takes a long time to make more.

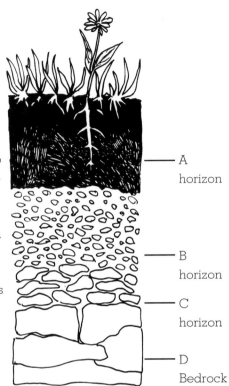

A horizon

B horizon

C horizon

D Bedrock

DON'T FORGET CLAY

■ One of the most important minerals found in soil—or anywhere else—is clay. Clay makes up about a third of all sediments on Earth. We use it to make so many things—bricks, pottery, tile, china, and cement, to name a few.

■ The most useful clay mineral is called *kaolin*; this is what we make pottery and china from. Another is *bauxite*, a tropical clay where most of our aluminum comes from. Another common clay is *montmorillonite*, mostly made from volcanic ash.

■ All clays are made of sheets of minerals that may slide apart when wet. If you're taking a rainy day hike and the trail has lots of clay in it, watch out: wet clay can be as slick as ice!

■ Where does clay come from? Like all other sediments, it comes from the breakdown of rocks. Clay minerals are formed when rainwater causes rocks containing feldspars to weather and fall apart. Some of the chemicals in feldspar wash away, and clay is what's left behind.

MOSS + ROCK GARDEN

DELICATE MOSSES IN VARIOUS SHADES OF GREEN CAN BE REPLANTED TO GROW OVER BEAUTIFUL ROCKS TO MAKE AN INTERESTING TABLETOP GARDEN. HUNT FOR MOSSES IN DAMP PLACES, BUT DON'T OVERLOOK CREVICES IN ROCK WALLS, CRACKS IN SIDEWALKS, AND THE BARK OF OLD, ROTTING TREES.

HAT YOU NEED

- *Collection of fresh mosses and lichens*
- *Shallow dish, such as a plant saucer or a dish garden planter*
- *2 to 3 handfuls of pebbles*
- *Several trowels of rich garden soil or well-rotted compost*
- *10 to 12 medium-sized rocks*

WHAT YOU DO

1. Collect mosses and lichens in wooded areas or parks or damp areas of a yard. There are many kinds of mosses and lichens. Some are fuzzy and green and look like velvet. Others look like tiny ferns. Lichens, which are really two plants that grow together—one an algae and the other a kind of fungus—often look like curly, leathery, gray-green skins attached to tree bark or rocks. Look around rotting tree stumps or on

rocks near streams or springs. As you collect, keep the plants in plastic bags with a little water in the bag to keep the plants damp.

2. Place a layer of pebbles in the bottom of the planter or dish. Then add a layer of soil. Arrange rocks over the soil and tuck the mosses in among the rocks. Finish by watering the garden.

3. It is important to water the moss garden often—every other day or even every day, depending on the dryness of the room. Mosses and lichens need dampness to live. They don't mind being cold (in fact, they do better in cool places than in hot, dry places) as long as they are wet. Try misting your garden every day with cool water, in addition to watering it.

Snowflake obsidian

HUNTING FOR Clay

You can buy clay in a craft-supply store, but you can find your own if you know what to look for and where to look. The nice thing about finding your own clay is that the pieces you make from it will have come from your own special place on the earth and will remind you of that place whenever you look at or use them.

WHAT YOU NEED

- *Trowel*
- *2 buckets*
- *Sieve or strainer: To make your own, nail four pieces of 1-by-2-inch (2.5 by 5 cm) lumber to form a square, and then use a staple gun to attach a square of hardware cloth to the wooden frame.*
- *Piece of window screening as big as the sieve or slightly larger*
- *Old T-shirt*
- *Piece of plywood at least 3 by 3 feet (91 by 91 cm)*

WHAT YOU DO

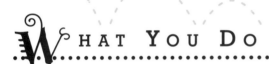

1. The best place to find clay is the banks of a creek. Walk in the shallow parts of the creek and watch for places, low on the bank, where the soil looks slick or slippery. Often clay is bluish gray or rusty orange. It will almost always be a different color from the regular soil nearby. The best test is to feel the clay. It should stick together and feel slippery when it's wet. Try rolling a chunk of it into a worm. If the worm holds together without completely crumbling, you have found clay.

2. Dig the clay, trying not to get ordinary soil or sand mixed in with it. Use a bucket to carry the clay.

3. Now you must clean the clay. Fill the bucket three-quarters full with clay; then add water almost to the top of the bucket. Use your hands to break up lumps of clay. The object is to mix the clay and water thoroughly. Take out any large rocks or twigs.

4. After the clay and water are mixed, you will have a bucket of what is called *slip*. Place the sieve over the second bucket, and pour the slip through. The sieve will catch any large or medium-sized rocks or twigs or other material.

5. Wash out the first bucket and the sieve. Spread the screen on the bottom of the sieve and place the sieve and screen on top of the bucket.

6. Pour the slip through the screen/sieve. This time smaller rocks and debris will be caught by the screen. The slip should be fairly smooth and clean by now. Some people stop after this step. If your slip feels silky smooth, go on to step 9. If it feels gritty, go to steps 7 and 8 first.

7. To get the slip even cleaner, you can sieve it through a cloth. Wash out the empty bucket and put it inside the old T-shirt so that a single thickness of cloth is stretched over the opening of the bucket.

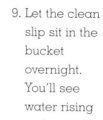

8. Slowly pour the slip through the cloth. The T-shirt will droop and stretch, so pour slowly. If it droops too much, pull it tighter. You may have to add some water to the slip so that it will go through

the T-shirt. It may take awhile for the slip to seep through the shirt. If the shirt becomes clogged, take it off the bucket and rinse it.

9. Let the clean slip sit in the bucket overnight. You'll see water rising to the top after a couple of hours. Pour or scoop the water off as it rises. Continue scooping off water until you get as much off as you can.

10. Pour the thick slip onto the piece of plywood so that even more water can evaporate. Put the plywood out in the sun, but be sure to cover it or bring it inside if it rains! Check the slip often. As soon as it is thick enough

for you to shape into a ball, roll or scrape it off the plywood, and store it in a plastic bag. Let it sit for a couple of weeks and it will be nicer to work with. Be sure to keep the bag sealed.

A Primitive Kiln

Did you know that you can bake or fire clay in your own backyard using a process that is thousands of years old? With help from an adult, you can build and use a simple primitive kiln that will turn your clay objects into hard, permanent pieces with a beautiful smokey gray or black color.

What You Need

- Hammer
- Awl or large nail
- Metal garbage can with a lid
- Large flat-head screwdriver
- Bricks or flat stones to put under the kiln
- Bucket of water
- Enough dry sawdust to fill the garbage can
- Old newspapers
- Matches
- 3 small wads of wet clay
- Hot pad
- Medium-sized rock to weight down the can lid

What You Do

1. Using the hammer and nail or awl, punch a row of three holes on each of four sides of the can. **1** Use the screwdriver to enlarge the holes until they are at least ½ inch (1.5 cm) across.

209

2. Place the bricks or stones on the ground for the kiln to stand on. It's best to put the kiln on ground that has no grass growing on it and to clear away any dry leaves or other things that could easily catch fire. Keep the bucket of water nearby to use in case of an emergency.

3. Put 4 inches (10 cm) of sawdust in the bottom of the kiln.

4. Carefully place the first layer of clay pieces you want to fire, leaving 2 to 3 inches (5 to 8 cm) between each piece and 4 inches (10 cm) between the pieces and the kiln walls. If you are firing bowls or pots, fill the insides of them with sawdust, too.

5. Cover the layer of clay pieces with 3 to 4 inches (8 to 10 cm) of sawdust, and place another layer of clay you want to fire.

6. Keep layering your clay pieces until you reach the top 6 inches (15 cm) of the can. Then add 2 inches (5 cm) of sawdust and finish off with twists of news-

paper. To make a twist of newspaper, first pleat half a sheet of newspaper. Then twist the folded paper, starting at the center. **2**

7. Place the twists of newspaper side by side to fill the top layer of the kiln.

8. Put three small wads of wet clay equal distances apart on the rim of the can. These will hold the lid up enough to vent the fire and let it breathe.

9. **Ask an adult to light the newspaper.** Once the twists have caught fire, rest the lid on the clay wads to cover the kiln.

10. Check the fire often until it is going smoothly. Make sure the sawdust lights after the newspaper twists burn out. If you see smoke coming from the can, the fire is lit. If the sawdust stops burning, add more newspaper twists and **have an adult relight them.** You should not see flames after the newspapers burn out, but you should continue to see smoke. Put a rock on the lid to hold it in place.

11. What you are aiming for is a slow, even smoldering that burns from top to bottom. Sometimes it takes several tries to get the kiln started. There is very little danger of a fire starting from a metal can kiln. Keep the cover on when you aren't around, and you can leave it for several hours and even overnight. Place a sign warning people not to touch it.

12. After 24 hours, when smoke is no longer coming from the kiln, remove the rock and lift off the lid. Be sure to use a hot pad for this operation. The sawdust should be black and the top layer of clay pieces should be visible. Let the pieces cool (may take several more hours), then carefully remove them. Brush off any remaining sawdust.

13. Pieces fired in a primitive kiln are not waterproof. They are stronger than they were before being fired, but they are still rather easily broken, so handle them with care. Rub the pieces with a soft rag to bring out the black, gray, or white shine.

Clay Beads

BEADS MADE OF CLAY AND FIRED IN A PRIMITIVE KILN HAVE A DARK SMOKEY GRAY, MYSTERIOUS LOOK. THEY MAKE BEAUTIFUL NECKLACES OR DECORATIONS ON BOOKS. IF YOU LEAVE OUT THE HOLES, YOU CAN USE THEM FOR GAME STONES.

WHAT YOU NEED

- Two large handfuls of clay
- 12-inch (31 cm) piece of dental floss
- 2 old corks
- Round toothpicks or uncooked spaghetti

WHAT YOU DO

1. Before making beads (or anything else out of clay), you need to wedge the clay in order to get rid of air bubbles that could cause it to break when it is fired. Wedge the clay by slamming it down on a tabletop, then pounding and lifting it, turning it, and pounding it again. Continue pounding-lifting-turning the clay for ten minutes.

2. To see if the clay is thoroughly wedged, try this: Tie each end of the dental floss to a cork. Hold the floss taut by pulling on the corks, and use it to cut through the lump of clay. Examine the flat sides where the slice was made: they should be smooth. If they are, slam them together and go on to the next step. If there are any holes or cracks, continue wedging for a few more minutes, then test again.

3. Take a small pinch of clay and roll it into a ball or a cylinder. If you want a square-sided bead, flatten each side and each end by gently tapping it on the table. Use a toothpick to draw designs on the bead.

4. Holding the bead gently between your thumb and index finger, poke a toothpick or a piece of uncooked spaghetti through the bead until it sticks out the other end. Leave the toothpick or spaghetti in there. It will burn away when the bead is fired, leaving a clean hole.

5. Place the finished beads in a single layer—not touching each other—on cookie sheets or old pie tins or on pieces of wood where they won't be disturbed. Let the beads dry for several days. To check for dryness, hold one of the biggest beads against your cheek. It should not feel cool. If it feels cool, put it back and let the beads dry for a few more days.

6. You are now ready to fire your beads. See the instructions on page 209 for making and using a primitive kiln.

Earth CRAYONS

Keep your eyes open for beautiful colors of soil and clay when you go for a walk. When you find some, scoop up a trowel or two, and store it in a plastic bag. When you have a good collection of several different colors of browns, reds, yellows, and oranges, you can make earth crayons.

What You Need

For each color:

- Sifter
- 1 cup (145 g) of sifted soil
- Heavy cloth, such as an old dish towel (optional)
- Hammer (optional)
- 2-quart-size (2 l) saucepan
- Piece of beeswax, about ½ by 2 by 2 inches (1.2 by 5 by 5 cm); sold at many craft-supply stores

- Piece of paraffin the same size as the beeswax; sold at grocery stores
- Clean empty tin can, 16-ounce-size (454 g) or larger
- Hot pad
- 4 teaspoons of turpentine
- Old wooden or stainless steel spoon; do not use sterling silver as it conducts heat
- Several sections of old newspaper

214

WHAT YOU DO

1. Sift the soil or clay to get out all pebbles and pieces of debris. The finer the particles, the better. If the soil is lumpy, break it up with your fingers first. For the finest soil, pour the soil into a heavy cloth and pound it with a hammer.

2. Fill the saucepan with 2 inches (5 cm) of water.

3. **Ask an adult to help you with the rest of this project.** Place the beeswax and the paraffin in the tin can and place the tin can in the pot of water. Carefully put the pot on a stove and bring the water to a boil. When the water begins to boil, turn down the heat so that it simmers but does not boil hard.

4. After a few minutes the wax and paraffin will melt. When this happens, carefully add the turpentine. Stir it, and then slowly add the cup of sifted soil. Stir until the soil is completely mixed into the wax and paraffin.

5. Use the spoon to scoop out the waxy soil. As it is scooped, it should be drained slightly against the side of the can. This mushy, waxy soil is VERY HOT. Be extremely careful when handling it. The mush should be placed in a couple of small mounds on several thicknesses of newspaper. Let the mush cool some, until you can see the liquid wax at the edges of the mound turning white and hard. While the mush is cooling, tap it lightly with the back of the spoon to make a patty, like a mudpie, so that it will cool faster.

6. After a few minutes the mush will be cool enough to handle, but still warm enough to be soft. **Ask your adult friend to test the mush for coolness.** When it is cool enough to handle (usually about ten minutes), scrape it into a pile and begin to form your crayons. Here's how to form them: Push the mush into a snake shape about 3 inches (8 cm) long. With your thumb on one side and your other fingers on the other side, pinch the top of the snake into a long wedge shape. Next, lift the snake (the bottom should be flat, the top pointy), and turn it so that the bottom becomes a side. Flatten and shape this side just like you did the first one. Finally, turn the snake to its third side and flatten and shape. You should now have a crayon that has three long, flat sides. Flatten the ends, and put it aside to cool completely while you form the other crayons.

7. To make other colors, clean out the tin can (or use another can) and repeat steps 1 through 4.

8. These crayons work best on rough, dull-finish paper, such as charcoal or construction paper. Experiment to see what works best with your crayons. Each type of soil will give a slightly different kind of crayon. If the soil that you use has mica dust in it, your crayons will have glitter dust in them! Because your colors will be limited to the colors that soil comes in, try combining them with cut or torn colored papers when you make pictures and designs. If you draw a picture of your backyard or the woods down the street, you'll have the satisfaction of showing the true colors of the rocks and soil in your neighborhood.

Rocks That Grow

*A*lthough lots of people have a favorite rock they carry in their pocket like a pampered pet, rocks aren't alive (oh, you knew that!). But did you know that some rocks can "grow"?

The most well-known type of growing rock is limestone, which grows into huge, thick *coral reefs*. The "coral" part, of course, is really a small, wormy animal that looks like a miniature sea anemone.

What does a wormy little animal have to do with rock, and why isn't it swept away by the ocean waves? This animal discovered the art of building construction way before we humans did. Corals are clever enough to secrete the mineral calcium carbonate to glue themselves together in sturdy underwater apartments. Some of these coral condos are called staghorn coral because they look like antlers. Others are called brain coral because they look like you-know-what, often several feet in diameter. These fancy structures provide shelter for colorful fish, crustaceans, and algae.

You may think that a tiny animal can't make all that much rock. The secret is... lots of tiny animals! Millions of little corals working for thousands of years can secrete a lot of limestone. If you have any doubts, check out the Great Barrier Reef, off the east coast of Australia. It's more than 1,200 miles (1,920 km) long—and all built by coral.

Corals sometimes live along the coast, and sometimes on the top of huge ocean islands called *atolls*. These atolls are the carcasses of giant volcanoes that are sinking slowly back into Earth's hot mantle. The coral animals need to be near sunlight, so they keep growing upward (and adding limestone) as fast as the island sinks. When they die, their limestone skeletons crumble in the waves, sink to the bottom, and are covered by more skeletons. This growing pile of sediment gradually becomes sedimentary rock (see page 62). Atolls may be a mile high—all underwater and all made by coral.

Another kind of rock that grows is *dripstone*, or cave rock—which is also limestone. When groundwater seeps through the limestone around a cave, it picks up the limestone mineral, calcium carbonate. If the water seeps through the roof of a cave and evaporates, it leaves behind its mineral load, a drop at a time. This mineral gradually builds into needle-shaped *stalactites* that hang from the ceiling like icicles. If the water drips to the floor, it builds up *stalagmites*—blunt, upside-down icicles.

This doesn't happen overnight; it may take dozens or even hundreds of years to grow an inch of dripstone. Sometimes stalactites and stalagmites join, forming thick *columns* from roof to floor. The dripstone formations in Carlsbad Caverns in New Mexico are so spectacular that visitors come to see them from all over the world.

Left: Coral reefs in the Virgin Islands

Top: Stalagmites and stalactites in the "Kings Palace" in Carlsbad Caverns National Park in New Mexico

Right: Other cave formations in Carlsbad Caverns

Limestone CAVE

This simple experiment lets you watch a process that takes many, many years in real life.

What You Need

- Scissors
- Clear plastic bottle, such as a small bottled-water container
- Piece of aluminum foil
- Large nail
- Glass bottle or jar with an opening larger than that of the plastic bottle
- 5 cups (725 g) of sand
- Spoon or trowel
- 1 cup (200 g) of granulated sugar or sugar cubes
- 1 cup (236.6 ml) of warm water

5. Put a 2-inch (5 cm) layer of damp sand in the plastic bottle. Press it down so there are no air spaces.

6. Put a 1-inch (2.5 cm) layer of sugar or sugar cubes on top of the sand. Be sure it is pressed against the side of the bottle and filled in solidly. The sugar represents limestone under the ground.

7. Put another 2- or 3-inch (5 or 8 cm) layer of sand on top of the sugar. Press out all spaces. You should be able to clearly see three layers.

8. Pour ½ cup (118.3 ml) of warm water on top of the top layer of sand. Wait until it drains down, and then pour the other ½ cup (118.3 ml) of water. Watch what happens to the limestone (the sugar) after two or three hours. What has caused the caves that you see? What does this show you about how caves form underground?

What You Do

1. Cut off the bottom half of the plastic bottle. Remove the cap.

2. Fit the piece of aluminum foil over the opening of the plastic bottle. Use the nail to punch a few small holes in the foil.

3. Place the plastic bottle inside the opening of the larger glass bottle.

Garden MARKERS

Brightly painted stones make cheerful garden markers. No more wondering what you planted when all those look-alike seedlings come up!

What You Need

- *Smooth potato-sized rocks, the flatter, the better*
- *Old pie pan*
- *Acrylic paints*
- *Paintbrushes*
- *Container for water*

What You Do

1. Wash the rocks and let them dry completely.

2. Paint a picture of a different plant on each rock.

3. Let the paint dry completely before placing the markers in your garden.

ROCK JEWELRY

A ROCK NECKLACE OR RING IS A WONDERFUL WAY TO SHOW OFF SOME OF THE MOST INTERESTING OR BEAUTIFUL ROCKS IN YOUR COLLECTION. IT TAKES PRACTICE TO USE NEEDLE NOSED PLIERS, AND AT FIRST THE ROCKS MIGHT KEEP JUMPING OUT OF THEIR WIRE CAGES. BUT WITH A LITTLE PATIENCE, YOU'LL SOON BE DESIGNING YOUR OWN ROCK JEWELRY.

WHAT YOU NEED

- *Assortment of interesting small rocks*
- *Roll of soft jewelry wire, gold- or silver-colored (sold in craft-supply stores)*
- *Wire cutters*
- *Needle nosed pliers*
- *Thin leather thong or heavy cotton string, 12 inches (31 cm) long*

WHAT YOU DO

To make a necklace

1. Place the rocks on a table in the order you would like them to hang from the necklace.

2. You must attach a wire to each rock. Use the wire cutters to cut 12 inches (31 cm) of wire. Place the rock on the wire near the middle of its length. Hold the rock down while you wrap one end of the wire

over the rock as in figure **1**. Now bring the other end of the wire over the rock, crossing over the first end of the wire. **2**

3. Turn the rock and wire over and repeat step 2. **3**

4. Twist the wire a few times as you pull the wire ends up toward one end of the rock. **4**

5. Use the needle nosed pliers to help twist one of the ends of wire into a small loop. **5**

6. Wrap the wire ends a few times to tighten the neck of the loop, then snip off both wires as close as possible to the loop neck. Use the needle nosed pliers to flatten the pointy ends of wire and to push them against the neck of the loop. **6**

7. Wrap all the other rocks with wire in the same way.

8. Slip the first rock by its wire loop onto the thong or string and place it where you want it to be. Carefully tie a knot to hold the rock loop in place. Twist the loop so that the front of the rock is facing front when the necklace is on the table.

9. Tie all the other rocks onto the necklace the same way.

10. Try on the necklace, tying it in back so that it hangs the way you want it to.

To make a ring

1. Use the wire cutters to cut two pieces of wire, each about 15 inches (38 cm) long.

2. Lay the wires side by side on the table and place a rock on top of both wires, midway along their lengths. **7**

3. Wrap both wires at once over the rock. Twist the wires. **8**

4. Now wrap the two wires on the left side all the way around the rock in the other direction from the first wrap, and meet the other wires at the same twisting spot. Twist all four wires again. **9**

5. Form a finger-sized loop with the two longer wires, twisting them a couple of times under the rock to hold the loop. **10**

6. Use the wire cutters to snip off all four wire ends as close as possible to the twist under the rock. Use the needle nosed pliers to flatten the short wire points and to press them into the twist.

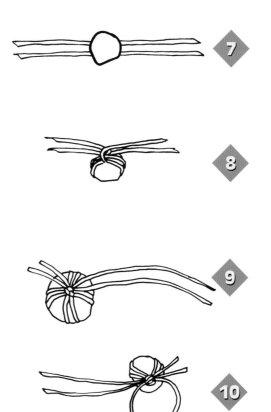

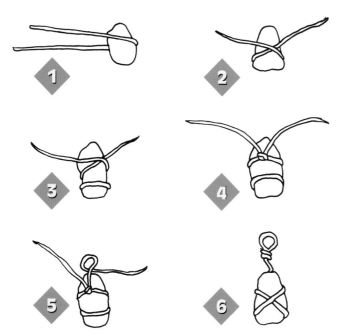

Fossils: Signs of Ancient Life

Some fossils look like their modern relatives, such as oysters, clams, possums, sharks, and horseshoe crabs. Others, such as flying reptiles and piglike, cud-chewing beasts, look more like extraterrestrial creatures from a bad dream!

*i*magine this: an insect becomes caught in the sticky resin of a pine tree. The tree blows down in a storm and is covered by a mud slide. Millions of years later the insect is found perfectly preserved in the resin, which has turned to a stone called *amber*.

But every fossil gives us clues about what—or who—lived on the earth millions of years ago.

And this: a dinosaur walks across a field, its huge feet sinking into soft sand. A dry wind blows and the footprints fill with dust. Later the prints are buried in sand, which hardens into sandstone. Millions of years later the sandstone erodes and exposes the footprint.

In a few places, paleontologists have found whole, large animals or plants. For example, a few woolly mammoths have been found perfectly preserved in permafrost in Siberia. Near Los Angeles, California, whole saber-toothed tigers and other large animals were fossilized when they fell into a big tar pit. And in the desert

And this: a young man is fishing on a lake shore in Africa three million years ago. A sudden noise frightens him and he falls into the lake and drowns. A storm covers him with mud, so that his bones are preserved and hardened into stone.

In all these stories, the insect, the dinosaur footprint, and the early human have become *fossils*. *Paleontologists*, the scientists who study fossils, roam the world finding teeth, bones, leaves, or footprints that have turned to rock.

of Arizona there are whole trees that have been turned to stone, or *petrified*.

Unfortunately, these fantastic signs of ancient life are very rare. It takes very special conditions to make a fossil, and most animals vanish without a trace.

Think of an ancient fish that dies. Chances are another fish would quickly eat it, or it would decay. The bones would probably fall apart and dissolve in water. Even if it were preserved, a flood might come along and wash it away or break it to bits.

For the fish to become a fossil, it has to be quickly buried in mud or shale. Then it has to be protected against erosion for many thousands of years while all the atoms of its bones are replaced by minerals. Finally it becomes a rock (a fossil) within a rock (a sedimentary rock).

This is why most fossils are formed in the ocean. On land, dead organisms are exposed to weathering by rain and wind—the forces that wear away rocks. In the ocean, dying organisms sink to the bottom where they are protected from the weather. Most ocean critters are tiny, floating plants or animals called *plankton* which have limestone shells; these shells easily harden into tiny limestone fossils.

We can learn a lot about the ancient world from fossils. For instance, if we find warm-water plankton all over the world in a certain time, we can be pretty sure the climate was warm when they lived. If we find cold-loving plankton, we can bet that this plankton lived in an ice age, when glaciers covered much of the earth.

Man pointing to dinosaur tracks east of Moenkopi. Coconino County, Arizona

Fossil Cast

FossiLS ARE INTERESTING RECORDS OF THE PAST, BUT THEY ARE ALSO BEAUTIFUL TO LOOK AT. IN THIS PROJECT YOU CAN SPEED UP TIME AND MAKE A FOSSIL MOLD OR CAST IN JUST A FEW HOURS. YOUR FOSSIL CAST WILL HAVE THE SAME DETAILS AND DELICATE PATTERNS THAT A REAL FOSSIL HAS.

What You Need

- *Chunk of plasticene (modeling) clay the size of your fist*
- *Dull table knife*
- *2 paper cups; bottom should be 2 to 3 inches (5 to 7 cm) in diameter*
- *A well-formed seashell, small bone, or seedpod*
- *About ½ cup (63 g) of plaster of Paris (sold at hardware and hobby- or craft-supply stores)*
- *¼ cup (59 ml) of water*
- *Spoon*

1. Make a ball of clay and flatten it until it's about 1 inch (2.54 cm) thick and smooth on top. Trim the circle of clay with the knife until it fits into the bottom of the cup.

2. Slide the clay into the cup, flat side up. Carefully press the object you want to fossilize into the clay until it's half buried. Then carefully lift the object out of the clay. You will be able to see an impression or print of the object.

3. Pour ½ cup (63 g) of plaster of Paris into the other paper cup. Add ¼ cup (59 ml) of water to the plaster of Paris and stir until the mixture is smooth. Leave it alone for five minutes.

4. After five minutes, the plaster of Paris mixture will have thickened. Pour it into the other paper cup right on top of the clay. Let this sit for an hour without touching it.

5. After an hour, the plaster of Paris should be almost completely hard. It will feel cool, and you will still be able to make marks in it, so be careful with the next step. Carefully tear away the sides of the paper cup and remove the clay and plaster. Holding the clay part with one hand and the plaster part with the other hand, gently separate them.

6. Clean off the clay part and put it away. You can use it for other projects. Use the knife to carefully trim away any rough edges from the plaster fossil cast. Smooth out the edges, then let it dry for a day or two until it no longer feels cool when you hold it against your cheek. Be sure to let it dry slowly and not in an oven or in the sun. Drying it too quickly could cause it to crack.

SEED CAST MEDALLIONS

USING THE PROCESS FOR MAKING A FOSSIL CAST (SEE OPPOSITE PAGE), YOU CAN MAKE CASTS OF SMALL LEAVES, SEEDPODS, DRIED FLOWERS, BONES, SHELLS, AND EVEN FEATHERS. A FEW EXTRA STEPS TRANSFORM THESE FOSSIL CASTS INTO MEDALLIONS TO USE AS HOLIDAY DECORATIONS, WINDOW ORNAMENTS, OR WALL HANGINGS.

WHAT YOU NEED

- *Chunk of plasticene (modeling) clay the size of your fist*
- *Scissors*
- *2 paper cups; bottom should be 2 to 3 inches (5 to 7 cm) in diameter*
- *Small, hard objects to cast, such as seedpods, leathery dried leaves, shells, bones, feathers*
- *¼ cup (59 ml) of water*
- *Food coloring*
- *Spoon*
- *½ cup (63 g) of plaster of Paris (sold at hardware and hobby- or craft-supply stores)*
- *Large nail*
- *Small container to hold glue*
- *Waterproof white craft glue*
- *Paintbrush*
- *Thin string or ribbon*

WHAT YOU DO

1. Make a ball of clay and flatten it on both sides so that it is smooth, round, and about 1/2 inch (1.5 cm) thick.

2. Cut a ring out of the paper cup, about 1/2 inch (1.5 cm) wide.

3. Press the ring into the flattened clay. Be sure the paper cuts slightly into the clay as this ring will form a container for the plaster of Paris.

4. Press the object that you want to cast into the clay so that it's at least half buried. If it is a thin object, such as a leaf or feather, use the flat bottom of a cup or glass to press.

5. Carefully remove the pressed object. Be sure to get out any crumbs or broken pieces.

6. Pour ¼ cup (59 ml) water into the second paper cup. Add a few drops of food coloring to the water and mix it in. Then pour ½ cup (63 g) plaster of Paris into the water. Stir quickly, and let the mixture sit for five minutes undisturbed.

7. After five minutes, the plaster of Paris mix will be slightly thickened. Stir it again, then pour a layer about ¼ inch (1 cm) thick into the paper ring on top of the clay. Let it sit undisturbed for one hour. Don't worry if some plaster of Paris leaks out from under the paper ring; just add a little more to the ring to replace what leaked out. The plaster will quickly thicken and stop leaking.

8. After one hour, carefully tear the paper ring away from the medallion and lift the medallion from the clay. The plaster will still be cool and wet, but it will be firm, and you will be able to see all the fine details of the fossil cast. Carefully poke a hole in the top of the medallion with the nail. Let the medallion dry for a day or two until it no longer feels cool when you hold it to your cheek.

9. When the medallion is completely dry, paint all surfaces with white glue. The glue will dry clear and will protect the medallion against water and dampness.

10. Put string through the hole in the top of the medallion and hang it in a window, on a holiday tree, or on a wall.

THE Big Time LINE

IT'S HARD TO UNDERSTAND THE ENORMOUS NUMBERS WE MUST USE WHEN WE TALK ABOUT THE AGE OF THE EARTH. THIS PROJECT WILL LET YOU SEE A MODEL OF THOSE BILLIONS OF YEARS.

WHAT YOU NEED

- *5 sheets of construction paper, each a different color*
- *Scissors*
- *Glue stick or white craft glue*
- *Markers or crayons*
- *2 empty toilet paper rolls or an empty paper towel roll*
- *Transparent tape*
- *Piece of ribbon, 2 feet (61 cm) long*

WHAT YOU DO

1. Fold each of the pieces of colored paper in half lengthwise. Press hard on the fold to make a good crease. **1**

2. Cut each piece of paper along the crease. Glue the two halves of each piece of paper together end to

228

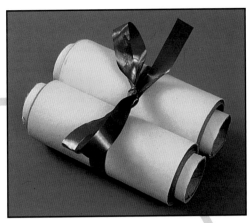

end. You should now have five long pieces of colored paper. Each piece represents 1 billion years. **2**

3. Now glue all five sheets end to end. You will now have one very long piece of paper.

4. Lay the piece of paper out on the floor. Begin marking at the left end of the strip of paper. Halfway across the first color (where the two pieces of paper are glued together) draw the Earth, for this is approximately when the earth was born—four and a half billion years ago.

5. Next move to the next color, and draw a fossil halfway across this color (again, in the place where the two sheets are glued together), for this is the time of the oldest fossils that have been found— three and a half billion years ago.

6. Leave the next two colors blank. These are the two billion years during which only a few organisms seem to have existed. If you want, you can draw a few more fossils in these colors, but only draw a few, and space them out widely.

7. Halfway across the last color draw some fish, for this is the time when abundant life seems to have started, around 500 million years ago.

8. Now things get crowded. Right after the fish, draw some reptiles and amphibians (snakes, frogs, and salamanders, for example). Keep them in a top-to-bottom row, because there are more creatures to draw in the few inches of space that you have left!

9. After the reptiles and amphibians, draw some mammals, such as wooly mammoths, tigers, or horses.

Right after the mammals, draw some dinosaurs, for they lived and died out between 200 and 100 million years ago.

10. Finally, at the very end of the time line, draw some humans, for it was not until the past 50 to 75 thousand years that humans have lived on the earth—as far as we know. Fifty thousand years sounds like a long time until you see how small that section of the time line is compared to four and a half billion years!

11. Tape a paper roller to each end of the time line to make a scroll. **3**

12. Roll the scroll from both ends toward the middle. **4**

13. Tie your scroll with the piece of ribbon. Find a big space on the floor to unroll it so that you get to see the whole long line at once. What a lot of years!

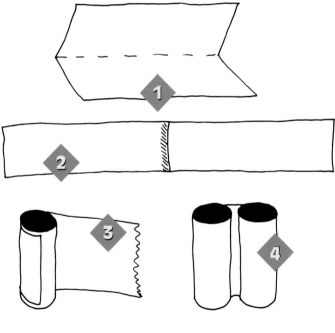

The Geologic Time Scale

For most of human history, people thought Earth was created only a few thousand years ago. Now we know that our story is a whole lot longer—and it's a story written in the rocks. But for a long time, nobody could "read" the rocks: they all looked, well, like rocks!

One of the first people to learn to read the rock record was William Smith, an engineer helping dig canals in England two centuries ago. As the work crew dug through sedimentary rock full of fossils, Smith could see that the rocks were arranged in layers, or *strata*. Some of these strata were paper-thin; others were several yards thick. After a while he realized that each stratum had to be younger than the ones below it and older than the ones above it. This makes sense—unless

someone is running around sliding young rocks underneath older ones!

The next thing Smith realized was that strata were piled up in the same order from one region to the next. He could tell partly by the way the rocks looked and

partly because each layer had its own special mix of fossil creatures. Smith became so familiar with these fossils that he could tell at a glance which layer a particular piece of rock came from. Little by little, geologists around the world found that rocks with the same fossil "fingerprints" are the same age no matter where they are found.

About a century after Smith's work came another big discovery: that many rocks contain tiny amounts of *radioactive elements*. These elements, such as uranium, decay at a steady rate into "daughter" elements, such as lead. Knowing the rate of decay and the amount of parent and daughter material, geologists have a "radioactive clock" for calculating a rock's age. This is how we know that Earth is about 4.6 billion years old.

Using these tools, geologists have been able to draw a chart of history called the *geological time scale*. This scale, which took a century and a half to construct, is

| Paleozoic Era ~ 345 million years | Mesozoic Era ~160 million years | Cenozoic Era ~ 65 million years |

divided into four large units of time called eras—the *Precambrian*, *Paleozoic*, *Mesozoic*, and *Cenozoic*, *Eras*—and each era is many millions of years long.

The first three eras are named after the Greek words for modern life, middle life, and ancient life. Each era is divided into smaller divisions called periods. These periods were named after the places where the rocks were first found: The *Devonian Period* was named for rocks found in Devon, England; *Permian* after the region of Perm in Russia; *Jurassic* for the Jura Mountains of Europe; and so on. The most recent (*Tertiary*) period is divided into shorter *epochs*.

The Precambrian Era is the longest part of the time scale: 80 to 85 percent of the entire age of the earth. This is everything that happened on earth from 4.5 billion years ago until 570 million years ago. Yet we know much less about that time. It was so long ago that most of the rocks—along with the evidence of what happened—have been weathered and eroded, or "morphed" into new rocks.

Far left: Part of star dunes. Northeastern part of Namid Desert, South West Africa

Left: Dunes in northwestern Namid Desert in South West Africa. The dune in the background is about 300 feet (92 m) high.

Above: U-shaped valley in Glacier National Park, Montana

Right: Yellowstone Canyon. Yellowstone National Park, Wyoming

Minerals, Minerals, Everywhere

*W*e find many reasons to study minerals. One is to enjoy their beauty. Another is to understand their structure.

A third reason is that so many of the things we use in modern life come from minerals, including all the metals and thousands of chemicals.

For example, iron is found in minerals such as *magnetite* and *hematite*. Aluminum is mined from the mineral *bauxite*. Titanium, used to strengthen the metal of the space shuttle, is refined from the minerals *ilmenite* and *rutile*.

Nonmetal minerals are equally important. How would our food taste without salt, evaporated from seawater? How would we plaster our walls without *gypsum*, another evaporite? How would we make glass without quartz? Or pottery without clay? Or lime without limestone?

The problem, of course, is to find places where there is plenty of the mineral we want. And that's what geologists spend a lot of their time doing.

In this chapter, we'll learn that rocks are made of minerals, and minerals are made of crystals, and crystals are made of atoms. And we'll also begin to see why so many minerals are so important to our lives.

Crumpled layers in evaporite salt deposits near the Dead Sea in Jordan

Building Blocks of Rocks

You know that a house is often built out of boards, nails, and bricks, but do you know what rocks are built out of? The building blocks of rocks are *minerals*. A rock like limestone is built mostly of a mineral called *calcite*; rocks like granite or gneiss are built out of several minerals.

Now comes the hard question: What is a mineral? The easy answer is that a mineral is a form of *matter*, like water or air or wood. But what do the *insides* of a mineral look like? If we had super-vision and could peer through any kind of matter, we'd see that a mineral is made of huge numbers of *atoms*. An atom is so small that if we enlarged one 100 million times, it would still be only about the size of a pea!

Until about a century ago, scientists thought atoms were the smallest possible particles. Now we know that each atom has a large *nucleus* at the center and tiny *electrons* that vibrate around the nucleus.

Halite

These electrons are like the nails of a house; they hold matter together. Here's how. Some atoms have "extra" electrons and some have "missing" electrons. When an atom of an element with extra electrons, such as sodium, meets an atom of an element that needs an electron, such as chlorine, the atoms join together by sharing an electron and becoming a *molecule* of sodium chloride. Sodium chloride is also known as the mineral *halite*, and when you find it in the grocery stores, it's called table salt.

When atoms are sharing electrons like this they are "charged up" with energy and are called *ions* (EYE-ons, from the Greek word "go"). The attraction between some ions can be as strong as...rock! These strong attractions, or *bonds*, between ions are what make a

mineral so hard and rigid—just like a house held together with strong nails.

Some ions have just one kind of matter, some have more. When atoms of carbon and oxygen bond together, they make an ion called *carbonate*; atoms of silicon and oxygen make an ion called *silicate*. These big ions can share electrons to make minerals just like smaller ions can. Carbonate ions can combine with calcium ions to form calcium carbonate, or *calcite*, the mineral of limestone. The chalk your teacher uses to write on a blackboard is a soft kind of calcite.

There are other common minerals in rocks—*oxides* (oxygen combined with other ions), carbonates, *sulfides* (sulfur combined with other ions), *sulfates* (sulfur-oxygen ions combined with other ions), and *phosphates* (phosphorus-oxygen ions combined with other ions).

That's too many minerals to keep straight, you say? How can anyone possibly understand rocks? Don't worry: most rocks only have a few different kinds of mineral building blocks, and more than half of the Earth's rocky crust is made up of silicate minerals. Whew! The commonest mineral of all is a silicate called *feldspar*, a name that comes from two Swedish words, feld (field) and spar (mineral). Swedish farmers gave it that name because their fields had so many feldspar rocks they could hardly plow through them.

Another really common mineral, *quartz*, has only silicon and oxygen ions. Most of the beach sand in the world is little specks of quartz. Feldspar and quartz together make up three-fourths of the Earth's crust. So if you look at the big picture, most rocks really aren't all that complicated.

Rock Candy

One type of crystal that you can grow not only looks pretty, but tastes good, too! If you have lots of patience, you can make rock candy out of sugar and water.

What You Need

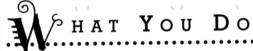

- 1 cup (200 g) of granulated sugar
- ½ cup (118 ml) of water
- Cooking pot
- Food coloring (optional)
- 2 heat-proof glass jars or small bowls
- Dull table knife

What You Do

1. Put 1 cup (200 g) of sugar into the pot. Add ½ cup (118 ml) of water, but do not stir the mixture.

2. **Ask an adult to help you put the pot on the stove over medium high heat.** Let the mixture come to a boil and let it boil for one minute without stirring.

3. If you want colored candy, add a few drops of food coloring as the mixture boils.

4. **Ask an adult to help you carefully pour the mixture into one or two glass jars or small bowls.**

5. Let the containers sit undisturbed for two weeks. Gradually crystals will begin to form. Check the candy every day. When a crust forms on the surface, tap it with a dull knife to break the crust so the water can continue to evaporate. Otherwise, don't move or disturb the containers.

6. When the crystals are as big as you want them to be, break the candy from the container with a table knife, and prepare yourself for a sweet and tasty treat. Yum!

Crystals and Their Shapes

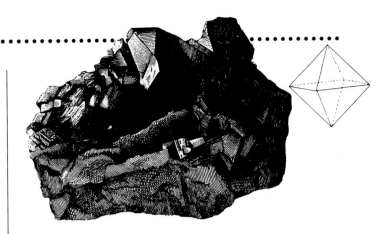

One way to understand minerals is to think about the way they're put together—their *structure*, or shape.

Think about water. When water is a liquid or a gas, the molecules can zoom around in any direction. The molecules don't have any structure. But when water temperature drops below 32°F (0°C), the molecules slow down and freeze into a rigid geometric shape, like eggs in a carton. This rigid shape is a *crystal structure*. Every time ice freezes, anywhere in the world, it always makes the same crystal structure. One way to describe a mineral is: a solid material that always has the same crystal structure.

Quartz cluster

If we could see into a crystal, we would see that all the ions are locked in little clusters called *unit cells*. The unit cell of the mineral halite (which we also call table salt) has four chloride ions and four sodium ions. Each unit cell is so small that in a single grain of salt there are more than 5 million million million of them, all arranged in regular patterns like bricks in a wall.

If we take a large chunk of halite and tap at it carefully with a hammer, we can break it into a squared-off piece that looks just like a life-sized ice cube. And here's the really amazing part: The shape of a large cube of halite is a life-sized version of the shape of its little, invisible unit cells! This is true for all minerals: the shape of a large piece is a gigantic version of its microscopic unit cells. (Pretty cool, eh?)

One more thing: knowing a mineral's crystal structure helps to explain why it breaks in a certain way. Minerals always break in the direction where the ionic bonds between unit cells are weakest. For example, the unit cells of mica are arranged in flat sheets, like playing cards. The bonds between the sheets are weak, and you can easily pull them apart with a fingernail. In other minerals, like quartz, the unit cells may be locked together in all directions—and they won't break at all.

To get a good idea of how beautiful some crystal patterns are, take a magnifying glass outside after it snows and look at a snowflake. When water freezes, its hydrogen and oxygen ions lock into many different hexagonal (six-sided) shapes. And it's true what they say about snow flakes: hexagons can be arranged in so many different ways that the crystal pattern of every flake is different!

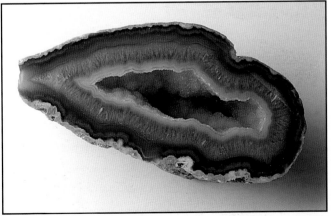

Geode crystals growing inside holes in rocks

How Crystals Grow: The Birth and Growth of Quartz

Most crystals are born in magma, that fiery liquid rock many miles below Earth's surface. There is so much heat in magma that atoms and molecules zing back and forth like angry bees. They have too much energy to hook up and form solid matter. But if the magma rises near the Earth's surface and starts to cool, all those particles lose energy, slow down, and look for partners.

The hot molecules that make quartz are called *silica*. The atoms of silica always lock into a shape called a *tetrahedron*, which means four-sided figure. A silica tetrahedron has one silicon ion sitting right in the middle of four oxygen ions, all of them sharing

Smoky quartz

electrons. That's why the chemical symbol for silica is written SiO_4—one silicon, four oxygens.

When magma cools, each silica tetrahedron starts to huddle up with another tetrahedron, then another, and another, up and down and sideways. Many millions of them all lock together in a growing crystal of solid quartz. If the magma cools too fast, like volcanic lava that is thrown onto the earth, the tetrahedra don't have time to get organized into crystals and instead they form a dark glass called *obsidian*.

The silica tetrahedra of quartz hold each other so tightly in so many directions that they are almost impossible to break apart. That's why quartz is so tough, and why we find quartz sand on beaches all over the world. All the other rock minerals have broken apart or dissolved in the rain, leaving the tough little crystals of quartz all by themselves.

Most quartz crystals don't grow big enough to see.

Rutilated quartz

That's because in a magma, lots of chemicals are trying to grow all at once, some faster than others, and they get in each other's way. But sometimes, in a protected pocket of rock where a crystal has plenty of room and no competition, it might grow to several inches or more. A really perfect quartz gemstone would look like a clear, six-sided cigar with hexagonal pyramids at each end; this is called *rock crystal*.

Sometimes atoms of other elements in the magma get mixed up with the silicon and oxygen. This can change the color of quartz to yellow, pink, brown, or even black. Violet quartz, which has tiny amounts of manganese or iron, is called *amethyst*, a semiprecious gem. When tiny air bubbles make the quartz cloudy, it's called *milky quartz*. Other gems of quartz are *agate* (with colored bands), *flint* (gray), *jasper* (red), and *opal* (quartz plus water). The best thing to do with these minerals is to make them into jewelry!

Quartz cluster

THE ATOMS IN A CRYSTAL
ARRANGE THEMSELVES IN AN
ORDERLY WAY. YOU CAN WATCH
HOW THIS HAPPENS IN THIS
EXPERIMENT. PRETEND THAT
THE MARBLES ARE THE ATOMS
IN THE CRYSTAL.

CRYSTAL Theory EXPERIMENT

WHAT YOU NEED

- *Between 40 and 100 marbles, all the same size*
- *Several round, shallow containers, such as large jar lids, plastic tub lids, and cake pans; the more marbles you have, the bigger the container you can use; if you have only 40 marbles, use jar lids and round plastic tub lids.*
- *Notebook and pencil*

WHAT YOU DO

1. Place a few marbles in a single layer in your smallest container. Notice whether or not they form a pattern all by themselves.

2. Continue adding marbles until no more will fit in a single layer. Now look for a pattern. Draw one if you see one.

3. Repeat steps 1 and 2 in a larger container. Notice any patterns and draw them, too. Compare them to the patterns you found in the smaller container.

4. Repeat steps 1 and 2 in the largest container that you have. What happens? Try taking out a few marbles

and stirring the others around so that the patterns are broken up. Now put the marbles back in until no more will fit in a single layer. What happens? Draw any patterns that you see. Compare the patterns in the biggest container with those from the other containers. What do you think would happen if you had twice as many marbles and a really big container?

5. A real crystal isn't flat, so an actual crystal pattern is not in a single layer and is deep as well as wide. This experiment does give you an idea of what happens in a crystal when atoms arrange themselves.

Growing CRYSTALS

You've probably come across directions for growing a crystal garden. Unfortunately, most crystal gardens don't look anything like gardens. They are fairly messy looking—not at all decorative like a small moss or cactus garden. So we aren't calling this project a garden at all. What it is, though, is a very interesting experiment that lets you get a good look at the fascinating patterns of crystals as they form.

What You Need

- *Minerals to grow into crystals:*
    Epsom salts (sold at drugstores)
    table salt
    alum (sold at many drugstores and craft stores)
- *Water*
- *Measuring cup*
- *Small pot*
- *Wooden spoon*
- *Food coloring (optional)*
- *Several small glass custard dishes or bowls*
- *Glass canning jars—one for each kind of crystal you want to grow*
- *Handful of clean rocks or pebbles*
- *String*
- *Scissors*
- *Pencils or thin sticks—one for each kind of crystal you want to grow*
- *Notebook and pencil*

WHAT YOU DO

1. First decide which kind of crystals you want to grow. Then make a solution of that mineral and water. Here are the "recipes" using the different minerals.

Epsom salts

Put 1 cup (200 g) of Epsom salts into ½ cup (118. 3 ml) of water in a pot. **Ask an adult to help you bring the mixture to a boil on the stove.** Stir the mixture to help dissolve the Epsom salts. What you are making is a saturated solution, which means that there is almost too much Epsom salts to stay in solution in the water.

Table salt

Mix ¾ cup (177.4 ml) of water and ½ cup (100 g) of salt in warm water. Stir until the salt dissolves. Again, this is a saturated solution, so some salt crystals may sink to the bottom and refuse to go into solution. That's okay.

Alum

Mix ¼ cup (50 g) of alum into 1 cup (236.6 ml) of hot water. Stir to dissolve the alum.

If you want to grow colored crystals, add a few drops of food coloring to each mixture now.

2. Now you have some choices to make. One way to grow crystals is simply to pour the solution over a few clean pebbles in the bottom of a glass bowl. Pour enough so that the solution reaches the top of the pebbles. Another way is to pour the solution into a glass jar and hang a string from a pencil so that the string dips into the solution. You might want to try both ways of growing crystals; pour half your solution in a bowl and half in a jar.

3. Here's your next choice. Crystals grow differently in a hot place than they do in a cool place. It might be interesting to put one container in the refrigerator and another in a warmer place, such as near (but not on) a heater, or in a sunny spot. If you are growing more than one kind of crystal, be sure to label each container by sitting it on top of a piece of paper with its name written on the paper.

4. Leave the crystal solution undisturbed for several hours. It's important not to move the container while crystals are forming. After a few hours, check to see what has happened. This would be a good time to make a drawing of whatever crystals have formed and to note the time, the temperature of the location, and any other facts that might be important.

5. Check the containers the next day and see what has happened. Make more notes and drawings. You may be able to come to some conclusions, such as what difference the temperature of the location makes to the way crystals grow. You can also note differences in the way crystals grow on rocks versus the way they grow on a string.

6. When some good-size crystals have formed, try scooping them out with a spoon. Many crystals will hold their wonderful shape as long as you don't get them wet. If you get a lot of pretty crystals, you could arrange them in a small glass bowl for a different kind of "crystal garden."

PAPER Crystal MODELS

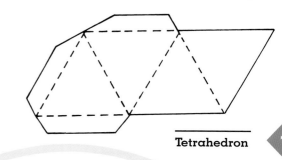

Tetrahedron ① 1

THE FORMS OF CRYSTALS HAVE FASCINATED PEOPLE SINCE THE TIME OF THE ANCIENT GREEKS. HUNDREDS OF YEARS AGO, SCIENTISTS BEGAN TO DEVELOP THE STUDY OF MATHEMATICS BY INVESTIGATING THE FORMS OF CRYSTALS. THE FOUR CRYSTAL FORMS IN THIS PROJECT APPEAR IN MANY MINERALS. YOU CAN HANG THESE CRYSTALS IN A WINDOW OR USE THEM FOR HOLIDAY DECORATIONS.

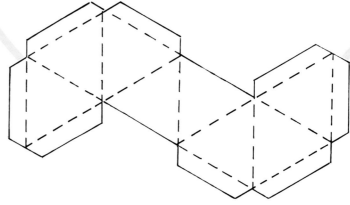

WHAT YOU NEED

Octahedron ② 2

- *Several sheets of tracing paper*
- *Sharp pencil*
- *Pencil sharpener*
- *Colored construction paper or origami paper*
- *Transparent tape*
- *Scissors*

- *Paper clip*
- *Ruler*
- *White craft glue*
- *Glitter (optional)*
- *Thread*
- *Sewing needle*

240

1. Enlarge the patterns on a copier by 200%. Then trace them carefully.

2. Turn over the sheet of tracing paper and color the entire back of the traced figure with pencil. Be sure to color the back of all lines.

3. Place the tracing paper, right side up, on top of the back of the colored paper. You want the pencil side to be against the back of the colored paper. Lay both sheets of paper on a hard surface, such as a tabletop. You may want to tape the tracing paper to the colored paper to hold it securely.

4. Trace over all the lines of the pattern, pressing hard with a freshly sharpened pencil. Your lines must be sharp and clean. Trace broken lines over the dotted lines, and solid lines over the solid lines.

5. When you have finished tracing, remove the tracing paper. You should be able to see the design in light lines. Use those lines as a guide to cut along all solid lines. Do not cut any dotted lines. Those are the fold lines.

6. When you have cut out the figure, use the ruler and paper clip to crease all the dotted lines. Creasing them will make them easier to fold. Using the ruler will insure that the lines are straight.

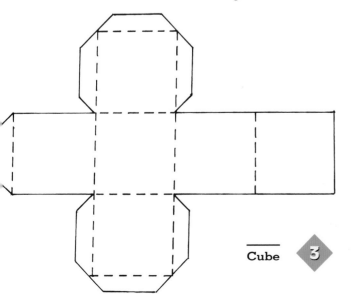

Cube 3

241

7. Fold all the dotted lines that you have creased. All folds should be made with the wrong side of the paper facing up. As you fold, you will easily see how to glue the tabs to form the figure.

8. After the figure is folded, put a few drops of glue on each tab. Now fold the figure, and when you come to a tab, press it against the side or tab that it is next to. On some of the forms, you may have to hold the tab for a few minutes while the glue sets. (The folds should be hidden inside the paper forms.) If you are making the dodecahedron, trace the pattern, and cut two pieces of paper at the same time, so that you have two identical patterns. When you fold and glue each of the two sides, you will see that they form bowl-like shapes with pointy edges. Put glue on the edge tabs of one of the bowls and fit the other into the jagged shapes to form one crystal.

9. If you want to decorate your crystals, use glue and glitter.

10. Thread the needle, knot the thread, and push it in and out of one point on each crystal. Hang the crystal from the thread.

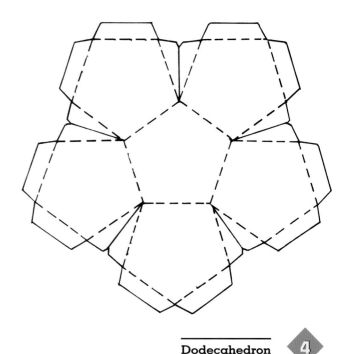

Dodecahedron 4

A Mineralogist: The Sherlock Holmes of Geology

Y ou've just used a rock hammer to carefully chisel out a golf ball-sized chunk of mineral from the side of a cliff. Its color and shape appeal to you, but what kind of mineral is it? There are hundreds of different minerals…how can anyone know what each one is?

Mineralogists are scientific detectives who use many clues to identify minerals. One of the best clues is *hardness*. You may think all minerals are hard—hard as a rock, right? Some are, some aren't. Quartz is too hard to scratch with a pocketknife, but gypsum is soft enough to scratch with your fingernail. Talc is the softest mineral known (it makes the talcum powder you may put on after a bath) and you can scrape it into powder with your fingernail.

Mineralogists use the *Mohs' scale*, shown on page 244, to rank minerals, from 1 (talc) to 10 (diamond). Any mineral on the scale will scratch any mineral below it. Topaz (#8) scratches quartz (#7); quartz scratches feldspar (#6); and so on.

What makes a mineral hard? Think about crystal structure and the strength of the bonds between atoms. The stronger the bonds between atoms in all directions, the harder the mineral.

Okay, some of you are now asking: If diamond is the hardest mineral, how can you cut a diamond to make diamond jewelry? Here's the answer: With another diamond!

Another clue to identify a mineral is its *cleavage*. Think of a butcher with a meat cleaver: he whacks a chunk of meat and makes a clean, flat cut. If you break a mineral by dropping it on a rock or breaking it with a hammer, it will cleave along flat surfaces, or planes. Each mineral has cleavage planes that are always at the same angle from one another. By measuring that angle a mineralogist has an important clue. (See "Crystals and Their Shapes," page 235.)

You might think the *color* of a mineral is a dead give-away. It is, for a few minerals, such as blue azurite, green malachite, yellow sulfur, or red cinnabar. But usually minerals occur in several colors. Fluorite may be colorless, yellow, brown, pink, greenish, blue, violet, or almost black.How can that be? It's because color is not something solid that's part of the mineral; it's really just light-wave information gathered by your eyes. The "color" of these light waves gives you information about how they've been bent and reflected as they pass

Fluorite

through the crystal structure of a mineral. If there is a tiny change in crystal structure, the light is bent differently and you see a different color. For example, the mineral corundum is made of aluminum oxide and usually has a white or grayish color. But when just a few atoms of chromium replace a few atoms of aluminum, it becomes blood red and we call it a ruby. Or when you add a dash of iron and titanium, corundum becomes a deep blue and we call it a sapphire. (And pay a lot of money for it!)

Because color isn't very reliable, mineralogists also use another clue called *streak*. A streak is a thin swipe of powder you can make by scraping a mineral against a white porcelain plate. If the mineral is really hard, you can scrape the mineral with a file to get some powder onto the streak plate. A streak may surprise you: The mineral magnetite has a blackish color, but its streak is always red! And the streak of the yellowish mineral pyrite is always greenish black.

Luster is another clue. Luster is what the surface looks like: metallic—a polished metal surface; vitreous—bright as glass; resinous—sticky as the sap on a pine tree; pearly—pretty as a pearl; and greasy—like a film of oil. Two minerals may have the same color but different lusters.

Still another clue is *density*—how heavy the rock feels. If you hold the same-size chunk of a light mineral like quartz in one hand and a heavy mineral like magnetite in the other, you can easily tell the difference. In heavy

Mohs' Scale

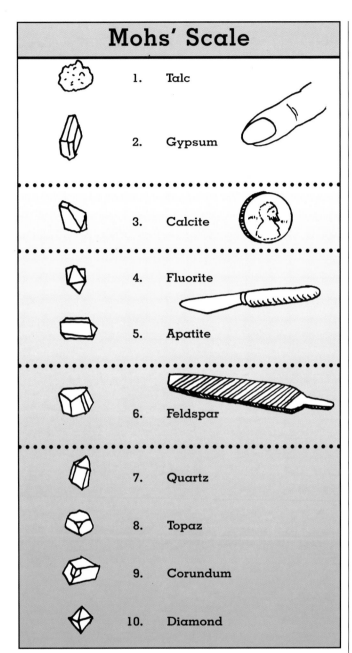

1. Talc
2. Gypsum
3. Calcite
4. Fluorite
5. Apatite
6. Feldspar
7. Quartz
8. Topaz
9. Corundum
10. Diamond

minerals (gold is one of the heaviest), the atoms are packed tightly together.

So, about that chunk of mineral you're holding. If you were a mineralogist, you'd put all these clues together to decide what this mineral is. Does it have a whitish streak, a vitreous luster, a density of 4, and hardness of 9? Then you're probably holding a chunk of corundum. Does it have a yellow streak, a metallic luster, a density of 17, and a hardness of 3? Then get on down to the bank: That's a nugget of gold in your hand!

What a Gem!

Aquamar

We all know what a *gem* is—the shiny, glittering stone found in jewelry. But what makes a gem a gem?

If you've read this far in the book, you probably know that a gem is a mineral. But not all minerals have what it takes to be a star: perfect crystals, beautiful colors, and sparkling lights. If there are any bubbles, cracks, or cavities—forget it! That mineral hasn't got what it takes! A gem is also rare.

A crystal of quartz, even a perfect one, wouldn't interest

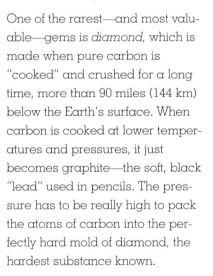

Opals

a picky gem collector. There is just too much quartz in the world.

One of the rarest—and most valuable—gems is *diamond*, which is made when pure carbon is "cooked" and crushed for a long time, more than 90 miles (144 km) below the Earth's surface. When carbon is cooked at lower temperatures and pressures, it just becomes graphite—the soft, black "lead" used in pencils. The pressure has to be really high to pack the atoms of carbon into the perfectly hard mold of diamond, the hardest substance known.

Now you're wondering—if diamonds come from so deep in the Earth, how do they get to the surface? No one knows for sure. But most diamonds are found in long volcanic channels called *kimberlite pipes*, named after the city of Kimberley, in South Africa. Very hot magma was probably pushed upward through these pipes by explosive gases—like the engine of a Saturn 5 rocket turned upside down. But the magma stopped and cooled (with its load of diamonds) before reaching the surface. The largest known diamond, which was found in a kimberlite pipe, weighed almost a pound and a half (681 g)!

Beryl (named for the rare metal beryllium) is usually a pale grayish or greenish mineral that may grow to enormous size: one crystal has been found that was 30 feet (9.2 m) long and weighed over 25 tons (27 t)! Even more interesting to us is the beryl that has just the right mix-

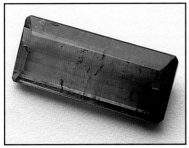

Termaline

ture of atoms to turn it bright green. This is the gem we call *emerald,* one of the most valuable on earth.

Corundum is a simple mineral containing just aluminum and oxygen. Like beryl, it may be a drab gray to yellow or colorless. But add a dash of the metal chromium and you've got yourself a *ruby!* Or a touch of iron and titanium and look out! It's a *sapphire!* Even ordinary corundum is so hard (9 on the Mohs scale) it is used to make emery paper, a very rough abrasive.

Opal is a class of gems that is just like quartz except that it doesn't have a crystal structure; it is more like glass. It may be pale pearly blue or pink to nearly black; the gem collector's favorite is milky white opal.

Sapphires

Topaz

A mineral needs one more thing to be a precious stone: it has to be really hard. Can you think why? Most gems are formed inside igneous or metamorphic rocks. The rocks gradually weather, fall apart, and dissolve, except for the hard quartz—and gems. Many gems are swept downhill by rain into rivers, where they tumble along with pebbles and rocks— which would chip or break them if they weren't really hard. At the end of their journey they often settle in piles of sand,

Ruby zoicite

Peridot

Citrine

pebbles, and rocks along the mouth or banks of a river. There they can be found by a hard-working (and very lucky!) rock hound— who could be you!

Amesite

Gems from a river bank look very different by the time they wind up in jewelry stores. About 400 years ago, people discovered that you can make a gem look even more brilliant and colorful by making small, flat cuts called *facets* in the surface. Jewelers figured out the exact angles of these facets so that the light that enters a gem is trapped for a while, bouncing back and forth inside the gem and increasing its brilliance.

Amethyst

Treasure Boxes

THESE BEAUTIFUL BOXES LOOK AS IF THEY WERE MADE OF GOLD, SILVER, AND PRECIOUS GEMS, BUT IN FACT THEY COST VERY LITTLE TO MAKE. THEY MAKE WONDERFUL GIFTS, OR YOU CAN USE THEM TO HOLD YOUR PERSONAL TREASURES.

What You Need

- *Variety of small, interesting boxes, such as egg crates, small wooden cheese boxes, or small cardboard boxes; don't use boxes with waxy, shiny surfaces*
- *Gold, silver, or copper acrylic paint (sold in art- or craft- supply stores)*
- *Paintbrush*
- *Aluminum foil*
- *White craft glue that dries hard and clear*
- *Small bowl*
- *Food coloring*
- *Spoon*
- *Scissors*

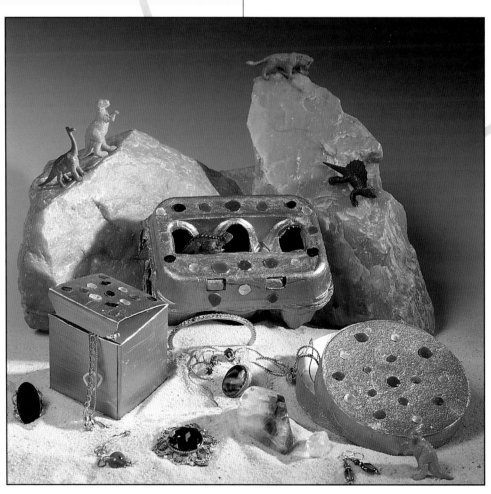

What You Do

1. Begin by painting the boxes with metallic paint. Paint all the surfaces, and let them dry.

2. While the boxes are drying, make your gems. On a table or countertop, spread out a piece of smooth, unwrinkled aluminum foil, about 12 inches (31 cm) long.

3. Pour a small amount of glue into the bowl and add a few drops of food coloring. Stir with the spoon to thoroughly mix the coloring. You can either use pure colors or mix colors, such as red and blue to make violet.

4. Drop blobs of colored glue onto the aluminum foil, keeping them at least 1 inch (2.5 cm) away from each other on all edges. The blobs will spread out a little, depending on how much food coloring you have added. If they spread until they are completely flat, mix more glue into the colored glue to thicken them. The blobs should form rounded ovals and circles on the aluminum foil.

5. When you finish with one color, wash out the bowl and spoon and make another color. Leave one batch white so that it will dry clear and you will have some "diamonds."

6. Let the gems dry for several days. You can tell they are dry because they will become glassy. At first the blobs will look like colored glue. As they dry, a clear colored, glasslike ring will form around the outside of each gem. The more the glue dries, the bigger the glassy ring will become. When the gems are completely dry, they will look like diamonds, rubies, topazes, or other gems.

7. After the gems are dry, cut them out with scissors into round, oval, or faceted shapes.

8. Glue the gems to your painted boxes. Fill the boxes with treasures!

Rock Mobile

A MOBILE MADE OF ROCKS SOUNDS STRANGE! ROCKS ARE HEAVY, AND OBJECTS IN A MOBILE SEEM TO FLOAT. BUT PRETTY ROCKS CAN BECOME AIRBORNE; TWISTING ON THE ENDS OF THIN PIECES OF THREAD, THEY CAN NICELY DECORATE A WINDOW.

What You Need

- Collection of small, pretty rocks
- Twig that has at least one branching fork
- Roll of silver- or gold-colored jeweler's wire (sold at craft-supply stores)
- Wire cutters
- Needle nosed pliers
- Spool of sturdy thread
- Scissors
- Craft glue
- Large metal paper clip

247

Wʜᴀᴛ Yᴏᴜ Dᴏ

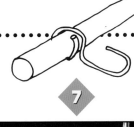

1. Select the rocks that you want to use. Place them on a table next to the twig and see if they look too big or too small.

2. You must attach a wire to each rock. To do this, begin by cutting 12 inches (31 cm) of wire. Place the rock on the wire near the middle of its length.

3. Hold the rock down while you wrap one end of the wire over the rock. **1** (Figures 1 through 6 are the same as for "Rock Jewelry" on page 222.)

4. Now bring the other end of the wire over the rock, crossing over the first end of the wire. **2**

5. Turn the rock and wire over and repeat steps 3 and 4. **3**

6. Twist the wire a few times as you pull the wire ends up toward one end of the rock. **4**

7. Use the needle nosed pliers to help twist one of the ends of wire into a small loop. **5**

8. Wrap the wire ends a few times to tighten the neck of the loop; then snip off both wires as close as possible to the loop neck. Use the needle nosed pliers to flatten the pointy ends of wire and to push them against the neck of the loop. **6**

9. Wrap all the other rocks with wire in the same way.

10. Tie a piece of thread about 10 inches (25 cm) long to the loop of each rock. Tie the other end of each thread to the twig in an arrangement that you like.

11. Dip your thumb and index finger of one hand in glue, and rub glue along the length of each piece of thread. Use the glue to stick the loose ends of thread to the main strings for a neater look.

12. Bend the paper clip into a large hook. Wrap one end of it around the middle of the twig, as in figure **7**. Use the other hooked end to hang the mobile.

How We Use Rocks and Minerals

You're sitting at the kitchen table, doing your homework or reading a newspaper. Ah, there's no place like home. But let's take a look around. Yikes! Better put on a hard hat! Your house is full of rocks and minerals!

Your family's stove and refrigerator and all the other metal appliances in your home are made from ores such as iron, chromite, and nickel. Those ceramic tile countertops, the linoleum floor covering, the dishes in your cupboard, even the paper you're reading contain clay minerals. There's quartz in your television, stereo, and watch. The "lead" in your pencil is made of a mineral called graphite.

Everything plastic and all the synthetic fabrics in your house—including, probably, the clothes and shoes you're wearing—are made of plant and animal fossils (better known as oil and gas). If your walls and ceiling are built of plaster or plasterboard, they contain gypsum—and if they're painted, they're covered with calcite and maybe some mica, too.

Even the food you eat is packed with minerals. Common table salt is actually tiny crystals of halite, or sodium chloride, formed thousands of years ago from evaporating prehistoric seas.

See? Your house really is full of rocks and minerals. Now take a look outdoors. (By the way, that glass window you're looking through is made of quartz sand.) Your sidewalk is paved with concrete (a mixture of crushed gravel, ground limestone, and sand). Most roads and streets are covered with asphalt (made from petroleum). Those cars driving by are running on gasoline extracted from fossils (oil). Automobiles, in fact, are a regular rock-and-mineral soup: glass from quartz, metal from ores, wire from copper, microprocessors from silicon chips, and plastic and fabric from petroleum. Why, the "rubber" tires alone contain zinc, sulfur, limestone, barite, magnesium, and a few different kinds of clays!

Above left: Mount Rushmore in South Dakota

Above: These skyscrapers are made almost entirely of rocks and minerals, from their cement foundation and marble walls, to their steel beams and glass windows. Charlotte, North Carolina

We use rocks and minerals in all sorts of ways: for building, for art, for tools, for medicine, for industry, for transportation. We make monuments of them to honor our heroes. We grind them into powder to make fertilizer and other chemicals. We wear them on our bodies, around our necks, and on our fingers. Why, rocks and minerals have been so important to humans for so long we even use them to describe our civilization's early history: The Stone Age, The Bronze Age, The Iron Age.

But whoa! Wait a minute! Earth's gifts to us, including its rocks and minerals, aren't endless. If we use them up, they'll be gone for good. Recycling the materials we've already used is a better idea than just digging up more.

Paperweight

When you become a rock collector, you will soon be faced with a problem: what to do with all the beautiful specimens you've found and just can't throw away. This paperweight is a good way to display small rocks because the water in it makes the colors and textures of the rocks look brighter and clearer.

What You Need

- *Clean, empty jar with a tight-fitting, screw-on lid*
- *Rocks, fossils, or seashells*
- *Enough water to fill the jar*
- *Chlorine laundry bleach*

What You Do

1. Remove the label from the jar by soaking the jar in warm water for 15 minutes.

2. Wash the rocks, fossils, or shells and place them in the jar.

3. Add water until the jar is three-quarters full. Then add bleach to completely fill the jar. (The bleach will keep algae from growing in the jar.)

4. Screw the lid on tightly. Wipe any water from the outside of the jar and the lid.

5. Turn the jar upside down to be sure it doesn't leak. If it does leak, try tightening the lid. If it still leaks, you may need to use a different jar and lid.

Sand Clock

CENTURIES AGO, BEFORE MECHANICAL CLOCKS WERE DEVELOPED, SAND WAS USED TO MEASURE TIME. YOU CAN BUILD A SAND CLOCK OF YOUR OWN TO TIME ALL KINDS OF THINGS— HOW LONG YOU WANT TO STAY ON THE TELEPHONE, HOW LONG TO COOK AN EGG, OR HOW MUCH TIME YOU WANT TO SPEND CLEANING YOUR ROOM!

What You Need

- *2 identical clear plastic bottles with screw-on tops, such as small bottled-water containers*
- *1 cup (96 g) of dry sand*
- *Sifter*
- *Bowl*
- *Funnel or piece of stiff paper rolled into a funnel*
- *Cork that fits snugly into the top of the bottles; use an old cork or buy one at a hardware store*
- *Plastic drinking straw*
- *Ruler*
- *Sharp knife*
- *⅛-inch (.5 cm) drill bit*
- *Hand drill or a brace and bit*
- *Clock or watch with a second hand*
- *Acrylic paints*
- *Paintbrush*

1. Wash the bottles and remove the labels. Remove and throw away the screw-on lids.

2. Sift the cup (96 g) of sand into the bowl. Be sure to get out all sticks, pebbles, and other debris. Also be sure the sand is completely dry. If it is damp, spread it out on a baking sheet for a day or so until it is dry.

3. Use the funnel (or the rolled piece of stiff paper) to help pour the clean sand into one of the bottles.

4. **Ask an adult to help you cut the end off the cork** so that it's about 1 inch (2.54 cm) long.

5. **Ask an adult to help you drill a hole down the center of the cork,** clear through to the other side. After you have drilled the hole, push the drill bit in and out of it a few times to clean out all crumbs of cork. This hole must be clean and smooth so that sand flows through it without sticking. To make it perfectly smooth, press a segment of the plastic drinking straw inside the hole as a liner. **1**

6. Plug the cork into the neck of the bottle that has the sand in it. Let half the cork stay sticking out. Now press the other bottle onto the cork, so that the two bottles are held together by the cork. **2**

7. The next step takes some patience. You must time the sand clock and adjust it so that it takes the right amount of time for the sand to drop from one bottle to the other. Turn the sand clock so that the bottle with the sand in it is on the top. Use your watch or clock to time how long it takes for all of the sand to drop down to the bottom bottle. If the sand stops flowing, carefully unplug the top bottle, and clean out the cork hole. Be sure to take out whatever was clogging up the hole. Then pour all the sand back into one bottle and start timing again from the beginning. It may take several tries before the sand flows smoothly. Once you know how long it takes the sand to travel from one bottle to the other, either add sand or take away sand to get the right amount for the time you want. For example, if you want your clock to be a five-minute clock, add or take away sand until it takes exactly five minutes for the sand in the top bottle to fall to the bottom bottle.

8. Decorate your sand clock with acrylic paints and enjoy watching the passing of time.

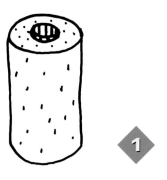

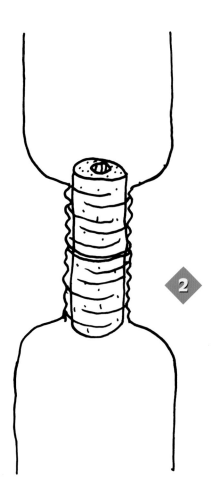

Trivet

Here's something useful and pretty to make when your collection of pebbles and rocks gets out of control! Use this trivet under hot dishes when you bring them to the table. You could also use it under a potted plant to catch drips of water.

What You Need

- *Sandpaper*
- *Piece of wood, about 6 by 6 inches (15 by 15 cm)*
- *Acrylic paint—any color that looks good with your pebbles*
- *2 paintbrushes, one thin, one fat*
- *Collection of pebbles of different colors, textures, and shapes: You can buy pebbles in pet stores that sell aquarium supplies if you don't have a collection of pebbles or can't find any you like.*
- *Waterproof craft glue*

What You Do

1. First sand the edges of the wood so they are smooth. Then use the thin paintbrush to paint one side and all four edges with acrylic paint.

2. While the paint is drying, plan your design. Move the pebbles around on a tabletop until you like the way they look. You might draw a sketch of your design to help yourself remember where to glue the pebbles.

3. When the paint is completely dry, use the fat paintbrush to spread a thick layer of glue in the first part of the design that you want to work on. Press the pebbles into the glue, making sure they are pressed against the board and surrounded by glue. The glue will dry clear, so don't worry about any glue globs!

4. Continue spreading glue and adding pebbles until the wood is completely covered. Fill in any open places or gaps between pebbles. Let the trivet dry overnight. It may take more than one day for the glue to dry depending on the weather. You can tell the glue is dry if it is clear.

Rocks for Building

Suppose you're an architect and your boss, the Pharaoh of all Egypt, wants you to build him something special, something big and impressive—and something that won't need painting or a new roof every few years. You suggest—a palm leaf and log pyramid? Off to the slave galleys, nincompoop! (Oh, now you say a stone pyramid...)

Rock buildings and steps on the volcanic island of Santorini, Greece.

The pyramids in Giza, Egypt.

For thousands of years, stone has been the natural choice for building. That's why the Egyptian pyramids and most other famous buildings and monuments from the past are still standing. Rock is tough, although, over millions of years, weather and other natural forces can wear down rock (see "Weather Wear," page 200).

The great pyramids of Egypt were built mostly of limestone taken from a quarry near Cairo. The largest of the pyramids, the Great Pyramid of King Khufu, has more than two million cut blocks of limestone, each weighing between two and four tons (1.8 and 3.6 t)! Most limestones used for building contain the fossils of shells from ancient seas. Because it's plentiful, limestone is the main ingredient in many famous structures, including the Notre Dame Cathedral in Paris.

Sandstone is another kind of sedimentary building rock used all over the world. Some types are too crumbly, but others are hard as, umm, rock. Different kinds are different colors, ranging from light to dark. Have you ever heard of New York City's famous "brownstone" houses and apartment buildings? They're made of brown sandstone. In Delhi, India, the spectacular impe-

rial palace called Red Fort is made of (you guessed it!) red sandstone. And the White House, in Washington, DC, is built of—well, actually, it's light-colored Virginia sandstone, painted white.

The fanciest of building rocks, marble, is limestone that has changed under pressure, becoming metamorphic. Pure marble is white, but other kinds of marbles have minerals in them that add color all over or in streaks or veins or swirls. Because of their handsome colors and smooth shiny surface, marbles give buildings an elegant look. One of the world's most impressive buildings, the Taj Mahal, is built of polished white marble decorated with inlaid gems!

Granite is harder than limestone, sandstone, or marble, so it stands up to weather best—but it's also the most difficult to cut into blocks. There are white, pink, red, gray, and black granites. Because it can be polished like marble but lasts longer, granite is a favorite for monuments and skyscrapers. The Greeks and Romans built many of their temples from granite. The Empire State Building is mostly granite.

These days, buildings are constructed mainly of manmade stone such as brick and concrete. But those materials begin with natural rock, too. Brick is made from soft clay that has been baked and hardened in a kiln. Concrete is a mixture of ground limestone, sand, gravel, and water. It was invented by the Romans, who used it to build such famous landmarks as the Colosseum in Rome, Italy.

MODEL Earth HOUSE

The earth is the most plentiful of all building materials. Many Native Americans living in the southwestern United States build adobe houses—houses made of mud and straw bricks. In this project you will make your own miniature adobe bricks and then use them to build model houses. The adults in your home will probably want to help with this project, because everyone likes to play in the mud. (Tell them to get their own bucket of clay!)

 ## WHAT YOU NEED

- Bucket
- Trowel
- Bucket of soil that is mostly clay
- Old newspapers
- Water
- Strainer made of coarse wire screen or a garden sifter

- Sturdy wooden spoon or stick
- Plastic dishpan
- Trowel of sand
- Scissors
- Handful of dried grass or straw
- Piece of cardboard about 2 by 3 feet (61 by 91 cm)
- Aluminum foil

- *Piece of wood approximately 1 inch (2.54 cm) thick, 2 inches (5 cm) wide, and 1 to 2 feet (31 to 61 cm) long; an old wooden ruler will do*
- *Metal spatula or dull dinner knife*
- *10 to 12 sticks as wide and long as pencils*
- *20 to 22 round sticks, slightly thinner than pencils, and about 10 inches (25 cm) long*
- *Several flat wooden sticks, such as frozen dessert sticks or wooden coffee stirrers*
- *Piece of black construction paper*

What You Do

1. Adobe bricks are made of clay, sand, straw, and water. When dried in the sun, they become hard. To make your miniature bricks, you need to find soil that has a lot of clay in it. (See "Hunting for Clay" on page 206).

2. Once you have your bucket of this kind of soil, you have to clean all big pebbles and other debris out of it. First, dump half the soil onto a pile of newspapers. Then, add water to the soil in the bucket and stir until the soil is completely mixed with the water. Next, pour the watery soil through the strainer into the dishpan. Throw away the pebbles and debris, and repeat the process until you have strained all of your soil. You now have a dishpan full of watery clay. Let it sit for a while until the soil settles to the bottom and you can scoop off most of the water.

3. Add a trowel of sand to the wet soil and stir until it is well mixed.

4. Use the scissors to cut the dry grass into tiny pieces, no longer than ¼ inch (1 cm)—the smaller, the better. Since your bricks will be small, the straw needs to be much smaller than real straw, too.

5. Add the straw to the brick mix and stir it well.

6. Cover the cardboard with aluminum foil. The foil will keep the bricks from sticking to the cardboard while they are drying.

7. Use the trowel to scoop out the wet mix onto the foil-covered cardboard. Drain off as much water as you can while lifting it out of the dishpan. Make a big flat cake, about ½ inch (1.5 cm) thick.

8. Put the cardboard in a sunny spot and let the clay and straw cake dry for about an hour.

9. After an hour, the cake should be partly dry. You will now cut it into bricks. First, use the flat stick to square up the edges of the big cake. Then use the spatula or knife to slice the cake into long strips, each about 1 inch (2.5 cm) wide.

may be too big. If the bricks crumble, mix up another batch but use less sand and smaller pieces of dried grass.

12. Now for the fun part. Peel the aluminum foil off the cardboard so you can use the cardboard as a base for your adobe house. Use some leftover adobe mud mixed with water for mortar to glue the bricks together. Here are some things to remember in building an adobe house:

~ *Lay the first row of bricks end to end, as in figure* **1**. *Lay the next row so that the bricks cover the cracks between the bricks on the first row.* **2**

~ *Put mortar on the bottom of each brick before you lay it in place. Simply hold the brick and press it into a puddle of wet mortar.*

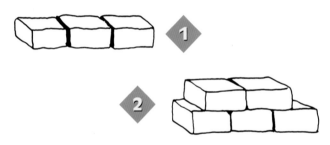

~ *For windows and doorways, lay a flat stick across the top of the opening (this is called a* lintel), *and then lay bricks on top of the lintel.* **3**

10. Now slice each long strip into ½ inch (1.5 cm) wide bricks. As you slice the bricks, use the knife to gently nudge the brick away from its neighbors so that all of its sides are open and it can dry better.

11. Place the cardboard full of bricks in a sunny spot to finish drying. This can take anywhere from another hour to another day, depending on the wetness of the mud and on the weather. When the bricks are dry, they will be hard and you can easily pick them up and handle them. If they are crumbly, they may have too much sand in them or the straw pieces

When you get to the top of the house, lay a row of peeled pencil-sized sticks across the walls, as in figure **4**. These sticks are called vegas, and they are made of peeled pine logs in real adobe houses. Place bricks between the vegas. **5**

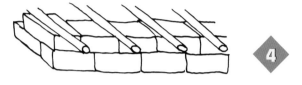

On top of the vegas, lay a roof of the thinner sticks. In a real adobe house, roofing paper would be placed over these sticks, so cut some black paper to the right size and place it on top to make the roof. Put a little mortar on top of some of the roof sticks to help hold the paper in place.

You can add a room or rooms to your house by building walls out from the first set of walls and laying vegas from wall to wall. **6**

Adobe houses usually have thick walls and not many windows. They are warm in winter and cool in summer because their thick walls provide good insulation. These houses are best suited to dry climates, because rain is their natural enemy. If heavy rains begin to wash away the walls, people can add more adobe mud to the walls to make them strong again.

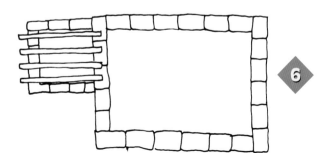

WINDOW Garden

SOME PLANTS STORE ENERGY AND FOOD IN ENLARGED ROOTS, SUCH AS BULBS AND TUBERS. YOU CAN GROW THESE PLANTS WITHOUT SOIL AS LONG AS YOU PROVIDE WATER AND A ROCKY BED FOR THEM. THIS IS A GOOD PROJECT TO SHOW OFF BEAUTIFUL COLORED OR UNUSUAL ROCKS THAT YOU FIND.

WHAT YOU NEED

- *Flower bulbs or carrots, radishes, turnips, or any other tuberous vegetable*
- *A collection of small- to medium-size pretty rocks*
- *A shallow bowl or an old pie tin*
- *Water*

WHAT YOU DO

1. If you are growing flower bulbs, you will first have to give the bulbs a cold period by putting them in a paper bag in the refrigerator for a few weeks. It is necessary to do this because bulbs naturally go through a cold winter outdoors before they sprout in spring. Making them sprout on a different schedule than their natural one is called *forcing bulbs*. Some garden centers sell precooled bulbs for forcing. They usually sell paper-white narcissus during late autumn. If you can't find these, or if you want to force tulip or other bulbs at a different time of year, simply give them a cool period in your own refrigerator.

2. Wash the rocks, then arrange them in the bowl or pie tin in a single layer.

3. If you are growing vegetables, trim off the bottom ½ inch (1.2 cm) or so of the fat part of the vegetable to give it a flat base to sit on.

4. Arrange the cooled bulbs or the trimmed vegetables on top of the rocks. If you are forcing bulbs, prop up the bulbs with rocks, but do not completely cover them. Be sure to plant the bulbs right side up.

5. Pour in enough water to wet the bottoms of the bulbs or vegetables.

6. Place your rock garden in a sunny window. Check it every day, and add water as needed. In a few days you should begin to see sprouts. Bulbs will take several weeks to bloom, but keep adding water, and your patience will be rewarded when you have beautiful flowers blooming in your house in the middle of winter!

TIN Lantern

LONG AGO PEOPLE MADE LANTERNS OUT OF TIN. THE TIN PROTECTED THE CANDLE FROM DRAFTS WHILE THE HOLES PUNCHED IN THE TIN LET LIGHT OUT IN A PRETTY PATTERN. THIS LANTERN IS SIMPLE TO MAKE AND, WHEN THE CANDLE INSIDE IS LIT, WILL CAST BEAUTIFUL DANCING LIGHT ON THE WALLS AND CEILING OF A DARKENED ROOM.

WHAT YOU NEED

- Empty aluminum can
- Black marker
- Sturdy log, nearly as wide as the can
- 2 or 3 nails of different widths
- Hammer
- Can opener—the type used to make triangular punctures
- Paintbrush
- Acrylic paints
- Small candle
- Candle holder

1. Thoroughly clean the can and dry it.

2. Lightly mark the outside of the can with dots where you want to create your pattern with holes. Your design should appear all around the can and on the unopened side.

3. Lay the can on the floor and slip the log inside it until the wood touches the unopened end. Use one of your legs to hold the log securely against the floor.

4. Use the hammer and nails to make holes through the can where you have made marks. Ask a friend or adult to hold the can still while you hammer.

5. Remove the log. Use the can opener to make large holes on the unopened end of the can (this will be the top of the lantern).

6. Paint a design all over the outside of the can.

7. Place the candle in the candle holder and put it on a table or mantle. **Ask an adult to light the candle.** Make sure the candle is at least 2 inches (5 cm) shorter than the height of the lantern. Place the can over the lit candle, turn out the lights, and enjoy the show!

Metals from Minerals

*i*magine you're a cave person thousands of years ago and you've just found a pretty blue or green rock. You figure you'll pound the rock into powder, mix in some grease, and make paint for decorating the cave walls. But sheesh, no matter how hard you hammer on it, the pesky rock won't break. Instead, it bends and flattens. What a worthless hunk of—hey, wait a minute. Maybe you could pound the stuff into the shape of a knife blade or scraper. That would be a lot easier than chipping away at flint. Hmmm....

Of course, nobody knows for sure, but that could be how the Stone Age ended and the Copper Age began. Scientists do know that humans began making tools of copper instead of stone about 10,000 years ago. A few thousand years later, someone discovered that you could make an even stronger metal by mixing a little *tin* with the copper. That mixture, the first *alloy*, was *bronze*. Bronze made sharper swords that could cut through a copper shield. Goodbye Copper Age, hello Bronze Age.

Eventually, about 4,000 years ago, ancient metalworkers learned to mine rock that contained iron, a super-strong and easy-to-sharpen metal. They heated

Copper

Pyrite

the ore in fire until the iron melted away from the rock, then hammered it into the shape of tools and weapons. That was the beginning of The Iron Age.

Many minerals, such as pyrite, magnetite, and marcasite, cointain small amounts of metals.

Minerals with large amounts of metals that can easily be separated are called *ore minerals*. These rocks are mined from the Earth's crust or dredged from lakes or streams. Then the ore is crushed and the metal is extracted from the "waste" rock and heated, or smelted, to make pure metal, like the eight major types described below.

Aluminum is the third most common element in Earth's crust and the most common metal. Aluminum is hard to take out of most rocks, except for the one called bauxite. Bauxite ore gives us strong, lightweight aluminum for buildings, cars and planes, foil, pots and pans, and lots of other uses.

Copper is the great-great-granddaddy of all metals. Workers used copper chisels to cut stone blocks for the pyramids! Today we still use copper for such things as wire and water pipes. We also mix copper with *zinc* to

Azurite / Malachite

make the alloy *brass*, and with tin to make bronze. Copper ores are colorful and look great in a collection. Some of the most important are chalcopyrite (gold-colored), *azurite* (blue), and *malachite* (green).

Iron is a really important metal. It's tough and hard but melts easily, so it can be poured into molds or flattened into sheets. We mix it with carbon and other elements to make alloys such as cast iron, wrought iron, and the most-used metal in the world: steel. *Hematite*, a bubbly looking mineral, is the main iron ore.

Magnesite

Lead is made from *galena*, a black, shiny mineral that's often found in limestone or with silver. Galena crystals are perfectly square and are used in crystal radio sets. Lead is used mostly in batteries and in materials that protect us against X rays and radioactivity.

Nickel is a strong, tough metal that stands up to high temperatures and hard wear. It's used mainly to add strength to alloys such as steel. It's also mixed with copper to make coins. The American nickel, or five-cent piece, has three times as much copper as nickel! The main nickel ores are *pyrrhotite* and *pentlandite*. Most meteorites contain nickel, too!

Tin comes from a hard, heavy ore called *cassiterite*. Tin is used mostly for plating metal products such as cans. It's also mixed with copper to make bronze, and with lead to make *pewter*.

Zinc is produced from an ore called *sphalerite*. The rock is usually dark black but can also be red, yellow, or green, so it's tricky to identify. Zinc is used to make brass and to give metals a protective coating.

Mercury is the only metal that's liquid even when it's not hot. It comes from an earthy red ore called cinnabar that is found in only a few places in the world, such as Spain, Italy, and the western United States. Mercury is used in thermometers, barometers, and as an ingredient in medicines and paint pigments.

Marcasite

Gold, Silver, and Platinum

Have you ever dreamed of finding a treasure chest? Eagerly, you open the lid and peer inside. It's full to the brim with pieces of—hey, what's this? Iron?

Not many people would jump for joy at finding a chest of iron or nickel or any of the other ordinary metals. But a box of gold! Wow!

For centuries we humans have valued *gold* and *silver* above all other metals. Over the past 100 years *platinum* has become an important precious metal, too. What makes them so special?

Platinum, gold, and silver aren't the rarest metals on earth. But they are uncommon—and, even more important—they're uncommonly beautiful. They glitter and shine. They're soft and easy to shape. And they don't rust or lose their beauty over the years.

Gold is especially good at keeping its spectacular appearance. When divers find gold coins from ancient shipwrecks, the coins are as bright and shiny as the day they were made—even after being buried in mud and sand and salt water for hundreds of years!

Silver is less valuable than gold partly because its surface reacts with the air around it and gradually darkens or tarnishes. Silver has to be polished occasionally to remove the tarnish and bring back its bright shine.

Platinum doesn't tarnish but also doesn't have the glamorous gleam of its cousins. Platinum is actually more valuable than gold, though, because it's in great demand in industry, for oil refining and for making low-pollution car exhaust systems.

It's no wonder that gold, silver, and platinum are prized for making jewelry, tableware, and other objects. All three are amazingly *ductile* (DUCK-tuhl). That means they can be hammered flat, stretched into wire, or molded into almost any imaginable shape. In 1902, a silversmith made a pair of silver water jugs for the Maharajah of Jaipur, India that are five feet three inches (160 cm) tall and hold 2,160 gallons (8,176 l) each!

Gold is the most workable of all the precious metals. It can be hammered into sheets, called gold leaf, so flat and thin that a stack of 250,000 is only one inch (2.5 cm) high! An ounce (or 28 grams) of gold can be heated and stretched to make a wire 60 miles (96 km) long! Egypt's famous King Tutanhkamun was buried in a coffin made of more than a ton of solid gold. China's emperors once wore robes woven of gold thread.

Of course, for centuries countries also have been using gold and silver for making coins. Platinum has been used for coins, too. Back in the days of Czar Nicholas I, Russian three-ruble pieces were platinum.

But precious metals are used for more than just money and luxuries. Over a third of all the silver mined in the United States is used for making and developing photographic film. Dentists use gold, silver, and platinum for fillings. And because they're terrific conductors of electricity, the metals also are used in electrical components, circuit boards, and computer chips.

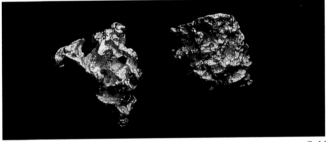

Gold

Platinum, silver, and gold are called *native* metals because they can be found in nature as pure metal. They don't always have to be processed into metal from mineral ore, the way aluminum has to be made from bauxite or lead from galena. Silver is mined either way; as "free" silver in *veins* or clumps, or in ores such as *argentite*. Most platinum occurs as small grains or flakes of free metal in nickel deposits. Gold is usually found in veins among quartz or with deposits of *pyrite*, a duller, brassy-looking mineral that's also called "fools' gold" because over-eager miners often mistake it for the real thing.

Collecting Rocks and Minerals

Have you ever picked up a really pretty or interesting rock and brought it home? Do you have a special box where you keep favorite rocks and other neat stuff? Then you've already started a collection!

Collecting rocks and minerals is a lot of fun. You can do it almost all the time, anytime: when you're walking with your friends, when you travel to different places, when you're exploring your neighborhood. After all, rocks are everywhere. You'll never run out of things to collect!

At first, you'll probably want to keep all sorts of rocks—anything that's especially beautiful or shiny or smooth or sparkly or bumpy or crumbly or...well, you get the idea. That's how most great collections start.

Sooner or later, though, you'll probably decide to specialize. Some people try to collect just one of as many different kinds of rocks and minerals as they can find. Others collect just certain types, such as igneous or metamorphic, or just rocks from certain places. You can build all sorts of different special collections: crystals, rocks from your home state or county, gemstones, rocks from your backyard; rocks from stream beds, fossils, rocks from the seashore, rocks you found on your summer vacation, rocks and minerals from foreign countries. The possibilities are endless!

Naturally, you'll want to show off your favorite specimens. You can build a collection box like the one on page 273, or you can buy plastic boxes with separate compartments.

Here are some other tips to help you build a terrific collection.

■ Don't worry if you can't figure out what kind of rocks or minerals you have. The pictures in field guides and geology books don't always look exactly like the specimens you find. Even professional geologists sometimes have a hard time identifying! Instead, label the rocks in your collection according to where you found them. Then, if you think you know what kind a specimen is, you can add that too.

■ Try not to gather too many rocks when you go collecting! Remember, rocks are a part of nature. Pick a few good specimens for your collection and leave the rest where you find them, undisturbed.

■ One of the best ways to learn more about collecting rocks and minerals is to join a rock hound club. Chances are there's one in your area. You'll learn the best places to go to look for specimens, and you might even be able to trade rocks with other members.

■ Look at other rock and mineral collections in museums, the geology department of a local college, and rock shops. Rock shops are an especially good place to buy hard-to-find specimens. Most also sell "starter" sets of mounted minerals for beginners.

■ Read books about geology and collecting rocks and minerals. Also, look in your local library or bookstore for collecting-site guides: books that describe and give directions to the best places in your region for finding good specimens.

Sand PAINTING

For hundreds of years, people from many cultures have created sand paintings as part of important ceremonies. Other sand paintings are not meant to last: they are made on the ground, and when the ceremony is over, the wind blows the art away. The sand painting in this project is one that you can keep. Designs made with colored sand have beautiful texture, as well as color.

WHAT YOU NEED

- *Coarse sifter or a piece of coarse window screen cloth*
- *Bucket of sand: If you want to use natural-colored sand and can find different shades of sand, collect a small container of each color; if you will need to add color to the sand, collect or buy a bucket of clean sand.*
- *Containers for each color of sand that you will use; paper cups or small plastic containers work well*
- *Powdered tempera paints; sold at craft-supply stores. If you can't find powdered tempera, liquid ones will work, but you will have to let the sand dry before you paint with it.*
- *Spoon*
- *Pencil*
- *Scissors*
- *Cardboard, cut to the size you want your finished painting to be*
- *White craft glue in a squeeze bottle*
- *Soft paintbrush*
- *Container of water*

WHAT YOU DO

1. Begin by sifting the sand to get rid of any pebbles, sticks, or pieces of leaves.

2. Now you are ready to color the sand. If you are using natural- colored sands, skip this step. To color sand, mix a spoonful of powdered tempera paint

266

into 1 cup (200 g) of sand. Stir until the sand is evenly colored. If you are using liquid tempera, stir the paint and sand until the sand is evenly colored. Then spread the sand out in a pie pan for a few hours so that it can dry before you use it.

3. Lightly draw your design onto the piece of cardboard. Plan where each color of sand will be.

4. Squeeze glue into the area where the first color will be.

5. Use the spoon to help pour sand onto the glue covered area. Completely cover the area with a thick layer of sand.

6. Wait a few minutes until the glue is almost dry, then gently tap the leftover, loose sand back into its container. When you do this, particles of sand will probably get in places where you don't want them. Don't worry; as long as these sand grains are not sitting on top of wet glue, you will be able to brush them off after everything has dried.

7. Brush any stray sand off the cardboard with the dry paintbrush, and put glue on the next area that you want to paint. Repeat steps 5 and 6 until the painting is finished.

8. If you want to add any colors on top of areas that are already painted, squeeze glue only where you want the added color to be, and pour sand onto the wet glue, just as you did with the first coatings of sand. You can continue to build up layers, but let the glue dry in between layers.

9. Let the entire painting dry overnight.

10. When the painting is dry, use the dry brush to gently brush colored sand off areas where it shouldn't be. If any sand sticks to the top of other colors, simply add a little bit of glue on top of these grains, and sprinkle on a thin layer of the right color sand; let that dry, too.

11. If the colors of your sand painting look dull, paint over each colored area with water. Clean the brush before moving to a different color.

Gearing Up

You don't need a lot of fancy equipment to collect rocks and minerals. You do need a few basic items, though, to make your hobby safer and to help you bring home top-notch specimens.

■ **Geologist's hammer.** Use the square end for breaking collection-size pieces from large rocks. The pointed or chisel-shaped end is for prying or splitting rocks and for chipping away small chunks. Don't try to use an ordinary carpenter's hammer: the hammer will break instead of the rocks!

■ **Safety glasses or plastic goggles.** Think of these as a part of your hammer and put them on every time you use that tool! They'll keep your eyes safe from sharp, flying bits of chipped rock. A good rock hound never forgets eye protection!

■ **Cold steel chisels.** These are made from extra-hard steel and are handy when you need to carefully chip out a specimen from the surrounding rock. Get a ¼-inch (1 cm) chisel for small work and a ¾-inch or 1-inch (2 or 2.5 cm) chisel for bigger jobs.

■ **Small backpack.** This is for carrying your equipment and the rocks and minerals you find. Look for a sturdy cloth pack with padded shoulder straps and at least one pocket for holding small items. Don't get a big pack or you'll be tempted to keep more rocks than you can comfortably carry! For a pack you can make yourself from an old pair of jeans, check out page 270.

■ **Protective clothing.** Think about where you're going and the kind of rock hunting you'll be doing. If you're picking pebbles or small stones from a streambed, you don't need much protection. But if you'll be hammering or handling large chunks of rock, you should wear boots, gloves, sturdy cloth pants, and a long-sleeved shirt. It's a good idea to wear a safety helmet, too. Just in case it rains, pack something to keep you dry.

■ **Hand lens or magnifying glass.** You'll need it for taking a close look at small crystals and fossils. Get one that folds into itself or has a case to protect the lens from accidental scratches.

■ **Newspaper or small bags.** Wrap each rock and mineral you find in its own sheet of newspaper or put it in a sandwich-size paper or plastic bag. You might also want to bring along some tissue paper or empty plastic pill bottles for delicate finds such as small crystals.

■ **Labels, a notebook, and pen or pencil.** You can buy small sticky-backed labels or use pieces of adhesive tape. For each specimen you bring home, put a number

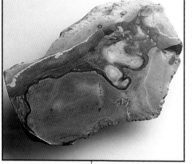

Picture jasper

on a label and stick the label on the rock before you wrap it. Then write the same number in your notebook, and next to it jot down where you found the specimen, the date, and any other information you think is important. A typical notebook entry might read: "No. 14— Fossil found in limestone boulder near south end of Flat Rock Creek. June 10." Don't skip this step! You won't always remember when and where you found each and every specimen. For a notebook you can make yourself, see page 138.

■ **Map and compass.** Always know exactly where you're going, how to get there, and how to get back!

■ **First-Aid Supplies.** For cuts and scratches, bring a supply of adhesive bandages and a tube of antibiotic ointment. On long field trips, carry a complete Red Cross–approved first-aid kit.

■ **Specimen Cleaning Tools.** Keep these at home for cleaning the rocks and minerals you find. Use a toothbrush or paintbrush to remove loose dirt and dust. A nail file or small knife works great for cleaning off hardened clay or mud. A dentist's pick or a large needle is handy for working with delicate fossils or crystals. Of course, you can wash most specimens with water—but be careful. Some minerals dissolve in water! If you're not sure about a specimen, soak a small piece in water for several hours to see if it shrinks or disappears.

Finding Rocks and Minerals

Where's the best place to look for rocks and minerals? Just look down! You can find at least a few rocks to examine almost anywhere. On the other hand, if you're hoping to discover some really great specimens, ones that are special enough to keep for your collection, you might need to look a little harder.

Rocks collect in places where the water slows down: behind boulders or other obstacles in the stream, for instance, and around sharp bends.

Ocean beaches can be good places to find pebble-size specimens. In places such as the Coastal Northwest in the United States, beachcombing rock hounds can pick up gemstones such as *onyx*, *agate*, and *jasper*, already smoothed and polished by the ocean waves! The best time to look is at low tide, especially just after a storm. The cliffs along rocky seashores also offer good places to search for specimens.

Lots of rock is exposed at quarries, where commercial types such as granite or marble or limestone are mined to be sold. Quarries can be excellent places for finding rocks, minerals, and fossils—but they also can be dangerous. **Be sure to get permission before entering a quarry, and never go without an adult.**

The best bets are places where nature, or humans, have already done some digging for you and have uncovered lots of rock. Cuts through hills or mountains where construction crews built highways or railroad beds are excellent prospecting sites. So are gullies, gulches, and ravines where rivers or streams have washed away the soil. Look carefully along the sides of these areas for rocks exposed by erosion. Other good places to look are natural outcrops, such as the stony faces of hills and mountains, where wind and rain have uncovered Earth's bedrock.

Streambeds can be great rock-hounding sites, too. Sometimes you'll find minerals that have tumbled along in the current for dozens or even hundreds of miles.

Of course, you won't find every kind of rock and mineral right in your own area. Different types of rocks and minerals come from different parts of the world. Try to include a few rock-hunting side trips when you travel or go on vacation.

Finally, there's one sort of rock-hunting site that's absolutely guaranteed to have great specimens: a rock shop! Finding your own rocks and minerals in the field is fun, but most rock hounds also buy specimens to add to their collections. Rock shops are great places to get a good look at many different kinds of rocks and minerals. The owners often are able to give you directions to good collecting sites, too.

Backpack

It's handy to keep all your rock collecting equipment packed and ready to go. You can make this sturdy pack out of an old pair of blue jeans, even if you've never sewn anything in your life!

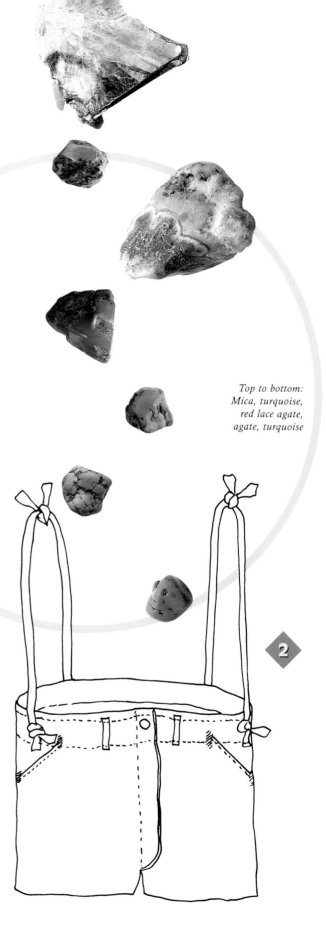

Top to bottom: Mica, turquoise, red lace agate, agate, turquoise

1

2

What You Need

- *Old pair of blue jeans*
- *Scissors*
- *Sewing needle*
- *Heavy thread, such as button thread*

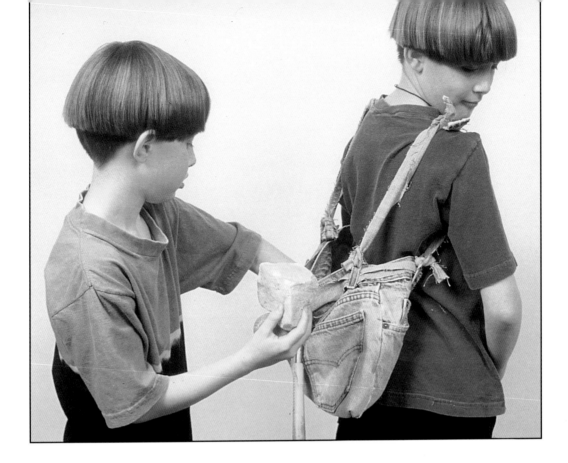

1. Cut off both legs of the jeans. Cut about 2 inches (5 cm) below the top of each leg.

2. Turn the jeans inside out.

3. Thread the needle with about 36 inches (91 cm) of thread. Tie a big knot in the end of the thread.

4. Make a running stitch going across each leg opening. To make a running stitch, poke the needle in near one edge. Pull the needle through the cloth, and stick it in again about ¼ inch (1 cm) away from the place where it came out of the first stitch. **1**

5. Repeat this step all the way across the leg. Tie a knot by poking the tip of the needle through a loop in the thread. Then cut the thread close to the knot.

6. After you have sewn both seams, trim the cloth about ½ inch (1.5 cm) away from the seams.

7. Turn the jeans right side out again. Now the seams will be on the inside and you won't be able to see them.

8. To make straps from the leg pieces of the jeans, cut a long strip from each leg seam, about 1 inch (2.5 cm) wide. You will have four long strips with a seam down the middle of each. The seams will make the pieces of cloth extra strong.

9. Tie one long strip of cloth to each of the four belt loops in the front and back of the jeans. Now tie each pair of strips together. **2** You can slip the straps over your shoulders to use the pack as a backpack, or carry it by the straps over one shoulder.

10. Cut one more long strip from the leg part of the jeans. Thread this strip through the belt loops like a belt. You can use this to tie the pack closed to keep things from falling out.

11. Use the pockets to store the gear listed in "Gearing Up" on page 268. Hang a small hammer from one of the belt loops. When you're ready to hit the trail, add a water bottle and a snack. (Be sure to leave plenty of room in the pack for all your rocks!)

Safety Tips to Remember

Thousands of kids and adults spend their spare time looking for and collecting rocks and minerals. It's a terrific hobby that takes you outdoors to all sorts of interesting places. Finding a beautiful crystal or a really good fossil or rock specimen is exciting! But you have to be careful. Working around rocks and using hammers and other tools can be tricky.

Always remember that the most important safety rule in everything you do is: Think before you act. Use your head and your own good common sense. If you're about to do something or go somewhere that you know deep down might not be safe, stop. Just don't do it!

Here are some more suggestions for keeping your hobby safe and fun.

■ Always get permission before going on private property. Tell the landowner what you want to do and where you want to go. If you ask nicely and mention that you'll be careful not to leave gates open or hurt anything, you'll probably get an okay. This is important. Entering private property without permission is against the law. Also, the landowner may be able to warn you about any dangerous places on the property.

■ Don't go on a field trip alone. It's always safer to have at least one friend along, just in case you need help. Besides, it's more fun.

■ Plan ahead. Be sure an adult knows where you intend to go and when you will be back. Better yet, have an adult go with you.

■ Wear protective clothing. Safety goggles are a must. (See "Gearing Up" on page 268 for a complete list.)

■ Pack food and fresh water. Rock collecting is fun, but it's also strenuous. You'll work up a big appetite and thirst. Don't drink from streams, lakes, or ponds, though. Bring your own water.

Children safely supervised by an experienced adult, Mammoth Cave National Park, Mammoth, Kentucky

■ Stay away from quarries and mines unless you're with an experienced adult and have the property owner's permission. These are dangerous places. Shaky rock walls, heavy equipment, and hard-to-see cliffs and pits are only some of the hazards. Also, never go in a cave or underground mine without the supervision of an experienced adult.

■ Don't work directly beneath a low, steep rock wall. Loose rocks can fall from above without warning.

■ Bring a first-aid kit (see page 268). Also, it's a good idea to take a first-aid course. Local Scouting organizations and Red Cross chapters offer courses for kids and adults. Knowing first aid means knowing how to help if someone is injured!

272

ROCK Collection Box

A COLLECTION BOX LETS YOU DISPLAY YOUR BEST ROCK SPECIMENS AND PROTECTS THEM FROM BEING THROWN OUTSIDE BY SOMEONE WHO THINKS THEY'RE JUST ORDINARY ROCKS. THIS BOX IS EASY TO FIND, AND YOU CAN TURN IT INTO A REAL TREASURE CHEST WITH A LITTLE IMAGINATION.

WHAT YOU NEED

- *Empty paper egg carton—any size will do; if you have too many rocks in your collection for the size of your egg carton, make more than one*
- *Water-soluble paints, such as acrylics or craft paints; look for bright metallic or pearlescent paints at a craft-supply store—watercolors DON'T work*
- *Paintbrush*
- *Container for water*
- *Scissors*
- *Stick-on labels*
- *Pen or marker*

WHAT YOU DO

1. Paint the egg carton inside and out with your favorite colors.

2. After the paint has dried, cut the labels into ½-inch (1.5 cm) square pieces. Write the name of each of your rocks on a label. Press each label into the bottom of one of the egg compartments.

3. Arrange your rocks in their compartments. That's all there is to it!

Geography Projects

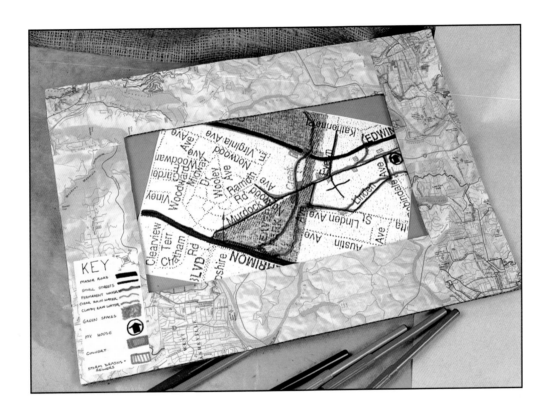

YOU ARE H

NOW WHAT?

Big question, eh? I mean, here you are, one person in a room in a home on a street in a neighborhood in a town, city, village, hamlet, or farmstead in a state, province, or territory in a country on a continent in a hemisphere all on this large rock that spins around an even bigger ball of burning gas located at the tail end of the Milky Way galaxy, which is one of who knows how many galaxies in the universe, and, and...where were we? Oh yes, now what? That's the question that starts us on this fabulous journey known as geography.

There's no one definition of geography, though if we were to give it a shot, we'd say geography is the where, why, who, what, and when of all things related to Earth and the life-forms that call Earth home. Geography can tell you why you're right where you are right now and how you got there. It explores why your ancestors settled where they did, why your parents moved to the home you live in, and why you're reading a book in the United States, Canada, Australia, New Zealand, England, or elsewhere, that was written in the United States (in a small city in North Carolina, in an office without any windows), printed in Hong Kong from paper and ink manufactured in Japan, that got shipped to a warehouse in New Jersey (U.S.A.).

Geography is the air you breathe, the clothes you wear, the roads you travel. It snoops around, explores, and starts finding answers. And it doesn't stop there. It also solves the world's mysteries, checks out what old, dusty people did on Earth long ago, and how what they did affects you. It's maps and charts, navigation and discovery, problems and solutions.

Finally, geography declares that you are one of 6,200,000,000 people on this planet, and yet instead of making you feel insignificant, geography lets you in on one of the biggest secrets of all: Not only does Earth affect you, but you, even just little old you all by yourself, affect Earth. It's an astounding thought. It's like going into the past in a time machine and telling your great-great grandmother not to marry your great-great grandfather. You'd change everything. Well, you're changing the world right now, without a time machine, by simply breathing.

This isn't a textbook—there's no memorizing rivers or towns, and who cares if you can't remember the difference between an isthmus and a peninsula or a gulf and a bay. This book also doesn't pretend to cover everything that geography has to offer—even textbooks couldn't do that—but we're here to show off a lot of cool things to do and make, and the only thing that ties all this stuff together is geography.

The five topics in this section all help define and explore different aspects of geography. Chapter One investigates how early explorers and geographers learned about, measured, and traveled the Earth, and gives you a head start on becoming a world explorer. No geography book is complete without lots of maps, so we've dedicated Chapter Two to the geographer's best friend: the map. Chapter Three explores world cultures and how even though the people of the world look, talk, and act differently, there are also a lot of similarities. Chapter Four delves into how Earth's weather, climate, landscape, and more affect human life and development, while Chapter Five shows how humans affect Earth.

One final thought: You may think Earth has pretty much been completely discovered, explored, and mapped. Well, that's what people thought 500 years ago, and little did they know what lay ahead of them!

Where in the World Are You?

YOU'RE LOST...DESPERATELY LOST. Your mom told your dad to turn left at the next intersection, but he turned right instead, and now, by the time you get to your dream beach vacation, it'll be time to turn around and go back home (at least that's what it feels like)! Even in this day of computer-generated directions, incredibly accurate maps, and global positioning devices that can pinpoint where you are to within 30 feet (9 m), we still get lost. And sure, you may lose some quality time at the ocean, but you know you'll get there as soon as your dad breaks down, stops driving around, and asks for some directions. Early explorers,

however, didn't have that sense of security. They had a few maps and some crude instruments to help them get around (either by foot or by ship), but if they went for more than a day or so without seeing the sun or the stars, there could be big trouble. It was risky business being an explorer back then, and these next several projects and activities give you a chance to walk around in the great and not-so-great explorers' shoes and to experience what it must have been like to go where no one you know had ever been. We've also included some fun projects that will help turn you into a world explorer in no time at all!

MARINER'S ASTROLABE

Up until only a few hundred years ago, the main focus of geographers was simply figuring out where places were, which is not such an easy thing on a spherical planet. And even though our ancestors weren't very good at knowing where they were, that didn't stop them from exploring. In order not to become completely lost out on the seas, mariners had to rely on some pretty crude instruments simply to tell them their latitude. (Until the 18th century, navigators couldn't find their longitude at sea at all!)

The astrolabe was originally used to determine the movements and positions of stars, but then somebody got the bright idea to try using it on a ship. And it worked! Okay, it worked well enough so that sailors sort of knew kind of where they were going. Create your own astrolabe and check out the information on latitude and longitude on page 285.

WHAT YOU NEED

- Piece of corrugated cardboard, 7 x 7 inches (17.8 x 17.8 cm)
- Round lid or something to draw a circle with a 6-inch (15.2 cm) diameter
- Pencil
- Scissors or craft knife
- Round lid or something to draw a circle with a 4-inch (10.2 cm) diameter
- Awl or nail
- Hex bolt with wing nut, 1/4 x 1 inch (6 mm x 2.5 cm)
- Ruler
- Protractor
- Acrylic paints, including metallic gold
- Paintbrush
- Black, fine-point, permanent marker
- Piece of wood, 5 x 1 x 1/2 inch (12.7 x 2.5 x 1.3 cm)
- Drill, with a bit slightly larger than the bolt
- 2 flat washers that fit around the bolt
- Plastic drinking straw
- Scissors
- 2 long, straight pins
- Piece of heavy thread or string, 20 inches (50.8 cm) long
- 2 nuts to use as weights

WHAT YOU DO

1. Make the dial by tracing a 6-inch (15.2 cm) circle on the piece of cardboard. Cut the circle out with the scissors.

2. Center the lid for the 4-inch (10.2 cm) circle on the circle you just cut, and trace this smaller circle (figure 1 on page 284).

3. Use the awl or nail to poke a hole through the exact center of the circle. Enlarge the hole by turning the awl until the bolt slides through the hole.

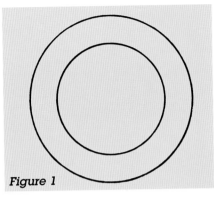

Figure 1

4. Use the ruler to help draw a straight line going from one edge of the cardboard circle to the other across the center hole. Label both ends of this line "0." Set the protractor on this line, with the center of the protractor over the center of the hole in the middle of the circle (figure 2).

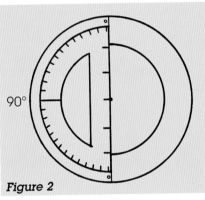

Figure 2

90°

5. The protractor is divided into numbered sections, beginning with 0 and going to 180, (straight up is 90°). Mark the place on the outer rim of the circle straight above 90. Place the ruler across the center hole and touching your 90 mark. Draw a line from edge to edge of the circle, going across the center and touching 90. Label both ends of this line "90."

6. Position the protractor again as you did in step 5. Mark the places on the outer rim above 60° and also above 30°. Draw lines and label the points as you did in Step 5. When

you're finished, your dial should look like figure 3.

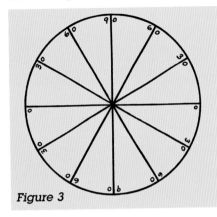

Figure 3

7. Paint the dial, and use a fine-point marker to number the angles.
8. To make the sighting arm, have an adult help you drill a hole in the middle of the wooden stick. Paint the sides and ends of the stick.
9. When the paint has dried completely, assemble the astrolabe. Put a washer on the bolt and slide the bolt into the hole in the wood. Slip another washer over the bolt, and then push the bolt through the hole in the center of the dial. Thread the wing nut onto the bolt end, and tighten it to keep the stick from moving around.
10. Use the scissors to cut the straw the same length as the stick.
11. Push the two pins through the straw about 1 inch (2.5 cm) in from each end, and then push the pins into the wooden stick.
12. Use the awl or nail to poke a small hole ¼ inch (6 mm) in from the edge of the cardboard at both of the 90° marks.
13. Loop a 10-inch (25.4 cm) piece of string through one of the holes. Slide the nuts onto the string and make a knot. Tie another 10-inch (25.4 cm) piece of string in a loop through the other hole.

HOW TO USE YOUR ASTROLABE

To use the astrolabe, hang it by the loop from your outstretched arm, a tree branch, or a large nail in the side of a building so that the instrument hangs freely. To measure the altitude of a star, move the wooden sighting arm so that you can sight the star through the straw. Read the angle that the arm is pointing to. That's the altitude of the star—the number of degrees above the horizon. If you want to measure your own latitude, see page 289.

You could do the same thing with the sun, but unless you want to end up like the blind sailors who frequented the crews of many ships way back when, don't ever stare directly at the sun. To measure the altitude of the sun, hold the astrolabe by the loop so that the sun casts a shadow either above or below the sighting arm. Move the arm until the shadow of the stick disappears. (You'll still be able to see the shadow of the spacer washers.) The arm will be pointing directly at the sun, and you can read the dial to learn the altitude of the sun without looking at it.

Oh, Drat, the World Ain't Flat

It isn't easy finding where you are on a sphere that's floating around in space (especially one with more than 196,000,000 square miles [509,600,000 km²] of land and sea!). There aren't any edges or corners, and technically speaking, there isn't a top or bottom either. And since we do live on a round world, a system had to be devised to help folks pinpoint exactly where they were. Most sane people agree these days that the North Pole is the top and the South Pole is the bottom. There's even an imaginary line that acts as the edge of the Earth. It's called the Prime Meridian, and it runs from the North Pole through Greenwich, England to the South Pole. This same line on the other side of the world is called the International Date Line (see page 290). Another line, drawn around the middle of the world, is the equator. After that, there are four lines both north and south of the equator and a total of 24 lines up and down. All these lines dissect the world into a useful grid that chops up the world into imaginary pieces.

The lines above and below the equator are called "latitude lines," and they're used to determine one's distance either north (N) or south (S) of the equator. They're measured in degrees 70 miles (112 km) apart. The up and down lines are called "meridians" or "longitude lines," and they're used to determine one's distance east (E) or west (W) of the Prime Meridian. These lines are measured in terms of the 360 degrees of a circle and are essential for pinpointing location, which is especially helpful if you're traveling one of the world's oceans and have no landmarks to help you. ("Take a left at the big school of dolphins!") Each 15 degrees represents one hour of rotation of the Earth.

If you have trouble keeping latitude and longitude straight in your mind (as most people who don't have to navigate on a regular basis do), remember that LATitude rhymes with FLATitude, and that latitude lines run flat, north or south of the equator. If that's too punny for you, make up your own (just don't make fun of ours—it works).

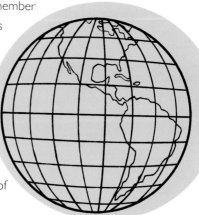

LATITUDE & LONGITUDE AROUND THE WORLD • LATITUDE & LONGIT

The equator: 0° latitude   The North Pole: 90° N   The South Pole: 90°S

The Prime Meridian: 0° longitude   The International Date Line: 180° longitude

More on page 289

The Gulf of Guinea: 0°, 0°   The Pacific Ocean, near the Gilbert Islands: 0°, 180° (where the equator and International Dateline meet)   Paris, France: 48° 50' N, 2° 20' E*

* Each degree of latitude or longitude can be broken down into 60 minutes, which look like this: 44'. These minutes help you pinpoint location even more accurately when a location doesn't appear exactly on the latitude or longitude line.

CROSS STAFF

If an old-time mariner didn't use an astrolabe while attempting a lengthy sea journey, chances are he used a cross staff instead. The cross staff, also called a "sighting stick" or "Jacob's staff," is regarded as one of the oldest navigational instruments, and it was used as early as the 1300s to measure the altitude of stars, which allowed sailors to find their latitude, tell time, and find their direction at night.

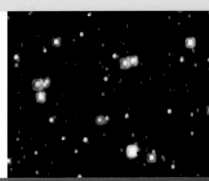

WHAT YOU NEED

- Piece of wood, 1 x 2 x 17 inches (2.5 x 5.1 x 43.2 cm)
- Handsaw
- Sandpaper
- Piece of wood, $^1/_4$ x $1^1/_2$ x 36 inches (.6 x 3.8 x 91.4 cm)
- Ruler
- Pencil
- Drill, with a bit slightly wider than the carriage bolts
- 2 carriage bolts, 2 inches (5.1 cm) long, with wing nuts
- Yardstick
- Protractor
- Acrylic craft paints
- Paintbrush
- Black, permanent marker

WHAT YOU DO

1. Saw the 17-inch-long (43.2 cm) piece of wood into two pieces—one

5 inches (12.7 cm) long and the other 12 inches (30.5 cm) long. Sand the ends of all the pieces of wood.

2. Use the ruler and the pencil to mark the center of the 5-inch (12.7 cm) piece of wood.

3. Lay the 36-inch (91.4 cm) piece of wood crossways over this center mark. Draw a line along each side of the long piece of wood. Remove the long piece of wood, and make two large dots. They should be centered and just outside each of the two lines you drew (see figure 1 on page 18).

4. Drill a hole through the 5-inch (12.7 cm) piece of wood at each of the two large dots.

5. Center the 12-inch (30.5 cm)

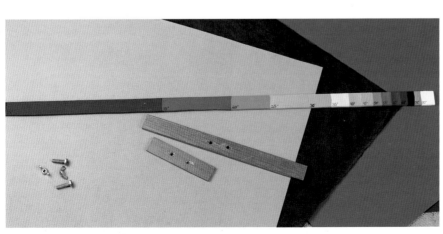

Figure 1

piece of wood under the 5-inch (12.7 cm) piece (figure 2). Stick the pencil down each drilled hole to

Figure 2

mark the wood underneath. Drill holes in the marked spots on this piece of wood, too.

6. Test the assembly by placing the 36-inch-long (91.4 cm) piece of wood between the holes in the two other pieces and slipping the bolts through the two pairs of holes. The wood should fit easily between the bolts. Tighten the wing nuts to hold the wood in position (figure 3).

Figure 3

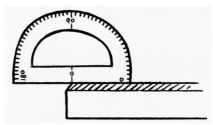

Figure 4

7. If everything fits, you can mark the angles on the staff. Lay the cross staff on the floor. Loosen the wing nuts, and slide the crosspiece—the two pieces of wood bolted together—down to about 4 inches (10.2 cm) from one end of the long stick. Place the protractor along the opposite end of the long stick (figure 4).

8. You'll notice that the protractor has angles marked going from 0 to 90 (straight up) to 180. Place the yardstick from the top of the crosspiece to the end of the long stick over the protractor. Slide the crosspiece (and push the yardstick so that it stays in contact with both crosspiece and long stick) so that the yardstick lies along the 10° line of the protractor (figure 5).

9. Draw a line across the flat surface of the long stick, using the side of the crosspiece that is closest to the

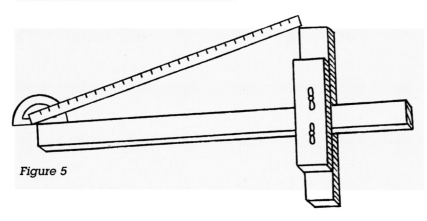

Figure 5

protractor as a guide. When the crosspiece is in this position, the reading will be 10°.

10. Now mark 15°, following the directions from steps 8 and 9. Continue marking every 5 degrees until you come to the end of the long stick. You should be able to get up to 65° or 70°.

11. Take the instrument completely apart to paint it. Paint one color between 0° and 10°, another color between 10° and 15°, and so on. After you have painted it, draw over the numbers with black marker so they can be easily read.

12. When the paint's completely dry, put the cross staff back together.

HOW TO USE YOUR CROSS STAFF

Go outside at night. Loosen the wing nuts a little so you can slide the crosspiece. Hold the long piece at eye level, with the higher numbers toward you. Sight a star along

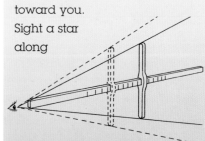

the edge of the staff and the top edge of the crosspiece. Slide the crosspiece until it lines up with your line of sight. Read the number closest to where the crosspiece crosses the long piece of wood. That is the altitude of the star. See page 289 to find your latitude.

288

LOST? THANK YOUR LUCKY STARS

Many an old-time sea dweller thanked his or her lucky stars while traveling the open seas. Why? Because without the stars, they'd be lost. North of the equator, seafaring travelers relied on the North Star (a.k.a. Polaris) since it always appears in the same direction and can help locate one's latitude. The North Star is at the end of the handle of the Little Dipper. Now, that's great for sailors north of the equator, but

what about folks south of the equator? They have their own stars to thank: the four stars of the Southern Cross constellation.

To find your latitude, measure the angle from the horizon to a pole star. (Use your astrolabe or cross staff.) Your latitude will be equal to the angle between the horizon and the pole star. If you're using the North Star as your pole star, your latitude is north of the equator, if you're using

the Southern Cross as your pole star, your latitude is south of the equator.

For example, you're lost somewhere north of the equator and all you have is your trusty astrolabe or cross staff with you (good thing you packed it!). You discover that the North Star is 30° above the horizon at dusk. That means you're 30° above the equator, or 30° N.

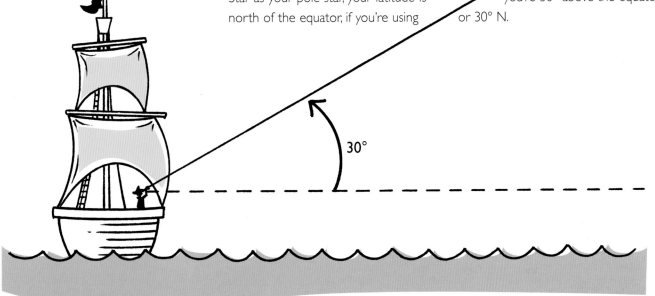

30°

ATITUDE & LONGITUDE AROUND THE WORLD • LATITUDE & LONGITUDE

Tokyo, Japan: 35° 40' N, 139° 30' E

Rio de Janeiro, Brazil: 22° 50' S, 43° W

Where the *Titanic* sank: 41° N, 50° W

Sydney, Australia: 33° 53' S, 151° 10'E

Where your authors live: 35° 36' N, 82° 33' W (look it up!)

Your hometown: _____ N or S, _____ E or W

To find the exact opposite side of the world of your hometown, take your latitude, and change its direction. For example, the opposite of 22 °N is 22° S. For longitude, take your longitude—for this example, let's say it's 43° W—and subtract it from 180° (180-43=137). Then switch directions. The longitude of this place is 137° E. So the location opposite of 22° N, 43° W is 22° S, 137° E.

A TOTALLY USEFUL COMPASS

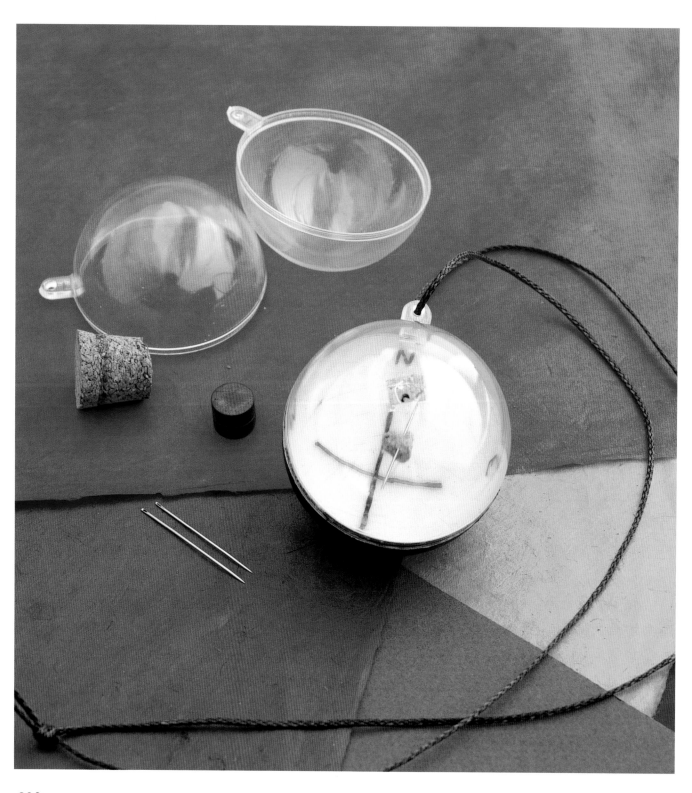

Nobody knows who invented the compass, though many cultures would like to take credit for it. The Chinese may have been using compasses for over 2,000 years. The Vikings used magnetized needles to guide them on their journeys. Whoever truly invented the compass, the truth remains that the compass was and still is an explorer's best friend.

Today's compass is a combination of the ancient compass rose, which had 32 points with the names of the winds, and a magnetized needle (a design that hasn't changed much in 800 years). That's all. Most make-it-yourself compasses are okay, but need water to make them work. This design is handy, compact, and pretty neat looking, if we do say so ourselves.

WHAT YOU NEED

- Two-piece plastic capsule with hang tab (available at craft stores)*
- White and black acrylic craft paint
- Paintbrush
- Ruler
- Permanent marker
- Metal sewing needle
- Thread
- Scissors
- $1/4$ x $1/4$-inch (6 x 6 mm) piece of cork
- Tape
- Refrigerator magnet
- Yarn or twine

*Make sure the two halves snap together tightly; if not, then you'll need to use glue or tape to keep them together.

WHAT YOU DO

1. Paint the outside of one of the capsule halves with white paint and let it dry. Next, paint over the white paint with black or another color of your choice. The inside of the capsule half should look white while the outside is black.

2. Use the ruler to make a cross over the open end of the capsule. Mark the letter for each direction at the ends of each line with the marker (figure 1).

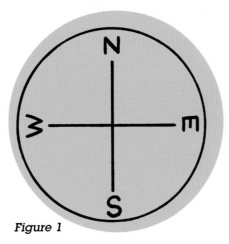

Figure 1

3. Thread the sewing needle with the thread and pass the needle through the center of the cork. Tie a knot in one end of the string so you can't pull it out of the cork (figure 2). Tape the other end of the string to the top of the unpainted half of the capsule.

4. Magnetize the sewing needle by rubbing the refrigerator magnet along it in one direction. Do not rub the magnet back and forth; rather, begin at the point close to you and sweep the magnet down the needle away from you several times.

5. Insert the sewing needle through the center of the cork so it's balanced when you let it hang freely.

6. Put the capsule halves together so the needle hangs freely. Make sure the needle doesn't touch the capsule walls (shorten the string or use a smaller needle if it does).

7. Rotate the capsule so the needle points to N. Find a commercial compass and compare. If they don't match within a few degrees, you may want to try to re-magnetize your needle.

8. Cut a piece of yarn, twine, or cord to make a strap for the compass to hang from. Pass the twine through the hang tab on the capsule, and tie the loose ends in a knot. Now go explore!

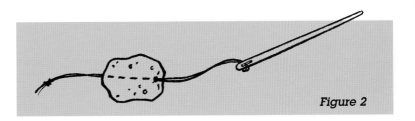

Figure 2

Happy Birthday

to You x 2

The few, lucky survivors of Magellan's voyage around the world (even Magellan didn't make it) realized something peculiar. They had kept very good records of the number of days they'd been away, and when they returned home, they realized they had lost a day! Where did it go? They lost their day when they crossed the International Date Line, an imaginary line that's on the opposite side of the Prime Meridian. If you're standing on one side of the IDL and your friend is standing on the other side, you'd be enjoying different days of the week. Technically, you could celebrate your birthday twice: stand just east of the line on your birthday, and then the next day, jump over the line and celebrate again. Don't hold your breath, though, waiting for more presents.

THE GREAT AGE OF DISCOVERY IN PERSPECTIVE

During the great age of exploration and discovery that helped end the dreadful Middle Ages, whole new worlds were discovered (though the people already living in these new worlds had, of course, already discovered them!). And each new discovery changed the world of the explorers and of the people already on the lands "discovered." It would be almost impossible to grasp today what it must have felt like to live during this time. So, try this: Imagine a space mission returning with news that they've found life on another planet, and they've brought some of these folks to Earth for a visit. What would your first reaction be? Surprise, shock, disbelief, fear, relief? What would you want to know about them? What could you learn from them? What could they learn from you? What do they have that could be of benefit to society? Can they play soccer? These are some questions that came to mind (okay, perhaps they didn't care much about soccer) as new worlds and people discovered each other on Earth. History, however, has shown that greed often got the best of many explorers, some of whom quickly became conquerors. Do you think we would seek to conquer new worlds in space today? Or do you think we've grown as a world society so that we'd instead seek to be peaceful neighbors who can learn and benefit from each other?

Soccer? Where I come from we call it football.

Amaze Your Friends
Prove the World Isn't Flat!

Okay, perhaps your friends will not be amazed, though it certainly is interesting that astronomers 2,000 years before Columbus's journeys not only knew Earth was spherical, but had accurately figured out its diameter. Anyway, if you have a friend who doubts the world is round, you can share this quick and easy activity to help him out. (He needs it!)

WHAT YOU NEED

- An ocean, with a ship sailing away toward the horizon
- A friend, preferably one who has lived in a cave much of his life
- A lunar eclipse (optional)

WHAT YOU DO

1. Bring your friend to the ocean and stand along the shoreline. Look for ships sailing out to sea. Watch the ship as it gets smaller and smaller. If the world was flat, you and your friend would see the whole ship get smaller and smaller until it was too far away to see. However, watch what happens. As the ship moves toward the horizon, the ship's hull disappears first—as if the ship were slowly slipping off the edge of the world!

2. If that doesn't convince your friend, find out when the next lunar eclipse is and make sure your friend checks out the shadow Earth casts on the moon. It's round!

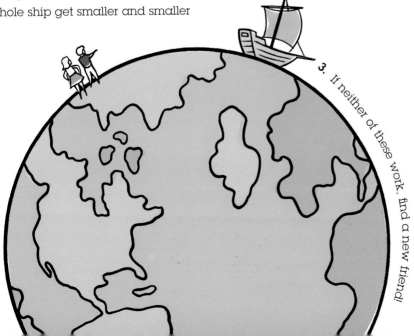

3. If neither of these work, find a new friend!

LOOK UP. SMILE. Gotcha! There are thousands of satellites up there in space taking pictures, recording information, and sending signals. But there are 24 super-cool satellites (called the Global Positioning System or GPS) orbiting 11,000 miles (17,600 km) above us that can help you figure out exactly where you're located. The GPS was developed for military purposes by the United States, but they now kindly let anyone use it. And for about the cost of three or four copies of this book, you could own a GPS receiver. It's a small, hand-held device that looks a little bit like a calculator, and it picks up signals from at least four of the 24 GPS satellites. These satellites send longitude, latitude, and altitude to the receiver. Most receivers then use a world map that's stored in its memory to pinpoint your location. It can be used anywhere on Earth: in a car, on a plane, on a boat, while hiking, or just standing around (as long as you're outside). Some receivers can also trace your path across a map as you travel and determine how fast you're going. A GPS receiver can be placed in a car and act as a speedometer and odometer. Some models will also figure out when you'll get where you're going.

HOUSE SUNDIAL CLOCK

Another ancient instrument that was important for early geographers was the sundial clock. These not only helped keep time, but could also figure out location, when the seasons changed, and the length of a day. A sundial was also instrumental in figuring out the circumference of the Earth 2,000 years before Columbus bumped into the Americas. You can turn your whole house into a sundial clock by observing the sun's movement around it throughout the day.

WHAT YOU NEED

- 10 x 10-inch (25.4 x 25.4 cm) piece of cardboard
- Pencil
- Old magazines
- Scissors
- Glue
- Compass
- Acrylic craft paint
- Paintbrush
- Journal or paper
- Tall, thin objects, such as rulers or vases
- 6-inch (15.2 cm) cardboard circle
- Foam brush
- Awl or nail
- $1/4$-inch (6 mm) quartz, battery-operated clock movement with hands*

*available at craft stores

WHAT YOU DO

1. On the cardboard square, draw a floor plan of all the rooms on the main floor of your home.

2. Cut out magazine images to match the rooms, and glue them in the appropriate place on the floor plan.

3. Stand in the center of the main floor of the house with a compass, and locate each of the four directions. Write N for north on the cardboard square in the northernmost room in your house, E for east in the room that faces east, and so on. Use paint or markers to make the letters stand out.

4. One morning, wake up at sunrise (come on, you can do it!) and write down the time as the sun moves through each room in the house. To help figure out when the sun is directly in line with a particular side of the house, place a tall, thin object on every windowsill and record the time when the object's shadow falls straight behind it (figure 1).

Figure 1

5. Decorate the cardboard circle to look like a clockface, and write the numbers 1 through 12 around the dial, with 6 at the top of the clock (see photo). We painted half of our dial yellow to represent daylight and midnight blue for night. Use another clockface as a guide for spacing the numbers, or follow the pattern on page 396.

6. Poke a hole through the centers of the cardboard square and circle, then slide the shaft of the clockworks through the hole in each. The dial should fit on top of the square and spin easily.

7. Spin the dial so that the hour for sunrise matches up with the room the sun first hits in the morning. Throughout the day, as the sun moves around your home, you should notice that the hour on the clock matches the room with the most sunlight. If this doesn't happen, try adjusting the size of your clockface and the distance between the numbers. **Note:** You'll have to adjust the number dial after a few days, since the sun rises at different times over the course of the year.

THIS AIN'T NO SUNDIAL!

Back in the time before wristwatches and other semi-accurate timepieces existed, if you asked someone what time it was, he or she might say, "My stomach's rumblin' so it must be suppertime." Today, relying on your stomach noises or even a digital watch you found in a cereal box could make you late for school or make you miss your favorite TV show. (You shouldn't be watching TV anyway.) Ever wonder how we know *exactly* what time it is? Well, there are atomic clocks that keep super-accurate time. So good, in fact, that the most accurate one, the NIST-F1 in Boulder, Colorado, won't lose or gain a second for around 20 million years. How does it work? Basically, instead of using a pendulum (like a grandfather clock), atomic clocks use (you guessed it) atoms to determine the duration of one second. These clocks are used to operate the Global Positioning System (see page 293), to help navigate spacecraft, and to synchronize telecommunication and computer operations. And although you can't fit one on your wrist, you can buy a clock that automatically synchronizes itself to an atomic clock.

The NIST F-1; courtesy of the National Institute of Standards and Technology; photo by Geoffrey Wheeler

STILL, STILL LOST?
FIND LONGITUDE & WIN BIG BUCKS!

It was one thing for early maritime explorers to be able to find their latitude, but without knowing their longitude it was still pretty dangerous to venture overseas. The problem? Even though longitude could be figured out on land, you needed an extremely accurate clock, and no such thing existed before the 18th century that could withstand the rough treatment of a sea voyage. It became such a huge problem that kings and governments offered big cash rewards for the first person who

could create an accurate timekeeper on a ship. (England's parliament offered 20,000 pounds, which is equivalent to about $1 million today!) Enter our hero, John Harrison (1693-1776), an uneducated (which bothered the snooty scientists back then) carpenter from Yorkshire, England.

Whoa, back up? A clock to help find location? Yup, that's right. Remember, longitude lines are the ones that go up and down from both poles. The Earth takes 24 hours to complete one 360° spin. If you divide 360 by 24 you get

This marine chronomether was made in Paris, France in 1776. Courtesy of the Clock and Watch Museum Beyer Zurich.

15. That's the number of degrees the Earth spins in one hour ($1/24$ of the Earth's full spin). So, if you know what time it is in one location, let's say Greenwich, England, home of the Prime Meridian, and you know what time it is where you are right now, you can figure out your longitude east or west of the Prime Meridian. Here's an example: If it's 4 p.m. in Greenwich and 12 p.m. where your ship is located, you're four time zones west of the Prime Meridian. That's 60° west longitude ($15 \times 4 = 60$) or 60° W. Or say it's 9 a.m. in Greenwich and 12 p.m. where you're located. That's three time zones or 45° E.

Though it took Harrison much of his adult life to create this precise clock (called a *chronometer*), it was a great success, though the best scientific minds of Europe had to have their arms twisted by King George before they coughed up the big bucks that Harrison so rightfully deserved.

Watch the news some time and see if the newsroom has a bunch of clocks with different times on them. They're showing the times in several different cities around the world. If you check out a map of the world's time zones, you'll notice that the time stays the same as you move along longitude lines, but changes as you move across latitudes. Create your own time-zone clock so you can keep track of what time it is in other countries where friends or family live.

TIME-ZONE CLOCK

WHAT YOU NEED

- Atlas
- Wooden board, ³/₄ x 5¹/₂ x 24 inches (1.9 x 14 x 61 cm)
- Ruler
- Pencil
- Drill, with a bit slightly wider than the shaft of the clockworks
- 4 sets of ³/₄-inch (1.9 cm) quartz, battery-operated clock movements with hands*
- Acrylic craft paint
- Paintbrush
- 5¹/₂-inch-diameter (14 cm) circle (a bowl or lid) for making the clock faces, or a compass (not the one for finding your direction)
- World times

*available at craft stores

WHAT YOU DO

1. Choose four places around the world that interest you and compare their times. Look for symbols in the atlas that represent those countries, cities, etc., to use as designs for your clock faces.

2. Using the ruler, find the center of the board, and draw a straight line across the center of the board from one end to the other.

3. Starting at one end of the wooden board, mark an X in the center of the board at 3, 9, 15, and 21 inches (7.6, 22.9, 38.1, and 53.3 cm).

4. Drill a hole through the X at each spot, and then check to make sure that the clockwork shafts fit in them. If your holes are too small, use a larger drill bit.

5. Paint the entire board with a color you like as a background for the clocks. Let it dry.

6. Make a 5¹/₂-inch-diameter (14 cm) circle around each of the drilled holes, using the bowl or lid as a pattern. If you have a compass, use that instead.

7. Paint the clock faces with symbols of the locations you chose. Here, we replicated the flags of China, Kenya, Argentina, and Australia.

8. Refer to a clock face, or use the figure on page 396 for spacing your numbers around each dial to match the speed of the clock.

9. Assemble the clockworks according to the manufacturer's directions. Set each clock to the current time for the locations you chose. You can use the atlas to help you figure out the times compared to local time, or you could search the Internet for "world times" to find accurate times for almost any location.

DREAM TRAVEL BOX

Though the world is now a familiar place for geographers, that doesn't mean the world is familiar to you! Imagine you could go anywhere in the world. Would you want to be someplace warm, or do you love snow? Do you dream of the ocean or trekking up in the mountains? What if you could go to a place where you could watch volcanoes erupt?

Whatever your dream place is, you can find information about it by searching on the Internet, looking for books at the library, and picking up brochures from travel agents. With a little planning, you could make it there one day. Until then, you can dream and collect all the things you find about this place in a special box to look through from time to time until your dream becomes reality.

WHAT YOU NEED

- Shoebox with lid
- Acrylic craft paint
- Paintbrush
- Images from magazines, books, brochures, or from the Internet that relate to your dream place
- Scissors or craft knife
- Small map of your dream location
- Craft glue
- Foam brush
- Decoupage glue

WHAT YOU DO

1. Paint the entire box a color you like.

2. With scissors, cut out the images you want on the box from the materials you've gathered. Place each image on the piece of cardboard and carefully cut along their outlines.

3. Glue the small map of the country you're hoping to travel to on the lid of the box.

4. Cut images to fit inside of the map, trimming the outside images to fit the contours of the border.

5. When you've filled in the map, outline it with a bright color of paint so it'll stand out. Decorate the rest of the box as you want.

7. Use the foam brush to cover each side of the box and lid with a thin layer of decoupage glue to seal and protect your collage.

8. Fill your box with information that can help you get to your dream location someday. Use your box and its contents to convince your parents that they may like to go there as well (and take you, of course)!

Before the World Was a Spherical Planet Orbiting the Sun...

A MYTH IS A STORY WITH A PURPOSE, and each ancient culture had its own set of stories that tried to explain why the world is the way it is. Stories were created to tell of how the world began, why storms happened, or why we die. Before science provided answers to some of the world's mysteries, people told stories to help explore these mysteries. These stories took the form of rituals, artworks, dances, or simple stories told to children before they went to bed. They helped the world seem more understandable, less scary, as well as more beautiful. And although they may seem farfetched, the message behind myths had an important meaning for those who told, listened, and believed them.

Some of the most fascinating myths include how ancient cultures thought the world began and what it looked like. The Vikings believed there were nine worlds, including Earth, all of which were arranged in three layers around Yggdrasil, a huge ash tree at the center of the universe. The ancient Egyptians thought the sky was a tent that stretched between mountains at the four corners of the Earth. The ancient Greeks believed Earth was a flat disk surrounded by a world ocean. In the Hindu Vedas tradition, a tree of knowledge held up the universe. Here's one particularly beautiful myth from the Iroquois of the northeast United States:

Before Earth as we know it was formed, all that existed was water, where many animals lived, and sky, where a chief and his people lived. One day the chief's young, pregnant wife went searching for some herbs for her husband. As she dug near the Great Tree, which bore fruits and flowers of all kinds, a hole opened up. Curious, she leaned forward, grabbing the tree for support, but she lost her balance and tumbled into the hole, holding only a handful of seeds.

The birds that flew over the water saw her falling and flew up and eased her fall with their outspread wings. Muskrat then quickly dove beneath the water and brought up handfuls of soft mud, which he placed on the back of a snapping turtle. The woman landed on the turtle's back, the mud became the earth, and trees and grass grew from the seeds in the woman's hand. To this day, the world rests on the back of the giant turtle, and when he moves, there are earthquakes and floods.

MARCO POLO TRAVEL JOURNAL

Marco Polo (1254-1324) didn't have a travel agent, nor did he have transportation. That didn't stop him, however, from traveling thousands of miles into the heart of Asia. Not bad for a guy who got around 600 years before anyone ever heard of airplanes and cars. However, Marco Polo did something else remarkable: He wrote down what he saw, heard, ate, learned, and experienced, and his writings continue to affect history today.

Now, once you've decided on a place to visit and figured out how to get there, you may want to keep a journal of your own. A journal will help you remember and enjoy your travels long after they're over. It can be part notebook, part sketchbook, and even part scrapbook, in which you record in words, pictures, and small souvenirs the events, places, and surprises you encountered. Marco would be proud.

WHAT YOU NEED

- Journal or sketchbook of your choice
- Pictures of old maps
- Scissors
- Craft glue
- Gold foil and adhesive
- Foam brush
- Ribbon
- Decoupage glue

WHAT YOU DO

1. Decide what you want to decorate your journal cover with, then cut the image(s) to size and arrange it/them on the cover.

2. Evenly spread glue on the back of the image you're using and carefully smooth it in place on the journal cover.

3. Cut three strips of gold foil, each long enough to fit along an edge of the journal that you want to cover. Spread the gold foil adhesive with a brush along the cover where you want the gold to stick, then wait a few minutes until it turns clear.

4. Place each strip of gold foil evenly along the edge of the journal. Use the handle end of the foam brush to rub back and forth on the foil to make it stick to the cover.

5. Carefully peel back the foil. Repeat steps 3 and 4 for a thicker layer of gold foil.

6. Measure the ribbon against the design on your cover and cut it to fit where you want it.

7. Spread a thin line of glue under the ribbon and press it in place.

8. With the foam brush, spread a thin coat of decoupage glue over the entire cover to seal and protect it. Fill your travel journal with sketches, photographs, poems, thoughts, and memories of places you visit, be they weekend trips with your family or long summer adventures.

"HEY, WHAT ABOUT ME?!"

Marco Polo's a pretty impressive guy, but we could have also called this journal the Chang Ch'ien Travel Journal. Sure "Chang Ch'ien" may not not be a household name, but when it comes to explorers, Chang Ch'ien is one of the greatest! *Huh?* That's right! Chang Ch'ien covered a lot of the same ground Polo did, but from the other direction! He left the capital of China in 138 B.C.E. as an ambassador, hoping to sign a treaty with a tribe 2,000 miles (3,200 km) away. After 13 years (many spent as a prisoner), he returned to China, not with the treaty, but with a ton of information on the history, geography, and culture of Central Asia, Persia, Arabia, and even the Roman Empire. Chang Ch'ien's travels led to increased trade and the most famous overland trade route ever: the Silk Road. So go ahead, give the guy a break and call your journal the Chang Ch'ien Travel Journal. He'd appreciate it.

WORLDLY PLACE MATS

When Christopher Columbus returned from the Americas, he needed to bring evidence that he had actually been somewhere. Though he didn't find gold or valuable spices, he did return with something that became quite a hit in Europe: sweet potatoes.

After you return from your traveling adventures and empty your pockets and bags, turn your valuable "evidence" into these lasting tributes to your dream vacation. You can even serve sweet potatoes on them.

WHAT YOU NEED

- Poster board
- Scissors
- Stencil letters (optional)
- Marker (optional)
- Craft knife (optional)
- Mementos from your trip
- Glue
- Clear adhesive shelf paper

WHAT YOU DO

1. Cut pieces of poster board to the size of your proposed place mats.
2. If you want, use the stencil letters to write the name of the country you visited on top of the place mat, and use the craft knife to cut out the letters.
3. Design your place mat by arranging your mementos on one of the pieces of poster board until you're happy with how it looks.
4. Remove the mementos, and one by one, glue them to the poster board.
5. Cut a piece of the shelf paper slightly larger than the place mat. Peel off the backing and place the shelf paper sticky side up onto your work surface.
6. Carefully lay your place mat on the shelf paper and smooth it down.
7. Cut a second piece of shelf paper and place it on top of the place mat.
8. Cut around the edges of the place mat until the shelf paper is the same length around the mat. Repeat until you have the number of place mats you want.

Maps, Maps, & Even More Maps

A MAP IS A PICTURE OF A PLACE. Sounds simple. However, if the map below looks a little strange to you, then maps aren't as simple as you may think. You see, there is absolutely nothing wrong with this map. It shows the continents accurately, and all the place names are correct. What? It's upside down?! Says you. There's no upside down in space. Plus, Earth is spherical, and sphere's don't generally have tops and bottoms. This map is just as accurate as any map you're used to seeing. So there! Knowing where you are is a fundamental concept of geography, and maps are pretty good tools for the job. However, as you can see, maps can be funny things. Sure, they're good at presenting information you need about a place, but since mapmakers have to make decisions about what to show and how to show them, maps also become good at *telling* us how to think about places. They also tell us about what people in the past knew and didn't know about the world, or what was important to them. Maps say a lot about who we are and hold clues about not only the mapmakers but the people who use the maps. This chapter explores maps (as you've probably already figured out): how to make them, how to use them, how to understand them, as well as how to have some fun with them.

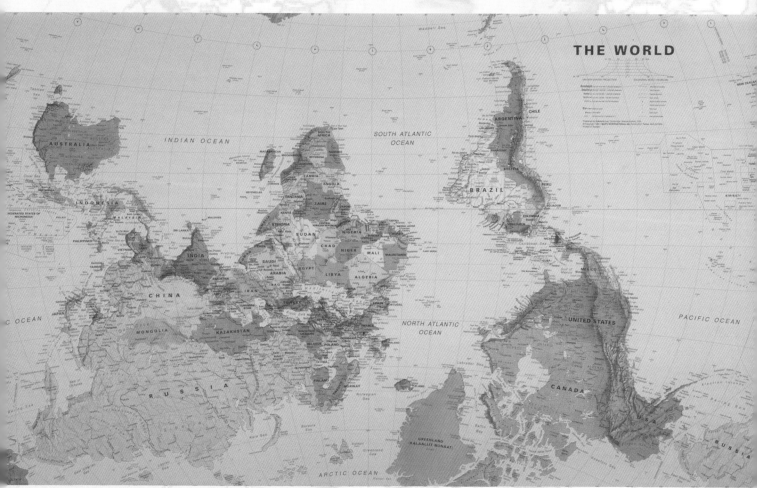

What's Up? South! Map (See page 398 for more information on this map.)

BECOME A CARTOGRAPHER IN ONE DAY
(Plus or Minus Several Years of Study and Practice)

It's a plain, old fact that some people would rather have a beautiful map that isn't all that accurate than a map that strictly gives good information about a location. A cartographer is another word for a mapmaker, and it's a cartographer's job to combine science and art to create the world's maps. This project delves into the science of making a map. For the art of making a map, see page 307. Now, most mapmakers would get upset at us if we said you could become a great cartographer simply by reading this book. So, we won't say that. (Angry mapmakers make us nervous.) However, we have no problem telling you how to make a simple map using only a compass, a tape measure, and a protractor. This map will be accurate and it's fun. If you run into any angry mapmakers, don't tell them where we live.

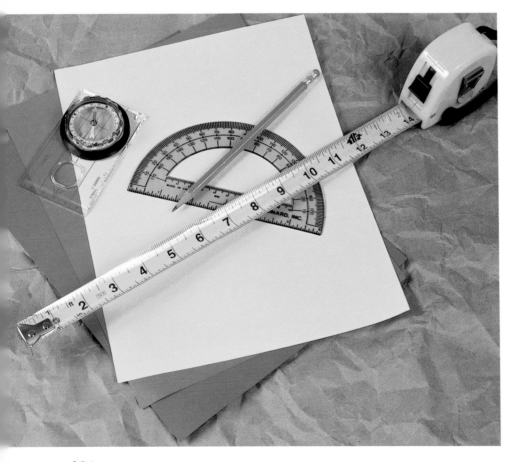

WHAT YOU NEED
- Tape measure
- Paper
- Clipboard
- Calculator (optional)
- Rock
- Pencil
- Compass, with degrees noted on the face
- Ruler
- Protractor

WHAT YOU DO

1. Find a good place to map. Pick a place that has some fun features, such as a park, playground, or backyard.

2. Find the scale of your map. To do this, first measure the perimeter of the area you wish to map. Then divide the size of the area by the size of your paper. Here are two examples, one for the ever-dwindling feet and inches crowd, and

N

X

1 inch = 12 feet 1 cm = 2 m

another for the vast metric crowd:
A. Say you want to map a playground that's 120 x 120 feet, and your paper is 10 x 10 inches. First, convert feet into inches by multiplying 120 by 12, which equals 1,440 inches. Then divide 1,440 inches by 10, which is 144 inches. The scale is

1:144. This means that 1 inch on the map equals 144 inches or 12 feet.
B. Say you want to map a playground that's 40 x 40 meters, and your paper is 20 x 20 centimeters. First, convert meters into centimeters by multiplying 40 by 100, which equals 4,000. Then divide 4,000

centimeters by 20, which equals 200 centimeters. The scale is 1:200. This means that 1 centimeter on the map equals 200 centimeters or 2 meters.
3. Locate the middle of the area you've chosen to map and mark it with the rock. This is the point where you will make your measurements.

Mark this spot on your paper. Use the clipboard to make drawing while standing easier.

4. Stand over the rock, and find north with the compass. Draw a line from the center point to show north. Use a ruler to get a straight line (figure 1).

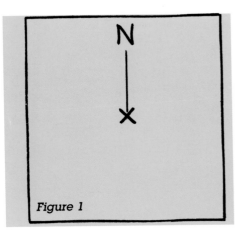

Figure 1

5. In order to figure out where to plot your objects on your map, you'll need to measure angles and distances. To measure an angle, you'll use the compass to measure how many degrees from north each object is. For example, say you're mapping out a playground, and the first item you want to plot is a slide. While you're standing at the center point, face the slide and hold the compass directly in front of you at eye level (figure 2). Notice where north is and then write down how

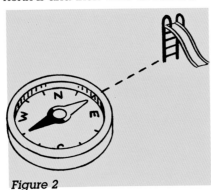

Figure 2

many degrees the slide is from north (say 60°).

6. Place the protractor over the center point on your map and mark the angle of your bearing with a pencil line. This is the direction of the slide (figure 3).

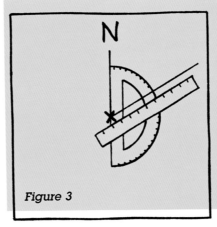

Figure 3

7. Measure how far away the object is from the center point (its distance) with the tape measure (let's say the slide was 10 meters] away).

8. Mark the distance, keeping in mind the scale you developed in step 2 —10 meters = 5 cm (figure 4).

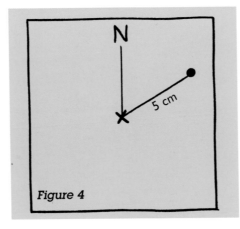

Figure 4

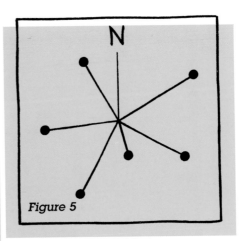

Figure 5

9. Follow steps 3 through 8 for every object you wish to include on your map (figure 5). When taking bearings on buildings or other large structures, take more than one bearing (use the buildings' corners). Since protractors have only 180 degrees, when you get a compass bearing that's more than 180° you'll have to do some subtracting. For example, say you take a bearing on a tree and it's 320° from north. Subtract 180 from 320 and you get 140. Place your protractor so that 180 is at the top of the map (pointing north) and read off 140°. This will end up being your 320° bearing.

10. After you've mapped all the objects in your area, you can draw in the objects and then erase your lines. Don't forget to show your scale on the map somewhere.

ANTIQUE MAP & CASE

This project focuses more on the art of mapmaking—in other words, making them pretty and cool. Most maps created during the Age of Exploration were stunning to look at, even if you couldn't find where in the world you were on it. If you're fascinated with these old maps, here's your chance to make one for yourself. You can use it to lead to the time capsule on page 343, or simply to decorate your room.

to the time capsule on page 343

WHAT YOU NEED

- Drawing paper
- Pens, markers, crayons, and/or colored pencils
- Ruler
- Black tea bag soaked in hot water
- Use of an oven
- Candle or lighter
- Mailing tube
- Scissors
- Fabric strips
- Paper
- Ribbon
- Craft glue

WHAT YOU DO

1. Draw your map on the drawing paper with markers, colored pencils, crayons, and/or pens. (See page 304 for information on creating maps.) Look at old maps for ideas for adding details, such as a compass rose in an antique-looking style.

2. When the ink on your map is dry, crumple the paper into a tight ball. Do this a few times until you think the map is sufficiently wrinkled.

3. Squeeze the excess water out of the tea bag, then blot the map with it. Wipe the tea bag all over the

paper, and firmly press the bag onto the paper in some spots to get darker stains.

4. Place the paper in the oven on the rack at 200°F (93°C) for a few

minutes until the paper is dry. Check the map often, as it'll dry quickly.

5. Ask a parent for help to use the lighter or candle to burn the edges of the paper to finish the antique look.

6. No treasure map is complete without its case. Cut a mailing tube so the rolled-up map fits into it. Save the caps for both ends of the original tube to close the case.

7. Glue fabric scraps, paper, ribbon, and other exotic-looking materials onto the tube to make the case look fit for a king or queen's map.

OLD MAP PILLOWCASE OR ADVENTURE BACKPACK

Some old maps are so awesome looking you may want to make your own exotic map patches to personalize your everyday belongings. With the help of a computer and color printer, you can download and print historical maps and imagery straight from the Internet. Since most of these maps are in the public domain (meaning the original creator long ago passed away or the images were produced by and for a government agency), you can use them for your projects.

WHAT YOU NEED

- Computer with Internet access
- Photo-editing software (optional)
- Ink-jet color printer
- Iron-on transfer paper (available at office supply stores)
- Lightly colored backpack, pillowcase, or other cloth item to decorate
- Iron
- Colored pens or fabric paint (optional)

WHAT YOU DO

1. Check out sources for old maps and public-domain images, or do your own subject search on the Internet for sites with images you can download and print. If you have photo-editing software, you can work with the digital images you find to change their size to fit the object you want to decorate. If you don't have this software, then look for images you can print directly. You should print the images you like on plain paper to judge the quality and actual layout of the images before using the transfer paper. If you have a scanner, you could also scan pictures you like and print them out.

2. When you've experimented with the image you want and have a good printed version, load the transfer paper into the printer and print the image again.

3. Cut the excess transfer paper from around the image and center it on your backpack or pillowcase to make sure it'll fit well.

4. Follow the directions provided by the manufacturer of the transfer paper for ironing your image onto the fabric. Some helpful tips include:

- Smooth out any wrinkles in the fabric you're going to transfer the image onto, and work on a firm, flat surface.
- Be especially careful to press the

iron down firmly for several seconds on the image, especially along the edges. Then run the iron over the entire surface for a few minutes to make sure the image has taken to the fabric.

- Let the transfer paper cool completely before trying to peel it off the object you're transferring to.
- Slowly and steadily peel the paper off the fabric. If you notice that the image has not completely transferred, stop pulling it up and smooth the paper back down and iron again.
- Make sure you're transferring onto light-colored fabrics, since images don't transfer well onto dark material.

5. You can highlight details of your image with permanent ink pens or fabric paint, or use paints and markers to add color to a black-and-white image.

GRID ART

WHAT YOU NEED
- Cool image you wish you could draw
- Tracing paper or graph paper
- Ruler
- Pencil
- Use of a photocopy machine

WHAT YOU DO

1. Cut a piece of tracing paper or graph paper to the size of the cool drawing you wish you could draw.

2. Draw straight, horizontal lines every 1 inch (2.5 cm) from one side of the page to the other. Use the ruler to make sure the lines are straight and spaced equally apart. Repeat with vertical lines every 1 inch (2.5 cm).

3. Decide whether you want your drawing to be bigger or smaller than the cool drawing, and enlarge or reduce the size of the grid you've drawn on the tracing paper with the photocopier. For example, if you want your image to be 20 percent larger, enlarge the size of the photocopied grid to 120 percent. Play with the "lighter/darker" buttons until your photocopied grid is very light.

4. Place the tracing paper over the cool drawing, and simply draw what you see in each square onto the same square on the photocopied paper. Voilà, you're an artist! We knew you had it in you. And that's how grids work on a map. Each square is simply a much smaller picture of the actual area it's showing.

Most maps that show locations in cities and towns have grids, which are horizontal and vertical lines that intersect to create boxes. These are not the same as latitude and longitude lines. This network of lines helps you find specific locations on the map. Usually columns are given numbers and rows are given letters, or vice versa. So if a road is located at B3, you can find the exact box in which that road is located. Here's a grid activity that not only shows you how grids work, but also how you can begin your career as an artist.

NEIGHBORHOOD MAP

As cool as maps are, they can't do and show everything. In fact, mapmakers are pretty particular about what they include in their maps. They can't possibly include everything there is to see—maps would be way too hard to read and decipher. So maps are drawn to show only what mapmakers and others consider very important.

That's one reason why your home most likely isn't highlighted on a map of your city. Sure your home's important to you, but it's not too important to the rest of the city. But sometimes maps omit too much, leaving you with a map that doesn't have enough information. You can fix that by personalizing a street map of your neighborhood to REALLY show what's there. You'll identify natural and cultural landmarks in your neighborhood not found on street maps, and talk with your neighbors and share your suggestions for the best routes for walking the dog, riding your bike, jogging, or skateboarding.

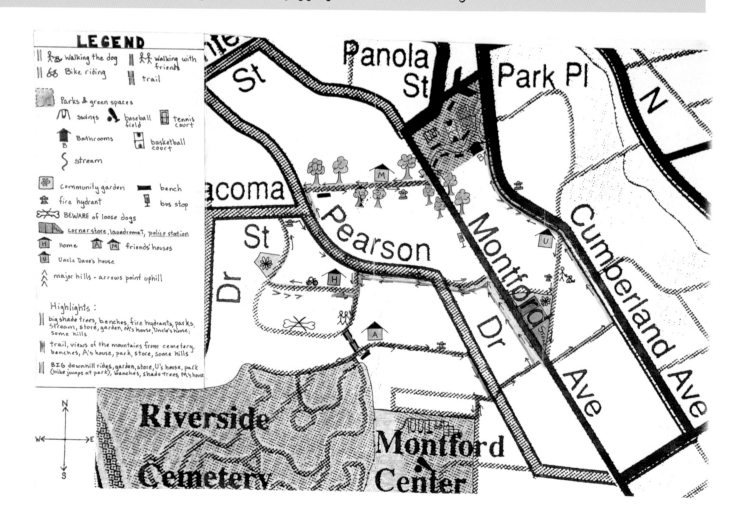

WHAT YOU NEED

- Notebook with a hard back or paper attached to a clipboard
- Street map that includes your neighborhood
- Use of a photocopy machine
- Ruler
- Colored pencils, crayons, or markers
- Pencil
- Eraser
- Black marker
- White correction fluid
- Glue
- Foam brush
- Compass

WHAT YOU DO

1. Let your dog take you for a walk (with guidance from you to stay on sidewalks and out of backyards). Let your dog lead the way around the neighborhood, and let your furry friend pick the next direction at intersections. Keep track of your route by writing it down in a notebook as you move from place to place. Write down the features your dog is attracted to, such as trees and fire hydrants, as well as the places you should avoid in the future. If you don't have a dog, keep reading.

2. Strap on a pair of inline skates, or hop on your bike, and highlight the best route through your neighborhood on the map. Highlight the best route for exploring with a friend. How are these routes different from the dog-walking route? Are any sections the same? How does landscape affect where and how roads are made and the shape of your neighborhood? What neighborhood improvements would you recommend to make the routes

even better and safer for walkers, dogs, or bike riders?

3. Use the zoom settings on a photocopier to enlarge the section of the street map that shows your neighborhood. Enlarge it until you can easily draw in details such as houses, trees, and signs. Your map will probably be large enough to work with when 3 inches equals 1 mile (7.6 cm equals 1.6 km). To figure this out, look at the original map and use the map scale to measure and locate a street that is 1 mile (1.6 km) long. Go to the enlarged map and measure the same street with a ruler. Keep enlarging this map until the street you're measuring becomes 3 inches (7.6 cm) long.

4. Refer to your notes and highlight your dog's path with a brightly colored marker, colored pencil, or crayon. Draw your house and other features that are important to your dog or to you.

5. In one corner of your map make a legend to explain all of the symbols you created for it. Cut a piece of blank paper and paste it over the part of your map where you want the legend to be. Decorate with the symbols you made and their meanings.

6. Fold your neighborhood map accordion-style into even sections for easy carrying.

7. Cut a photocopy of the original map to fit on the front of your map when it's folded up. Use the foam brush to spread the glue on the back of the photocopy and paste it to the front of your map.

8. Make a circle around your neighborhood. Decorate as you like.

9. Present your map to neighbors and share your suggestions for neighborhood improvements. If your neighborhood has an organized council or a representative who works with your town's government, send a map to them with your suggestions, and maybe your effort will make the improvements happen.

FAMILY MAPS

WHAT YOU NEED
- Your family
- Paper
- Markers

WHAT YOU DO

1. Have each family member map the same area, with your home as the center. Give them the streets they should map, and ask each of them to mark locations and landmarks. While they're doing the activity, you can do one yourself.

2. After everyone's done, compare the maps. What landmarks did a sibling choose that your dad or mom didn't choose? Why do you think that happened? Well, the same thing happens to real mapmakers. They may map the same area, but highlight different landmarks, due to their knowledge of the area or their reason for making the map.

"Hey, Dad, this is Heather. I'm in front of the candy shop. Can you pick me up? It's raining."

"No problem, tell me how to get to the candy shop."

"Take a left onto 9th Street, and then turn right when you see the bicycle shop."

"The what?"

"You know, the bicycle shop on 9th."

"Oh, you mean the shop next to the bank. Okay, I'll be right there."

Have you ever had to give directions to one of your parents and had trouble because they didn't know the landmarks you were using to direct them? Doesn't it seem odd to you that you can live in the same place as the rest of your family, and yet notice completely different landmarks? Try this map experiment with your family and see how the same thing could happen to cartographers.

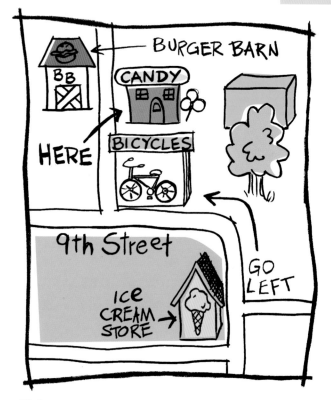

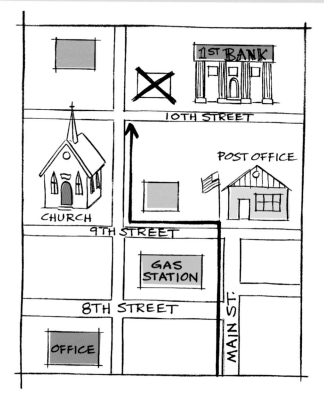

GLOBE YOUR FRIENDS

As you taught your friend in Chapter 1, the world is round (okay, technically it's a sphere). So, the only truly accurate map of Earth is a globe. (The best way to map a round object is with a round map.) Now, globes are great for classrooms and bedrooms, but they can get pretty hard to handle during a car trip or while out exploring. That's why we need flat maps, which are called "projections." These are great because you can fold them up and put them in your pocket. The only problem with flat maps is that when those nice cartographers take the time to project the curved earth onto a flat piece of paper, funny things start happening. Countries and oceans get stretched out and distorted. In fact, no matter how hard you try, a flat map will not be as accurate as a globe. Draw a map of the world on a grapefruit, and then carefully peel it. Go ahead, try it out. We'll wait....

...Now, try placing the rind onto a table. Not so easy, is it? First of all, there are gaps at the top and bottom. If you stretch the top and bottom so that they come together, the world at those places becomes distorted, and they appear much bigger than they actually are. In fact, if you stretch the globe out on a flat surface, almost all directions and distances between things are out of their proper places.

In this activity, you'll start with a flat photograph and cut away pieces until you can create a globe. Those extra pieces you end up cutting away represent all the extra pieces that have to be added to a flat map to make it look good! See page 319 for more on flat maps.

WHAT YOU NEED
- Template on page 397
- Use of a photocopy machine
- Pencil
- Your class picture or other image enlarged to 11 x 14 inches (27.9 x 35.6 cm)
- Cereal box
- 1 piece of colored paper, 11 x 14 inches (27.9 x 35.6 cm)
- Scissors or craft knife
- Craft glue
- Awl or nail
- Large sewing needle
- String

WHAT YOU DO
1. Enlarge the template on page 397 to 11 x 14 inches (26.9 x 35.6 cm) with the photocopy machine.
2. Trace the template onto the back of the picture you had enlarged, the cereal box, and the colored paper, then cut out the pattern from each.

3. Glue the picture to one side of the cereal box template and the colored paper to the other side.
4. Use the awl to poke a hole through each end of the "petals"

316

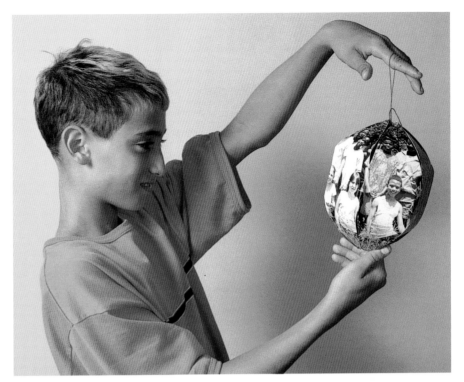

so that when the ends are matched up, the holes line up together.

5. Thread the string through the needle and sew the bottom of the globe together by passing the needle through the holes at each end of the petals. You'll need to fold the petals over each other, and in the process, your globe will begin to take shape. Tie a knot in the string and cut off any excess string.

6. Thread another piece of string through the needle and sew the top of the globe together by passing the needle through the holes in the petal tops. Tie a knot, but leave extra sting so you can hang the globe up. Before you recycle the parts you cut away, remember, that's all the extra stuff that needs to be added to a flat map!

WHERE THE RIVERS FLOW

Here's a question that proves that maps can often influence you in ways you didn't expect.

Which way do rivers flow? You probably answered north to south, except for the Nile. Why do they flow north to south? Perhaps you said because you think rivers should flow from top to bottom. If you look at a map, that would make sense; however, rivers move where there's less resistance, which means they take advantage of gravity. So even though it *feels* right that things should move from north to south or up to down and not the other way around, rivers flow down hills and mountains, not down maps. Do some research and check out all the rivers that actually flow south to north. You'll be surprised by what you find.

317

THE CENTER OF THE WORLD

Congratulations! Right now you're standing at the center of the world. Pretty cool, eh?! But don't get too excited. Though we're used to seeing the world the way maps present it, there are actually an infinite number of centers of the world. If you live in the United States, your world looks like this:

Or if you're from a tiny island in the Pacific Ocean, your world looks like this:

Not too many neighbors!

If you live at the South Pole, the center of the world looks like this:

When you look at a world map or even a satellite photo of Earth, make a note of what countries are featured in the center, and which ones get cut off on one side and appear again on the other side. Think to yourself, "Hmmm, wonder who made this map?" If your answer is, "It was probably somebody who lives in one of the countries in the center of the map," you're probably right.

A note on these photos: These are computer-generated relief globe images of the Earth showing land and undersea topography. They're from the National Geophysical Data Center.

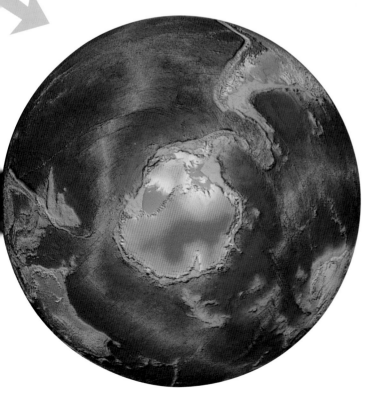

The Flat Map Flap

As you saw on page 315, trying to map something round on a flat piece of paper can be troublesome. Many cartographers have tried and had some success, but something screwy always happens. The cartographer's problem is that you cannot show accurate shape, size, distance, and direction at the same time. Take a look at these four popular world maps *and* what happens to poor old Greenland in each map.

THE MERCATOR PROJECTION

Until recently, this map is the one you've probably seen and worked with. It appeared in most classrooms, atlases, and geography textbooks as a pretty good map of the world. This map was created in 1569 by a cartographer (named Mercator) who wanted to create a map that kept all the directions correct so navigators on ships wouldn't get lost. He decided to create a projection in which direction was represented accurately and the land near the poles would be distorted. So Mercator ended up keeping the continents' shapes accurate while he stretched

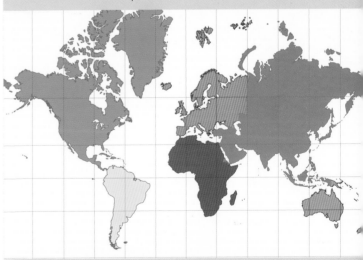

and distorted their sizes. Mercator knew this was going to happen, and though he probably would be proud to have his map in classrooms all over the world, he probably would pitch a fit if he found out that his distortions were not being explained. Most people, after looking at his map, came to believe Greenland was the same size as Africa, even though Africa is 14 times bigger! Plus, the center of the map is western Europe, not the equator.

THE PETERS PROJECTION

This map, first introduced by cartographer Dr. Arno Peters in 1974, attempts to correct the distortions created by the Mercator Projection. It's called an "equal area map" because it shows all areas according to their actual size (one square inch anywhere on the map equals a constant number of square miles), though their shapes become distorted, making the continents look strange to us. This map is not good for navigating, but it's great for people who want to show all of the areas of the world according to their size and location. It also corrects the perception created by the Mercator projection that the Northern Hemisphere is larger than the Southern Hemisphere.

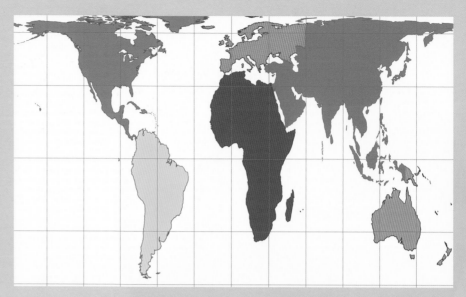

THE ROBINSON PROJECTION

This map was created in 1963 by cartographer Arthur H. Robinson. It's considered a compromise between other maps. It isn't reliable for navigating, and though it minimizes size and shape distortions, some distortions still exist, especially in the polar regions. Distances are also distorted. This map attempts to show a more accurate picture of the world by distorting size, shape, scale, and area. Sounds like a paradox, but it works.

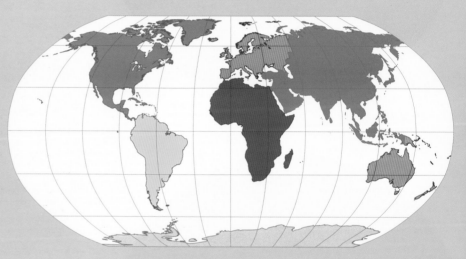

THE WINKEL TRIPEL PROJECTION

The Winkel Tripel improves on the Robinson projection by distorting the polar areas less to give an even more accurate perspective of the world.

FORGET LATITUDE AND LONGITUDE, GIVE US SOME SEA MONSTERS, UNICORNS, AND MEN WITHOUT NOSES!

Back during that miserable time known to most as the Middle or Dark Ages, before the world had been explored (and much of what had already been discovered about the world had been lost and forgotten), mapmakers had a lot in common with fiction writers. Absurd, you say?! Well, mapmakers back then based most of their maps on pure fantasy. Sometimes they'd draw what little

they knew and fill in the empty spaces with doodlings, imagined lands, or whatever came into their heads—none of which had anything to do with rivers, mountains, or cities. Sometimes cartographers didn't know anything about a place and simply drew their maps from stories they overheard, which could include far-fetched tales about sea creatures that swallowed ships whole, mermaids, unicorns, and more! Mapmakers soon found that their colorful, almost entirely unusable, maps sparked people's imaginations and became quite popular. So they kept turning out maps that had less to do with trying to find your way from one

place to another than with entertaining. Many maps from this period were based on the absolutely, positively, unconditionally silly and insane notions put forth by Julius Solinus. His book, *Gallery of Wonderful Things*, was first published around A.D. 235. In this so-called geography book, he wrote detailed descriptions of places he never visited and people he never met. Some of Solinus's best whoppers include:

• A race of dog-headed people ruled by a dog-king

• People with four eyes

• Ants as big as dogs

• A mule-like creature with an upper lip so long that it must walk backwards in order to eat

• Tribes who had eight-toed feet that were turned backwards

• People with only one leg, but with a foot so large that it protected them from the hot sun by serving as an umbrella

• People with ears so long that they used them as blankets at night

• People with only one eye just above their noses

• People without noses

• And our favorite one of all: people whose eyes and mouths were on their chests

Funny, yes, but unfortunately, some of these stories were considered fact for up to a thousand years. So the next time someone asks you why the Dark Ages were "Dark," tell them about this guy Solinus.

TOPOGRAPHIC MAP OF A FRIEND'S FACE

Topographic maps solve the problem cartographers have when they attempt to show elevation on a flat map. A favorite of hikers, "topo" maps show the height off the ground of hills, valleys, and cliffs using *contour lines* to give the appearance of height.

Contour lines are imaginary lines on the ground that join places of the same height. Think of them as lines that will go anywhere in order to maintain a constant elevation. If the contours are close together, then the slope is steep; if they're spaced wide apart, then the slope is more gentle. If you see hardly any contours at all, then the area is almost flat. For another perspective, think of a region completely underwater in your tub. As you slowly let the water out, the water leaves rings. Those rings are contours.

You can create contours on a map using lines, but nothing says contours quite like face paints!

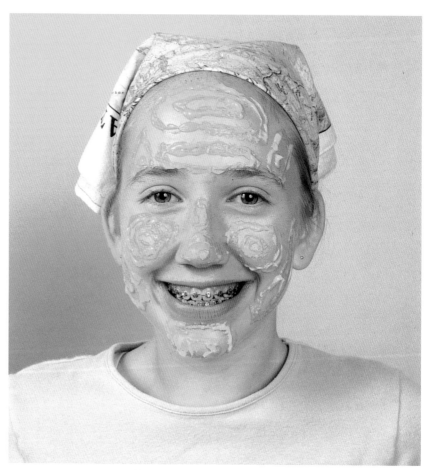

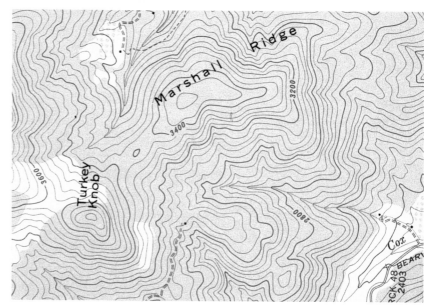

A topographic map

WHAT YOU NEED

- 1 tablespoon (14 g) cornstarch
- 1 1/2 teaspoons (7.5 mL) of water
- 4 1/2 teaspoons (22.5 mL) cold cream
- Bowl
- Spoon
- Food coloring
- Tissue paper

WHAT YOU DO

1. Mix the cornstarch, water, and cold cream in the bowl until smooth. Add a few drops of the food coloring of your choice.

2. Examine the different features on your friend's face. Imagine her nose is like a mountain, her eyes are like valleys, and her eyebrows are like ridges.

3. With your finger or a small paintbrush, mark the highest point on her face. Then move down from there approximately 1/4 inch (6 mm), and trace the highest features at this level. Continue moving down from the highest point on your friend's face in 1/4-inch (6 mm) intervals until you feel you've thoroughly mapped her face.

4. Carefully lay a piece of tissue paper over your friend's face, and press it against her skin so it sticks to all of her contours.

5. In one swift motion, peel the paper off her face and lay it flat on a table to dry.

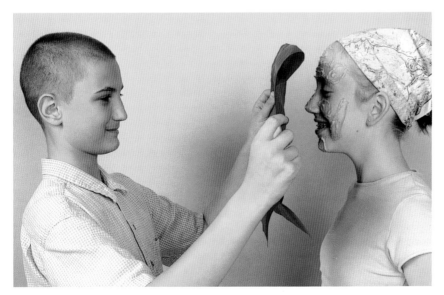

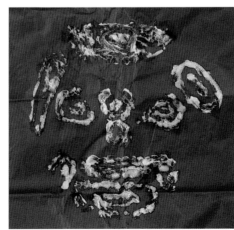

There's Cool, California and Frostproof, Florida. There's Gas, Kansas and Flushing, New York. You may have a good time in Yeehaw Junction, Florida or Celebration, Florida, but don't expect much in Boring, Oregon or Boring, Maryland. Don't get lost in North, South Carolina, and watch where you're walking in Dead Horse, Alaska. There might be some self-esteem problems in Oddville, Kentucky; Odd, West Virginia; Only, Tennessee; Nowhere, Oklahoma; Nameless, Tennessee; and No Name, Colorado. And you may just find the answers to the world's biggest questions in Why, Arizona and Whynot, Mississippi. After visiting Cut and Shoot, Texas, spend some time in Notrees, Texas. Slap Out, Illinois sounds like a good town to skip, though Zook, Kansas and Zap, North Dakota don't sound much better. As for Santa Claus, Indiana; Monkey's Eyebrow, Arizona; Muleshoe, Texas; Experiment, Georgia; and Rough-And-Ready, California; well, let's just say at least they don't have big egos, like the folks in Earth, Texas.

DEEP MAP

A deep map is a map that shows something different. Instead of showing roads, boundaries, and cities far and wide, a deep map goes beneath the surface and tells about what used to be in one place, about the plants and animals that live there, about the people who live there now and who used to live there, about the feel, sounds, and smells of a place. A deep map can be as deep as you want it to be. You might want to tell a lot about the very earliest people who lived there, or you might want to tell where the squirrels that live there now like to congregate. You can also include the geography, natural environment, culture, and spirit of that place and the people who have lived there over time.

WHAT YOU NEED

- Paper for pages, any size you want
- Drawing materials
- Piece of heavy paper for the cover, it should be at least two-and-a-half times as wide as the text pages, and the same height as the text pages
- Ruler
- Scissors
- Small paper clip
- Strong paper clamp
- Awl or nail
- Rubber band, 2 to 3 inches (5.1 to 7.6 cm) long
- Stick, 3 inches (7.6 cm) long, about as thick as a pencil

WHAT YOU DO

1. Begin collecting information about the place you want to deep map. What does the land look like today? What can you find out about the way the land used to look? Go to the library and ask for copies of any maps that include this place. Old maps are especially interesting. Look in old city directories to see who used to live and work in the place years ago. Look in the current directory to see who lives and works there now.

2. Take a walk in the place. What plants grow there? What animals live there? Can you find any animal homes? What kinds of houses and other buildings are there? Talk to the people who live and work there. What can you learn from their stories about the place? What are the special sounds, songs, smells, foods, holidays of this place? Are there any cemeteries? What can you learn about who used to live there? Make drawings and maps of your own, and take notes and photographs.

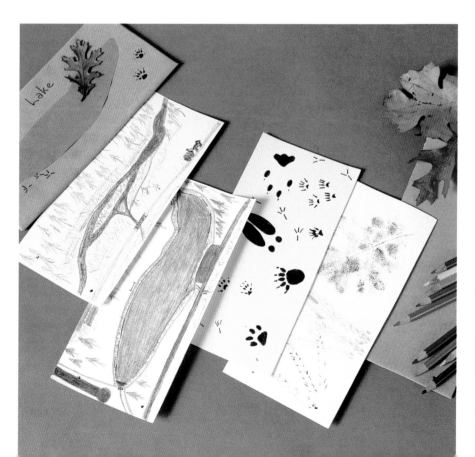

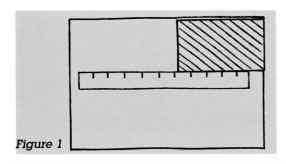

Figure 1

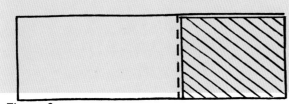

Figure 2

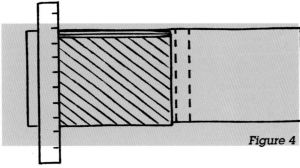

Figure 3

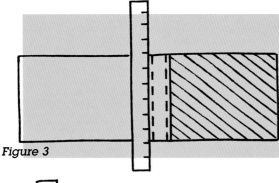

Figure 4

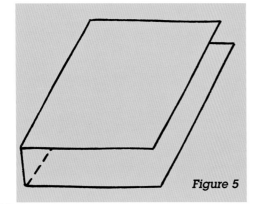

Figure 5

3. When you have lots of information about the place, think about how you want to put it all in the book. Decide how big the pages need to be. What will it take to give a good, deep picture of this special place? Do you need any pages that are extra long and will fold out? Do you need any that have special shapes? Decide which pictures, photographs, or drawings you'd like to include. Write up the stories you want to tell. Make time lines, charts, and diagrams to give other information.

4. Start putting your book together. Don't continue until you know exactly where you want to put everything.

5. Gather all your blank sheets of paper, and write and draw on each page. Be sure to leave a space at least $1^1/_2$ inches (3.8 cm) wide at the left side of each sheet because that's where the binding will be. Assemble all the sheets of paper in the order you want them. Fold in any extra long sheets. Be sure to

include a title page and maybe a blank page at the beginning and at the end of the book.

6. Make a cover for the book out of the heavy paper. To do so, place the stack of pages in one corner of the cover. Place the ruler across the top (figure 1).

7. Remove the stack of pages, but don't move the ruler. Draw a line along the bottom edge of the ruler. Cut the paper along that line.

8. Place the stack of pages at one end of the piece of cover paper that you have just cut (figure 2). Use the small paper clip to score a line on the cover paper along the side of the stack of paper. Remove the stack and use the ruler and paper clip to score another line as far away from the first one as the book is thick (figure 3).

9. Lay the stack of pages on the cover so that its left edge lines up with the second scored line (figure 4). Score along the right edge of the stack. Remove the stack and cut along the line you've just scored. Fold the cover along the other two scored lines as shown in figure 5. Slip the pages into the cover.

10. Tap the book on a tabletop so the pages all line up. Clip the book with the paper clamp along the right edge to hold the pages in place while you bind it (figure 6).

11. Use the awl to poke a hole through the cover and all the pages at one time (figure 6). Keep the awl straight up and down while pressing hard and screwing it back and forth. Poke through from one end, then turn the book over and widen out the hole from the other side.

Figure 6

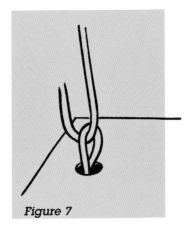

Figure 7

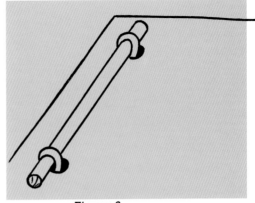

Figure 8

12. Poke this hole around ¹/₂ inch (1.3 cm) down from the top edge and ¹/₂ inch (1.3 cm) from the spine. Poke a second hole ¹/₂ inch (1.3 cm) up from the bottom and ¹/₂ inch (1.3 cm) in from the spine.

13. Unbend the small paper clip; then squeeze a narrow bend or hook in one end. This hook will help you thread the rubber band through the holes. With the front cover facing you, slip the hook through one of the holes. Put the rubber band on the hook, and pull the hook and rubber band about ¹/₂ inch (1.3 cm) through the hole (figure 7).

14. Slip one end of the stick through this loop of the rubber band. Now stick the hook through the other hole, and hook the other end of the rubber band. Pull this end through the hole, and slip this loop onto the other end of the stick (figure 8). Decorate the cover to finish your deep map.

Take a Deep Breath and Say...

"Llanfairpwllgwyngyllgogerychwyrndrobwyll-llantysiliogogogoch."

That's the name of a town in North Wales. But if you think that's a cartographer's nightmare, there's a small hill in New Zealand called Taumatawhakatangihangakoauauotamatea-turipukakapikimaungahoronukupokaiwhenuakitanatahu. Hmmm...nice place to visit, but I wouldn't want to pronounce it.

CREATE A FAVORITE NOVEL MAP

What's your favorite book of all time? Where did the story take place? Most likely there's quite a lot of detail about the "where" of the story. See if you can create a map of the book's location. You might be able to map a whole world, part of a city, a small village, or even every house on a block. You might notice some interesting items, but, even more importantly, you might notice things that are missing. Harper Lee's *To Kill a Mockingbird* is one of those books that teachers make you read in school that's actually awesome. And not only is it one of the coolest books around, but the location of the story is very important, and drawing a map actually helps understand the story. All you have to do is read the book and start adding details to your map as you come across them.

MAIL MAP

As we said before, maps can be created to show you just about anything: trade routes, population growth, or even where your mail comes from. In fact, if you take a close look at postmarks and business addresses, you might learn that certain business activities are concentrated in some regions of your country more than others. Perhaps it's due to the physical topography or how highways and railroads are situated.

Collect the mail that arrives at your home for a few weeks, and clip the postmarks and return addresses from the envelopes and backs of catalogs. Plot them on a national map that includes highways and major cities, and see where all that mail is coming from.

WHAT YOU NEED
- National road map
- A large sheet of cardboard to fit behind the map
- Mail
- Tape
- Pushpins
- Scissors
- String

WHAT YOU DO
1. Tape the road map to the large sheet of cardboard, and find a place to hang your map. Keep the pushpins and string near it.

2. Locate your town or city and mark it with a pushpin.

3. As mail arrives at your home (bills, letters, junk mail) cut out the postmarks and return addresses from the envelopes.

4. Pin the postmarks and return addresses to their matching cities on the map, and connect a piece of string between each new pushpin and the pin on your town or city. You've just created a mail map that tells you something you didn't know before: where all that mail is coming from.

RECYCLED MAP SHADE

With the way the world keeps changing, with islands disappearing and countries forming and changing names, maps become outdated rather quickly. That leaves map stores with large supplies of old maps that are probably slated for recycling. With this project, you can salvage an old map and give it a new use as an inspiring view for daydreaming in your room during long homework assignments.

WHAT YOU NEED

- Fabric-lined window shade
- Newspapers or painter's drop cloth
- Acrylic craft paint
- Large paintbrush, 2 or 3 inches (5 to 7.5 cm) wide
- Map to fit the shade
- Ruler
- Pencil
- Decoupage glue
- Water-based varnish
- 1/4-inch (6 mm) paintbrush

WHAT YOU DO

1. Unroll the window shade on top of a layer of newspapers or a painter's drop cloth. Spread a thin layer of paint across it with the large paintbrush until you've covered the shade. When dry, flip the shade over and paint the back of it.

2. Center the map on the side of the shade that'll face into your room. You can use the ruler to line the map up evenly by measuring the distance between the edge of the shade and the edge of the map in three places on each side. Use the pencil to mark the corners of the map on the window shade. Then set the map aside.

3. With the large paintbrush, spread an even and thin layer of decoupage glue across the shade, keeping inside of the box where the map was centered. Use the marks you made at the corners as guides.

4. Ask a friend to help you carefully lay the map back in place on the shade. Beginning in the center, smooth the map against the shade with your hands. Try to flatten out any air bubbles or creases in the map as you work around it. Some of the glue may soak through the map so that it looks wet or dark in color in some spots. Decoupage glue dries clear, so the color differences should go away once the glue has dried.

5. You may notice some spots along the edges where the map didn't stick to the shade.

Use the small paintbrush to spread a thin layer of glue under these areas, and press the map in place.

6. Spread a thin coat of varnish over the entire map and shade to seal it.

7. Hang your shade, sit back, and admire the new view you just created.

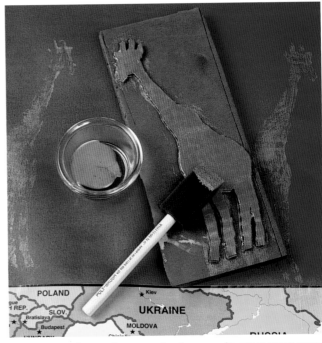

To further decorate your shade, create your very own stamp by cutting out a cardboard or foam shape, gluing it to a square piece of cardboard, and using a foam brush to cover the stamp with ink or paint.

331

We Are Different; We Are the Same

A PARADOX IS A STATEMENT that seems to be contradictory, or saying opposite things, but is true anyway. The title of this chapter is a paradox because even though it's contradicting itself, there's no better way to describe you and your world neighbors. If you took an imaginary walk down your world block, you'd run into all sorts of people wearing all sorts of clothing and speaking all sorts of languages. Some people might look strange to you. Maybe even weird. And the funny thing is, those people would be looking at you and thinking how weird you look. And what's even funnier is that all of these weird people staring at each other share 99.9 percent of their DNA! That's only one example of this "different sameness" we're talking about here. Geography isn't just a science, it's also a celebration of everything that's different and not so different about the 6 billion and then some inhabitants of Earth, and this chapter explores people (including you), how we live in our different corners (okay, okay, that's just an expression) of the world, what we share in common, how we relate our experiences, and what's important to us.

THE TOOTH RAT?

A custom is another word for a tradition or a practice that people of a particular group or region do. For example, when you were around six years old and lost your first primary tooth, your parents probably told you to put it under your pillow, and a tooth fairy would take it during the night and leave you some cash. Pretty good deal. Too bad you only had 20 primary teeth! Most of your friends had the same cool arrangement. That's a custom. Now, if you lost your tooth somewhere else in the world, a completely different creature may have taken your tooth, including a rat, mouse, hyena, rabbit, dog, beaver, crow, squirrel, or sparrow. Another popular custom, especially in Africa, is to throw your tooth on the roof. And there's usually no cash involved! You're just making sure a new tooth comes in. If you lived in Central or South America, your mom might make an earring or necklace out of your tooth. Other customs include burying the tooth, throwing it out a window, and placing it in a slipper. Just be glad you didn't lose your teeth in Germany. They don't do anything at all with their teeth. Investigate other cultural differences. How do people around the world celebrate birthdays, New Year's, the seasons? What about coming-of-age celebrations?

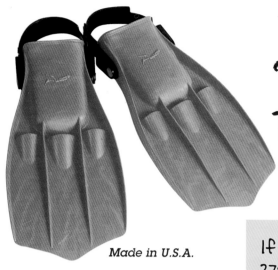
Made in U.S.A.

"MADE IN..." TREASURE HUNT

Made in China

Made in China

If you've read the introduction way back on page 275, you already realize that this book has been places. Stop reading for a moment and look around your room. Okay, now keep reading. Chances are your stuff, like this book, has been places you've only dreamed of visiting. In fact, there may be nothing in your room that was actually made in your own hometown or country! So even if you've never stepped foot outside your home your entire life, you've still been influenced by most of the world through your stuff. Check out this "treasure hunt" to see all the cool places your stuff has been (try not to get too jealous).

Made in ?

Made in Korea

Made in Canada

Made in China

Made in Pakistan

Made in U.S.A.

WHAT YOU NEED

- Your room
- World map
- Cardboard (optional)
- Glue (optional)
- Piece of paper
- Pen
- Markers or pushpins

WHAT YOU DO

1. Choose any room in your home as your treasure site.

2. Lay your map flat on a table or other hard surface. If you're using pushpins, first glue the map to a thick piece of cardboard.

3. Pick one area of the room and look for the labels on every object in that area, including clothing, furniture, games, electronic equipment, curtains, shoes, and books. Write down the country the object was "made in" on the piece of paper. Keep score of how many objects came from each country.

4. After you've recorded every object in the area, move on to the next area in the room and repeat step 3. Continue until you've checked as many objects as possible in the room.

5. If you're using a marker, develop a legend for the number of objects for each country. For example, place a large red dot on countries that contributed 20 or more objects to your room, a smaller blue dot on countries that contributed 15 to 19 objects, an even smaller green dot on countries that contributed 10 to 14 objects, and so on.

6. Did you notice anything unusual about your results? Was anything made in your country? If so, what? Was one type of object (CDs, clothing) made in one country? Did some objects have different parts that were made in different countries? Once you've looked over your results, research the countries your stuff came from and how they make their money.

Made in Japan

Made in China

WORLD SNACKS

Circle the correct words and fill in the blank:

There's nothing better than a nice

cold/hot   plate/bowl   of sticky/crunchy/smooth/tangy/hot/

_____ to satisfy my hunger after a long day at school.

Students worldwide will choose different words to describe their afternoon snacks, but the fact remains that everyone needs a snack when they get home from school. Here is a delicious selection of after-school snacks from around the world. Hit the kitchen and decide which you like best.

OATY BARS (NEW ZEALAND)

WHAT YOU NEED
$1/2$ cup butter or margarine (1 stick)
$1/4$ cup sugar
2 cups rolled oats
Use up to four of the following:
1 tablespoon peanut butter
$1/4$ cup raisins
$1/4$ cup banana chips
$1/4$ cup diced dried apricots
$1/4$ cup diced dried apples
$1/4$ cup chocolate chips
$1/4$ cup shredded coconut

WHAT YOU DO
1. Microwave the butter or margarine in a microwave-safe bowl on high for 1 minute.
2. Add the sugar and oats to the melted butter. Stir in up to 4 of the rest of the ingredients.
3. Press the mixture into a 9 x 9-inch microwave-safe dish. Microwave on high for $3^{1}/2$ minutes.
4. Cool, then refrigerate at least 30 minutes.
5. Cut into squares. Oaty Bars taste best at room temperature. Makes 16 bars.

WATERMELON SLUSHES (THAILAND)

What You Need
6 ice cubes
2 cups seedless watermelon, cubed
1 tablespoon (15 g) sugar or honey

What You Do
1. Crush the ice cubes in a blender or food processor.

2. Add the watermelon pieces, and blend for about 1 minute until the mixture is slushy.
3. Add the sugar or honey, and blend for 10 seconds. Pour the slush into tall glasses. Serves four.

PAIN AU CHOCOLAT (FRANCE)

WHAT YOU NEED

1 hard roll
Butter, softened (optional)
1 bar of milk chocolate

WHAT YOU DO

1. Slice the roll in half.
2. If using butter, spread it on one half of the roll.
3. Sandwich the chocolate bar between the bread.
4. Heat the sandwich in a toaster oven until the chocolate melts. Serves one.

FIVE-SPICE POPCORN (CHINA)

WHAT YOU NEED

$^1/_3$ cup popcorn kernels
1 cup chow mein noodles (optional)
$^1/_2$ cup peanuts
$^1/_3$ cup peanut oil
2 tablespoons soy sauce
1 teaspoon five-spice powder
$^1/_2$ teaspoon garlic powder
$^1/_2$ teaspoon sesame salt or salt
$^1/_2$ teaspoon ground ginger
$^1/_4$ teaspoon cayenne pepper
$^1/_8$ teaspoon sugar

WHAT YOU DO

1. Pop the popcorn kernels according to the instructions on the package.
2. Immediately after popping the popcorn, toss in the chow mein noodles and peanuts.
3. Combine the remaining ingredients in a bowl, and mix thoroughly.
4. Slowly pour the mixture over the popcorn, and mix.
5. Pour the popcorn into a large roasting pan. Heat the popcorn in the oven at 300°F (149°C) for 5 to 10 minutes, stir once.

BEANS AND CHIPS (MEXICO)

WHAT YOU NEED

15-ounce can refried beans
$^1/_2$ cup shredded cheddar cheese
1 tomato, washed and diced (optional)
$^1/_4$ cup sour cream (optional)
$^1/_4$ cup guacamole (optional)
Tortilla chips

WHAT YOU DO

1. Mix the beans and cheese in a microwave-safe container. Microwave on high for 45 seconds. Stir, then microwave for another minute and stir again.
2. If desired, layer the diced tomato, the guacamole, and the sour cream over the bean mixture.
3. To eat, scoop out with the tortilla chips. Serves four to six.

STAMP BOX

If you think a stamp is merely a small piece of paper that tells a postal carrier that you've paid to have a piece of mail delivered, oh how wrong you are! Stamps are tiny windows to the countries of the world.

Pick a country, and collect as many of its stamps as you can. By simply studying a country's stamps you can learn about its history, natural resources, political system, culture, places, citizens, birds, music, theater, dance, science, sports, and more. Many countries put a lot of time and effort into creating beautiful stamps, so that people will buy them and never use them. In fact, creating stamps for collectors is one of the main ways many small countries, such as San Marino—the entire country is 24 square miles—make money. Collect stamps from one country or collect stamps from many countries that have the same theme, and turn an ordinary box into a really awesome keepsake box.

WHAT YOU NEED

- Your choice of box
- Paint (optional)
- Small paintbrush
- Stamps
- Decoupage glue
- Craft knife
- Clear acrylic spray paint
- Small hinges with nails
- Hammer
- Decorative trim or upholstery tacks (optional)
- Glue

WHAT YOU DO

1. If your box already has hinges, remove them.

2. Paint the inside of the box, if you wish.

3. Decide how you want to decorate the box, and separate 15 to 20 of your most interesting stamps and set them aside. These will be your final layer on the box, and you don't want to use the coolest ones first.

4. Using the small paintbrush, apply the decoupage glue to the backside of the stamps and place them randomly on the box one at a time.

5. When your box is completely covered, place the lid on the box (without hinges) and apply the favorite stamps, allowing some to overlap the line between the top and bottom of the box. Allow the stamps to dry completely.

6. Find the line between the box and the lid, and press all the way around with your thumbnail. Next, place the craft knife in the groove you made and cut the lid away from the box.

7. Apply two to three coats of decoupage glue to the lid and bottom of the box, allowing each coat to dry thoroughly.

8. Spray the box with two to three coats of clear acrylic spray.

9. Reattach the hinges to the back of the box.

10. Add the decorative trim with the glue, if desired. Fill your box with treasures and enjoy!

FAMILY TREE BATIK BANNER

Who are you? The answers to that question are as varied as the number of people in the world. Many choose to answer this question by stating what nationality they are or what country they live in. Others, however, may state their ethnicity, or what culture or group of people in which their family originated.

Figuring out what your background is can become a fascinating world journey, which means that asking where your parents came from, where their parents came from, where their parents came from, and where their parents came from, until you run out of information, may lead you to many different lands. So, if you need further proof that we live in a global community, trace back your family tree as far as you can. Once you've done your research, "publish" your results on this fabric tree you can hang in your room or give to a relative as a gift.

WHAT YOU NEED
- Paper
- Pencil
- 100% cotton sheet (washed)
- Chalk
- Craft glue
- Paintbrush
- Large piece of cardboard (to fit under the banner)
- Fabric dye
- Salt
- Water
- Spray bottle
- Newspaper
- Rubber gloves
- Wash bin
- Dish soap
- Fusible webbing
- Iron
- 1/4-inch (6 mm) wooden dowel
- Permanent marker

WHAT YOU DO
1. Call your relatives and talk with your parents to get the information you need to draw your family tree on paper. Start with yourself as the trunk, then add two large branches (your parents), then add two branches to each of their branches (your grandparents), and so on as far back as you can trace your history. In doing this, you'll discover that your family has probably moved quite a bit and may even have roots on other continents.

2. Redraw your tree on the fabric with chalk. Leave 1 inch (2.5 cm) around each side of the banner to fold under for a hem later in the project.

3. Use the paintbrush to paint your entire tree with craft glue. Flip the banner over, and paint the tree on this side as well. The glue will block the dye from reaching the fabric wherever it's applied. Lay the banner on the large piece of cardboard, and let the glue dry.

4. Follow the manufacturer's directions, and mix up the dye, salt, and water in the spray bottle. Then, move the cardboard to a spread of newspapers on your driveway or in your yard, and spray the entire banner. You may want to spray the banner several times, as the dye will lighten as it dries and with washing. Let the banner dry before moving to the next step.

5. With rubber gloves on, rinse the banner in a wash tub or metal sink with cold water until the water runs clear from the fabric.

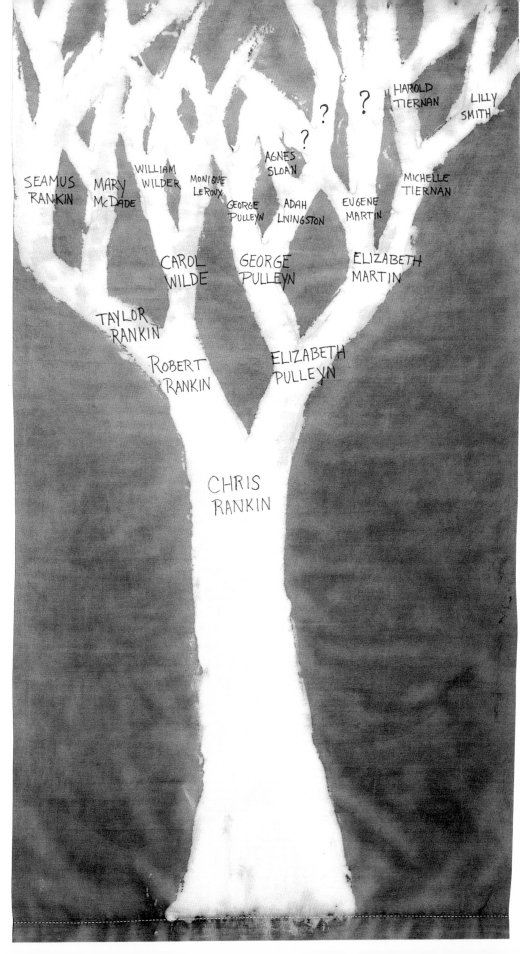

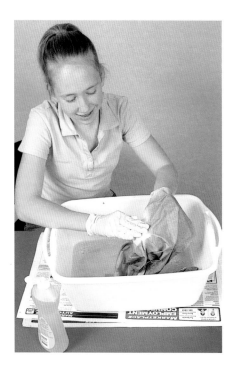

6. Squirt dish soap over the tree design, and in warm water, scrub the glue off the fabric. It should dissolve easily.

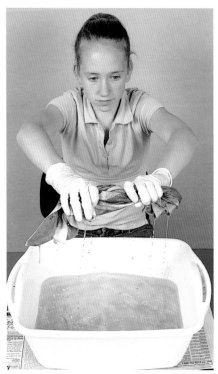

7. Wring out the batik and hang it to dry.

8. Cut four pieces of fusible webbing $1/8$ inch (3 mm) shorter than each side of the banner. Set your iron to the setting recommended by the fusible webbing manufacturer.

9. Flip the banner so the wrong side faces up, and place a piece of webbing along each side. Fold the sides of the banner over the webbing to make the trim. At the top of the banner, fold enough fabric over to make a pocket for the dowel to slide through above the fusible webbing strip.

10. Press the hot iron against the hems for at least 10 seconds in each spot as you move around the banner. The heat causes the webbing fibers to bind with the sheet to hold the hem in place.

11. Use the permanent marker to write your ancestors' names on the family tree.

Geographers are very interested in the past as well as what's going on today. By studying the past, they can learn about what people thought was important and how that affected how they lived on Earth. You can make tomorrow's geographers' jobs very easy by creating a time capsule that preserves this time in history you're experiencing by including stuff that's important to you and your friends. Or, you can dig it up yourselves years from now, and laugh at the things you thought were important way back then.

WHAT YOU NEED
- Large container with airtight lid
- Paint
- Paintbrushes
- Acid-free tissue paper
- Plastic bags
- Time capsule items
- Shovel

WHAT YOU DO
1. You can use many different containers for your time capsule. Choose something that is made of a nonbiodegradable material, such as plastic or metal. The plastic barrel used here has an airtight lid.

TIME CAPSULE

3. Place each item in a plastic bag to further protect them from rotting (especially paper items).

4. Decorate the capsule.

5. Place the items chosen into the capsule, and seal it.

6. Bury the capsule at least 3 feet (.9 m) underground.

7. Draw a map of the capsule's location (see page 304), and hide it someplace, and if you're going to open it yourself, decide on a date in the future to dig it up.

2. When deciding what to put in your time capsule, think of interesting topics that are important to you, your friends, your community, and your world. Include newspaper headlines, items of social and scientific interest, everyday objects such as a picture of your bike or your parents' car, or even a grocery store receipt. Include mementos of your favorite bands, fashions, and movie stars. Create audio and video tapes. You can even write a letter to the future and tell people what life is like today.

CLAY BOWL

There are some things all humans need to survive: food, water, air, shelter, clothing...but, what about the extras? There are some objects humans have perfected and passed around the world and through generations of people, and no, we're not talking about video games.

Archaeologists, anthropologists, and many geographers learn about past lifestyles based on the ways people decorated and used some of these universal objects, such as baskets, knives, and well...bowls. It may not seem so exciting, but the bowl has a pretty important place on the list of things people around the world choose to have. In other words, just about every ancient culture had cool bowls, and all over the world, people figured out that clay, wood, pounded stone, and woven grasses could be shaped to do something so simple—hold stuff. Mostly they're useful for keeping food together, but at best, they're beautiful pieces of sculpture.

So grab some clay and carry on an ancient tradition, and imagine what someone thousands of years from now would learn about you when they unearth your bowl.

WHAT YOU NEED
- Paper
- Pencil
- Wax paper
- Plastic wrap
- Oven bake clay
- Small bucket of water
- Rolling pin or flat-bottomed pan
- Fork
- Acrylic craft paints
- Paintbrush
- Charms and objects to glue to your finished bowl
- Craft glue or clear-drying, water-based sealant

*available at craft stores

WHAT YOU DO

1. Design your bowl on paper first, and decide how you'll decorate it. Choose symbols or items that are important to you or best describe who and what you are and what you like to do.

2. Cover your work surface with wax paper or plastic wrap.

3. Break off chunks of the clay and work it with your hands to warm it up and make it flexible. Throw it on the table several times, and smoosh it out and squish it back together. When it feels easy to work with, roll the clay into a ball with your hands.

4. Roll the ball on the table to make a long coil. Make a circle with the coil to see how wide your bowl will be. If you want it wider, roll the coil longer. If you want it shorter, cut some clay off the coil. If the clay starts to crack, dip your hands in water and smooth out the cracks with your fingers. You can also spread some water on the clay and then wrap the coil in plastic wrap to absorb the moisture.

5. Make several more coils, wrapping each one in plastic wrap so they don't dry out. The coils should all be the same size so they'll dry evenly.

6. Take a ball of clay and flatten it out with the rolling pin (or use a flat-bottomed pan to press the clay evenly) as wide as you want the base of the bowl to be.

7. Take one of the coils and shape it into a circle. Place it on the clay base, and trim the base to fit the outside edge of the coil.

8. To attach the coil to the base and the coils to each other, use the

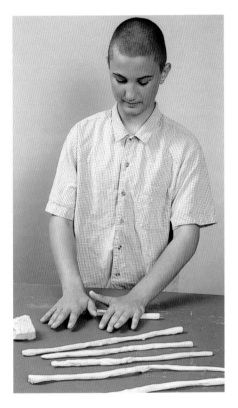

fork to roughen up the sides of the pieces you're going to connect. Pat the roughed-up sides with a little water and then press the pieces together. Smooth the coils together with wet fingers as you move up the bowl. If the clay starts to get dry, wet it with your fingers and let it sit under plastic wrap for a little while to moisten it up. Your finished bowl should be about the same thickness through the walls and the base so it will dry evenly.

9. Use the pencil to make impressions in your finished bowl, and outline the images you want to paint.

10. Follow the clay manufacturer's directions for drying and baking the clay. It's essential that the clay be dry before you bake it or else it'll crack. Small cracks can be patched with some craft glue or covered with paint.

11. Paint your bowl, glue charms onto it, and otherwise decorate it so it becomes an expression of who you are.

12. Seal and protect the inside and outside of the bowl by painting the entire surface with a thin layer of clear-drying craft glue or water-based sealant.

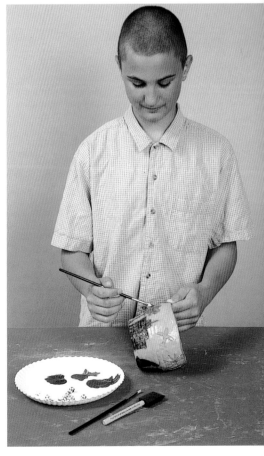

Baa, Moo, Kuk-kurri-kuu

Not only do different cultures see things differently, but they also apparently hear the same things differently. Even something as seemingly easy to "translate" as animal sounds are pronounced differently around the world, even though a cow in Belgium sounds the same as one in China. See if you can match the animal sounds below with the correct animal (answers are at the bottom of the page). Here's a hint: Read the sounds out loud a few times before giving up. The language the sound comes from is in parentheses.

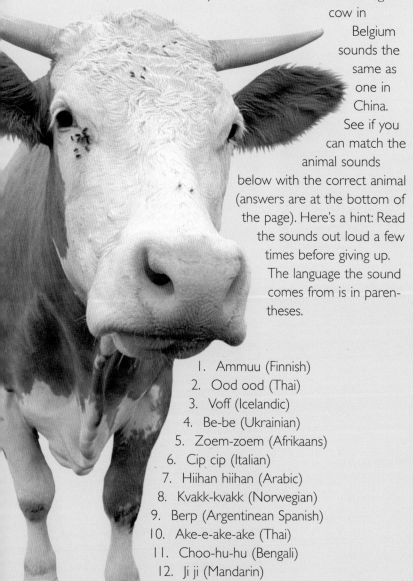

1. Ammuu (Finnish)
2. Ood ood (Thai)
3. Voff (Icelandic)
4. Be-be (Ukrainian)
5. Zoem-zoem (Afrikaans)
6. Cip cip (Italian)
7. Hiihan hiihan (Arabic)
8. Kvakk-kvakk (Norwegian)
9. Berp (Argentinean Spanish)
10. Ake-e-ake-ake (Thai)
11. Choo-hu-hu (Bengali)
12. Ji ji (Mandarin)
13. Qip qip (Albanian)
14. Sss (French) (Okay, some animal sounds are easier than others)
15. Auuuuuuu (Croatian)

Answers: 1. Cow; 2. Pig; 3. Dog; 4. Sheep; 5. Bee; 6. Bird; 7. Donkey; 8. Duck; 9. Frog; 10. Rooster; 11. Horse; 12. Monkey; 13. Mouse; 14. Snake; 15. Wolf

WORLD DRUM

We don't know why, but there's something in our human nature that likes to bang on things. Try passing up a drum in a store without testing it out—it's hard not to at least tap on it. Drums are as old as humans. The oldest drums found so far are from 6,000 B.C.E. and were made from hollowed tree trunks and gourds with animal skins over the top.

Now, what's a drum doing in a geography book? Well, drums, like bowls, appear in almost every culture, without these cultures having had any contact with one another. Drums represent the universal language of music; we may not understand each other's language, but no one can fail to be moved by the sound of a drum. Used in ceremonies as music, speech, or as a healing tool, percussion is the most basic form of music known to humans around the world. Release the ancient rhythm in your hands with this simple-to-make drum.

WHAT YOU NEED

- Cardboard food canister with lid
- Acrylic craft paint
- Paintbrush
- Large, heavy-duty rubber glove
- Scissors
- Elastic band
- Craft knife
- Twine or yarn

WHAT YOU DO

1. Paint the food canister with an even coat of paint, and let it dry.

2. Cut a circle from the wrist portion of the rubber glove so that the rubber circle is approximately 1 inch (2.5 cm) wider in diameter than the canister lid.

3. Stretch the rubber circle across the mouth of the canister so that it's taut, then secure it with the lid rim (figure 1). You can also use an elastic band to hold the rubber circle in place.

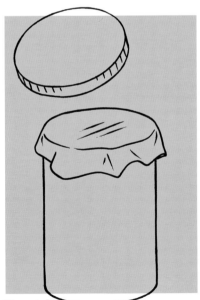

Figure 1

4. Beginning just under the edge of the lid, wrap the twine tightly around the canister until all of the loose rubber is covered (figure 2).

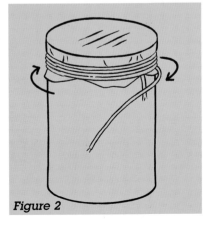

Figure 2

Hold the starting end of the twine diagonally across the can so you can wrap the rest of the twine over it. Tie a knot at the bottom of the wrapped section of the canister. Do the same for the bottom of the canister, but leave enough loose twine so you can use it as a strap for carrying and hanging the drum.

5. Paint the open areas of the drum.

347

The Earth Shapes You

THINK ABOUT IT. If the Earth shakes, you shake. And although it's obvious that storms, earthquakes, and other natural phenomena can have a severe impact on our lives, geographers are also fascinated with the not-so-obvious ways in which Earth affects us. Geographers pay close attention to our relationship to Earth and can often tell us why certain towns were built, why a once-booming tourist attraction is now nearly a ghost town, or even how a geological phenomenon that started millions of

years ago affects us to this day. Just because we've explored and mapped most of the world, including ocean floors and mountaintops, doesn't mean geographers are sitting around twiddling their thumbs. They're out there visiting supposedly familiar places and digging up new and amazing information. This relationship between Earth and its dwellers is at the heart of this chapter. Explore weather patterns, how natural landmarks affect your life, why your hometown is where it is, and more by simply turning the page!

WHERE YOU LIVE BROCHURE

How did you end up where you are? Did your parents move to your town, or has your family lived there awhile? Ask your family what drew them to this particular place you now call home.

Great civilizations started out as small groups of people who realized that they had found a good place to call home, whether it was because they had access to a river or the soil was good for planting, or there was good access to other kinds of food. Do some research, call your city leaders, talk to your family, and find out what makes your hometown such a cool place to live, and create a fun brochure advertising your hometown's natural and cultural features that make it distinct and appealing to visitors.

WHAT YOU NEED

- Travel brochures, newspapers, postcards, and photographs from your hometown, plus additional magazines for cutting pictures out
- Scissors
- 11 x 17-inch (27.9 x 43.2 cm) poster paper
- Craft glue
- Foam brush

WHAT YOU DO

1. Take a few minutes to think about what there is to do in your town and surrounding areas. What would be fun to do with a friend who came to visit for a week? Find out why your parents chose to live in your town, and what they like about the area.

2. Go through all of the brochures, magazines, and photographs you've gathered, and cut out images and words that relate to your region. Keep in mind the things you'd want to do with your friend. Look for both man-made attractions (amusement parks, movies, museums) and natural attractions (beaches, scenic views, wildlife) to include in your brochure.

3. Fold the 11 x 17-inch (27.9 x 43.2 cm) piece of poster paper into three equal parts. Then open it back up and lay it down flat in front of you.

4. Arrange the pictures and words on the paper as you like. You may want to overlap images, trim around some of them with the scissors, and leave spaces between others.

5. When you're happy with your arrangement, break out the glue! Working with the bottom layer of images first, use the foam brush to smooth glue over the backs of each image, and press them in place on the poster paper. Continue gluing all the images in place until your brochure is complete. How many of your town's attractions are natural?

6. If you wish, take your finished brochure to a copy center and make several color copies on glossy paper to make your brochure even more appealing. Or with the proper software and some assistance, you can scan your finished brochure into a computer and print a copy on a color printer.

7. Send your brochure to a pen pal or friend to encourage him to visit.

HOMETOWN DETECTIVE

Do you ever wonder about the place where you live? Was it always the way it is now? Where did people go before the mall was built? What was there before the mall was built? When did it all begin? Whether you live in a small town or a section of a big city, some time in the past it was just beginning. Folks came by ship, train, or even covered wagon and created your town. Maybe the old railroad station or the historic water mill is where it began.

If you like detective work and know a little bit about maps, it's a good bet that you may be able to find why your town was built and exactly where it all began.

WHAT YOU NEED
- Journal for note taking
- Camera

WHAT YOU DO
Here are some suggestions on how to get started:

- What natural resources (forests, fish, game, building stone, arable land, etc.) made the location of your town desirable? Chances are some sort of natural resource first attracted settlers to your town. Or perhaps your town grew because it was located between two major cities and became a good resting place. The topographic conditions of your town may have been perfect for a rail line or an airport.
- Did the town grow as natural resources were needed? Did demand for these resources diminish over time, or did your town run out of these resources?

- Most towns start off in a central place like a crossroad or railway depot and spread outward. They usually begin on "Main Street" or a similar name and go from there.

- Take a walk through the oldest part of town (ask your grandparents) and begin to look for clues. Bring along a notebook, and be ready to sketch a homemade map. It's a good idea to bring your camera, too. Be prepared to find old building signs, dates on the tops or cornerstones of the buildings—look for any indications of what kind of business took place there. There may be unusual structures such as storage tanks, silos, and docks. Don't miss the old stone roads, partially covered trolley car tracks, and monuments along the way.

- The names of the streets give wonderful hints to your town's beginnings. First Avenue, Main Street, or Central Boulevard may not be important today, but their names alone tell of past importance. The names of the founders of the town or important historical figures who played a part in the town's history can usually be found on a corner street sign.

- The best part of your investigation is to take your findings to the local library and discuss them with the librarian. Most local libraries are filled with histories, photos, and maps of your town, and the librarian will surely be able to help you.

- There's a good chance other folks are doing the same thing that you're doing, so ask lots of questions and enjoy your search.

Listen to Your Landscape

Before and After: On September 5, 1996, Hurricane Fran made landfall on the North Carolina coast at Cape Fear. The photo on top was taken before the storm, and the photo below was taken just after the storm.

It used to be that land features influenced where builders put their houses. In other words, you didn't build a town too close to the ocean or a flood plain. With technological advances and incredible population growth, however, people can and do live just about anywhere—at least until nature strikes back.

In developing countries, people are often forced to live in dangerous places such as bare hills where landslides are likely. In other situations, nature is "contained" in order to build. For example, if you want to get closer to a river that tends to flood, you build levees and dams that keep the river from overflowing its banks. And that works fine, until it doesn't work. You see, rivers have this way of continuing to do what they've done for thousands of years.

SALT-DOUGH LANDSCAPE MODEL

To get a good sense of where you live, you need a bird's-eye view to see the bigger picture. From up high you can see population centers clustered together, factories dotting the landscape by the river, desert areas nearly devoid of life, or mountains and hills rising from the ground. Maps often provide you with a good overall view of an area, though even topographic maps don't provide a good three-dimensional look at your town.

With this project you can move mountains, carve valleys, and divert rivers—all with your fingertips. Mix up a batch of dough, and with guidance from a topographic map (page 322), recreate your town's landscape and examine where you live.

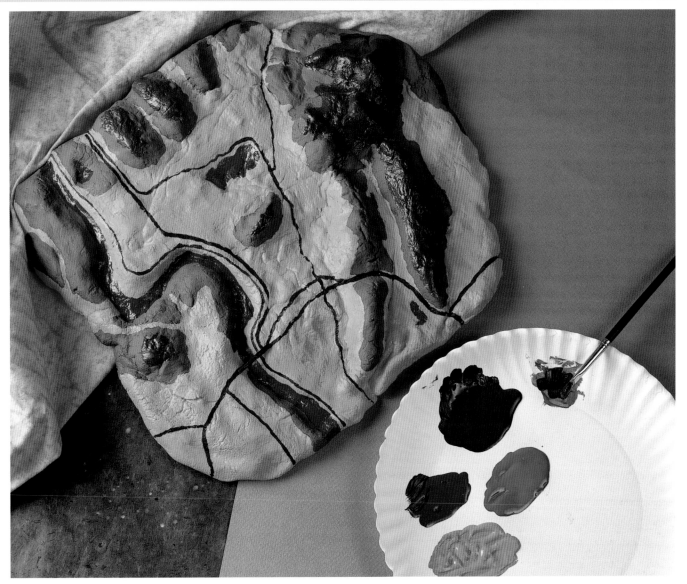

WHAT YOU NEED

- Aluminum foil
- 4 cups (560 g) all-purpose flour
- 2 cups (400 g) non-iodized salt
- Large bowl
- Spoon
- 2 cups (.48 L) water
- Topographic map of your area (a map that shows elevations)
- Oven mitts
- Acrylic craft paints, at least three colors
- Paintbrush
- Pencil
- Ice cream sticks, toothpicks, or twigs (for making bridges)

WHAT YOU DO

1. Cover a counter or a tabletop with aluminum foil. (You may need to overlap several sheets of foil to make sure your work surface is completely covered.)

2. Sprinkle a light layer of flour over the foil—this will keep the dough from sticking as you shape it.

3. Mix the flour and salt together in a large bowl. Slowly add the water while you stir the mixture. Set down your spoon and dig in with your hands. Break up any lumps, and knead the dough until it's smooth.

4. Break off a clump of dough, and work it with your hands until it's warm and easy to shape. Form the handful into a ball, and set it aside on the aluminum foil. Shape the rest of the dough the same way.

5. Examine your topographic map, and plan where you'll need more or less dough to make the land features. Flatten some of the dough balls, and press them together to make the base of your model. The base should be approximately ¼ inch (6 mm) thick, but it can be as long and as wide as you want to make it. The model in the picture is 12 x 13 inches (30.5 x 33 cm).

6. Using your topographic map as a guide, add more dough where needed, and shape the model with your fingers to show the most obvious landscape features in your area.

7. To add dough to the model, moisten the piece you want to attach by dipping your finger in water and wiping over it; then press the piece into place. Smooth out the creases and lines where you added the new dough. Continue shaping the model until you can recognize it as your area's landscape.

8. Heat your oven to 250°F (121°C). Carefully set the model with its foil on the center rack.

9. After about two hours, carefully remove the model from the oven. Don't forget to wear oven mitts! At this point, parts of the model will still be wet.

10. Peel the aluminum foil off the bottom of the model.

11. Place the model back in the oven (on the center rack), and bake it until the whole model is dry. It will probably need to bake for a total of four hours. You'll know it's done when you can't make marks in it with your fingernails. It's okay if the bottom's still a little soft.

12. While the model cools, study your topographic map. Notice the places with the most buildings and roads, the areas with only a few houses and roads, and those areas with no roads or houses at all. How does the shape of the landscape affect where people locate? What water features do you see on the map, and what kind of development is around them? What natural features do people seem to be attracted to in your area? What do they avoid?

13. Choose a different color to represent each type of area on your model: one for heavily developed areas (lots of roads and houses), one for lightly developed areas (few roads and houses, some farms and forest), and one for undeveloped areas (no houses or roads). On our model, orange-pink represents heavily developed areas; light green represents lightly developed areas with some houses, roads, farms, and forests; and dark green represents places that haven't been developed. Parks and green spaces are also painted light green. Paint on any water features, such as rivers, lakes, ponds, and marshes. If you live near the ocean, paint an edge of the model to represent the shore. Locate any major roads, especially highways, that cross through your area and paint these on the map as well. To make a bridge, cut a toothpick, ice cream stick, or a thin twig to the size you need, paint it to match the color of your roads, and glue it in place.

PREDICT THE FUTURE!

You don't need a crystal ball to find out how your neighborhood will change in the coming years. Call your local chamber of commerce or town hall, and ask for the latest statistics on population growth and housing development in your area. Examine your model and figure out where you would put the additional people, houses, roads, schools, and businesses, if growth continues. What will happen to parks and the undeveloped areas on your model? How could you add more people without taking up more undeveloped space?

PANGEA PUDDING PUZZLE

Once upon a time (about 4.5 billion years ago) Earth was a big, red fireball. As it cooled off some, it rained for a couple thousand years, until all of Earth was one big ocean. Slowly some of the water evaporated, and around 500 million years ago, land chunks emerged and floated around until they came together along the equator, forming one continent that we call *Pangea,* which means "all lands" in Greek. One hundred million years later, the continent began to break up, fractured by shifts in the molten core of the planet. We now have seven continents, which are still shifting, due to *plate tectonics*, the interaction of the moving slabs of rigid rock called plates, which make up Earth's hard shell (see page 358).

Here's a yummy way to travel back to the good old days when you could grow apples in Antarctica and walk to Europe from North America.

WHAT YOU NEED

- 2 large packages of instant pudding
- 1 quart (.95 L) of milk
- Premade cookie dough
- Measuring cup
- Large bowl
- Whisk or fork
- Cookie sheet
- Use of an oven

WHAT YOU DO

1. Combine the pudding ingredients in the bowl, and stir with the fork until it's smooth and thick. Put the pudding in the refrigerator until you're ready to serve it.

2. Flatten the cookie dough out on the cookie sheet until the dough is about ¼ inch (6 mm) thick, and then place it in the oven to bake.

Follow the directions on the dough package for baking times and temperatures.

3. When the cookie dough's done, remove it from the oven. While it's still warm and soft, use a knife to outline the shape of Pangea in the dough (see illustration). Pull the extra cookie from the Pangea outline. Next, draw the fault lines

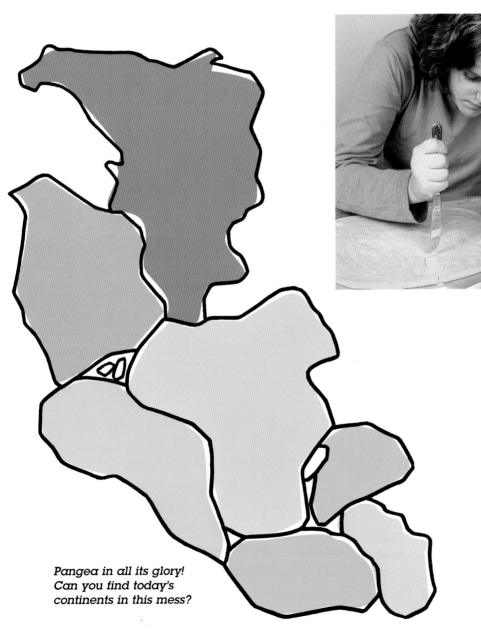

Pangea in all its glory! Can you find today's continents in this mess?

where the continents we know today tore away from the giant land mass. This time, don't go all the way through the cookie with the knife, but carve about halfway into it.

4. When the dough has completely cooled, slide a knife under it to loosen it from the cookie sheet in one whole piece. Place the giant Pangea cookie on top of the pudding.

5. Dig into the dessert by breaking apart the supercontinent and passing out the new, young landmasses that we float around on today.

SERVING UP SOME PLATE TECTONICS

If you live in California, U.S.A., you're moving to Alaska, whether you like it or not. According to the theory of plate tectonics, California is moving north and will crash into Alaska in around 200 million years. So don't pack your long underwear quite yet.

Earth's crust (outermost layer) isn't a solid shell, but instead, a series of large blocks or plates that drift upon Earth's mantle (first inner layer). According to plate tectonics, these plates are in constant motion, though with an annual speed anywhere from 1/2 to 4 inches (1.3 to 10.2 cm), this isn't something you can feel. These plates may include both oceans and continents, and when they move, the continents and ocean floor above them move as well. Earthquakes and volcanoes are most active where these plates meet, and mountain ranges are formed where plates have collided.

So, what's in store for Earth's continents in the next 100 to 200 million years?

• The Mediterranean Sea may disappear, connecting Africa with Europe.

• India will continue to push into southern Asia, pushing the Himalayas even higher.

• Asia and America may become one continent.

• The Indian Ocean could rise a little and cover the 1,000-plus islands of the Maldives.

• Africa could be split into two continents.

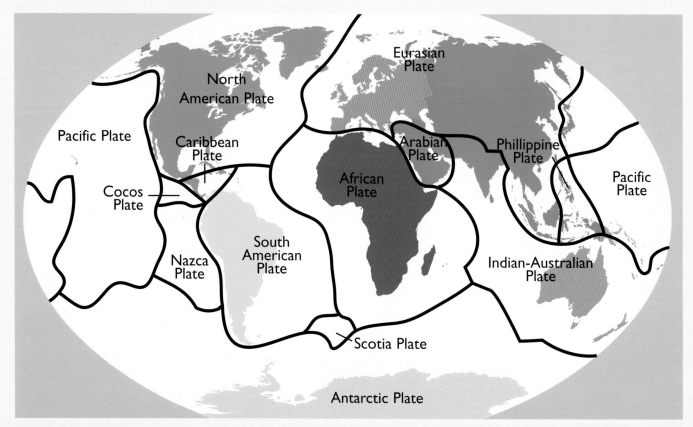

CLIMATE STUDY WITH TREE RINGS

Weather is what's happening outside your window right now. Climate, on the other hand, is the overall weather of an area, including average temperatures for months and years, temperature highs and lows, average precipitation, general directions and speeds of winds, and severe weather. And believe it or not, trees are some of the most accurate climate record keepers, able to record evidence of floods, droughts, temperature, lightning strikes, insect attacks, and even earthquakes. How do they do it? If you cut down a tree, you'll notice its growth layers or tree rings—one for each year the tree was alive. The width of each tree ring can tell what conditions were like during that year of growth. The study of tree rings is called *dendrochronology*, and with a tree stump and a ruler you can figure out how the climate changed over the years in your area and compare it to the history of your area.

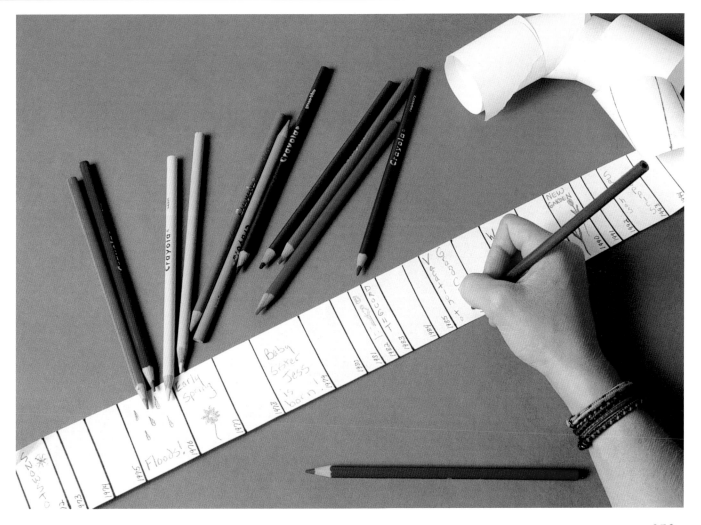

WHAT YOU NEED

- Tree stump in your neighborhood
- Tape measure or ruler
- Journal or piece of paper
- Adding machine tape
- Markers

WHAT YOU DO

1. Find the stump of a tree that has been cut down in your neighborhood. Ask around until you find out what year it was cut down.

2. The outermost ring represents the year the tree was cut down. Measure the width and record the measurement in your journal, along with the year the tree was cut down.

3. List the previous year in your journal and measure the second ring, and so on until you've reached the core. See "Reading Tree Rings" below. When was the tree "born"?

4. Create a time line with the adding machine tape. Record each year the tree was alive from the earliest year to the most recent. Identify years that were good growing years (wide widths) for the tree and those that were poor (narrow widths) by allotting more space on the tape for the good growing years.

5. Ask your parents, grandparents, local librarians, or neighbors about the years on your tape, and fill in each year with information on local weather, history, farming seasons, droughts, and any extreme weather. See if this information matches up with the tree's growing season. For example, your grandparents might recall a three-year drought that corresponds to three consecutive narrow rings. You can

also see if your library has archived copies of your local newspaper. If so, check out the headlines and the weather section for more information. Can you pinpoint specific incidents in your town's history that may have affected the tree's growth?

6. Decorate your time line when you're done.

READING TREE RINGS

- Trees grow from the middle out, so the ring closest to the center is the oldest and the outer rings near the bark are the youngest.
- The dark lines represent the end of growing seasons, and the lighter colored rings represent the actual growing period.
- Wide rings indicate a good growth year, while narrow bands indicate a poor growth year.

360

WEATHER STATION

Weather can be a pain in the neck. It's always there, threatening your skiing trip or soccer practice or promising one thing and delivering something entirely different— like the predicted GIANT SNOWSTORM that produces only a dusting of snow or the lovely weekend that turns into a swampy, rainy mess. Weather defines where and how you live; it determines what you'll wear and what you'll end up doing. Here's your chance to set up your own weather station and practice the art and science of predicting what kind of weather is heading your way.

WHAT YOU NEED
- Barometer (measures air pressure) (see instructions on page 362)
- Anemometer (measures wind speed) (see instructions on page 364)
- Wind vane (measures wind direction) (see instructions on page 363)
- Thermometer
- Notebook

WHAT YOU DO
1. Once you have made and/or gathered all of your weather instruments, put them in appropriate locations for observing the weather. The wind vane and anemometer should be placed far from buildings and other objects, in an open area. The thermometer should be set up outside, but sheltered from direct sunlight and wind. You can tape it to the inside of a white box (the white will reflect sunlight) and set it on a porch for an accurate reading. The barometer should be set up indoors in a calm area of the house where it won't get knocked over.

2. Set up the pages in your notebook to record each of the following, three times a day: date, time of day, temperature, air pressure, wind direction, wind speed, and cloud type as you have observed them (see page 365 for cloud chart). Plan to observe the weather for at least 14 days or longer.

3. At the end of each day, write your weather prediction for the next day based on your observations. It'll probably take you a few days to get familiar with using your weather instruments, but after two weeks you should have a keen sense of the weather. Wind direction, air pressure, temperature, and cloud cover are basic factors that interact to produce the weather in your region at any given time of day. Careful observation of these factors can forewarn the type of weather that's headed your way. Wind from warmer, wetter regions will bring moisture to your area and may produce precipitation if it meets up with a significantly colder mass of air. Wind from arctic regions will often move in quickly as the colder, denser air mass pushes out the lighter, warmer air mass. Where cold and warm air masses meet, a "front" is produced. Fronts are where all the activity happens as the two air masses struggle with each other—their arrival and intensity announced by the cloud development that accompanies them. The more extreme the difference is between the colliding masses, the more exciting the weather.

Air pressure (measured with a barometer) is the weight of the air on the earth. One square inch (6.5 cm^2) column of still air that rises from sea level to the top of the atmosphere weighs 14.7 pounds (6.6 kg)—that's about as heavy as a day's worth of homework packed in your backpack. But the air doesn't just sit in one place over the earth—it's constantly moving. Warm air masses are less dense, and therefore put less pressure on the earth than cold, dense air masses. Tornados, hurricanes, and storms are low-pressure systems. The strong winds that accompany them are caused by air rushing from surrounding high pressure areas to fill the space in the low pressure area. When there's only a slight difference in air pressure between the two masses, you'll measure a gentle breeze with your anemometer, as air calmly moves from areas of high pressure to low pressure. The barometer reflects the degree of pressure being exerted by the air at any given moment. It's one of the fundamental tools meteorologists have used for predicting changes in the weather.

4. Look for patterns in your weather data. What changes seem to go together? Did you notice that wind from a certain direction usually brings rain? What did the cloud formations tell you about incoming weather? Were your weather observations the same or different from the local meteorologist's? If your observations were different from the meteorologist's, what land features and other factors do you suspect influenced the differences?

Making a Barometer

WHAT YOU NEED
- Balloon
- 1 glass jar
- Rubber band
- Drinking straw
- Scissors
- Piece of paper
- Ruler
- Tape
- Pencil

WHAT YOU DO
1. Cut a piece of rubber from the balloon to stretch across the top of the jar. Secure the rubber around the neck of the jar with a rubber band.

2. Snip one end of the straw to make a point. Tape the other end of the straw to the center of the rubber piece that covers the jar.

3. Tape the ruler to the piece of paper lengthwise. Tape the paper to a wall, and place the jar barometer next to it so the pointer is just a hair away from the paper.

4. Three times each day, check the level of the pointer against the paper and make a mark. Use the ruler to compare the distances between the marks. Each time you check the barometer, record where the mark lines up with the ruler.

Making a Wind Vane

(Figure 1)

WHAT YOU NEED

- Thin, long nail
- Drinking straw
- Wood glue

- $5/8$ inch-diameter (1.57 cm) metal washer
- $1/2$ inch-diameter (1.27 cm) wooden dowel, 3 feet (91.4 cm) long
- Hammer
- Scissors
- Index card
- Thin, bendable wire
- Wire cutters
- Compass

WHAT YOU DO

1. Use the scissors to make 1-inch-long (2.5 cm) vertical slits in the top and bottom of one end of the straw.

2. Slip the index card into the slit in the straw, and glue or tape it in place. This end will catch the wind, and the other end of the straw will serve as the pointer.

3. Glue the washer, flat down, to one end of the dowel.

4. Try to balance the straw on your

(Figure 1)

finger and pinch the straw where it rests on your finger when you finally get it to balance. Press the nail through the straw where you pinched it, without crushing the straw.

5. Center the nail in the straw over the circle in the washer, and hammer the nail into the dowel. Leave enough of the nail exposed so the straw can spin freely.

6. Hold the dowel vertically, and center the wire horizontally across it, approximately 6 inches (15.2 cm) below the spinner.

7. Wrap the wire around the dowel to hold it in place (this should resemble a cross). Wrap a second piece of wire below the first in the same manner, perpendicular to the first wire. Now you should have four arms of wire extending out from the dowel.

363

8. Bend the tip of each wire in the shape of a letter for one of the four directions, North, South, East, West. Be sure to follow the order of the directions.

9. Stick the bottom of the dowel in a planter or in the ground, and rotate it as needed so the directions of the wires point in the same directions as the compass.

10. To read the wind direction, just note the direction the pointer end of the weather vane faces. The wind will push the index card away from it, so the pointer end will tell you where the wind is coming from. If the pointer lines up between the direction wires, then record your wind as coming from the northeast, southeast, southwest, or northwest.

Building the Anemometer
(Figure 2)
WHAT YOU NEED

- ³/₄ inch (1.8 cm) x 3 foot (90 cm) piece of wood
- 5¹/₂ x 5¹/₂ inch (13.8 x 13.8 cm) block of wood, ³/₄ inch (1.9 cm) thick
- Hammer
- 2 nails, 1¹/₂ inches (3.8 cm) long
- Pencil or pen
- Scissors
- ⁵/₈-inch (1.6 cm) metal washer
- Wood glue
- 2 pieces of wood trim, ¹/₄ inch x 1 inch x 36 inch (.62 x 2.5 x 90 cm)
- Vegetable oil
- 4 yogurt cups or other plastic cups
- Acrylic craft paint
- Paintbrush
- 4 tacks

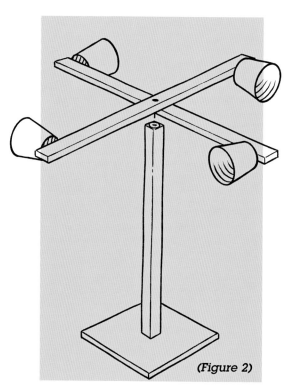

(Figure 2)

WHAT YOU DO

1. Stand the ³/₄ inch (1.8 cm) x 3 foot (90 cm) piece of wood on one end, and center the wood block on top of it. Have an adult help you hammer one of the nails through the center of the block into the end of the piece of wood. This will be the stand for the anemometer. Flip the stand so the wood block is on the ground.

2. Glue the washer, centered, on top of the post.

3. Take the two pieces of wood trim and make a cross. Hammer the remaining nail straight through the hole in the washer and into the top of the post. Leave a ¹/₂ inch of the nail exposed above the post so that the cross-pieces can spin.

4. Give the cross a whirl to see if it spins smoothly. You may want to rub vegetable oil on the washer to reduce friction between the parts.

5. Paint the outside of one of the

yogurt cups with the acrylic paint, and let it dry.

6. Tack the side of a yogurt cup to one of the cross ends, as shown in the illustration. Use glue between the cup and the wood for reinforcement in addition to the tack. Glue and tack the remaining cups to each of the ends of the cross so that the open ends of the cups face the same direction.

MEASURING AND CALCULATING WIND SPEED

1. Ask your partner to time you for one minute as you count the number of times the colored yogurt cup makes a complete circle. Record this number as X revolutions per minute (rpm).

2. Next, find the circumference of the anemometer (the distance around the circle of yogurt cups): circumference = 3.14 (pi) x diameter (the distance across the center of the circle). The circumference calculated for the illustrated anemometer is 56.5 inches (141.3 cm) (3.14 x 18 inches [45 cm] = 56.5 inches [141.3 cm]).

3. Multiply the circumference by the revolutions per minute (X rpm) to get the wind speed in feet (cm) per minute.

4. Convert the wind speed from feet (cm) per minute to miles (km) per hour by multiplying the wind speed by .0114: X ft (cm)/min. (.0114) = X miles (km)/hr.

CLOUD CHART

Many times you can identify the current (or future) weather situation by analysis of cloud type and coverage.

Stratus are low, dull gray clouds that usually cause overcast skies and steady precipitation.

Cirrus are high clouds that appear feather-like. They are fair-weather clouds and signal the approach of a warm front.

Cumulus prevail during fair, sunny, dry weather.

Nimbostratus are usually the predominant cloud forms during continuous, widespread precipitation.

Stratocumulus often appear ominous, but they typically occur during fair weather.

Cumulonimbus are formed when warm, humid air rises and turns to water, which can lead to thunderstorms and tornadoes.

Altocumulus are similar to cumulus clouds, though they are often arranged in lines.

Altostratus form a uniform gray sheet in the sky. Sometimes you can see the sun faintly.

MORE WEATHER FORECASTING TIPS

- Though weather forecasting is a science, sometimes, based on experience, you have a hunch what's going to happen. Follow your hunches.

- Know the climate (highs/lows, average temperature for the time of year, and average rainfall) of your area. This will keep you from predicting a temperature that's 30° lower than the average.

- Once you have a basic understanding of where your weather is coming from, you can note areas that have the same temperature as your region that are experiencing the weather you'll be getting soon and make predictions based on what's happening in those areas.

- Low-pressure areas are probably close to a front and therefore precipitation. High-pressure areas are probably not associated with precipitation. If there's a rapid change in pressure over a short distance, strong winds will result.

- High humidity is usually located ahead of a front, and low humidity is usually behind a front.

RAIN MAP

The movement of the Earth's many plates is not the only way the earth's surface was and continues to be shaped. These great blocks of stone have been chiseled by wind, sunlight, oceans, rivers, and ice. Water may not seem like a good chiseling material, but ice can bust boulders and carve out hollows in mountains. Rain can dissolve limestone, and rivers can cut through a mountain over the course of many years. The next time you look at a topographic map, notice how the rivers have carved out the valleys over thousands of years of traveling through the landscape.

Water also has the power to transform your neighborhood in minutes, when rainstorms send torrents of water rushing down the streets, filling streambeds, and creating puddles. Get outside with this activity and look for signs of the excavating power of water.

WHAT YOU NEED

- Street map or topographic map
- Use of a photocopy machine
- Clipboard
- Assorted blue, brown, green, and red markers
- 2 pieces of cardboard
- Pencil
- Ruler
- Scissors or craft knife
- Glue
- Paint
- Paintbrush

WHAT YOU DO

1. Enlarge a portion of a street map of your neighborhood so it's large enough to draw in streams and ponds in your area. A topographic map is even better since it already includes some larger water sources.

2. Put your map on the clipboard, and along with your blue, brown, green, and red markers, go for a walk. Look for other sources of water not included on the map. Draw these additional streams or ponds on the map, and use the blue, brown, or green marker, depending on the color of the water you find. Whenever you come across a sewer drain or you notice a water culvert that redirects a stream, draw it on the map with the red marker.

3. Wait for rain.

4. Go back outside with your map and markers right after a rainstorm and look for new sources of water. If you notice that a stream is flooded, use a different color blue to outline the original stream to show that it floods. Draw in puddles and rainwater streams on the streets. Try to match the color of these water features when you draw them. Where does it all go? You've probably

noticed that the sky can drop a whole lot of water on your neighborhood, and almost as soon as it appears it starts to disappear. Did you notice too that sewer drains are placed in areas where the water tends to naturally collect because of the Earth's contours and the pull of gravity? These sewer drains lead to a whole network of pipes that eventually release the rainwater into nearby rivers, which in turn pass the water (and all that it carries) into the ocean. Sometimes the rainwater passes through a treatment plant, but more often it goes untreated, and all of the trash and pollutants it picks up in your neighborhood are passed on down the line.

5. Look for *vernal pools*, which are temporary ponds of water that nourish life such as frogs, salamanders, and insects. They appear in the spring when fresh rain raises the water table in the ground to support large puddles in low spots in the terrain. During dry seasons, the water evaporates and the organisms that

lived there hop, slither, or slide to new homes. A shallow depression in the ground and dried mud is a clue that there may have once been a pool of life there.

6. To make a frame for your rain map, trace the outside edges of your map onto one of the larger pieces of cardboard.

7. Use the ruler and pencil to measure and mark a 3-inch (7.6 cm) border on the cardboard around the rectangle you just drew, then cut the center rectangle from the cardboard.

8. Paint the second piece of cardboard a color you like as a background for your map. Let it dry.

9. Use a brush to evenly spread glue across the back of your map. Then smooth your map in place on the painted piece of cardboard. Glue the frame on top of this.

10. Cut up a local topographic map to fit the frame, and glue it so the entire frame is covered. Spread a final, thin layer of glue over the frame.

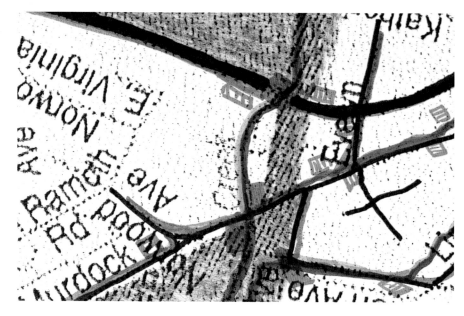

You Shape the Earth

IN ORDER TO PRESERVE the environment they're exploring, hikers and backpackers live by the rule "leave only footprints." That way the natural environment will still be there for the next visitors. Earth has over 6 billion "hikers," and we're leaving behind some pretty big footprints. Some of these footprints include greenhouse gases, pollution, garbage, enormous parking lots, and malls, all at the expense of Earth's natural resources. Even you alone affect the environment every time you flush the toilet or drink a can of cola. And the only way to explore how we can live lightly on the Earth is to start with ourselves, by looking at what we're doing and how we can do it more responsibly. This chapter explores the ways humans are shaping and changing the Earth and ways we can leave Earth a better place for the next visitors.

SOLAR OVEN

When someone asks to describe a world problem, a common answer is "energy consumption." We are heavily dependent on nonrenewable fossil fuels, and someday we're going to simply run out. And you need an awful lot of energy just to get you through your day. You need electricity to power your alarm clock; gas, oil, or coal to heat the water for your shower; gas to power the car that takes you to school, and so on.

What are some solutions? One answer is right outside your door. Stop reading for a minute and go outside, and you'll instantly feel the power of the sun. Solar technology may be one of the better ways people can produce the energy they need with fewer resources and less pollution. Put it this way, if the sun can transform a couple of pizza boxes and some aluminum foil into an oven, just think of the huge possibilities more advanced solar equipment can offer. See page 115 for another type of solar oven.

WHAT YOU NEED
- 2 pizza boxes, one larger than the other
- Pencil
- Craft knife
- Aluminum foil
- Newspaper or polystyrene foam
- Nontoxic, black paint
- Paintbrush
- Nontoxic glue
- Sunglasses
- String
- Tape
- Cooking pan
- Piece of clear plastic sheeting that will cover the large pizza box

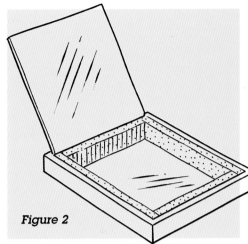

Figure 2

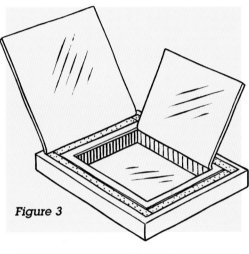

Figure 3

WHAT YOU DO

1. As you work with the solar oven, remember that the point is for it to get hot enough to cook food—in other words, you should treat it like a real oven and exercise some caution when using it. Center the small pizza box on top of the large one with one side touching (figure 1).

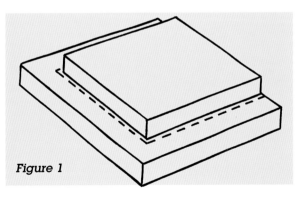

Figure 1

2. Use the pencil to outline all four sides of the smaller pizza box on the lid of the larger box. Set the small box aside and, with the craft knife, cut out three sides of the square you just drew. Leave the fourth side

attached so you still have a connected lid.

3. Line the inside of the large box with aluminum foil, then stuff around the sides with newspaper, or cut polystyrene foam to fill the space (figure 2). This layer of stuffing acts as insulation to help hold the heat in the oven.

4. Fit the small box into the large box, and add more stuffing if needed to fill the space between the two boxes (figure 3).

5. Paint the inside bottom of the small box, and the outside edges of the large box with nontoxic, black paint. Black absorbs heat and will increase the heat in the oven. Line the rest of the box with aluminum foil, and use nontoxic glue to hold it in place.

6. Spread some glue on each of the pizza box flaps, and smooth a large

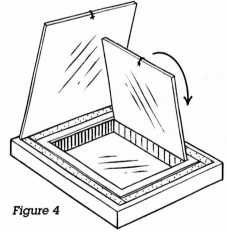

Figure 4

piece of aluminum foil on each (shiny side up). Try to keep the foil as wrinkle free as possible, so sunlight hitting it reflects into the box and doesn't get caught bouncing around wrinkles in the aluminum foil.

7. Adjust the flaps so that they reflect light directly into the box when you line the oven up with the sun. Try not to look directly at the aluminum foil, and wear sunglasses while you adjust the flaps.

8. Poke a hole in the top of each flap, and tie a piece of string through each hole. Tape the other end of each piece of string to the outside of the large box to hold each lid in place at the best angle for reflection (figure 4).

9. Place the food you want to cook on a pan in the oven, and cover the oven with the clear plastic sheeting to trap the heat. Select foods that cook at low to medium temperatures. Cookies, biscuits, pizza, nachos, and other simple foods are perfect for the solar oven. It may take 20 minutes to 2 hours for the food to cook depending on what you're making, so plan ahead and record the baking times for each thing you try.

10. You can use an old cooler as a solar oven by lining it with aluminum foil and painting the inside bottom black. Cover the lid with aluminum foil, and angle it for the best reflection into the cooler. Cover the cooler with a large piece of clear plastic sheeting. Or, use two packing boxes, one large and one small, and fit them together like the pizza boxes. Tear the flaps off the smaller box, but cover the four flaps of the outside box with foil for maximum reflection into the oven.

WATER FILTER

Over one-sixth of the world's population doesn't have access to clean water, due to erosion, pollution, chemical spills, and other environmental disasters, and 80 percent of all diseases in developing countries are transmitted through unsafe water. Boiling water is one way to make water safe to use, but that's not always possible in areas where wood and other fuels are scarce and/or expensive. Desalinating salt water (removing the salt from ocean water) is another possible solution, though at this point it's quite expensive. Other ways are being developed and tested, including using the power of the sun to "pasteurize" water. This project shows you one way water can be filtered, and though this is a cool project, don't use the water from this activity for drinking or cooking.

WHAT YOU NEED

- Small rocks (but too big to fit through the opening of the bottles)
- Sand
- 2 large plastic bottles (2 liter soda bottles work well)
- Scissors
- Charcoal
- Cotton or synthetic stuffing
- Can or pitcher
- Water
- Food coloring
- Spoon
- Strainer

WHAT YOU DO

1. Rinse the rocks, charcoal, and sand to remove dust and residue.

2. Cut the bottom off one of the soda bottles, and cut the neck off the other.

3. Balance the bottomless bottle upside down in the second bottle (see illustration).

4. Fill the bottom third of the top bottle with stuffing, on top of the stuffing add 2 inches (5 cm) of sand, 1 inch (2.5 cm) of charcoal, then fill the rest with rocks.

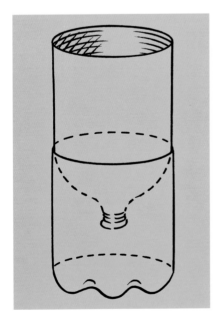

5. Fill the pitcher with water, add a few drops of food coloring, and stir with the spoon.

6. Slowly pour the colored water into the open end of the bottle and watch how it moves through the different layers. Check out the color of the water that collects in the bottom bottle. While we don't recommend you use this to treat water for drinking, you could certainly experiment with using it to treat the "gray water" in your home for reuse to water plants or paint with watercolors. Gray water is the water leftover after washing dishes, brushing your teeth, or doing laundry, that can be reused for other household chores and projects that don't involve drinking or cooking.

CD MOBILE

As technology changes, so does our garbage. Companies are always on the lookout for faster and cheaper ways to deliver their goods and information. Years ago, milk was delivered in glass containers that were dropped off in front of people's homes. The empty containers were then collected, washed, and used again. Today, you buy milk at grocery stores in cartons made from a specially coated paper that's not easy to recycle, leading to more milk cartons in landfills.

What do you predict will be in your garbage cans in the future? Are there ways to figure out how to recycle these products before they end up in landfills? For this project, you'll be collecting old compact disks (CDs): scratched music CDs or CD-roms, data CDs, or even junk mail CDs, and recycling them into a mobile to brighten up a dreary corner of your room.

WHAT YOU NEED

- Old compact disks
- Fabric paints in squeezable bottles
- Craft glue
- Bamboo sticks or wooden dowels
- Fishing line
- Scissors
- Yarn

WHAT YOU DO

1. Lay the CDs label-side down, so the shimmery side is facing you. Draw your designs on them with the fabric paint. Note: Squeezable fabric paints are fun to use, but it can be tricky drawing and keeping an even pressure on the bottle at the same time. Practice first on a thick piece of paper or old fabric.

2. After the CDs are dry, glue them together, back to back, so that a painted design shows on either side.

3. To prepare the CDs to hang, cut a long piece of fishing line (up to 3 feet [.9 m] long) for each CD. Tie each line through the centers of the CDs. Tie several knots so the lines don't slip, and leave a long tail to hang the CDs to the mobile.

4. You may have an idea of what you want your mobile to look like, or you may have even drawn a picture. If not, now's the time to experiment. How many sticks do you want to use? How many CDs do you wish to hang off each stick? The trickiest thing about making a mobile is *balance*. Be prepared to spend some time making tiny adjustments to the spacing of each CD in order to get the mobile to swing freely and evenly.

5. Tie a piece of fishing line to the main branch of your mobile and hang it from a hook in your ceiling. You may need a stepladder. Hang the other branches to the main

branch so they're balanced.

6. To hang the decorated CDs from each branch, begin tying CDs to the branches, varying the length of the lines. At this point, the mobile will probably sag on one side and not be balanced.

7. Move the CD lines along the branches until the mobile's balanced and you're happy with the design. You may have to add or remove a CD to make the mobile work. Also, use this time to decide if you like where the CDs are located. You may want to shorten some of the lines or take a CD off and give it a longer line.

8. Cut several short pieces of yarn. To secure the lines to the branches, hold a loop in place on the branch, and spread glue on both sides of it, about ¹/₂ inch (1.3 cm) on each side. Wrap the yarn around the branch, beginning on one side of the loop (at the edge of the glue), passing over the fishing line loop and continuing to the other side. Make sure the yarn is wound tightly since this is what will hold your loops in place. Do this for all the CD and branch strings. You can still make minor adjustments while the glue dries.

TRASH TRIVIA

☞ The world produces up to 1 billion tons (.9 billion t) of solid waste each year.

☞ If we recycle, we can reduce the amount of waste going to landfills and incinerators by 20 to 50 percent.

☞ The United States has 5 percent of the world's population and produces half of the world's garbage.

☞ 17 trees are saved when 1 ton (.9 t) of paper is recycled.

☞ Each American uses about 100 pounds (45 kg) of glass per year.

☞ Almost one-third of the waste generated in developed countries is packaging.

☞ There are over 100,000 pieces of man-made litter in space.

☞ We throw away 2.5 million plastic bottles every hour.

☞ Recycling an aluminum soda can saves 96 percent of the energy used to make a can from ore, and produces 95 percent less air pollution and 97 percent less water pollution.

☞ Over 100,000 marine mammals and over 2 million seabirds die every year by ingesting improperly disposed of plastic.

☞ It takes your trashed paper 2 months to biodegrade; your orange peels, 5 months; milk carton, 6 months; plastic bag, 11 years; shoe, up to 40 years; aluminum can, up to 500 years; polystyrene foam (packing peanuts, etc.), never.

DEBATE BOOK

You hear about the state of the world's environment all the time in the news. Don't you ever wonder why governments and organizations don't just take care of the problems once and for all? The next time you're troubled by a report in the news about the environment or any other world issue, find out more about the issue. You'll probably realize that the problem is a lot more complex than you imagined. Perhaps protecting an endangered animal means restricting access to water a city needs. Or maybe there are people whose lives depend on the grazing land created by cutting down rain forests. This three-part debate book is designed to hold two conflicting points of view on an issue that concerns you, along with possible solutions.

and crease them firmly. Slide them inside each other to make three booklets, one for each section of the book.

4. Fold the long piece of cardboard for the cover into three sections (figure 1).

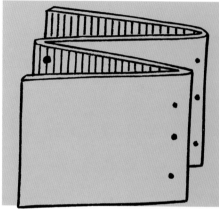

Figure 1

5. Place each signature in position in the cover, and hold them in place with paper clips.

6. Use the awl or sharp nail to poke three holes in the center of each signature and through the cover.

7. Sew the thread into each signature in place as shown in figure 2. Don't tie a knot in the thread. Poke the needle from the outside through the center hole to the inside of the book. Pull the thread through, but

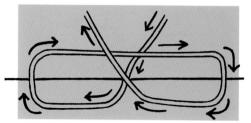

Figure 2

leave about 4 inches (10.2 cm) of string on the outside.

8. Poke the needle through the top hole and out the back of the book,

WHAT YOU NEED

- Pictures, news articles, summaries of information from all sides of your issue
- Several sheets of paper, 6 x 14$^1/_2$ inches (15.2 x 36.8 cm)
- Piece of corrugated cardboard, 6$^1/_2$ x 22 inches (16.5 x 55.9 cm)
- Paper clips
- Awl or sharp nail
- Thread or waxed linen
- Large sewing needle
- 6 beads
- Markers, pens, and/or acrylic craft paint
- Scissors or craft knife
- Craft glue
- Foam brush
- Stamps and ink (optional)

WHAT YOU DO

1. Spend some time exploring the issue that has caught your attention. Hit the library, read magazines, or do an Internet search. Collect information from both sides of the issue, and also start thinking about how you'd solve the problem. Remember, learning about the other side of the issue isn't the same as agreeing with it.

2. Sort through the materials you've gathered, and separate them into three piles: one side of the issue, the other side of the issue, and solutions.

3. Fold the 6 x 14$^1/_2$-inch (15.2 x 36.8 cm) pages in half sideways

then down to the bottom hole and in through to the inside of the book. Poke the needle back into the center hole and out the back. Pull both ends of the thread tight, and make a knot (figure 3).

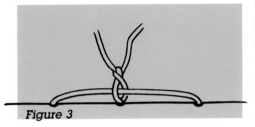

Figure 3

9. Decorate the excess string with beads (tie knots below the beads to keep them in place).

10. Decorate the inside and outside of the cover to make it appealing and to provoke curiosity.

11. Use one section to place your information on one side of the issue. Use the last section to place your information on the other side of the issue. And use the middle to provide solutions you've learned about or thought of on your own. Use a foam brush to smooth glue onto the backs of pictures and information that you plan to stick to the inside pages. Include charts, graphs, statistics, letters to the editor, and whatever else you find that tackles the issue. If you're going to use this book to help others understand the issue, use plenty of colorful images and lots of facts, so people will be drawn to the book and will want to look through it. In your solutions section include information people could take away with them. Sample letters, names and addresses of related organizations they can join, and tips and advice people can easily act on, are key for empowering others to help out with your effort. Share your book with classmates, family members, friends, and community decision makers. At the very least, you'll learn about something that matters to you, and who knows, you may even inspire a movement.

12. You can make your own stamp to use as a symbol and as decoration on your book. Simply draw a figure on a piece of foam or cardboard. Cut away the excess material, and you've got yourself an image to print with.

TO FISH OR NOT TO FISH: A DEBATE

One world issue that has gotten a lot of attention is what to do about fishing the world's oceans, lakes, and rivers. It's an issue that not only focuses on how our world appetite can affect whole species, but also how attempting to fix a problem can cause more problems.

ONE SIDE OF THE PROBLEM

When you think of fishing, an image of a couple of people on a boat casting lines from their fishing poles may come to mind. However, that's not how most of the world's fish are caught. The majority of the fish you find in supermarkets have been caught by fleets of huge ships that cast out gigantic nets in the deep ocean in order to capture entire schools of tuna and other popular fish. These nets also capture whatever else is in their way. While some nations have laws that discourage taking non-fish species, on the open ocean (which means free from national borders and their laws), fishing fleets are able to act as they desire. The huge nets don't discriminate tuna from dolphins, sea turtles, or wading birds, and by the time the nets are emptied and cleaned, it's usually too late for anything that accidently got tied up in them. This

type of fishing also quickly leads to overfishing, to the point where it would take years for some aquatic life to build up their population numbers again. Overfishing and catching large numbers of fish in nets should be outlawed.

ANOTHER SIDE OF THE PROBLEM

The world demands fish. Fishing has been a way of life for thousands of years, and in some parts of the world, it's the cornerstone of local diets, providing important nutrients for humans. In the United States alone, consumers spend almost $50 billion on seafood. Eating fish has been linked to brain growth in children, heart attack reductions, and a decrease in dyslexia and other learning problems. Also, there are hundreds of thousands of independent fishermen that depend on fishing for their livelihood. Fishing is a hard life, and any and every advantage should be used. By severely limiting how fishing can be done, you're not only denying the world of the fish it needs, but you're also preventing fishermen from making a decent living.

WHAT'S YOUR SOLUTION?

Food for Thought

The Hunger Banquet on page 382 is a modified version of the one created by Oxfam, a nonprofit organization that seeks solutions to hunger, poverty, and social injustice around the world. What does Oxfam suggest you do to help fight world hunger and poverty?

• Teach others about the causes of, and solutions to, these problems.

• Shop wisely; buy only what you need, and get it from socially responsible companies.

• Raise money or volunteer for organizations that work with poor people to improve their lives.

You can find out more about Oxfam by checking out their website, www.oxfamamerica.org, or write to Oxfam, 26 West Street, Boston, MA 02111-1206.

Where's Your Slice?

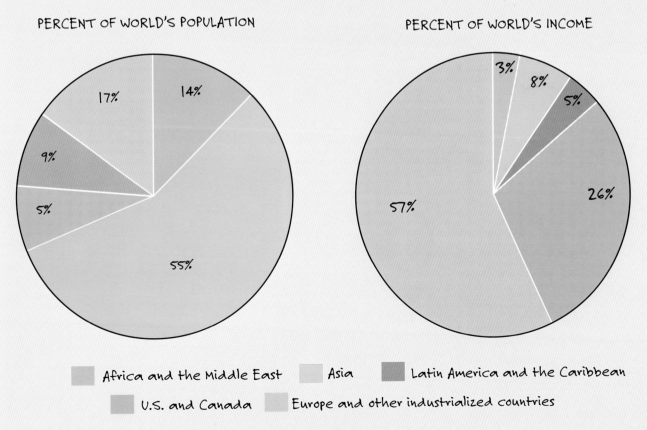

PERCENT OF WORLD'S POPULATION

PERCENT OF WORLD'S INCOME

Africa and the Middle East   Asia   Latin America and the Caribbean

U.S. and Canada   Europe and other industrialized countries

WORLD HUNGER BANQUET

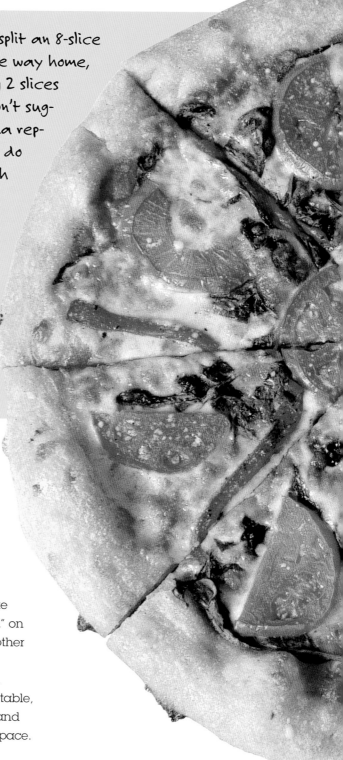

Let's say you and nine friends are going to split an 8-slice pizza. You and one friend go to pick it up. On the way home, you and your friend eat 6 of the slices, leaving 2 slices for your 8 friends. Some friends you are! We don't suggest you try this at home, but let's say this pizza represents all of the world's food and energy. Who do you and your one hungry friend represent? North America, Europe, and parts of South Asia and the Pacific. Who do your other eight friends represent? What's called the developing countries that represent 80 percent of the world's population, including South and Central America, Asia, and Africa. The world's pizza is big enough for everyone, it's just that much of the world doesn't have access to it. Host a hunger banquet with your friends to drive this thought home.

WHAT YOU NEED

- 100 pieces of candy (gum, lollipops, jelly beans, malt balls, etc.)
- 9 friends and yourself
- 5 index cards
- 10 small slips of paper
- A pencil or marker

WHAT YOU DO

1. Write "Africa and the Middle East" on one index card. Write "Asia" on the second card, "Latin America and the Caribbean" on the third, "U.S. and Canada" on the fourth, and "Europe and other industrialized countries" on the last card.

2. Place the index cards around the room, with the "U.S. and Canada" and "Europe and other industrialized countries" at a table, "Latin America and the Caribbean" on a rug or floor pillows, and "Africa and the Middle East" and "Asia" in a small, crowded space.

3. Write "Africa and the Middle East" on one of the small slips of paper, "U.S. and Canada" on another, and "Latin America and the Caribbean" on another. Write "Asia" on five slips, and "Europe and other industrialized countries" on two slips. These slips represent the population of each "continent" as a percentage of the world's total. For example, Asia has about half of the world's total population, so it gets five of the 10 slips.

4. Fold up the slips of paper, and have each guest draw one as they arrive at the banquet. Once they open the slips of paper, have them go to that "continent's" designated area.

5. Distribute the candy to each "continent," telling the guests not to eat it. "Africa and the Middle East" gets three pieces of candy, "Asia" gets eight pieces, "Latin America and the Caribbean" gets five pieces, "U.S. and Canada" gets 26 pieces and "Europe and other industrialized countries" gets 57 pieces. The candy represents the wealth of each "continent" as a percentage of the world's total. For example, "Europe and other industrialized countries" has over half of the world's total wealth.

6. After the candy gets passed out, guests can take turns explaining how they think the candy should be divided. Some guests (most likely the ones with a lot of candy) may not want the distribution to change. Other guests might suggest giving each person an equal amount. Talk about why food and wealth aren't equally distributed around the world. Should that be changed? If so, try to come up with ideas on how to do it.

POPULATION NUMBERS

Though the world's poverty problem is more about access than it is about resources, that may not always be the case, since the more people you have on Earth, the more resources are needed for them to live. Consider this: It took from the beginning of time until 1830 for the world's population to reach 1 billion; the second billion took 100 years; the third billion took 30 years; the fourth billion took 14 years; the fifth billion took 13 years; the sixth billion took 12 years; and unless there's a tremendous effort to slow the population down (birthrates), the next billion will show up in less than 12 years. By the year 2050 there may be over 9 billion people crowding this planet, which will severely strain Earth's already depleted resources. And where will most of these people that will be born in the next decade live? Over 95 percent of this increase in population will take place in the less-developed countries of Africa, Asia, and Latin America.

MORE NUMBERS

- 30 percent of the people living in developing countries live in poverty.
- 70 percent of the world's poor are female.
- 23 percent of the population live on less than $1 a day.
- 2 billion people have no electricity.
- 2.6 billion people lack basic sanitation.
- 1.1 billion people lack adequate housing.

LUMINARY OF EARTH AT NIGHT

If you could get up out of bed one night and travel to the moon and look back at Earth, what do you think you'd see? To tell you the truth, the Earth's surface would look like a bunch of stars. Satellite images, such as the one on pages 386 and 387 help us to better understand where and how we manage to squeeze onto our planet.

Most of the light reflected into space is generated by urban areas where approximately half of the world's population lives and works. But what about those bright lights in Siberia and in the deserts of Africa? Forest fires, natural gas burn off at oil refineries, and major transportation routes like the Trans-Siberian Railroad (which looks like a string of lights across an otherwise dark landscape) all glow at night and look like huge metropolises from space. With this luminary, you can lie on your bed and imagine that you're up in space, circling the dark side of Earth. Where would you want to land?

EARTH FROM SPACE:
A Global Map of City Lights at Night

With this map, it's pretty easy to tell where most of the world's cities are located. This image was pieced together from several satellite shots of the Earth at night. NASA scientists use this map to measure the size of cities and how these cities affect the Earth. Image by Craig Mayhew and Robert Simmon, NASA GSFC; based on data from the Defense Meteorological Satellite Program courtesy Christopher Elvidge, NOAA National Geophysical Data Center

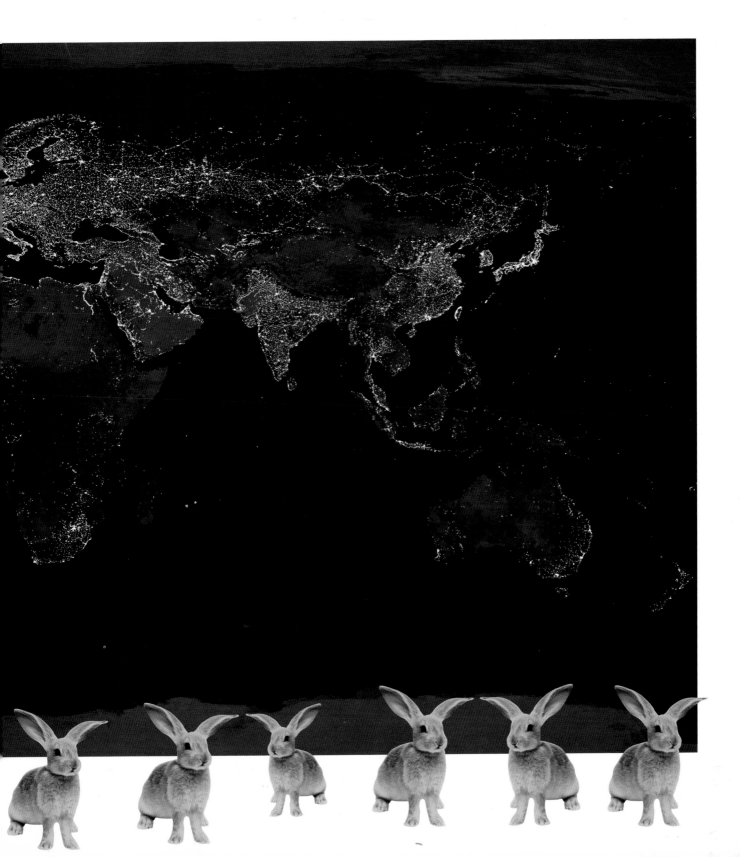

WHAT YOU NEED

- Cardboard cylinder (oatmeal and cocoa containers work great)
- Ruler
- Rag
- Pencil
- Tape measure
- Photocopy of the world map (template on page 397)
- Marker
- Thin, white chalk
- Tape
- Paintbrush
- Dark blue acrylic craft paint
- Pen
- Safety pin, thick sewing needle, and assorted nails
- Scissors or craft knife
- Flashlight

WHAT YOU DO

1. Remove the wrapping from around the cardboard container, and wipe any dust from the surface with a rag.

2. With the ruler and pencil, measure and mark a line around the center of the upright container. This line represents the equator. Wrap the measuring tape around the cylinder to draw the equator line.

3. Measure the circumference of your container with the tape measure. Compare this measurement with the length of the template map, and enlarge or reduce the map as needed with a photocopier. Wrap your photocopied map around the container to make sure it fits.

4. You now need to transfer the map onto the cardboard container. First, outline the continents on the map with a dark marker so that you can see the map when you turn the paper facedown. With the paper facedown, trace the reverse image of continents with the white chalk. If you're right-handed, you should start tracing from the left, and if left-handed you should begin tracing from the right so you don't smear all your hard work across the page with your shirt sleeve.

5. When the chalk outline is complete, match the equator on the map with the equator line on the container, and tape the map to the container so the chalk side is against the cardboard (you'll want to work with the bottom of the container facing up).

6. With the handle end of the paintbrush, rub along the outline of the continents so the chalk makes a print on the cardboard cylinder.

7. Carefully, peel back one corner of the paper to see that the chalk is leaving an outline; if not, you may need to start over.

8. Trace the finished chalk outline on the cardboard container with a pen to make the chalk lines permanent.

9. Use paint or markers to outline the continents and represent oceans and other major bodies of water. Let the paint dry.

10. Compare your cylinder map with the satellite image of the Earth at night (see pages 390 and 391). Use a safety pin or tack to punch through the cardboard to make pinholes in the locations on Earth that match the light spots shown on the satellite image. Can you identify these cities? Can you guess which spots are due to forest or gas fires? Use the large sewing needle or nail to re-punch the cardboard to emphasize the brightest spots on the map.

11. Cut out a circle in the back of the container, near the base, and slide your flashlight inside the hole to illuminate the container. Don't use your map as a lampshade, and don't use a candle.

12. Compare your luminary to a population map. What major population centers are not represented by the nighttime satellite image? What does this comparison tell you about rural versus urban lifestyles in different regions of the world?

Top 25 Largest Cities on Earth

See if you can find these megacities on the Earth-at-Night satellite image on pages 386 and 387. No cheating. Now check how well you did by comparing the satellite image to a world map. How'd you do?

1.	Tokyo, Japan	35 million people
2.	New York, USA	21 million people
3.	Seoul, South Korea	20 million people
4.	Mexico City, Mexico	19 million people
5.	Bombay, India	19 million people
6.	São Paulo, Brazil	19 million people
7.	Osaka, Japan	18 million people
8.	Los Angeles, USA	17 million people
9.	Cairo, Egypt	15 million people
10.	Manila, Philippines	14 million people
11.	Buenos Aires, Argentina	13 million people
12.	Jakarta, Indonesia	13 million people
13.	Moscow, Russia	13 million people
14.	Calcutta, India	13 million people
15.	Delhi, India	12 million people
16.	London, U.K.	12 million people
17.	Shanghai, China	12 million people
18.	Rio de Janeiro, Brazil	11 million people
19.	Karachi, Pakistan	11 million people
20.	Istanbul, Turkey	11 million people
21.	Teheran, Iran	11 million people
22.	Dhaka, Bangladesh	10 million people
23.	Paris, France	10 million people
24.	Chicago, USA	9 million people
25.	Beijing, China	9 million people

NATIVE HABITAT GARDEN

Just as earthquakes can topple bridges and buildings, and tornadoes can tear up houses, so too do humans have the power to destroy the homes of the wildlife that are native to our neighborhoods. What used to live in your neighborhood before the houses were built and the streets paved? What still survives there? Animals play an important role in the natural world, keeping populations of other living things under control. Birds eat insects and mosquitoes, weasels eat birds' eggs, and foxes eat weasels in some ecosystems. But take part of that formula out, and things grow out of proportion. Mosquitoes might take over the world if it weren't for hungry birds, bats, and frogs. So, investigate the plants and animals that would be beneficial to encourage in your backyard and neighborhood. Build shelters, plant the things they like to eat, provide some water, and see what flourishes around you.

WHAT YOU NEED

- Permission from your parents to turn a part of your backyard into a habitat garden
- Nature field guide (see instructions on page 392)
- Toad houses (see instructions on page 393)
- Yard debris
- Ladybug house
- Butterfly house
- Bird Feeder (see instructions on page 393)

WHAT YOU DO

1. Begin by planning out where you're going to put your habitat garden and what wildlife you wish to attract. The activities below are only a few of the hundreds of ideas available for attracting animals and insects. You can do any or all of these activities to get your habitat garden growing!

2. Look into what animals and insects are native to your area, and write down ways to attract them in your field guide. Also research what plants are native to your area, and plant them where you think they'll grow best.

3. Frogs, toads, and salamanders are disappearing at alarming rates around the globe. Habitat destruction, disease, and climate change are all suspects. Encourage a safe place for these sensitive and threatened creatures to live in your yard. Toads and salamanders love moist, dark places so they can hide safely from predators. Provide some shelter for these bug-eating critters in your yard with a few homemade toad houses (see page 393).

4. If you've ever helped with yard work, raking leaves, cutting

branches, pruning shrubs, then you know how much garden debris can pile up. Instead of burning your yard waste or putting it in bags to haul to the dump, create a fort for animals such as field mice, hedgehogs, rabbits, foxes, birds, and other small critters. These animals can be beneficial for controlling rat populations and insects, and they're interesting to watch. Imagine a rabbit hopping through your backyard or a hedgehog munching on dandelion flowers outside your window.

5. Ladybugs are wonderful helpers in your garden or flowerbed. Their favorite food is the green aphid—the same creature that likes to eat and destroy your plants. Invite ladybugs to hang around your yard by providing them with a shelter they can enjoy. You can

buy a ladybug house at most garden centers. Paint it, then place it in a sunny spot off the ground.

6. Butterflies, those beautiful, graceful pollinators of plants, are threatened. They're disappearing as the native and wild plants they depend on disappear, as yards are planted with grass and fields are turned into parking lots. Because butterflies migrate, new buildings or roads anywhere along their route can affect their survival. Imagine going on a trip across country and then discovering that all the grocery stores and restaurants were closed along the way. You could probably figure out a different route to take, but what if it was a day or more off your path? This is the problem many migrating animals face as they fly into familiar feeding and resting areas, only to discover their resting spots have disappeared. Help butterflies out with a butterfly box. Then research local plantings that attract butterflies.

7. Welcome feathered friends to fuel up at a well-stocked birdfeeder in your yard (see page 393). In return, visiting birds will feast on pesky gnats and mosquitoes and help pollinate flowers to support your growing habitat garden.

8. Observe your garden, and note your new wild neighbors you meet in your field guide.

Field Guide

WHAT YOU NEED
- 5¹/₂ x 10-inch (14 x 25.4 cm) sheets of paper
- 6 x 14-inch (15.2 x 35.6 cm) piece of corrugated cardboard
- Thread
- Large sewing needle
- Craft glue
- 1 small envelope with clasp
- Tape
- Leaves
- Paint
- Twine

WHAT YOU DO

1. Line the stack of paper 3 inches (7.6 cm) from one end of the cardboard.

2. Use the binding method shown on page 378 to sew the pages to the cover.

3. Fold the papers in half to expose the rest of the inside of the cover.

4. Glue the envelope to the inside front cover. You may need to cut the envelope to make it fit in the space. Use tape to reseal the envelope where you've cut it.

5. To decorate your nature journal with leaf prints, simply spread a thin layer of paint on a leaf, and press it in place.

6. Keep your journal closed by tying a piece of twine around it.

Toad House

WHAT YOU NEED
- Terra-cotta flowerpot, whole or broken
- Acrylic paints
- Paintbrush
- Small shovel

WHAT YOU DO

1. Wash and dry the flowerpot.

2. Paint your pot until you're happy with it, and let the paint dry.

3. Find a good, shady hiding place, such as under a bush. Use the shovel to dig out a hole big enough to bury the pot on its side halfway.

4. Make sure the dirt inside the pot is a little wet. Place a few dead leaves and twigs inside too. You'll know when a toad moves in by the way the dirt at the front of the house gets worn down. That's where the toad sits and waits for its dinner to fly by.

Twiggy Bird Feeder

WHAT YOU NEED
- Plastic bottle
- Scissors or craft knife
- Lots of small twigs
- Glue gun and glue sticks
- Bendable wire

WHAT YOU DO

1. Cut the neck off the bottle with the scissors or craft knife.

2. Carve two holes, opposite from each other, 1 inch (2.5 cm) from the bottom of the bottle.

3. Heat up the glue in the glue gun, then drizzle some over a section of the bottle.

4. While the glue on the bottle is still warm, press twigs flat against the bottle and close together. Cover the entire bottle, working in sections around it with the glue and twigs.

5. Poke a stick through the two holes in the bottom so that some of the stick hangs out on both sides of the bottle. These are the perches the birds balance on while they eat from the bottle.

6. Fill your twiggy feeder with birdseed, and hang it somewhere you can see it.

WHAT'S UP WITH ALL THESE RABBITS?

An unwanted visitor is someone who visits and refuses to leave, sort of like a friend who overstays his welcome in your room. In the environment, however, unwanted visitors are also known as eco-invaders or alien species: plants and animals that come from somewhere else (a different country) and are not native to the area. In their natural surroundings, they may be harmless, but they can completely ruin a different environment. Alien plants and animals can disrupt the natural balance, reduce biodiversity, and transmit diseases. And when the aliens have no natural enemies or predators in their new home, they can reproduce at will, creating a population explosion, which can cause a total ecological nightmare.

Here are some examples of alien species that have wreaked havoc around the world:

• Europeans introduced rabbits to Australia in the 1800s so they'd have something to hunt. Unfortunately, rabbits loved their new home, and their population soon grew to half a billion, ruining grasslands and displacing native species. They still cause problems to this day.

• The East Asian long-horned beetle, who entered the United States in wooden crates from its native China, has already devoured thousands of maple trees in Chicago and New York City.

• Non-native plants can sweep through an area, clogging waterways and reducing the amount of land available for farming. The South American water hyacinth has done this in Southeast Asia.

With travel, transportation, and trade becoming easier and easier in this ever-shrinking world, many of these invaders are coming along for the ride, on ships, in wooden crates, and even in luggage. They're one of the biggest causes of biodiversity loss in the world, and though stricter regulations on imported plants and animals will help, as will better inspections of ships and their cargo, this remains a multi-billion dollar problem.

ONE FINAL THOUGHT: THE ULTIMATE WORLD HERITAGE SITE

A UNESCO (United Nations Educational, Scientific, and Cultural Organization) World Heritage Site is a natural or cultural location that has such great value to the world that it's protected against the threat of damage. This means no one can change it around, knock it down, or otherwise mess with it. There are nearly 700 sites around the world, with more added to the list every year. Some sites include the Great Wall of China, the stone circle of Stonehenge (in the U.K), and Grand Canyon National Park in Arizona (U.S.A).

Can you think of a heritage site in your neighborhood? What can you do to help protect it? And here's a thought: Maybe we should just go ahead and declare Earth THE World Heritage Site, with each one of us as site managers. Hey, it can't hurt. We can't help but shape the Earth, but if we

The Great Wall of China. Photo by Thom Gaines

begin walking on it a bit more carefully, leaving lighter footprints, Earth will continue to be a nourishing, flourishing home planet for us and for future generations. We hope you've enjoyed this geographic journey and that it gave you something fun to do as well as something important to think about. Whatever you end up doing on this Earth, please remember that you can always make a difference.

TEMPLATES

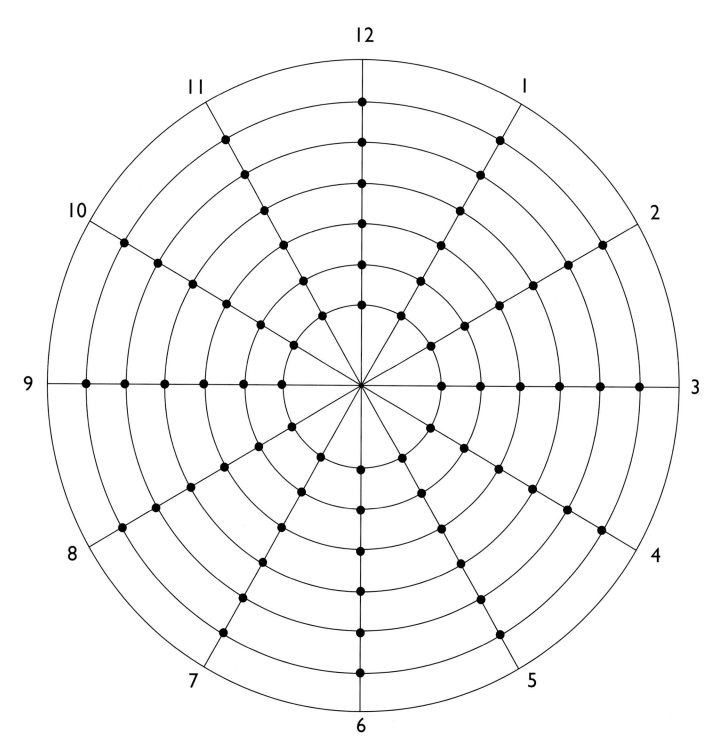

Positioning Guide for Placing Hour Markers for the House Sundial Clock (page 294) and the Time-Zone Clock (page 297)

World map template for Luminary of Earth at Night (page 385)

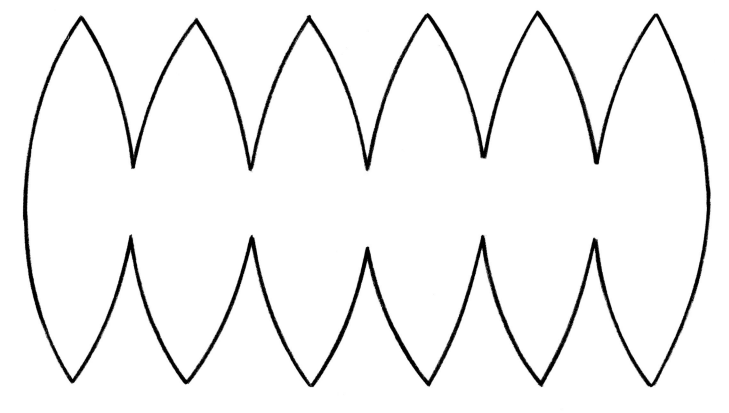

Globe Your Friends (page 315) globe template; enlarge 220%

iNDEX

Acids, 87

Adventure Backpack, 309-310

Air, 63, 71

Alien species, 394

Aliens, 292

Amber, 223

Andesite magma, 188

Antique Map & Case, 307-308

Archaeology, 36

Asthenosphere, 148

Astrolabe, 133-135, 282-284, 289

Atolls, 216

Atomic clock, 295

Baa, Moo, Kuk-kurri-kuu, 346

Balloon, hot air, 55-58

Barometer, 64-65

Basalt, 144, 188

Bases, 87

Beaufort scale, 73-74

Bird hide, 18-20

Boats, clay, 107-108;
    model, 104-105

Books, 324-325, 377-379, 392

Bronze Age, 261

Camouflage, 22-24

Cartography, 304, 321

CD Mobile, 374-376

Cenozoic Era, 230

Ch'ien, Chang, 301

Cities, 385-389

Clay Bowl, 344-345

Clay, 203, 206-208, beads, 212-213

Climate Study With Tree Rings,
    359-360

Clocks, 294-295, 297

Clocks, fire, 126-127;
    solar, 112-113

Cloud chart, 365-366

Color spinners, 124

Colors, 125, 131

Columbus, Christopher, 294, 302

Compass, 290-291

Continental drift, 152

Convection currents and cells, 148,
    150-152

Copper Age, 261

Coral reefs, 216

Core-inner and outer, 244, 148;
    temperature, 144-145

Cross Staff, 286-287

Crust-continental and oceanic, 144

Crystals, 188; how created, 236;
    shape, 235;

Customs, 333

Debate Book, 377-379

Deep Map, 324-327

Definition of geography, 280, 332

Devonian Period, 230

Diamond 243-245

Dream Travel Box, 298

Dried apple garland, 128

Dripstone, 216

Drums, 346-347

Earth, 16, age, shape, and size,
    136-137; creation myths, 299;
    facts, 280, 285, 356, 358;
    night view, 386-387

Earthquakes, 149, 156-157, 183

Earthworm, 27-29

Energy, 370-372

Equator, 285, 289

Erosion, 166-167, 201-203

Explorers, 292, 296, 301

Family Maps, 314

Family Tree Batik Banner, 340-342

Fault lines, 156

Feldspar, 196, 233

Fire, 110

Fish, 380

Floating, how it works, 109

Food, 336-337, 370-372,
    380, 381-383

Fossils, 38, 223-224

Fungi, 27

Gears, 97

Gems, 243-245

Geologic time, 183;
    time scale, 230

Geological map, 175

Geysers, 164, 188

Glaciers, 167

Global Positioning System
    (GPS), 293

Globe Your Friends, 315-317

Gluep, 100-101

Gneiss, 166

Gondwana, 152

Granite, 188, 254

Grid Art, 311

Grist mill, 93-96

Harrison, John, 296

Helicopter, 70-71

Hometown Detective, 351-352

Hot springs, 164

House Sundial Clock, 294-295

Hovercraft, 68-69

Hurricane damage, 352

Hydrosphere, 144

Hypsometer, 42-44

Ice Age, 167

Igneous rock, 188

International Date Line, 292

Iron Age, 262

Jurassic Period, 230

Kiln, 209-211

Kites, centipede, 61-63; rocket jet, 58-59

Landslides, 149, 157

Latitude and longitude, 285, 289; finding yours, 289; Listen to Your Landscape, 352

Laurasia, 152

Lava, 161

Light catcher, 129-131

Light, 131

Lightning, 77

Limestone, 192, 216, 254

Lithosphere, 144

Llanfairpwllgwyngyllgogerychwyrn drobwyllllantysilio-gogogoch, 327

Loess, 167

Luminary of Earth at Night, 385-388

"Made In…" Treasure Hunt, 334-335

Magellan, Ferdinand, 292

Magma, 160, 188, 196

Mail Map, 329

Mantle, 144, 148, 188, 196

Maps, antique, 307-308; Flat Map Flap, 319; making, 304-306, 307-308, 311, 312-314, 328, 329; perspective, 303, 312-314, 318-321, 324-327; 175-182; projections, 319-320; scale, 311; topo graphic, 178-179, 322-323; transferring, 309-310; world, 303, 318-320, 386

Marble, 196, 254

Marco Polo Travel Journal, 300-301

Mariner's Astrolabe, 282-284; how to use, 284, 289

Mercator, 319

Mesozoic Era, 230

Metals, 131; precious, 263

Metamorphic rock, 195-196

Mica, 196

Migration, 340-341

Minerals, 192, 232-233; identifying, 243; precious, 244-245; ore, 242; use of, 249

Mini-pond, 90-91

Mohs' scale, 243

Mold garden, 25-26

Moraines, 167

Moss, 204

Mountains, 166-167

Myths, 299

Native Habitat Garden, 390-393

Navigation, 283-291, 293, 296; measuring altitude of stars, 284, 289

Neighborhood Map, 312-313

Nephoscope, 53-54

Nome, Alaska, 325

Novel Map, 328

Obsidian, 188, 236

Old Map Pillowcase, 309-310

Oobleck, 100-101

Opal, 245

Oxfam, 381

Paleozoic Era, 230

Pangaea, 152

Pangea Pudding Puzzle, 356-357

Paper, red cabbage indicator, 85-86; marbled, 88-89

Periscope, 22-23

Permian Period, 230

Peters, Dr. Arno, 320

Pit Kiln, 209-211

Plant tepee, 122-123

Plate tectonics, 148, 166, 358

Plates, 148, 161, 183, 196

Plutons, 188

Polar bears, 119

Polo, Marco, 301

Population, 280, 384, 389

Precambrian Era, 230

Prime Meridian, 285, 296

Prove the World Isn't Flat, 293

Puzzles, 106

Quartz, 196, 233, 236, 243-245

Radioactive elements, 230

Recycled Map Shade, 330-331

Resources, 370, 372, 376,
    380-384,

Rivers, 317

Robinson, Arthur H., 320

Rock cycle, 183, 200

Rockets, 60

Rocks, 36, 183

Root viewer, 32-33

Salt-Dough Landscape Model,
353-355

Sandstone, 192, 254

Schist, 196

Science log, 14-15

Sea monsters, 321

Sediment, 192

Sedimentary rock, 192, 216

Seed cast tiles, 34-35

Seismograph, 158-159

Shale, 196

Silica, 236

Skimmer net, 98

Slate, 196

Smith, William, 230

Soil formation, 203

Solar Oven, 370-372

Solar, collectors, 119;
    food dryer, 120-121; oven,
    115-118; stone, 131-132

Solinus, Julius, 321

Sound viewer, 51-52

Sound, 48, 50

Spider webs, 39-41

Spiders, 41

Stalagmites and stalactites, 216

Stamp Box, 338-339

Stamps, 329, 330, 338-339

Stone Age, 261

Strange Place Names in the United
    States, 324

Strata, 230

Sun, 114

Temperature, 54

Templates, 396-397

Tertiary Period, 230

Thunder stick, 75-76

Thunder, 77

Time Capsule, 342-343

Time, 292, 294-297

Toad house, 30, 393

Tooth Rat, The, 333

Topographic Map of a Friend's
    Face, 322-323

Topographical maps, 175

Totally Useful Compass, 290-291

Trash, 374, 376

Tree rings, 359-360

Twiggy Bird Feeder, 393

Underwater viewer, 92

Valleys, 166-167

Volcanoes, 148, 160-161, 183,
    188; submarine, 166

Water, 78, 372; Filter, 372-373;
    lens, 102-103

Water's skin, 99

Waterspout, 82-83

Wave in a bottle, 80

Waves, 81

Weather, anemometer, 364;
    barometer, 362-363; clouds,
    365-366; rain map, 367-
    368; station, 361-362;
    forecasting, 359, 366; wind
    vane, 363-364

Weathering, 20

Wegener, Alfred, 152

What's Up? South! Map, 303, 398

Where You Live Brochure,
    349-350

Whirlpools, 84

Wildlife, 390-394

Wind, 65; chimes, 47-48; sock,
    66-67; speed meter, 72-73

Winkel Tripel, 320

World Drum, 346-347; Heritage
    Sites, 395; Hunger Banquet,
    382-383; Snacks, 336-337

Worldly Place Mats, 302

Wormery, 28-29

Worms, 27

Xylophone, 49-50